Turkey Hunting Digest

WORDS OF WISDOM ON A GRAND SPRING SPORT

Call em close

Jim Spencer

Jim Spencer

Published by

kp krause publications
An F&W Publications Company

700 East State Street • Iola, WI 54990-0001
715-445-2214 • 888-457-2873
www.krause.com

Please call or write us for our free catalog of publications.
Our toll-free number to place an order or obtain a free catalog is (800)-258-0929
or please use our regular business telephone (715)-445-2214.

ISBN: 0-87349-506-3
Library of Congress Number: 2002113127
Printed in the United States of America

Dedication

To Tommy Aycock, Harold McAlpine and Sid Riley –
three of the best friends anyone could ever ask for;
and to my late father, Truman Spencer,
who took the time
out of his own too-few free hours
to instill in his son a love and respect
for things
wild and free.

Acknowledgments

Acknowledgments, I've discovered in the past few hours of trying to write this one, are tough. There's always the danger – the certainty, actually – of leaving someone out. So to begin with, my apologies to all of you who should be mentioned in the following paragraphs, but due to sloppiness on the part of my mental processes have been omitted.

Thanks to the various magazine and newspaper editors I've worked with over the past three decades of my rocky career as a freelance writer. There are too many to mention, but a few who deserve special thanks are Bill Rooney (who helped me get started when he was at *Outdoor Life*, helped me improve my craft when he was at *American Forests*, and helped me keep the bills paid by buying my stuff when he was at *American Hunter*), Gerry Bethge, Gordy Krahn, Ken Duke, Aaron Pass, John Zent, Mitch Cox, Brian Lovett and Jim Schlender.

Thanks to all my fellow outdoor writers who have helped me in various ways over the course of my career. Notable among them are Tom Kelly, Jim Casada, Wade Bourne, John Phillips, Monte Burch, Larry Dablemont, M.D. and Julia Johnson, Glynn Harris, Bob Marshall, Mike Pearce and especially Keith Sutton. Being a writer is a lonely business, but you folks make it a little less so. We're all competitors, but we don't let that get in the way of helping each other.

Thanks to the various turkey hunters, both well-known and otherwise, who've helped me get better at this mystifying sport. Here's a very abbreviated list of folks in this category: Joe Lorinc, Bill White, John Spore, Alan Stone, Brad Harris, Ray and Marty Eye, Mark Drury, Tad Brown, Harold Knight, David Hale, Eddie Salter, Bill Jordan, Toxey Haas, Barney LaRue, Ronnie "Cuz" Strickland, David Blanton, Michael Waddell, Glenn Garner, Larry Norton, Bob Walker, Bo Pittman, Don Shipp. Thank you, guys. I've learned from you all.

Thanks to my editors at Krause Publications: Don Gulbrandsen for encouraging and helping in the early stages, Kevin Michalowski for the middle stages, and Larry Teague for doing the actual grunt work of putting this book together. Thanks, fellows, it's a pleasure to work with you.

Special thanks to Bill Hailey for his nitpickiness and excellent suggestions during the proofreading of the manuscript. Nobody could have done a better job, Bill.

Even more special thanks to Jill Easton, my partner, who also fits into several of the categories above – editor, fellow outdoor writer, hunting partner and in general the best friend I've ever had.

And finally, both thanks and brickbats to Robert Steinmetz, who long ago called up my first turkey and got this whole thing started.

Contents

Section 5 — Putting Something Back

Section 6 — Lagniappe

Foreword

By Tom Kelly

Tom Kelly interacting with one of his other loves – in this case, a 300-year-old longleaf pine.

As a general rule, there are three separate kinds of hunting and fishing stories.

The first group, and by far the most common, are those epics that take the reader along on a trip simply as a bystander to the action.

"Me and Sam went hunting/fishing and we killed/caught a hell of a pile and this is a picture of both of us." Here will be a picture of two guys simpering over an impressive string of fish, or a picture of a dead animal with one of the party standing over the remains with his foot on the neck of the dead critter and his rifle held at high port.

If it were to be exhibited in a gallery, it would be hung, lighted and entitled, "Man with Antlers."

As a reader of one of these Type One epics, all you are privileged to do is attend the story. The way you used to sit in the back row in the 5th-grade English class while the teacher read poetry aloud. You were there, but you did not contribute.

You are really not considered part of a Type One story. It is the equivalent of saying hello to the individual in the Robert Service poem, who… *"had filled whole halls with antlers, and slaughtered herds of gnu, And sought the Cassowary on the plains of Timbuktu."*

Some of these tales of the distant and the far away make an attempt to lead you into the action at the end of the story by first asking and then answering the unspoken and rhetorical question, "Do you want to go?" They then list locations, guide services, airlines, seasons, etc., etc. More or less a travel brochure kind of arrangement, laying out the details of a trip you can take if you are so minded.

The second group of the usual hunting/fishing stories are those that bristle with what has come to be called "how-to" in the trade. In these Type Two stories, you are positively buried under layers of instruction.

You are force-fed details not only on tactics and techniques, but also you're inflicted with exhaustive discussions concerning rod weights, fly patterns, barrel lengths and gauges, shot sizes, muzzle velocities, camping gear and tools. Type Two stories, in short, become U.S. Army field manuals in color, rather than plain old government black and white.

Most of these stories seem to be written by the kind of people who would rather travel than arrive.

But every once in a while you find an author who takes you into his head and makes you a part of the system, whether you happened to be in attendance at the action or not. He gives you a present, composed of ink, of a piece of the memory.

Jim Spencer, in *Turkey Hunter's Digest,* is an outstanding example of an author of this third class.

Before you go much farther (assuming you have gotten this far because some people skip forewords altogether), turn to the chapter he calls "Advice for a Rookie," which he has misnamed on purpose.

Read the part about the first time he ever hooted on a turkey hunt and got answered by three turkeys at his first hoot and by five turkeys only moments later, and remember the time when every man jack among us has been there himself.

Remember how back in the beginning you were never confident that the noises you were making on the turkey call you had just bought would sound anything like turkeys, to other turkeys. Turkey-calling contests were no help at all because they simply solidified your feelings of inferiority, like watching golfers on the pro tour hit fades and hooks and straight shots at will. And the very thought of going around making noises like owls, in the simplistic expectation of actually fooling a turkey into gobbling at your pitiful noises, was clearly out of the question.

Notice in that passage in this chapter how he calls with four notes, half a hoot, because half a hoot only seems half as silly as the full eight-note call, even if there is nobody else there to be embarrassed in front of. And then, when he is actually answered by three turkeys, and then right after that by two more, it becomes an embarrassment of riches.

He has figuratively gone to the beach, walked around the first sand dune past the parking lot, and stumbled over most of the Swedish bikini team lying on beach towels. They all said yes at once, and he cannot, for the life of him, figure out what to do and where to start. You are not supposed to win that big.

Turkey hunting is not a sport. It is an intellectual exercise. Not only does Jim Spencer know this, he knows how to let you share the experience with him, rather than simply s howing you pictures of dead turkeys, complete with footnotes as to weight, beard and spur lengths.

Neither does he break your heart with inch-by-inch and note-by-note descriptions of the affair, beginning with what he had for breakfast before he went to the woods.

Read this book. It will make you a better turkey hunter.

If you can't afford to buy a copy, steal one. From the standpoint of an author, borrowing books is an outrage that simply cuts into his royalties. A stolen book, on the other hand, means a replacement sale, and all sales, original or replacement, are of equal value and a consummation devoutly to be wished.

Old farmhouses and turkey hunting go together like grits and cheese. Tom Kelly and Jill Easton discuss the day's events on the porch of an antebellum Alabama home.

Preface

The Romance of the Road

Drivin' my life away, lookin' for a better way, sang Eddie Rabbit a long time ago. Those words fit my psyche like a crawdad fits its hole. I love to travel in the spring of the year, when the earth is renewing itself, searching out new places to hunt turkeys, always "lookin' for a better way." If my destination lies a thousand miles from my driveway, so much the better.

Yeah, I know, that's weird. My home state of Arkansas contains 52,000 square miles, more or less, and within that range are an estimated 200,000 turkeys. As much time as I've spent chasing gobblers right here in my home state, I still haven't seen a hundredth of the available turkey territory.

It torments me to know I'm going to die without having enough time and money to alter that percentage very much. You'd think, with that much of the turkey range in my home state still unseen, I'd be more inclined to stick around and see more of it.

And I love doing just that. We have both the Ozarks *and* the Ouachitas, two of the best-known mountain ranges among turkey hunting circles, not to mention a wealth of good turkey hunting in both the Gulf Coastal Plain in the southern part of the state and the Delta in the east. I like not only exploring new territory in the Arkansas turkey woods, but also revisiting old, familiar places.

There are several favorite spots to which I return every year, and next spring will be no different.

It's just that ... well ... there's a lot of good turkey hunting in other states, too. And if I've only seen a hundredth of what's available right here at home, how tiny is the fraction I've seen elsewhere?

It's not just the turkey hunting opportunities in other states that regularly draw me onto the road. That's usually my excuse, of course, since I am what I am. But in addition, a big part of the appeal of the road – for me, at least – is simply the road itself. The pure adrenaline-rush adventure of just being Out There.

Windshield wipers slappin' out a tempo, keepin' perfect rhythm with the song on the radio, sang old Eddie. The "song on the radio" can be as varied as the places I'm going, but in order to fit the mood, it must have a hard, driving beat. The artists, too, must have a certain ... I don't know, for lack of something better, call it defiance. Bob Marley, Waylon Jennings, Sheryl Crow, Toby Keith, Vonda Shepard, Warren Zevon, Hank Jr., Hank the Third, that kind of people. Those folks provide appropriate music for the beginning of a trip. Yeah, Eddie Rabbit, too. Toward the end of a journey, when the truck is full of that scratchy, edgy sadness that comes on when it's almost over but there's still a hard two-day drive staring you in the face, it'll be time for Enya, John Coltrane,

In order to fit the mood of "heading out," the music needs a hard, driving beat and a defiant attitude: Waylon, Jerry Jeff, Buffett, Palmer.

George Winston, Linda Ronstadt. But not at the beginning. Not on the way Out.

On the way Out, the trip is still perfect. It won't stay that way, of course, but for now, nothing has gone wrong. The rain hasn't fallen in buckets on opening day, the turkeys haven't dummied up, the gobbler I've traveled halfway across the country to kill hasn't ring-around-the-rosied me and gone his merry way. So far, everything is going according to plan.

There are sights from journeys past I carry with me always, and I can summon them with no effort. Some involve people and/or turkeys: the old Navajo woman selling the prettiest jewelry you ever saw along a hot roadside in northern Arizona, with desert sage in front of her and a Merriam's turkey gobbling on the ponderosa pine hillside at her back; the seven Rio-Eastern hybrid strutters that came a half-mile across a field to me in Kansas; the three Osceolas that duked it out less than 20 yards in front of me in a palmetto thicket near Yeehaw Junction down in Florida; the kid who hauled the huge triple-bearded gobbler into the rural Missouri check station, wearing a grin a foot wide; the grumpy black bear that ran off the only gobbler I called in during eight hard days of hunting in the mountains of West Virginia.

But most of these burned-in, on-the-road memories involve geography: the surprising first glimpse of the Great Salt Lake basin as you drop out of the Wasatch Range heading west toward Salt Lake City; the vast sweep of sawgrass flats as you roar along Alligator Alley through the Everglades; the molten-lava color of the northern New Mexico mesas as you weave through them on U.S. 84 between Santa Fe and Chama; the breathtaking drive up the California coastline on Wonderful One between Big Sur and Monterey; the lush, green softness of the Natchez Trace; the arid harshness of the cactus/mesquite landscape between Corpus Christi and Brownsville; the hostile, above-timberline, snow-flurries-in-August moonscape of Beartooth Pass in northwest Wyoming.

There's plenty of memorable geography here in Arkansas, too, of course. I've already mentioned the Ozarks and Ouachitas, and it's not my intent here to minimize the beauty of those places. But all of that is close to home, and though the destinations are every bit as nice, the trips don't afford the same sense of raw adventure.

That's why I'll be heading farther afield than is really necessary this spring and every spring for as long as I'm able, chasing gobblers in distant places, making footprints where I've never made them before. I'll be prowling the river bottoms and mountains of Arkansas quite a bit, too, but every now and then I simply have to jump in my old truck and head somewhere, for no other reason than those places are Out There.

We'll talk about some of those places in the pages that follow. Buckle up your seat belt, punch the cassette with Eddie or Hank or Waylon on it into the slot, and settle back. It's gonna be a long, leisurely, enjoyable ride, but keep the map handy. We'll probably make a detour or two.

Hey, waitress, pour me another cup of coffee, pop it down, jack me up, shoot me out, flyin' down the highway; lookin' for the morning.

Always, always, lookin' for the morning.

The places turkeys live are almost as varied as the hunters who pursue them, and the only way to see and enjoy these variations is to hit the road.

Author's Note

Author Jim Spencer, trying to get the words right.

As you read this book, if you are observant enough to have what it takes to be a turkey hunter, you are going to notice repetition, redundancy, contradiction, equivocation, maybe a little confusion, and sometimes out-and-out waffling on the part of the guy whose name is on the cover. Those things are in this book for a very good reason: They're in turkey hunting, too.

I wrote each chapter of this book to the best of my ability, following my own lights, saying the things I truly believed (or at least suspected) about turkeys and about turkey hunting at the time I wrote each chapter. The trouble is, you can't write a book of this size in one sitting. And, as became abundantly clear during this exercise, when you're writing about a subject as complex as turkey hunting, your viewpoint and opinions change from year to year. Even, sometimes, from day to day.

The world is not stable, and neither should be a thinking turkey hunter's take on things. As you gain experience as a turkey hunter, your opinions will change. By the time this appears in print, I'm quite sure I won't feel the same way about some of the things I've said in the following pages.

This is not, by the way, an apology. It's simply the way things are. You are perfectly free to accept everything in this book as gospel, or reject all of it, or (if you are wise) pay attention to some parts, modify other parts to suit your own style and philosophy, and either disagree with or flatly ignore the rest.

If you are very, very wise, you may even be able to figure out which parts of this book to do which of those things with. Personally, I'm not smart enough to make that determination.

Introduction

In the Grip of Our Compulsion

Three guys die and show up at the Pearly Gates. "We have a simple test to see whether you get in," St. Peter says. "We just compare your IQ with your accomplishments in life, and if they compare favorably, you're in. If they don't, you go to hell."

The first guy's IQ turns out to be 103. "What did you do with your life, Mr. Smith?" St. Peter asks.

"Diesel mechanic," says Smith. "Worked in the same shop 35 years and was part owner when a truck fell off the rack and crushed me."

"Very good," says St. Peter. "Go on in."

The second guy's IQ is 162, or some such ridiculous thing. "How about you, Mr. Jones?" St. Peter asks. "What did you accomplish?"

"PhD at 22. Rocket scientist. Worked on the space shuttle. Much of the technology in today's space program is of my design."

"Go on in, Mr. Jones, and welcome. Now, Mr. Johnson, I see here your IQ is 61. I have only one thing to ask you: How long have you been a turkey hunter?"

*   *   *

Yeah, I know. It's a silly joke. But every time I've told it to a turkey hunter, I've gotten a belly laugh in response. People laugh at what rings true.

And, as experienced turkey hunters know, that one rings true. If you become a hunter of these big birds, you eventually come to wonder just how deep is this streak of masochism and stupidity that makes you keep at it. You won't feel this way all the time, but you will most assuredly feel this way some of the time. Probably a lot of the time.

As Tom Kelly wrote in his marvelous book *Tenth Legion*: "I do not hunt turkeys because I want to, I hunt them because I have to. I

Sackcloth and ashes comes in many forms on a turkey hunt. Saplings have an uncanny way of jumping in front of a charge of shot.

would really rather not do it, but I am helpless in the grip of my compulsion."

It's a sentiment most of us share. With the possible exception of golf, turkey hunting contains a larger potential for frustration than any other sport I can think of.

Trust me here. That pronouncement comes from the firm footing of a moderately jockish background – baseball, softball, track, tennis, and yes, golf – and I know whereof I speak. Ice-skating or the balance beam might also be exceptions, judging from what you see on TV, but I have no experience there and can't say for sure.

But this I can say: If you've been so successful in sports, business or any other endeavor that you're jaded and bored and looking for a challenge, then you should consider becoming a turkey hunter. (If you already are one, you're no longer in need of a challenge.) I've been hunting turkeys since the late 1970s, and I highly recommend it if you're in the market for a dose of sackcloth and ashes.

Those who do try turkey hunting are affected in one of only two possible ways: Either the whole thing leaves them unmoved, in which case they come away wondering what's the big deal and never feel the vaguest desire to ever go turkey hunting again; or they become hopelessly addicted, in which case they chase these elusive, aggravating, magnificent birds for the rest of their lives.

Where turkey hunting is concerned, there is no in between. There is no halfway. There are no casual, ho-hum, take-it-or-leave-it turkey hunters; where this grand sport is concerned, either you is or you ain't. And so we is, beset with all the attendant joys and sorrows, highs and lows, ups and downs, that are part and parcel to this peculiar pastime.

That is not a complaint. Like Tom Kelly, I, too, am helpless in the grip of my compulsion, but Lord help me, I wouldn't have it any other way.

We modern-day turkey hunters, as you will read about in Chapter 2, almost didn't have the opportunity to take up this frustrating sport. Turkey hunting is a born-again enterprise, a phoenix risen from its own ashes. To sum it up in a single sentence: Turkeys were plentiful when European settlers arrived, and we nearly wiped them off the face of the earth. Then we learned how to manage them and brought them back from the brink.

Long story short: This big bird is back. Turkeys are now legal game in every state except Alaska, which is too cold for turkeys to survive. And next spring in 49 states, several Canadian provinces and across much of northern Mexico, turkey hunters by the millions are going to go out and, more often than not, get frustrated.

But it won't all be frustration. There will be days when the turkey gods smile – or at least, do not frown – and the gobbler will do what he's supposed to do. But even when the birds don't cooperate, every turkey hunt is special and unique. There are rewards, plenty of them, even on those hunts when we get beat.

Maybe especially on those hunts when we get beat.

That's why, as you read the words on the following pages, you're going to notice a pretty high proportion of narratives in which the gobbler wins the day. I'm not ashamed of getting regularly beat by turkeys; they regularly beat hunters a lot more skilled than me.

If you're a turkey hunter, you already accept that. If you're not yet a turkey hunter, you'll come to accept it as you become one. Those who are unable to accept it will get disgusted and quit.

I doubt that many of you who are reading these words fall into that second category. The fact that you've decided to read this book tells me otherwise.

Section 1

The Games & the Players

Chapter 1

The Turkey Hunt

Feasting on a holiday bird awakens the urge, but it's still a long time until opening day.

Sometimes the urge holds off until after New Year's Day. More often, though, it starts pulling at me around Thanksgiving, when our family feasts on the succulent flesh of a wild turkey gobbler, one saved from the previous spring's hunting efforts. So far, we haven't had to get our Thanksgiving bird from the supermarket, but once or twice the Christmas bird has come from there.

Regardless of their pedigree, these holiday birds are still turkeys, and wild or tame, they set the cognitive wheels turning. Before our family has even digested the bird, the familiar fever has begun its insidious work. By day's end I've dug slate calls, diaphragms and the trusty Lohman box with all the notches in its side out of the drawers and closets where they've been since May. The house and yard are once again filled with clucks, purrs, yelps, cackles and cutts – rusty-sounding at first, but then sweeter and surer as the old skills resurface and the muscle memory kicks in.

By the time the last of the inevitable turkey salad is gone, everyone within earshot is tired of the discordant-to-them, lovely-to-me sounds of hen turkeys in love. This, mind you, is in November, with the spring turkey season still four months away. It doesn't get better.

Non-turkey hunters just don't get it. They can no more understand our compulsion than they can understand Chinese slang. But they're not alone in this; we who are afflicted don't understand, either.

We aren't unhappy about it, though. We may make noises to that effect from time to time, especially when the turkey gods are against us and/or the season is 4 weeks old and we're well into the ravages of sleep deprivation, but by and large we've come to accept our lot. We are turkey hunters, for better or worse … and it usually gets worse.

Even among outdoor types, non-turkey hunters outnumber turkey hunters by a wide margin. This being the case, some of you reading these words may have no clue what we're talking about here. If you've never experienced the rush of turkey hunting, there's no way you can understand it through reading a book. I know this for a fact, since for the first three decades of my life, I didn't have a clue, either.

So go with me on your first spring turkey hunt, the way I did with another guy in 1978, and learn firsthand what this business is all about:

*   *   *

Turkey hunters get up *early*. Three o'clock is about right, if you're going to meet me at the crossroads by half past 4. I'm not trying to threaten you here, but know this now: If you're late, I'll leave without you. Gobbling turkeys aren't tolerant of tardy hunters, and neither am I.

Lock your car and ride with me. Yours looks too shiny and new to go where we're heading. Old Blue is used to the rough roads, and another ding or two won't even be noticeable. Don't forget any of your gear – shotgun, shells, camouflage, calls, gloves, coffee thermos, small water bottle. Just throw everything except the coffee in the back of the truck, on top of my stuff, but hurry up. We're

burning precious time, and there's still 20 miles of rough road between us and our bird.

I roosted him late yesterday evening. In turkey hunter's lingo, that means I heard him fly up to his roost and gobble a time or two after he got there. I already know where he is, and that gives us a little edge on hunting him this morning. But it's only an edge if we get there early enough to take advantage of it. Come on!

A turkey hunt isn't so much a hunt as it is a military maneuver, and while we're driving through the inky night over these rough roads, we have time to review the morning's battle plan. If he's gobbling, or if you've roosted him the night before, as I did with this one, you already know the bird's location so you're not actually *hunting* him in the strictest sense of the word. Rather, you're trying to get in a good position and entice him to overcome his inbred reluctance to come to an unseen hen, instead of holding his ground and letting the hen come to him, as is the normal course of things. You're trying to outsmart him.

No, excuse me. I misspoke. You can't outsmart him because he isn't smart. What you're trying to do is outmaneuver him, to bend his will to yours, to get him to do something his instincts are screaming at him not to do. You have to overcome his native caution in order to achieve success, and to do so, you must contend with a set of senses – hearing and eyesight – so incredibly sharp, even veteran turkey hunters are continually amazed. It's

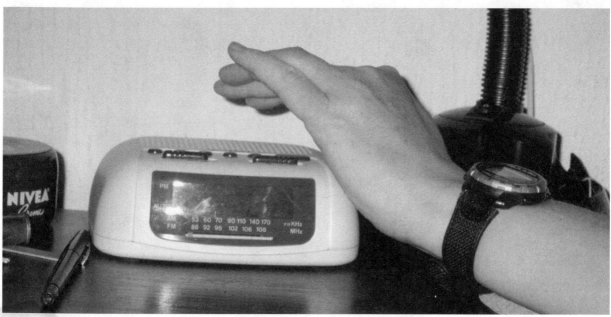

Turkey hunters get up early.

been said a turkey can see through a thin rock, but of course that's ridiculous. What they really do is see *around* them.

Philosophy and semantics aside, we're here to kill this turkey, and now it's time to leave the truck pinging in the cool morning air and hike through the dark woods to where he slept last night. It's a classic case of good news/bad news: It's not far as the crow flies, but we're not crows. We have two deep valleys and two steep ridges to negotiate, and not much time left to do it. So let's go.

What? You forgot your face mask? Hold still, then, and let me put some of this face paint on you. It's better than a mask, anyway. A mask restricts your peripheral vision and doesn't do your hearing any good, either. A turkey hunter needs every edge he can get.

We'll be able to use our flashlights for about half the trip, because the bird is roosted on the top of the second ridge, and he won't be able to see us or hear us until we crest the first one. Before we start, though, put on this orange hat. We'll take off the deer hunting garb when we sit down to work the bird, but it's best to wear it while we're moving, even though it's still dark right now. There'll be some daylight when we get where we're going,

and we're not the only hunters in these woods. Not all of them are as careful about target identification as they ought to be.

I'm joking, of course, but be careful anyway. No sense ruining a hunt by getting hurt before it starts.

What did you say? We're moving too fast? You're tired? Hmmm. Listen close: There's a turkey gobbler sleeping in a pine tree two ridges from here, and I intend to be over there with him when he wakes up. Whether you're there or not is entirely up to you.

OK. We've climbed out of the first valley onto the middle ridge, and I see you're still with me. It's time to turn off the lights. Don't worry, your eyes will adjust to the dark in a few minutes, and there's an old logging trace that'll take us down this ridge and up the next one pretty close to the turkey.

Here's the road now. It slants up the ridge, following the easier slopes, and it'll be fast going and not too hard. Not as hard as the last ridge, anyway. Load your gun now, but do it quietly and don't forget it's loaded. We don't want to make any unnecessary noise once we get in close.

We're getting close to the top now. Keep your voice to a whisper, and don't talk any more than necessary. Remember that sharp hearing. It's not a myth.

When you're hunting with a partner, always sit close enough together to be able to communicate in whispers.

When we sit down to this turkey, we'll lean against the same tree if we can find one big enough. You'll be on my left, because you shoot right-handed and I don't, and that way we'll each have our best swing radius to work with. We're getting pretty close to where we need to be now. Don't break any sticks underfoot or I'll twist your neck in a knot.

Here, this is close enough. Let's sit against this old red oak. It's big enough for both of us, and we'll be able to communicate in low whispers – which I've learned the hard way is highly desirable when you're hunting with a buddy.

The gobbler is roosted down the slope to the left – your direction – in a small group of big shortleaf pines on the edge of an old clear-cut. The cut is too brushy for him to fly down into, so we've got a real good chance of him coming our way. He's 100 yards away and maybe 25 yards downhill, and there's nothing between us but mature, wide-open woods.

It's a textbook setup. I just hope this old boy hasn't read the book.

Take a few seconds to rake back the leaves and smooth the ground where you're going to sit. Then take off your orange vest and use it for a cushion.

You need to be as comfortable as possible, because we might have to be as motionless as this oak tree we're leaning against, and we might have to be that way for a long time. That's hard enough to do even when your butt doesn't hurt.

After you're sitting down, get your knees up and rest the gun across them, to make sure that's going to be a comfortable position when the time comes. Got a rock under where your right foot wants to rest, you say? Well, that's why you rehearsed the shooting position ahead of time. You've got time to dig it up and move it out of the way. But do it quietly.

Everything ready? Good, now we can relax for a few minutes and enjoy the coming of the day … and we didn't get here a minute too soon. There's already a strong reddish glow in the east and, while the cardinals haven't started yet, I expect they're clearing their throats. The turkeys start gobbling not long after the cardinals start singing – that is, if they gobble at all.

There's the first cardinal. Their song even *sounds* red, have you ever noticed? He ought to gobble any minute. Maybe I ought to hoot like a barred owl …

Hooooo-awwwww!

Take a few extra seconds to make your setup spot as comfortable as possible. You might be nailed down there a long time, and it's no fun if there's a rock under your hindquarters.

If you're lucky enough, a real owl may be in the neighborhood to do your locator calling for you, but don't depend on it. Practice owling the same way you practice turkey calling.

Ah, good. My owling's not all that great, but that real owl did the honors for me.

Hooooo-awwwww!

Gobble, will you? What's the matter with him, anyway? Please gobble.

There he is! Right where I left him last night, but that's never a sure thing. I've had lots of roosted birds move on me during the night, and I don't know why. But I know they sometimes do it, so I'm always a little nervous at first.

We'll let him sound off a few more times, if he will, and then we'll give him a tree cluck or two. We want to make him think there's a sleepy hen over here that's just waking up.

He's gobbling pretty good now, isn't he? I could sit here and listen to him all day, but I'm sure he's got other plans, so we've got work to do. Soft stuff first, since he's still in the tree. I like a slate for the soft stuff. Here goes. Cross your fingers; I'm not very good at tree clucks …

Good. That sounded good. The turkey seemed to think so, too. Did you hear how he walked all over me as soon as I made the first cluck? We'll let him gobble once more on his own, and maybe I'll tree cluck to him one more time, and then we'll shut up until he flies down. He knows where we are, and there's no sense in overplaying our hand. Calling too much tends to make a gobbler stay in the tree, probably waiting for the eager hen to come walking underneath him. We want him to think a hen is here, but leave him with the impression she's not too eager.

There he is again. Now, two or three more soft clucks and we're set.

Boy, he gobbled back fast at that series, even though that first cluck was a little sour. We've got his attention, so now we wait him out …

There! Did you hear him fly down? That was a long 15 minutes, wasn't it? I bet he gobbled 50 times, and it was a strain not to call to him some more. But now he's down here with us, and it's time to call to him again. I'm gonna yelp at him a little and see what happens. You be ready. He might come running, or it might take him two hours to cover this 100 yards. And then again, he might go the other way. With a turkey, you just never know.

Ah, that's what I was hoping for. He gobbled back before I even finished the yelp. In turkey hunting parlance, that's known as "cutting your call," and it's a very good sign. We might get a look at this bird.

Oh, boy, I can hear him drumming. Listen and you'll hear it; it sounds like a log truck a long way off, right out at the limit of hearing, pulling a hill in granny low. When I can hear it, the turkey is just about shootable. Keep your eyes ... oops, there he is! Don't move. He's about 60 yards out, just to the left of that double-trunk dogwood about 45 degrees to the right of your gun barrel. He's strutting, and he's getting a little closer, but he's not in any hurry. Don't move.

All right. Less than 50 yards now. You see him? Good. Getting to watch the show is the best part of the hunt. Look at him, blown up as big as a Russian boar and just as black. Wait until he goes behind that white oak, and then shift your gun around.

Good. He didn't see the movement. If we don't screw it up, you're about to kill this turkey. Let him come on at least until he's even with that stump. It's about 40 yards, and that'll put him in range. If he wants to come closer, though, let him. Thirty yards would be better. If he gobbles, try not to flinch. It'll be pretty loud at this range.

He's even with the stump now, but he's still coming, so let him. Lordy, isn't he something! Look at that beard, thick as a bell rope. I bet he weighs 22 pounds. You've done everything right so far, so just stay as calm as you can and think things through. Don't blow it by making a mistake at this late stage of the game, the way I've done so many times.

Let him come. Let him come ...

Thirty yards now, more or less. Perfect killing range. Don't shoot him while he's strutting; his brain stem is all pulled down into his chest, and it's a smaller target now. Also, you're liable to shoot most of his beard off. Be ready, though. I'm gonna let him come another yard or so, and then I'll cluck at him pretty loud. That ought to make him break strut and stretch his neck to take a look, and that's when you need to shoot him. Aim at the base of his wattle, where it's biggest and reddest. That'll put the upper part of your pattern in his neck and head.

Here we go. Show time.
Cluck!

Don't call too much to a gobbler until he's on the ground. Overcalling at this stage will often cause the bird to stay in his tree and wait for the "hen" to walk under him.

Chapter 2

The Fall and Rise of Turkey Populations

Most turkey hunters have a few preferred listening spots. This remote ridgeline in Missouri is one of the author's favorites.

T he morning was still, and it was quite a bit cooler than normal for a late-April morning in the Missouri Ozarks. There was no frost, but it had been a near thing. The heavy dew stung my skin like powdered snow when I brushed a weed with the back of my hand.

Bill and I had our doubts as to whether the turkeys would gobble that morning, but it was the day before the second week of Missouri's spring season, we'd both filled our first-week tags, and we wanted to go out and listen. Our excuse was that we needed to locate birds to hunt the following morning, when we were both once again eligible to harvest a gobbler.

But you know better, as surely as Bill and I knew better while we were saying it to each other. We went out to listen that morning because we are turkey hunters of the most virulent sort, and we could no more have stayed in camp and slept late than we could have wiggled our noses and jumped over the moon.

We left the truck at the edge of the woods and started the 2-mile hike to the listening spot we'd chosen that morning, a long hogback that extended like a knife blade into a big expanse of good turkey country. It's a terrible place from which to launch a hunt, because all the country you can see is difficult to reach from there. But it's a great place to listen for turkeys, if your objective is just to hear them and not shoot any.

We reached the listening spot a few minutes before gobbling time, and we used the interval to gather a few branches and build a small fire. Once it was crackling merrily, we sat back and prepared to listen, a thermos of hot coffee between us, feeling as rich as Bill Gates.

To say we had plenty to listen to that morning would be low-balling it. This sounds like a lie, but I can't help it: On that cool April morning, while the fire warmed our outsides and the coffee warmed our insides, Bill and I heard more than 30 different gobblers. We tried to count the individual gobbles at first, but lost track and gave it up somewhere around 600.

This, mind you, was without any calling, owl-hooting or other encouragement on our part. All we did was listen. Those turkeys were gobbling at airplanes, owls, crows, distant gunshots and each other. They didn't need any prompting from our little corner, so we kept mum and enjoyed the symphony.

It was without a doubt the most turkey talk I've heard, before or since, from Eastern turkeys or any other kind. That morning stands out as one of the most remarkable mornings I've ever spent in the turkey woods.

That day was amazing in its own right, but what makes it even more notable is that less than 50 years before it happened, turkeys were almost completely gone from the entire Ozark Mountain region. It wasn't just in the Ozarks, either; turkeys were in a pickle almost everywhere. It was a sorry state of affairs.

In pre-settlement days, wild turkeys were unbelievably abundant in the vast hardwood forest that blanketed the Eastern United States. Turkey bones are among the most common animal remains in the kitchen middens of American Indians, proving turkeys were a common and important part of their diet. In fact, turkeys were so numerous and unwary, many Indian tribes considered them fit game only for beginners, and sent young boys out with bows and arrows or blowguns to bring home a turkey for supper.

When the first European settlers arrived in America, they made expeditious use of this immense population of wild turkeys inhabiting the vast forest that blanketed the Eastern half of the continent. DeSoto and his men dined frequently on wild turkeys as they tramped through the Lower Mississippi Valley in 1541 and 1542, as did the Spanish, French and English explorers who followed them two centuries later. In the decades just before the Civil War, Featherstonaugh, Audubon, Schoolcraft and other explorer/adventurers of that era chronicled the continuing abundance and relative unwariness of wild turkeys throughout the East.

One early adventurer named Rasles, who prowled the Illinois River region south of present-day Chicago in 1723, reported seeing numerous flocks of as many as 200 turkeys. "Prodigious multitudes" are the words he used to describe the numbers he saw. William Bartram, the famous naturalist/explorer/adventurer who was roaming the wild country that is now Alabama, Georgia and South Carolina about the time the 13 colonies were declaring their independence from England, wrote time and again about the abundance of turkeys in

Today's turkey is the descendant of the wiliest of the original birds. No wonder we have a hard time dealing with him.

Unregulated year-round hunting for market and sport just about wiped out the American wild turkey by shortly after 1900.

his book *Travels*. And Frederick Gerstaeker, a German shootist who wandered through the Arkansas and Missouri Ozarks in the mid-1700s and who might well have listened to turkeys from that same ridge Bill and I sat on that morning, talked of turkeys, too. He claimed that from daylight till nearly noon, for two solid months during the spring, the woods were in a constant uproar from the incessant gobbling of turkeys.

On a more personal level, the yellowed journal of my great-great-great grandfather Poynter also has passages referring to turkeys. Grandpa Poynter was a courier for the Confederate Army in the White River bottoms of eastern Arkansas, and he wrote in his crabbed, backslanted hand of how he fed himself on wild turkeys without firing his gun and alerting Yankee soldiers: "In the evenin, the turks would fly up, and a fellowe sittin quite could hear them for a ways. Come dark, I take a club and a torch in to the place, and could nock one out more times than not." Maybe Grandpa had a little trouble spelling the King's English, but he provided a graphic picture of turkey abundance in the 1860s.

But we brought this super-abundance of turkeys to near extinction, and we did it pretty quick. The open, mature stands of mast-bearing trees provided ideal turkey habitat, but when man came along, something had to give. That "something" was the very warp and weft of the land itself, and the settlers started converting those vast forests to towns and pastures and farms and roads. It was what Mississippi novelist William Faulkner was talking about in *The Bear*, when he referred to "... the doomed wilderness whose edges were being constantly and punily gnawed at by men with axes and plows." Puny the early settlers may have been; ineffective and lazy they were not. Faulkner's wilderness truly was doomed. Swarms of settlers followed close behind the trailblazers and trappers, and plumes of smoke began to rise here and there as pioneers laboriously hacked tiny holes in the unending forest canopy. Many of the early settlers died from scarlet fever, yellow fever, malaria and a dozen other diseases, or from accident or Indian attack. Others were defeated by the land and went back East. But a dozen new wagons rumbled in for every one that left, and the holes in the doomed wilderness grew larger and more numerous.

The result was inevitable. The abundance of wildlife with which the New World was blessed began to disappear. The biggest game – bison, elk, black bear – went first, and then the wolves, cougars, deer … and Grandpa Poynter's "turks."

In the lightning flash of a few generations, man found himself paying for all the drastic changes he'd brought to the natural order of things: the frantic clearing and draining; the cut-out-and-get-out logging; the inappropriate and damaging farming practices; the thoughtless pollution of air, soil and water. Added to these ecological outrages were the triple threat of unregulated year-round hunting for the urban market, unregulated year-round subsistence hunting to feed the numerous large rural families, and (following the Civil War) unregulated year-round "sport" hunting in which enjoyment and success were measured mainly by body counts.

No wonder the turkeys disappeared. Logically enough, they disappeared first from the more accessible, first-settled areas. For example, they were gone from Long Island, N.Y., by the late 1700s, from Connecticut by 1813, and from Massachusetts by 1851 – appropriately enough, from a place called Mount Tom.

But in most of the Eastern United States, turkeys held on for a while longer. Kansas lost its last native wild turkeys by 1871; Ohio by 1880; Iowa by 1907. By 1910, these great birds had vanished from more than 70 percent of their original range east of the Great Plains. Even where flocks managed to hang on, their numbers were a pitiful fraction of the former abundance. From the original untold millions, the nationwide turkey population had fallen to an estimated 30,000 birds by the late 1930s.

Populations languished at that approximate level for the next 20 years or so, and the early students of the brand-new profession known as wildlife management were generally of the opinion that the live wild turkey was a dead duck.

It was about this time, though, that the conservation ethic began to find favor in America, fueled largely by sportsman/President Teddy Roosevelt's inner fire and vision. We began to evolve from a nation of greedy takers into a populace a little more willing to put something back – or, at least, to quit taking quite so rapaciously. Roosevelt established the Ouachita National Forest (then called the Arkansas National Forest)

Turkey hunters know the value of "putting something back." Through license purchases, donations, volunteer work and membership in organizations like the National Wild Turkey Federation, turkeys are once again common throughout most of the United States.

The cannon net and later the rocket net, adapted for use on wild turkeys, set the stage for the reintroduction of wild turkeys – not only to their former range, but also to much suitable habitat outside the historical turkey range.

and the first national wildlife refuge (Pelican Island in Florida) in 1903. State conservation agencies were formed, and these infant organizations made the first attempts at regulating the harvest of wildlife populations through the enactment of primitive game laws.

It was a start, but it wasn't enough. Remnant turkey flocks stopped dwindling and began to hold their own, but just barely. Despite the protection, the birds had been hammered so hard and their habitats and habits altered so drastically that little range expansion took place during the first three decades of the 1900s. Vast tracts of suitable turkey habitat continued to stand empty of turkeys.

Enter the era of the game-farm bird. Pennsylvania, Arkansas, Alabama, Missouri, Louisiana and other states began to raise semi-wild turkeys by the thousands, turning them loose willy-nilly into the wild. Most of these birds quickly disappeared down the throats of bobcats and foxes and therefore caused no great harm. But a few of these inferior birds, released in areas already populated with remnant flocks, survived

long enough to interact and/or breed with the wild birds, and this weakened the genetic superiority of the wild stock and also infected them with diseases such as avian cholera and blackhead.

Things continued to look bleak for the bird, which Benjamin Franklin once proposed, only half-jokingly, as our national symbol.

But then came the Depression, and what was devastating for the works of man was a godsend for the struggling turkey population. Rural America lost a great deal of its human population as farmer after farmer went bust, abandoned his farm and moved on to find work in the cities or to start a new life on the West Coast.

The heavy hand this large rural population had been laying on the turkey population through illegal hunting and continued habitat destruction suddenly wasn't there any more. Abandoned farms began to revert. Cutover forests began to establish a second growth of mast-bearing trees. And turkeys began to expand their range, although the expansion was barely perceptible at first. Squirrel hunters and woods workers started seeing turkeys

Restoration work was slow and laborious at first. These crates contain wild turkeys trapped along the Mississippi River, transported by train across Arkansas and released in the Ouachita Mountains near Waldron.

and turkey sign where none had been seen for a half-century.

Furthermore, the wild turkey proved to be considerably more versatile than wildlife managers had once thought. Conventional wisdom held that a wild turkey flock needed a block of at least 50,000 acres of contiguous forest habitat to survive, and the biologists of the 1930s pretty much believed that daunting rule of thumb … that is, until turkeys started thumbing their snoods at it and showing up in thin ribbons of woods bordering creeks, and in small woodlots surrounded by pasture and row crops. They weren't supposed to be able to make a go of it in these small, remnant woodlands, but they did.

The crisis was over. The birds were coming back.

Natural flock expansion was an unacceptably slow process, though. Before any significant range expansion could take place, a local turkey population had to grow until it saturated its existing range. Only then would population pressure force birds outward and into new territory. One or

two bad hatches could reduce the population and set the whole process back to square one.

Looking for a solution, biologists borrowed a page from the book of waterfowl management. Waterfowl researchers in the 1940s developed the cannon net and used it to capture ducks and geese for banding studies. Turkey biologists found the technique worked equally well on large gallinaceous birds with wattles under their chins.

Trapping and transplanting didn't hurt the original core turkey populations, since the number of birds removed from any area was small. But the standard release of two or three adult gobblers and 10 to 12 hens paid huge dividends in re-establishing turkeys to former, still-suitable habitats. Massachusetts, for instance, hadn't had a wild turkey since 1851. Biologists there made the first release in 1972, and the first Massachusetts spring turkey season took place in 1980.

Nobody actually knows how many turkeys are in the United States today, but it's over 5.6 million and still growing. We hunt them in every state except Alaska. Some states have populations of

Today's gobblers are good at giving us the slip because we killed all the unwary ones a hundred years ago.

300,000 to 500,000 or more – Georgia, Alabama, Texas and Missouri, for example.

These aren't bad statistics we're throwing around here. Especially considering that we're talking about a bird that professional wildlifers had written off only 70 years ago. Urban encroachment, habitat destruction, pollution, illegal hunting and excessive predation still cause problems for wild turkeys. But today there are more pluses than minuses, and the population continues to grow.

Today's Eastern wild turkey is a vastly different critter from the turks that fed my Grandpa Poynter during the Civil War. This computer-age bird we have to contend with is a descendant of the wariest and most elusive of the original population. He's good at giving us the slip because his predecessors were the turkeys that panicked and flew away from my Grandpa in 1863, not the ones that sat there in the glare of his torch and waited for the club. The modern wild turkey is more adapt-able than most of the original flock, and he's that way because the few survivors that spawned him were the ones able to adapt well enough to their rapidly changing world to survive. In short, today's bird is wary and cautious because only the wariest and most cautious of his kind survived to pass their traits down the line.

Today's wild turkey is as much a product of the modern age as Hevi-Shot and microchips. He is what he is because his ancestors were baptized by fire and lived to tell the tale. He is magnificent and he belongs to you and to me. But we can possess him only if we are skillful enough – and lucky enough – to beat him on his own court and at his own game.

Chapter 3

The Bird Himself

Today's wild turkey is a more wary, more elusive bird than the one Indian boys and settlers' sons sharpened their hunting skills on two centuries ago. Our 21st century turkey is a descendant not of the many that were stupid and died, but of the pitiful few that were smart and lived.

No, not smart; that's not the right word. A wild turkey is, after all, a bird, possessed of a brain that would rattle around in a ping-pong ball. How smart can he be?

What he is, is paranoid. He's suspicious of his own shadow, and if the least little thing is out of whack – or if he even suspects it might be – he

A wild turkey isn't smart. What he is, is paranoid.

doesn't stick around to confirm his suspicions. He simply leaves. And he leaves so quickly and sometimes so silently you wonder if he was ever there at all.

A good part of the frustration built into turkey hunting is born of just that one thing, but plenty of other factors also contribute. Even when the bird isn't spooked, he's generally hesitant to come to your calling. Frequently, a gobbler will stand 80 to 100 yards away, sometimes quite a bit closer, maybe in sight and maybe not, and strut and gobble like crazy at your calling and never break that magic 40-yard circle that marks the outer limit of effective shotgun range.

And very often, you never know why he doesn't come, either, because it can be any of a jillion things. Turkey hunting is a game of infinite variables, played on a field of unlimited dimension, against an opponent that doesn't know the rules and wouldn't play by them if he did. Every hunt differs from every other hunt in a hundred little ways, and every turkey reacts differently than every other turkey … in a hundred little ways.

Already, that's enough to give any turkey hunter a lifetime supply of angst. But there's still another wrinkle: Not even the same bird will react the same way from one day to the next, even under seemingly identical circumstances. Find a turkey gobbling from the same spot two days in a row, under the same weather conditions and at the same time of day, call to him the same way both days, and one day he's liable to clam up and sneak away in the opposite direction. The next day, he might gobble his head off and come at you on a dead run, forcing you to throw your gun to your shoulder and shoot him more or less in self-defense.

It's already been mentioned that golf is a frustrating sport. But in golf, at least the ball holds still while you're swinging at it. The difficulties you encounter on the golf course are invariably of your own manufacture.

Turkeys don't. Hold still, that is. They have a disconcerting habit of jinking and juking all over the landscape, and many a hapless hunter has spent half the morning calling to a gobbler that's gone off to visit relatives in the next township.

A turkey hunt doesn't have rules, except for the ones we impose on ourselves as sportsmen and sportswomen to keep it ethical and within bounds. A turkey has no such constraints; he'll beat you any way he can.

Another thing turkeys don't do is what you expect them to do. Balance a golf ball on a tee and whack it true, with the club face perpendicular to the axis of the ball and your arm straight and your head down and all that Tiger Woods stuff, and it will fly straight as an arrow down the fairway. Angle the head of your club in or out a little, or bend your elbow or lift your head, and you'll impart a crooked spin to the ball and it'll curve giddily either right, which is a hook, or left, which is a slice. Or maybe it's the other way around.

In other words, the ball acts predictably according to the way you attack it with the club. Hit it straight and it goes straight. Put some English on it and it'll bite the air unevenly and veer off course. Every time. Guaranteed.

There's no such cause-and-effect relationship in turkey hunting. Sometimes you can do everything exactly right and still lose. You just never can tell with a turkey, and that's where the extra measure of frustration comes from. You can call to a gobbler in world-class fashion, and not make a single stupid tiny error such as blinking at the wrong time or letting your heart beat too loud, and still everything might go for naught. The turkey won't go straight down the fairway when you strike him true. Instead, he'll invent his own English and hook or slice on you – sometimes simultaneously.

Turkeys will sometimes do exactly what you expect them to do, but not often enough that you can depend on it. They do it just enough to keep you off stride. Switching the analogy to another sport, a turkey usually makes a hunter feel like a batter who stepped into the box looking for a fastball but got a knuckleball instead. You think the pitch is your meat, and you get a good, level swing, but you get too much of the top of the blasted ball and send a little dribbler back to the mound. You're out before you're halfway down the line.

Given all these elements of difficulty, the outsider looking in is left to wonder how come there are turkey hunters at all. If it's that frustrating and aggravating, if it's that difficult, then why are there such things as turkey hunting veterans? Why does anyone ever go the second time?

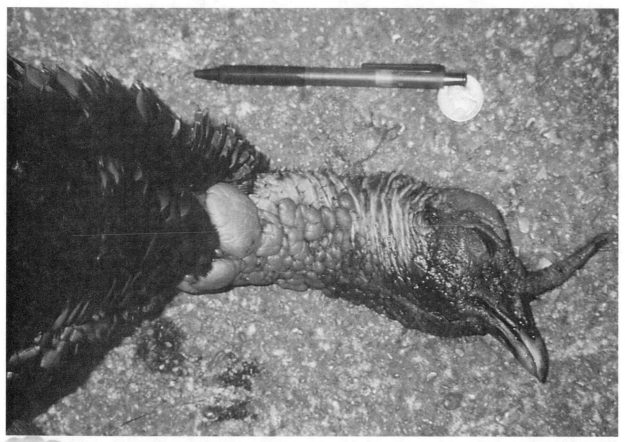

A turkey's brain is about the size of a quarter, and its spinal cord isn't any bigger than a standard ink pen. That's the target you must hit to make a clean kill.

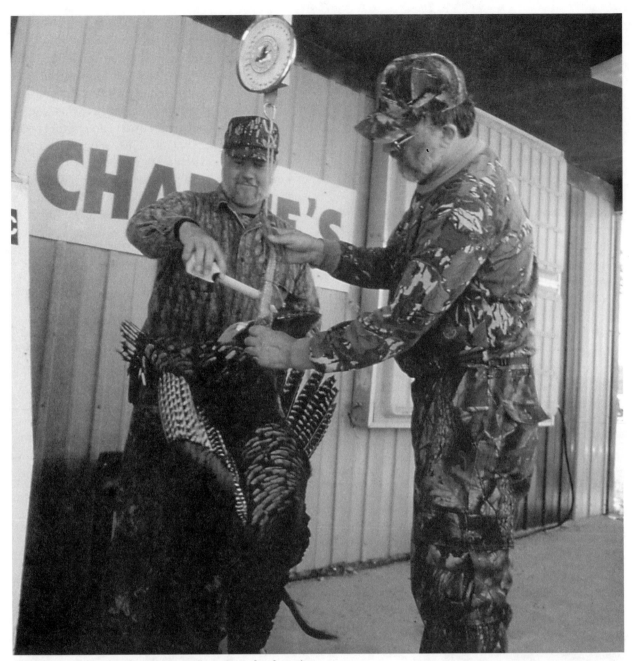

Sometimes the turkey hunter wins. Sometimes he doesn't.

Well, because it's not always frustrating and aggravating. Sometimes the turkey hunter wins. Sometimes you find an easy one. Or sometimes, after hunting the same gobbler for a few hours, days or weeks – even a few seasons, in some extreme examples – after trying every trick in your book and borrowing a few pages from the books of other hunters, you finally punch his hot button. You finally hit the right combination of calling, location, time of day, terrain and the mood of the bird … and he begins, unbelievably, to come.

And when he gets there, gobbling and drumming and strutting his stuff, it will have been worth all the frustration and aggravation. It's at this point that a turkey hunter tries to remain calm enough to enjoy the show; after all, it's one of nature's most stirring performances. And by the time most of us get to see it, we've more than paid the price of admission.

Section 2

Getting Off on the Right Foot

Chapter 4

Lessons From the Spring Woods

Young gobblers grow up into big boys, and most experienced hunters pass them up, but there's no biological reason for not taking jakes. Even the young ones can put on a good show.

I remember quite well the first two wild turkeys I ever saw. It was during the spring of 1953, and I was in my sixth year. The birds were dead in the back of a pickup truck, brought to town by two proud and rough-hewn rivermen. Although none of us who gathered around the truck to admire the birds knew it at the time, we were looking at 1 percent of the total Arkansas turkey harvest for that year.

One of the birds was a mature gobbler, and the other was a jake – a "blue john" in the parlance of the southeast Arkansas River delta country where

these two long-ago birds lived and died. The adult had a fine bushy beard and a wicked set of hooked spurs, and I realized, despite my tender years and abysmal lack of knowledge about turkeys, that I was looking at a genuine trophy.

It was a long time before I saw another turkey, living or dead. Turkeys didn't grow many to the hill during my youth and early adulthood, in my home state or anywhere else.

Even so, thanks to the resurgence of turkey populations related in Chapter 2, the wide-eyed boy who peered at the two gobblers in the bed of the pickup truck in 1953 has become a veteran – and inveterate – turkey hunter. Each spring, these grand birds lure me into the greening woods and teach me a few new lessons …

… such as the one about moving. Or, more correctly, about not moving. It happens to me every spring, and I have no doubt it'll happen next year, too: I'll be sitting against a big tree somewhere, calling to a turkey that hasn't gobbled for the past 30 minutes, and a root will grow under my butt and I'll shift ever so slightly to relieve the agony. And the turkey, which will have come ghosting into easy gun range (as likely as not from directly behind me), will yell *putt!* in my ear and vanish from my life forever.

The obvious solution is to remain completely motionless, but that's so difficult I can't even understand how dead people do it. For me at least, it's easier to climb steep mountains all day long than remain perfectly motionless for one lousy hour.

But since turkeys are allergic to motion, it pays to make the effort. You can't eliminate movement entirely, of course, but I try to minimize it. Still, I always seem to not be able to minimize it quite enough, and there's often a turkey hanging around to call my shortcomings to my attention.

Over the years, though, I've developed a compromise that works fairly well. When things are slow and I'm sitting around in the woods doing a little blind calling in the hopes a turkey will hear it and come to investigate, I remove my wrist watch at the start of the session and prop it up so I can see it without having to move my head. Then I try to remain completely motionless for 15-minute intervals. When each 15-minute segment is over, I carefully scan the woods one final time and then take a five-minute "break." I stretch, scratch, move my head and neck, shift my legs and scratch my back against my setup tree. Sometimes I even stand up for a bit. Then I sit down and repetrify for another 15 minutes. I still spook incoming turkeys from time to time, but not as many as before.

Calling too much is another trap I usually manage to fall into every year, and it takes a hung-up gobbler or two to get me out of the habit. The problem is, calling is a lot of fun, and I love to do it. And so, like so many other turkey hunters, I tend to come across like an overly eager hen. Gobblers often approach to that maddening 70-yard marker and stop, expecting me to come the

It's impossible to remain absolutely motionless, but the stiller you can be, the more turkeys you'll kill.

rest of the distance since I'm so hot-to-trot and all. They'll walk around out there and strut and drum and gobble and crane their necks to look toward me, but perversely maintain that distance – too far to kill, too close for me to change calling positions or do anything else that might help me kill them. It's a Mexican stand-off in the classic tradition, and rarely is there a dead gobbler at the end of it.

Some turkey hunters believe a hung-up turkey is a spooked turkey, but that's ridiculous. When a gobbler is spooked, he doesn't hang around gobbling, barely out of gun range of the thing that spooked him. When a turkey is spooked, he leaves, and he does so quicker than you can tell someone about it.

No, a hung-up turkey is only living according to his lights. His job in nature is to find a good strutting area – which is to say, an area from which he can be easily and plainly seen by approaching hens – and then stand around in that area and gobble and look handsome until a hen comes to visit. When a gobbler hangs up, it's often because he's reached a strutting area and is waiting for the hen to meet him halfway.

The gobbler's job is to find a good strutting area from which he can easily be seen, and then wait for the hens to come to him. The turkey hunter's job is to convince him to do otherwise.

The proper course of action in such a situation depends largely on whether the gobbler is in sight or not. If there's a fold of ground or some other terrain feature between you and the turkey, you can try changing calling positions. It doesn't have to be a move closer to the turkey; just moving is the important part. A hen turkey isn't nailed to the ground, so when you change positions and resume calling, it simulates the normal movement of an unrestrained hen. Sometimes it's just the ticket for breaking a hung-up gobbler loose and bringing him to the gun.

If the turkey is in sight when he hangs up, of course, moving is out of the question. That's another lesson. I usually manage to run off a gobbler or two each spring by moving on them when I think they're out of sight but they're apparently not.

Continuing to call to a gobbler that's close but hung up is the wrong thing to do, but it's yet another lesson I have to relearn every spring. It's hard not to do it. One of the reasons it's hard not to do is because every so often, it's the exact thing

you ought to do. Sometimes when you yelp or cackle or cutt or purr right in the face of a hung-up gobbler – especially if you've been giving him the silent treatment for a while – he'll come marching straight at you.

Or not.

On the other hand, it's entirely possible to call too little to a gobbler in this situation. I have a loosely developed theory about this whole scenario: No matter how little or how much you think you should call, there are days when it will be exactly right and days when it will be wrong, and there's not much you can do about it either way. The lesson here is that it takes experimentation to find the right style of calling for most gobblers you'll encounter, and the hard part of the lesson for me is that it's almost always best to start conservatively. It's easier to increase the intensity of your calling than to back off on it.

Not getting too close to a gobbler is another lesson I have to relearn each spring. It's hard to keep from trying to close the gap between those

You can call too much to an approaching gobbler, but you can also call too little. Experienced hunters develop some ability to "take the temperature" of a gobbler and then call appropriately, but all of us make mistakes.

final few yards to that perfect setup tree just ahead, but if you get just one step too close, the game is over. Here's a handy rule of thumb: If you have a gut feeling you can't make it to a given setup tree without spooking your gobbler, you're probably right.

The sword cuts both ways, of course, and the other side of the blade is that you ought to get as close to a bird as you can before calling to him. Setting up too far away has cost otherwise good turkey hunters many a gobbler.

One long-ago spring in the Missouri Ozarks, a friend and I climbed a ridge to position ourselves between four gobblers on our right and two gobblers on our left. The turkeys were about 500 yards apart, and we split the difference and set up dead between them. It was late in the season and plenty green enough for us to have gotten closer to either group, but we didn't.

It was a serious mistake. While it's sometimes possible to pull a gobbler a half-mile to your calling, other times you can't pull one a dozen feet.

That was the case on this occasion. The two groups of birds held their ground, and Bill and I held ours, and we all talked excitedly back and forth for the better part of three hours. It was very entertaining, but in the end it was just frustrating. One group of gobblers went east, one went west, but none flew over the cuckoo's nest. After the turkeys were all gone, the cuckoos in question went back to camp and poured themselves a couple of stiff drinks.

This uncertain and inexact aspect of the hunt known as setting up assumes even greater importance when the gobbler you're trying to get close to is still on the roost. Set up too far away from the still-roosted turkey, and chances are excellent there'll be a hen closer to him than you are. Get too close, though, and he'll see you. If either of those things happens, you're history.

In article after article on turkey hunting, you'll read stuff like, "Always get within 150 yards before setting up on a roosted turkey." Maybe the figure will be 100 yards, or 200.

35

When everything works as planned and he's lying there dead at your feet, all the difficulties seem worthwhile.

can, and go to work. You'll spook some turkeys, all right, and in the process relearn a lesson or two, but after a while you'll begin to develop a feel for this delicate and iffy part of the hunt. You'll still bump turkeys, but not quite so often.

How to work a turkey that's still on the roost is another iffy thing. If there's a constant in turkey hunting, it's this: If you call too much to a turkey that's still in a tree, he will stay in that tree longer than you want him to. The rub, of course, is it's hard to resist calling to a roosted gobbler, especially when he's in the mood to gobble.

Sure, you usually need to call to him while he's still in the tree to let him know you're in the neighborhood. But once you've done that and he's answered you, your best course of action is to dummy up and wait until he's on the ground. He might fly down in your direction; then again, he might not. You just never know. But wait until he's down before you call again; it's the best percentage play. And yes, it's another example of the lessons I have to relearn each spring.

It's a frustrating classroom, these spring woods. And a wise old turkey gobbler is the most perverse teacher you'll ever have. He delights when you fail. He's willing to help you at every step along the road to ruin.

But when things work out as planned and he's lying there dead at your feet, the difficulty of the lessons seems worthwhile. There'll be other hard taskmasters in the future, and plenty of other times when you'll fail in a most miserable fashion, but for now, for this moment, you've passed with honors.

Whatever the figure given, it's a crock. Every situation is different, and in some cases you'll have to settle for a 200-yard setup (or more), while at other times you can get within 50 yards of the roost tree. Closer is almost always better, but don't fret about it too much, and don't push the envelope. Get as close as you think you safely

Enjoy the moment. It will be fleeting.

Chapter 5

Advice for a Rookie

The world is dark, and you're out there in it. Alone.

As you stand there waiting for first light, shivers of anticipation ripple along your skin. Optimism runs high, but it's a feeling based thus far on emotion rather than success; this is only your second season as a turkey hunter, and you've yet to pull the trigger.

Your listening spot is the crest of a steep ridge, and you've never laid eyes on the place except on paper. You found it during an armchair scouting expedition one cold evening last winter, sitting by the fire and poring over a stack of maps. You're not an experienced turkey hunter, but you know how to read a topo map. The place "lays good" and it's been pulling at you ever since.

It caught your attention because the end of the ridge is broad and flat as a football field, and because three narrow, steep-sided spur ridges like the toes of a chicken's foot (or a turkey's) jut off the end of the ridge. The three spurs descend gradually to the river that loops around this devil's backbone of limestone, providing easy climbing from the bottom of the valley to the top of the ridge. The place almost screams turkey, judging from everything you've read and heard. The flat area on the end of the ridge is a made-to-order strutting area, the hollows between the spur ridges provide good roosting places, and the spurs themselves give the turkeys easy access to both.

You'd intended to scout the place prior to the season, of course. But there was deer season and duck season, and the holidays and then the Super Bowl. February was cold and short, and March was windy and hectic, and with one thing and another you never found time. Now April is here ... and it's time to hunt.

Waiting for first light and, if you're lucky, the first gobble.

Almost time, anyway. You're a half-hour early; you didn't know exactly how long it would take, in the dark, to pull the two ridges between here and the truck, so you allowed a little cushion. It's always better to be early than late, but the down side is that the last minutes you spend standing around in the dark are an eternity.

You stand and fidget, then sit and fidget, and still the night lingers. Finally the new day begins to grow in the east. The light gains intensity so gradually, you can't detect the change from minute to minute … but somehow, it's suddenly light enough to see things: trees, rocks, leaves. A cardinal wakes up and burbles his music, and it's gobbling time.

But the turkeys of Chicken Foot Ridge evidently don't know it, because none within your limits of hearing utters a peep. *Maybe there aren't any turkeys here*, you think with mild panic. Maybe you made the wrong choice. Maybe you should have forgotten about this place and gone back to the south slope of Blowout Mountain, where you saw the two flocks of gobblers last deer season.

Two barred owls have been calling back and forth far down the valley, but if a turkey has answered them, you've failed to hear it. You're thinking about going on a forced march to another listening spot, but before you commit to Plan B, you decide to try a hoot or two yourself.

As new as you are to turkey hunting, though, you're even newer to the peripherals of the sport like owl-hooting, and you're still pretty self-conscious in front of witnesses about purposefully trying to sound like a nocturnal bird. That's why you haven't practiced owling very much, and it shows in the sounds you make.

But the only witnesses out here this morning are the trees, and you'll never get good at it if you don't start doing it. So you square your shoulders, draw in a breath and belt out an abbreviated four-note call: *Hoo-hoo-ho-hooooo!* Somehow it seems less silly than the full-roll, eight-note standard hoot.

They say a turkey gobbles at an owl because the sound "shocks" him. Train whistles, thunder, airplanes and even gunshots can elicit the same

In order to wrap turkey tags around many turkey legs, hunters must learn to make quick decisions and be flexible enough to change plans in the middle of the hunt.

response. But no turkey has ever been more shocked than you at this moment, because not one but three gobblers immediately roar back at your tentative call. All are close to your position on the main ridge, but they're spread out, each roosted by himself. If you managed to course them accurately, there's one bird on each of the chicken toes.

You're trying to decide which of them to go after, but it's a paralyzing decision and you don't know how to make it. Things get even more complicated a minute later. One of the turkeys gobbles again, the other two answer it … and then two more gobblers crank up on the main ridge, one in either direction, neither of them more than 300 yards away. Now you have five gobblers calling back and forth, and you're pretty much surrounded.

You're still wet behind the ears, you've never looked down the gun barrel at a turkey, you're hunting unfamiliar territory and you're in the middle of five talkative gobblers. What would you do in a situation like that?

Not, I hope, what I did when it happened to me in 1979. I spent the first 45 minutes of precious hunting time rushing back and forth across the flat top of that ridge in erratic, indecisive zigzags, heading first toward one turkey and then another. I never got more than 100 feet from my starting point the whole time, though I must have trotted a mile or more.

By the time I forced myself to pick a single gobbler and go to him, all five had flown down and dummied up, and the party was over. I heard a few scattered gobbles over the next three hours, but I'd blown my chance and I knew it. I failed to seize the moment and it cost me the day. I laugh about it now, but my sense of humor comes from the perspective of time. For several years, it wasn't a bit funny.

Now, let's roll back the clock, go back to that morning and talk about some things I might have done to give the hunt a more satisfactory outcome:

That awkward, four-note owl hoot may have been the only thing I did right that morning, aside from map-scouting to find the spot in the first place. Many beginners get so caught up in the mystique of "raising" a gobbler, they forget that

Is there a fence between you and your bird? Even if the gobbler crosses it every day of his life, he might not do so to answer your calling. Get on the same side as the gobbler and take the potential obstacle out of play.

the objective is not to fill the woods with owl music, but to actually get a turkey to gobble … and furthermore, to be able to hear him when he does. If you're busy making owl noise, you're going to miss hearing some turkeys.

The most effective hoot – and the same applies to crow calls, coyote calls or any other artificial sound you might make to get a turkey to gobble – is abrupt, loud … and short. Short is important in this context. Make your locator call, then shut up and listen.

If there are two of you hunting together, the person not making the locator call should stand 5 to 10 yards away from the one who's calling, with ears focused in a different direction from the caller. It's much easier for the listener to hear a gobbler if he "walks on the call" – that is, if he starts gobbling before the noise of the locator call dies away. And a hot turkey will often do just that.

One of the identifying characteristics of a good turkey hunter is his or her ability to make quick decisions based on the information he has to work with in a given hunting situation. My best play that morning, with five gobblers around me, would have been to sit down pretty much where I was and start calling to all five. None was more than a quarter-mile away. Although I could have gotten closer to any one of them, doing so would have put me farther away from the other four. It was a catbird-seat situation, and I was too inexperienced to realize it.

Usually, though, your morning isn't going to be quite that target-rich. In a more common scenario, you'll only have one gobbler responding, and that makes the "which-one" decision unnecessary. But suppose there are two or more gobblers from which to choose. How do you go about it?

Distance is one obvious factor. If Gobbler A is a half-mile away across a deep valley, and Gobbler B is 100 yards from you along the same ridge you're standing on, it's a no-brainer.

But in other situations you won't be able to make your decision based solely on distance. If a more distant turkey seems more eager to answer your calls or is gobbling a lot more than a closer bird, maybe he's the better choice even though he's farther away. Most veteran turkey hunters will take a hot gobbler at a half-mile over a disinterested one at 100 yards any old day.

The terrain between you and the birds can be a big factor, too.

"Knowing the lay of the land is about half the battle," says my old friend Eddie Salter, who knows more about what a turkey's going to do than the turkey does. "There might be something between you and the gobbler he doesn't want to cross – a fence, a creek, a ditch, a thicket or something else. And if he doesn't want to cross it, there's nothing you can do to make him."

Knowing about these potential obstacles can mean the difference between a successful hunt and just another frustrating conversation with a long-distance gobbler. If the closest gobbler is on the other side of a creek or a clear-cut and the distant one is in open woods, it might be another case where the more-distant bird is the better candidate. That is, unless you know the land well enough to move to a calling location that provides the near gobbler with an easier approach.

These and other factors can weigh in your decision when you have two or more birds to choose from, but there are no hard-and-fast rules in any aspect of turkey hunting. You have to assess each situation on its own merits and make what amounts to an educated guess. (Like Eddie Salter says, you can't actually *make* a turkey do anything.) And you need to make this educated guess very quickly. Seconds are often precious in turkey hunting situations, especially at first light when the birds are gobbling from the roost. You gain a lot of advantage if you can move into a good position and set up on a gobbler before he leaves his roost tree.

Once the decision is made and you're moving into position, try to get as close as you can without spooking the turkey. That's easy to say, but it can be tricky, and again, there are no hard-and-fast rules. That old advice you've heard about always getting within 100 yards, or 200 yards, or whatever, before setting up is as ridiculous as it is useless. Every situation is different and you must deal with them differently.

Possibly the best piece of turkey hunting wisdom I've ever heard was imparted to me by Brad Harris, my friend and turkey hunting mentor and one of the nation's best hunters. "The difference between getting close enough to a turkey and too close to a turkey is one step," is the way Brad put it. "The closer you can get, the better your chances. But only as long as you're not detected."

Getting close is important for a couple of reasons. First, it can remove many of the obstacles that might sabotage your hunt – those draws,

Bill Jordan is not one of the old-style "yelp-three-times-and-wait-till-noon" hunters. He believes in either getting a bird fired up, or going in search of one that wants to play.

creeks, fences, thickets and other bugaboos we talked about a few paragraphs ago. If you're 300 yards from a bird and there's a ravine or fence between you, you're probably beaten before you make your first tree call. Get closer, put the obstacle behind you and take it out of play.

OK. Let's assume you've made what you think is a good setup on a roosted turkey. Now, how much should you call to him?

Again, it's a tricky thing. Probably the best answer is "not much."

Although most veteran hunters feel it's important to call to a roosted gobbler before he leaves the tree, so he'll think there's a hen in the area, most of them also feel it's equally important to not overdo it. Overcalling to a gobbler that's still in his roost tree can, and usually does, cause him to remain in the tree past normal fly-down time,

41

waiting and watching from his elevated viewpoint for the eager hen to show herself.

My usual game plan – and this is true of most of the really good hunters I've shared the woods with – is to call sparingly and softly to a roosted gobbler, but only until he answers. Then I shut up until the bird flies down, at which time I start to get more aggressive.

This, by the way, can be a real test of your resolve. A good percentage of the time, once you pull a gobble out of a roosted bird, he won't shut up. Your impulse is to call back to him some more, to engage him in a conversation, but it's almost always the wrong thing to do because he'll just sit there stubbornly in his tree and gobble at you all the more. This increases the risk not only of attracting other hunters, but also of attracting an honest-to-goodness hen, which won't be constrained by that 100- or 200- or whatever yard limit, and will walk right under your gobbler. The gobbler will then drop out of his tree and go off with her, almost never in your direction.

The only consistent exception to the don't-call-much-to-a-roosted-gobbler rule is when the gobbler is roosted over water. In this case, he knows no hen is going to swim out there to him like a wood duck, so you can go ahead and call to the gobbler if you want. Even here, though, I've found it's not a good idea to overdo it. If I'm set up on a gobbler that's roosted over a backwater area or over a cypress brake, I'll usually set up within 50 yards of the edge of the backwater and try to get the gobbler excited and well-fired with a few minutes of aggressive back-and-forth calling. Then I'll shut up and let him gobble. It works about as often and anything else does in turkey hunting, which is to say just often enough to keep me trying it.

Once the gobbler is out of the tree, regardless of where he was roosted, you can, and usually should, get more vocal. And this is where the different personalities and styles of turkey hunters come into play.

One of the old-time hunters I used to know – and he was a very good one – didn't call as much in a whole season as most of us do in two hours. If Abner ever got a gobbler to answer his beat-up old slate call, he never called to that turkey again. He would sit down, shut up, get his gun on his knees, and wait. And wait, and *wait*. Furthermore, while he was waiting he would never call to that bird again, not so much as a cluck. "If a turkey

ever answers you, he'll eventually come looking for you," he used to say. "All you have to do is be patient."

Ab killed his limit of turkeys every spring, so there's bound to be some merit to his system. But he was an old game warden, accustomed to long, silent vigils while he waited for the bad guys to show up and do their thing. It's good training for this low-key style of turkey hunting, but I could no more wait that long for either a bad guy or a gobbler than I could kiss my elbow and turn into a prince. I require a little more active participation, thank you. I've killed a few – a very few – gobblers using Ab's call-once-and-wait-till-moss-grows-on-your-north-side tactics, but it's about the closest I've ever come to not having fun while turkey hunting. Spending half of a perfectly good spring morning sitting as motionless and as quiet as a rock isn't my idea of a good way to spend it. If a turkey that's answered my call will eventually come, but it takes him three hours to do it, I won't fool with him. If I can't call to a gobbler except on alternate Tuesdays, then I won't fool with him again. If I wanted that much frustration, I'd stay home and work on my income taxes.

Having vented my spleen in such an unmistakable manner, let me now say that this snail's pace, wait-'em-out style can come in handy if you're hunting a small area and can't move around. But for the average turkey hunting conditions, most of us just don't have that kind of patience.

For example, there's Will Primos, president of Primos Hunting Calls in Mississippi. As Will often says in his *Truth About Spring Turkey Hunting* video series, he calls too much and he calls too loud. But in Primos' style of aggressive turkey hunting, it works.

"There was a time when I thought knowing the terrain was 70 to 80 percent of playing the game," Primos says. "But as time went on and I got better at calling, things changed dramatically. Now I think calling can be 70 to 80 percent of it, but only if you can call *well*. If you can't, then knowing the terrain is still the most important thing."

Somewhere between Abner and Will lies the appropriate calling plan for most hunting situations. The best way to settle on that appropriate calling regime is by paying attention to what the gobbler is telling you. Some birds want a lot of calling, while others are put off by it. There's no way to tell at first what type of turkey you've

Switch calls on a reluctant gobbler before making the more risky decision to change calling locations. Sometimes switching from box to slate, or slate to diaphragm, is just what the gobbler is waiting for.

drawn, so it's wise to start out like Abner – conservatively, with soft yelps and clucks and not very many of them. If that doesn't work (and you can usually tell pretty quickly whether it's working or not), you can always pick up the pace and become more aggressive. But if you start out with the loud, aggressive stuff, you'll run off some timid, cautious or experienced gobblers you might otherwise have killed – and these birds, unfortunately, are the ones most likely to have those hay-hook spurs.

One more thing about calling: If Will Primos' remarks about calling *well* didn't register, go back and read those words again. Average calling, even poor calling, will let you kill some turkeys, if you work hard enough at the other facets of turkey hunting and get lucky every now and then. But good calling will let you kill a lot more.

Going back to our imaginary turkey hunt for a minute, let's say the gobbler you've set up on has flown down, and you've engaged him in conversation. But that's as far as things have gone, and the whole encounter seems to be at stalemate. For more than an hour, the gobbler has stood out there at 150 yards, gobbling lustily, considerably beyond the distance where you'd be able to see him. This is bad. Another hunter or a real hen could come to the gobbling, and either way it would dash your chances at tagging this particular bird on this particular day.

What to do now?

Well, first, try a different call. Sometimes, the solution is just that simple; switching from a box call to a slate, or from a slate to a diaphragm, or from a diaphragm to a box, may be all it takes. But if you run through two or three calls and the bird still won't move, it's time to consider the obstacle factor.

"If a bird seems interested in your calling but still won't come, there's probably an obstacle between you," says Eddie Salter. "That's when it's time to try calling from a different position. Sometimes a hung-up gobbler will come in fast if you'll change calling locations."

Of course, there will be times when this isn't possible. The gobbler may hang up too close to your position for you to risk a move, or maybe the terrain is too open, or maybe you're on the edge of the property you have permission to hunt and you're trying to pull the bird into legal territory.

But if you're confronted with a hung-up gobbler and conditions are such that you can move, then by all means, do it. And don't fool with the bird for an hour before you do, either. I generally switch calling locations within 15 minutes of a gobbler's first sign of hanging up. Sometimes you can eventually break a hung-up gobbler loose without moving – and sometimes, as mentioned, that'll be your only option – but the odds are against you. No sense putting a big investment into a long shot.

Moving on a hung-up gobbler is far from being a cure-all. For one thing, it always carries an element of risk. You might spook the gobbler while you're changing setups, or there might be another gobbler or hen near you when you move and you could spook it. Or, the hung-up gobbler might lose interest and vanish while you're moving and not calling.

Anyway, your new setup might be no more attractive to the gobbler than the one he just refused. Sometimes, you can change locations six or seven times on a hung-up gobbler and he'll still balk. Or, he might come running in, twirling his beard like a walking stick, the first time you move.

I once killed a longbeard in southern Missouri after moving on him 23 times over a three-day period. That part of the Ozarks is plateau country, with relatively flat expanses carved by abrupt, steep, deep hollows. This particular bird had staked out a strutting area on a 10-acre wooded knob that would have been called a mesa if it had been in New Mexico instead of Missouri – an island, a flat-as-a-tabletop place with scattered, open oaks and short-grass pasture surrounded by a valley that led eventually to the Norfork River.

The place was too open for me to get up on top with him, so I'd get as close as I could to the top and set up, and he'd gobble and come right to the edge but wouldn't stick his head over the side no matter what. After a while I'd shut up and he'd wander back toward the center of the mesa, and I'd reposition at another spot along the edge, set up just below the top and try again. He'd always come, but he'd always hang up just short of letting me see him over the edge.

For two days we played this game, and I swore after the second day I was giving up on him. But you know what happened: He pulled me back to the mesa the third morning, and we were well into a repeat performance when I happened to stumble onto a blown-down oak limb right on the edge of the flat. There were a few dried leaves still clinging to the limb, and it provided just enough cover so that I could wiggle on my belly and break over the crest of the ridge. I could see the gobbler as I snaked carefully into position, and he gobbled and headed my way at the first string of yelps. Once he was headed my way, I never called again until I putted at him to bring him out of strut at 20 yards. He wasn't a remarkable turkey, weight/beard/spur-wise, but he's one of the gobblers I'm proudest of.

The lesson to be learned here is persistence pays, and that's something to keep in mind whether you're dealing with a hung-up gobbler or are simply going through one of those frustrating periods when the turkeys don't gobble and/or everything you try turns out to be a mistake. Persistence is one of the most important attributes a turkey hunter can have, but it's a hard lesson to learn. Especially for a newcomer.

"After you've hunted a few seasons, you begin to see the importance of sticking with it," Brad Harris says. "You'll begin to kill a gobbler every once in a while after a long, unproductive morn-

And suddenly, there he is …

ing, or after three hours or three days of working the same bird and thinking he's never going to come. Don't quit. It's easy to give up when the turkeys stop gobbling at 8 a.m., or when a turkey refuses to come no matter what you try, but it's the wrong thing to do."

Back to our imaginary hunt: Your gobbler is on the ground. He answers your calls but he's hung up. You've switched calls several times with no luck. You've also switched locations several times, and still no luck.

But on your fourth setup, you notice the gobbler sounds considerably closer after your second series of calls. Surprised, you think, *this bird is coming!* Your heartbeat suddenly becomes noticeable in your chest. You ease the gun onto your left knee and shift your body slightly to the right, so the gobbler's likely approach is at a 45-degree angle off your left shoulder – the most desirable direction for a gobbler to approach a right-handed shooter.

He gobbles again just as you're thinking about making another soft call, and the sound is so

Once he's in the open, under the gun and in good shotgun range, the hunt is basically over. Unless you do something stupid, the trigger pull is a mere technicality, like tipping over your opponent's king after declaring checkmate.

close, so fierce, you nearly drop the corncob striker you were just about to touch to the slate call. You cut your eyes frantically back and forth. *Where is he? He ought to be in sight by now.*

And suddenly there he is, already in easy range at 25 yards, black as a buzzard in the midmorning sun. How he got there without you seeing him is one of those sweet mysteries that so fascinate turkey hunters all over the country, but there he is all the same.

There's only one problem: He's 90 degrees off your gun barrel, almost past you to the right. He must have come in behind that oak tree and popped around it just as he gobbled, or surely you'd have seen him coming.

No matter; the fact is, he's here. Don't move. Don't even breathe too deeply if you can help it.

The gobbler struts back and forth while you watch him out of the corner of your right eye. He gobbles explosively three more times, but your pulse rate is already redlined and the in-your-face gobbles have no additional effect. Finally, just when you think you won't be able to take the strain any more, the gobbler spins away from you, still in strut, his white head disappearing for a moment behind his tail fan.

It's now or never. You swing the gun around quickly but quietly, and you get away with it. The gobbler makes another half-turn, and now you're looking at the side of the head – or at least you would be if the bead on your gun barrel wasn't eclipsing it.

Unless you do something stupid, the game is over at this point. You've won, and the trigger pull is a mere technicality, like tipping over your opponent's king after you've declared checkmate. Don't let your guard down for a second, though, because you could repopulate a lot of territory with the gobblers that have gotten away clean after they've been dead to rights at the end of a gun barrel. Even a point-blank gobbler can disappear like smoke if you give him half a chance.

So, don't give him that half a chance. Keep him under the gun, stay still and either wait until he raises his head on his own or cluck sharply on your diaphragm call to make him do it.

But wait a while before you do that, if you can stand it. You invested a lot of time and effort, and probably no trifling amount of money as well, to arrive at the situation in which you now find yourself. Enjoy it for a minute or two before bringing it to an end.

It's what this whole enterprise is all about.

Chapter 6

A Checklist for Spring Turkey Hunting

A string of spurs like this one tells you only one thing for sure: The turkey hunter who owns them has spent a lot of time getting beat by gobblers.

Hard-and-fast rules are scarce where turkey hunting is concerned, but here comes one: No matter how skillful a turkey hunter you are, no matter how many cigar boxes full of beards you accumulate during the course of your turkey hunting career, you're going to get beaten by a good percentage of the gobblers you challenge. One of the undeniable truths of this wacky business is the turkey wins a lot more often than his hickory-nut-size brain should allow him to.

It happens to novices and veterans alike. Pick a name: Brad Harris, Ray Eye, Mark Drury, Tad Brown, Larry Norton, Bob Walker, Harold Knight, Toxey Haas, David Hale, Bill Jordan, Eddie Salter, Ronnie Strickland, Tom Kelly, Bo

Pittman, Mike Waddell – no matter how famous you are, no matter how well you can run a box or a slate or a triple-reed diaphragm, no matter how many turkey videos you've starred in, and no matter how many gobblers you've called to the gun, a lot of gobblers are going to get the best of you. Those big-name boys I just mentioned don't tag every bird they set up on, not by a long shot. I know this first-hand, because I've hunted with every one of them. If those guys get beat regularly, it's going to happen even more often to the likes of you and me.

Sure, those fellows account for more gobblers each year than the vast majority of the rest of us. And a big part of the reason for that is they're unquestionably better turkey hunters than we are.

But there's another equally important reason: They spend a lot more time in the woods than we do. To illustrate the point, here's a comparison: One spring in the late 1980s, when I was still fairly new to the turkey hunting game, I suffered through a run of the worst luck you could imagine. I'll spare you the details, but it wasn't pretty, and when the season was over I had one scrawny jake to show for my efforts in two top turkey-producing states. That summer, I ran into Wayne

Gendron, a world-class turkey caller and expert turkey hunter whose name could be inserted into the above list save for the fact that I've never hunted with him. Wayne is a Missourian but hunts just about everywhere, and he told me he tagged 10 gobblers during the same spring I was getting dumped on by every turkey I came across.

OK, it doesn't bother me to acknowledge Wayne Gendron was then and probably still is now a better turkey hunter than me. I can live with that. But I bristle at the notion he's 10 times better, even back then, when what I didn't know about turkey hunting would have filled a book a lot bigger than this one. Part of that difference was one of opportunity. Gendron hunted more than 50 days that spring. My logbook shows I hunted 11.

That's a big part of being successful. Put in the time in the woods, and not only will the odds swing in your favor, but you'll also become a better turkey hunter. It's a double-win situation.

Of course, most of us can't hunt as much as the Wayne Gendrons of the world. We must cram most of our turkey hunting into weekends and brief vacations, while pro-staffers like Gendron are in the woods almost every day of the season. Since we must make do with less hunting time, it

Most of us have to work through most of the turkey season, and that automatically disqualifies us from killing as many turkeys as the Wayne Gendrons and Cuz Stricklands of the world. Of course, there's also the skill and ability factor ... but a lot of that comes from having enough time and desire to be in the woods 40 to 50 days every spring in five to 10 states

becomes more important that we capitalize on as many turkey encounters as possible.

Easier said than done, of course. Every turkey hunter, regardless of his or her level of experience, knows there are endless variables that make every hunt different. That's part of the attraction of turkey hunting, but it complicates things.

That's why a hunter should, to rework an overworked phrase from the corporate business world, "think outside the season." The brief time when spring turkey season is open is too precious to waste any of it doing things you could have done earlier.

Replacing and/or repairing equipment is the first thing on the list, and this needs to be done right *after*, not right before, turkey season. That's when your equipment deficiencies will be fresh on your mind, and that's the time to do something about them. If you sat on your favorite box call or slate and broke it, you have time to try to repair it and see if it still sounds OK. If not, you have plenty of time to replace it.

Clean out your turkey vest as soon as the season is over. It's amazing how many candy wrappers, leaves, twigs, grass seeds and unidentifiable forest detritus can accumulate in the pockets of a turkey vest during the course of a season, and all that stuff needs to be dumped and shaken out. Also, a forgotten apple or banana in a vest pocket can make an awful mess when it has an 11-month off-season to do it in. Trust me on this one. It's not quite as bad as a dove forgotten in a shooting vest (trust me on this one, too), but it's close.

Remove all of the equipment you normally carry in your vest and clean or refurbish it as necessary. Then, when the vest is emptied of both gear and trash, replace all that stuff and *put the vest away until next turkey season.* Do not, repeat, do not use the vest for squirrel hunting, duck hunting or anything else. A well-designed, well-equipped turkey vest is one of the turkey hunter's most useful tools, and it doesn't need to be cross-contaminated with things like duck calls and squirrel loads. Set it up the way that works best for you (this will be a continually evolving process, by the way), and don't mess with it during the off-season.

Hanging your vest in the back of a closet is one acceptable way to store it during the off-season, but I prefer to put mine in a plastic storage bin that's airtight and mouseproof, and store it in a climate-controlled, out-of-the-way place. When I get it out to start running my calls in February, every-

Today's turkey hunters have access to an unlimited supply of knowledge and tips in the form of books, magazines, videos and in-person seminars. Still, there's no substitute for in-the-woods experience.

49

Keep a journal of your hunts, both successful and unsuccessful. After a few seasons, you'll begin to pick up on patterns and techniques that work for you, and in many cases the only way to pick out these patterns is by writing down your experiences.

thing is ready to go because I made sure it was that way before I put it up the previous May.

Which leads us neatly to the next topic: practicing your calling. Do it. Your family may complain, because face it: A turkey call is music to the ears of no one else but a turkey hunter. If that's the case, find a place where you won't bother anybody. You can practice with a diaphragm call while driving around in your car, and even in the largest cities there are places where you can run a box, slate or tube call without doing anything more than attracting curious glances. On my only visit to New York City (it was late March), I visited Central Park. While strolling along one of the paths, dodging rollerbladers and winos, I heard the unmistakable sounds of someone stroking out yelps on a slate call – and pretty good ones, at that. I coursed the sound to its source: a suit-and-tie Wall Street type with a lunch sack and three friction calls on the park bench beside him. Nobody was paying him any attention at all. He hunted upstate in the Adirondacks, he said, and he wanted to be ready.

Attending state or national turkey conventions is another form of pre-season preparation too many hunters fail to take advantage of when the opportunity presents. These events are built around turkey-calling contests, which in themselves are valuable for the lessons on cadence and subtleties of calling the contestants demonstrate on the stage. The conventions are also attended by turkey hunting equipment vendors, and they're an

excellent place to do some comparison shopping, check out new products and stock up on needed (or just plain wanted) supplies. Most conventions also have a seminar schedule, and these are also excellent learning places for turkey hunters at all stages of development.

But the real value of these get-togethers is the informal give-and-take of turkey hunters talking among themselves about this grand thing that brings them together at these conventions. If you'll engage in conversations with other hunters and keep your ears open, you can pick up more tips and tricks and general knowledge on turkeys and turkey hunting in a two-day convention than you can learn in five seasons of hunting on your own.

Watching turkey videos is another way to climb the learning curve as a turkey hunter. There are scores of these tapes on the market, and another dozen or so are produced each year. Some of them are poorly done, but in general they're pretty good, and even the worst of them can teach you something about turkey hunting or about turkey behavior if you'll just pay attention.

One of the most valuable things I've ever learned from watching turkey videos is the body language of turkeys. There are so many gobblers shown on a turkey video, almost all of them in front of the gun, that the observant viewer can learn the subtleties of turkey movements and actions and incorporate that knowledge into his or her hunts. For example, it was through watching

When patterning your turkey gun, shoot from the position you'll most likely be using in a hunting situation – flat on your butt, with knees up.

turkey videos that I first became aware of the fact that when a gobbler is alerted but not panicked, one of the first things he does is refold his wings. Then, almost always, he turns and starts to leave.

That's a valuable thing to know, and I probably would have eventually figured it out without the videos. But watching those videos gave me a several-year jump on figuring it out, and knowing it has made me a better turkey hunter. I know when a gobbler sets his wings that I'd better set him to flopping at the earliest opportunity.

Along the same lines as turkey videos is reading magazine articles and books like this one. The visual stuff isn't there, but books and magazine articles have a lot more detail than videos. Both have their place in a hunter's education.

Keep a journal of your hunts, both successful and unsuccessful. After a few years, you'll begin to pick up on patterns and techniques that work for you, and in many cases the only way to notice these patterns is by writing down your experiences. Aside from the educational value of this exercise, it has an entertainment value as well; I re-read my turkey journal every winter, and it helps me relive past hunts that would have been lost if I'd tried to rely on memory alone.

During the off-season, pattern your shotgun at different distances and with different loads to find out which one shoots best through your particular combination of gun, choke and barrel length. It isn't necessary to do this every year if you've already done it once and you're shooting the same

gun, choke and load, but it's been my experience that few hunters ever actually do this exercise properly. (Shooting offhand at a crude turkey-head outline drawn on a paper plate does not constitute a proper patterning exercise.)

Last but not least, get yourself into some semblance of physical conditioning before the season opens. I'm no Schwarzenegger and never will be, but I try to step up my level of physical activity between the holidays and the beginning of the turkey season. I've learned the hard way that going into the season looking like Homer Simpson is a good way to not have a good time.

This is a lot more important for the mountain hunter than for the guy who stays in the flatlands, but getting rid of a little of the overwintering lard before the birds start gobbling will make anybody a more effective hunter. When you hear a bird, you need to be able to get to him, and sometimes you must do it very quickly. Being couch-potato soft isn't going to help.

In reality, a serious turkey hunter's season never ends. There's always something to do – new country to scout, maps to buy and study, videos to watch and rewatch, lies to swap with your buddies. All this is important to your overall game plan and to your continuing education as a turkey hunter.

Don't neglect any of it.

The Right Stuff

Sometimes turkeys are easy, but more often a hunt is slow and difficult. Get comfortable in your setups, and when hunting with a partner, face in slightly different directions so you can cover more approaches. Gobblers have a bad habit of not coming in from the direction you expected them.

The gobbler stayed down in that hole in Mississippi's Homochitto National Forest for most of the morning, responding well to our calls but steadfastly refusing to climb up out of there so we could shoot him. It was early in the season, with little green-up in evidence, and the hollow was small. That combination of factors made it unadvisable for us to try to go down there with him. We were almost certain to get burned.

So Bill and I stayed above him, circling the rim of that little Tunica Hills canyon, trying different setups and different calling techniques. Over the course of three hours, we circled and called to that stubborn gobbler from a dozen different positions that covered more than 270 degrees of the compass. For all the good it did us, we might as well have been blowing kazoos.

Finally, though, we found a spot he was willing to approach. He was reluctant, but he came. It was like pulling teeth, though, and a peppy snail could have covered the distance as fast as that turkey did. We sat in that last setup spot for what seemed a lifetime as the gobbler climbed 100 vertical feet and advanced something less than 200 horizontal yards. When he finally stuck his wrinkled old head over the top and Bill uncapped it for him, I looked at my watch. We'd been sitting in the same spot for nearly four hours.

Aside from the sight of that gobbler's white head cresting the ridge in the early-afternoon sun, what I remember most about that grueling hunt was the incredible volume of gear littering the ground around both of us when Bill finally got the opportunity to pull the trigger. You could have started a respectable yard sale with it.

Surrounding the seat cushions at each of our setup positions were box calls, slate calls, diaphragm-call carrying cases, water bottles, half-eaten candy bars, cameras, gloves, head nets, a small bottle of bug dope and I don't remember what all. Suffice it to say it was a whole bunch of stuff.

After, we'd packed all that gear back into our vests and were walking back to the truck, we talked about that impressive amount of equipment we'd scattered around us during the hunt.

"Yeah," Bill said, shifting the gobbler to a more comfortable position over his shoulder, "it would really be nice if somebody would design a turkey vest that had a game pouch big enough to hold all that gear *and* a turkey."

*   *   *

That's the problem, all right. A well-equipped turkey hunter carries so much gear, there's often not enough room for a gobbler in his vest, and so he winds up carrying his bird home over his shoulder.

Ray Eye and Brad Harris are two such hunters. Both are Missouri boys, products of the Ozarks, and they're two of the best turkey hunters in the business. As friendly competitors in the game-call and hunting-equipment industry, both men have earned envious reputations as masters of the art of getting gobblers in front of the gun.

I've hunted with both, and you'd be hard-pressed to get me to venture an opinion as to which is the better hunter. That's not because I'm afraid of making either of them mad; it's simply because it's too close to call. Let's just say that when either of these fellows goes hunting, the local gobbler populace had better be careful.

While Eye and Harris have much in common when it comes to hunting techniques and style, they also have differences of opinion. One of these is the proper way to equip a turkey vest.

Part of this, of course, is a simple matter of brand names – Brad works for Outland Sports, while Ray is affiliated with Hunter's Specialties. Because of product loyalty, you won't catch either of them carrying the other's equipment. But their differences go beyond Brad using Lohman stuff and Ray using H.S. products. Here's the scoop on their differing "what-to-carry" philosophies:

Ray Eye

"I believe in carrying a lot of stuff on a turkey hunt," Eye says. "I guess I believe that, anyway, because I sure seem to carry a lot of it."

That may be the understatement of the century. Here's a more or less complete list of the equipment Eye carries on a typical spring turkey hunt, along with his comments on each:

• H.S.'s Bun-Saver seat cushion – "If you've ever had to sit on a root or a rock for two hours while a gobbler had you pinned down, you know the importance of this item."

• Six mouth calls (three to hunt with and three as backups) – "I use a waterproof pen to put numbers on my calls – one, two, three – so I can quickly find the one I want."

• A two-sided box call

• Two slate calls (H.S.' Black Magic and Li'l Deuce)

• Three strikers (carbon, wood and glass) – "With two slates and three strikers, I can vary the sounds almost infinitely."

• Chalk, sandpaper and steel wool for the friction calls

• A Red Wolf gobble tube

• Three locator calls: crow, hawk and Palmer Hoot Tube – "I usually use my natural voice for owling, but sometimes they'll respond to the tube better."

• Four extra shotgun shells besides the ones in the gun –"Use a Magic Marker to write the shot size on the brass of each shell, because the writing will eventually wear off and you won't know what you've got."

• A sturdy folding knife

• Pruning shears – "It seems redundant to carry both a knife and shears, but the shears are much quieter and quicker for getting rid of unwanted limbs or cutting limbs to build a makeshift blind,

Ray Eye carries a lot of stuff and finds room for most of it.

or for cutting a shooting lane in thick cover. Quiet and quick are both important for a turkey hunter."

• Gerber Multi-Tool

• H.S.' strap-on knee gun rest

• A set of shooting sticks – "Handy for those long periods of gun-up waiting. You don't have to scrooch down as far as you do when the gun's on your knee, and you can stay more comfortable."

• Two small flashlights – "If your batteries have ever gone dead, you understand the reason for carrying two."

• Two half-mask head nets

• Two pairs of fingerless gloves – "After you've left as many gloves, head nets and flashlights in the turkey woods as I have, you learn to carry spares."

• A Bug-Out head net

• Insect repellent

• Walker's Game Ear – "I use it a lot for listening for birds to fly up, or for listening for approaching birds drumming or walking in the leaves. I don't wear it when I'm walking, though, because the amplified sound drowns out everything else."

• Compact binoculars – "Much more useful in open country, but you'd be surprised how often they come in handy in heavy cover, too."

• Compass – "I'm trying to learn to use a GPS, but I haven't played with it enough yet to become proficient. I don't think a GPS will ever fully take the place of a plain old compass, though."

• Topo map of the area being hunted – "No matter how well you think you know your hunting area, a topo map knows it better."

• Six-foot length of camo netting with a hole cut in the middle – "You can make a blind anywhere."

• Toilet paper –"Nature does call, you know."

• Handi-Wipes – "Ditto."

• Digital scale

• Point-and-shoot pocket camera

• H.S.'s orange safety bag, for carrying a turkey

• Roll of orange flagging – "Useful for marking a good listening spot, a creek crossing or a route to or from a hunting area."

• H.S. Limb Lights – "These are handy when I've roosted a bird and want to go back to him the next morning. By putting them close to the ground, I can follow the trail back to my position without having to shine my light all over the woods. Also, they give me the option of sending someone else into that position without having to go in with them and show them the way."

• Wallet with hunting license and driver's license

• Pen and notepad – "My memory's not what it ought to be, and when you're turkey hunting you think of all sorts of things you need to check into later."

• Snacks and drinks – "I freeze boxed drinks and carry them, and sandwiches, too. By the time you're ready for them, they're thawed but still cold."

• Clean pair of socks – "No matter what, your feet will eventually sweat. Or you might get your feet wet or get thorns or beggar lice in your socks. A fresh pair can make a world of difference in your comfort level on a long hunt."

• Mesh mushroom sack – "Morels don't carry well in a head net, and you might need the net to put on your head."

Brad Harris

Compared to Ray Eye's, Brad Harris' turkey vest is almost empty when he sets off on a typical turkey hunt. But I've hunted with him numerous times, and I think I know the reason: Harris covers a lot of ground when he hunts turkeys, whereas Eye is more deliberate, moves slower and covers less ground in an average hunt than Harris. Therefore, Harris needs to travel lighter.

"My list of necessary items keeps growing, though," Harris says. "I remember when I went to the woods with a shotgun and a few shells, a couple of mouth calls and a box call and a hat and head net and gloves. Now I carry a peach basket full of stuff, and every item is there because it increases my effectiveness, my comfort level or my safety."

Here's Brad's normal equipment list, along with explanations for selected items:

• Lohman's Wing Thing – "As turkeys get pressured more and more, they get harder and harder to fool. Imitating natural sounds, such as the wing-flapping of a turkey as it flies down, can often be the difference between success and failure."

• Lohman's Spit-n-Drum call – "Dominance and territorial instincts may even be more important than the mating instinct when it comes to getting a response from a spring gobbler. If a gobbler has a bunch of hens already, he probably won't be too interested in coming to your hen calls. But challenge him with the sounds of another dominant gobbler, and you might get a look at him."

• Lohman box call

• Assorted mouth calls

• Aluminum Thunder Dome and two strikers – "Aluminum friction calls produce the highest-

Brad Harris travels a lot lighter than Ray Eye does on a hunt. He doesn't carry a magazine along, either.

One of the bad things about having a roomy turkey vest is that we can carry too much stuff. Think about the things you take on your turkey hunts, and eliminate those you find you don't use, or that you can get along without.

pitched yelps available in mechanical calls today. Sometimes, that high-frequency sound will work when nothing else will."

• Pruning shears – "Ray is right; pruners work faster and quieter than a knife. Try to set up against an open-growth cedar bush with about a hundred dead, brittle limbs low on its trunk, and you'll understand why this tool is handy."

• Compass – "I don't use it very much, but I've observed over the years that when I do need a compass, I need it pretty bad."

• Topo map, if hunting unfamiliar ground – "I use these mostly from the road when I'm scouting or hunting new territory. I usually don't carry one

into the woods with me unless I'm planning to cover a lot of ground."

• Flashlight

• Hen & jake decoys – "This goes back to the dominance instinct. A jake/hen combination is by far the most effective decoy setup I've ever tried

• Ink pen/notebook – "I use these items all the time to make notes as things pop into my head during a hunt. The pen is especially important, since many states require you to write something on a turkey tag at the time of the kill. It's hard to do this with a blackened twig."

• Coyote Howler: "Excellent for pre-flydown and post-flyup locating."

• Crow Call: "My favorite midday locator call."
• Orange flagging
• Camo gloves
• Ninja-style head net
• Seat cushion, if vest doesn't have one
• Five shotgun shells (plus the three in the gun)
• Orange hat, if hunting public land – "I don't wear it when I'm working a bird, but if I'm moving through the woods on public land, I've got it on my head."
• Water – "I use just plain old water in a plastic bottle. Soft drinks or juice tend to gum up my calls, and don't quench my thirst as well, either. I don't fool with snacks; I don't have time to eat when I'm turkey hunting."

*   *   *

I don't carry as much equipment as either of these two guys, but my turkey vest still seems to be pretty full most of the time. Everything has its place – box call here, slate calls there, gloves in this pocket, bug dope in that one – and I religiously return each item to its designated place after each use. There are few things more aggravating than searching frantically through the multitude of pockets in your turkey vest for some essential item (a head net, for example) while a hot-to-trot 2-year-old longbeard comes hurrying toward you, gobbling with every breath.

Aside from creating and adhering to a nit-picky system of organizing the equipment in your vest, there's one other important consideration before you include or discard an item. Ask yourself: Is this item really necessary? If the answer is a definite yes, by all means keep it on your list. If your answer is less positive, think again.

"There are an awful lot of good turkey hunters who carry little more than a gun and the shells in it, plus some ratty camouflage and one or maybe two turkey calls," says Brad Harris. "They kill turkeys, too. A good hunter without much equipment is going to kill a lot more birds than a poor or mediocre hunter with a lot of equipment."

"That's entirely accurate," Ray Eye agrees. "But a good hunter with the right equipment will kill a lot more turkeys than an equally good hunter without the right stuff."

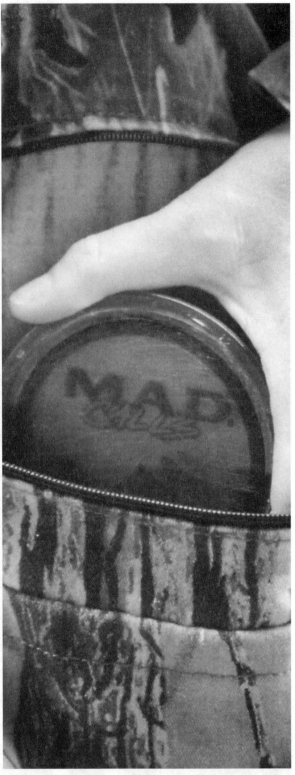

Develop a system for stuffing your vest, keeping each item in its own designated pocket. It doesn't matter what the system is as long as you have one. When a turkey's thundering at you from 60 yards away is not the time to be looking for your diaphragm call case.

Section 3

The Noises
We Make

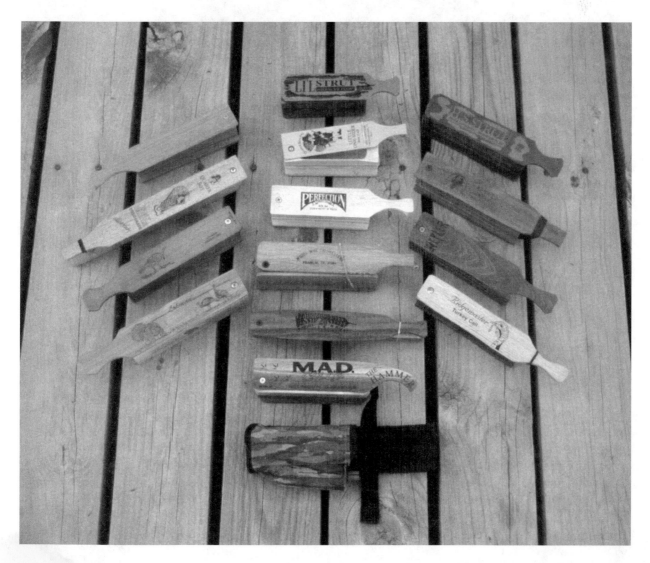

Chapter 8

Calling

There are so many types, styles and brands of calls on the market, it's impossible to even list them, and no hunter needs to carry them all. On the other hand, becoming proficient with many styles of calls will make you a more effective turkey hunter.

Get two turkey hunters together – any two turkey hunters – and you'll have more differences of opinion than they had in Florida during the 2000 presidential election. Every facet of the hunt provokes heated argument among veterans and rookies alike, but calling tops them all for generating dissension in the ranks. Some hunters swear by box calls, while others are dedicated slate, wingbone or diaphragm users. Some are proponents of soft calling, while others like to really pour it on. Some call every 30 minutes; some have a hard time shutting up for 30 seconds.

Part of the reason for all this difference of opinion is that there are so wretched many turkey-calling instruments on the market these days. There are hinged-lid box calls, peg-and-pot calls, scratch boxes, wingbone calls, tube calls, bellows calls, push-button calls and more. Within each of those broad categories are hundreds, sometimes thousands, of variations and brands. A turkey hunter who sets out to collect one of each type of call on the market had better have lots of money and a big, big house.

I'm not a collector of turkey calls, exactly, but I seem to have accumulated quite a few. They occu-

The "best" turkey call for any given situation is ultimately determined by this guy.

py the better part of three large storage crates in my catch-all closet. Each February, I get the crates out and spread the calls all over the living room floor and spend the better part of an afternoon fiddling with them. I try a couple dozen pegs on a couple dozen slates, running through possible combinations. I run three dozen or so box calls through a series of yelps, clucks and cutts. I toot and yelp pretty amateurishly on a dozen or so wingbones and twice that many tube calls.

Then I carefully pack them all away again and go get my turkey vest and take out the small battery of calls that live there year-round. They're the calls I knew I was going to use all along, before I ever started playing with the others. They're the ones I use every year: two wallets of assorted diaphragm calls, a custom-made wingbone, a tube call made from a plastic film canister, two slates and four strikers, and one particular beat-up old box call I wouldn't part with for $10,000.

That's my calling arsenal in its entirety. I replace the diaphragms each year, as needed, and I often carry an extra box call to give me a little more tonal versatility, but the rest have been almost constant companions on turkey hunts for many years. They're as familiar to me as the knots on my head, and I can run them in the dark with my eyes closed. I know where their sweet spots are, and I'd feel underequipped if I left any one of them behind.

I know many hunters who use only one or two calls, and some of them are very good hunters. I know other hunters who carry three times as many calls as me, and some of them are very good, too. But the very best hunters of my acquaintance carry about the same number I do – one or two of several types of calls, plus an assortment of diaphragms.

Furthermore, these best-of-the-best hunters are excellent callers with each and every one of the calls they carry. They know the truth about the which-call-is-best controversy mentioned at the start of this chapter, and the truth is this: There is no "best" turkey caller, just as there is no "best" method of calling turkeys. Every hunt shakes out a little differently, and every gobbler reacts differently to different calls and calling styles. In fact, the same gobbler will often react differently to the same call and calling style on different days, or even at different times on the same day.

So the very best turkey hunters carry a representative assortment of calls, and they take the time during the off-season to practice with those calls until they can make them sound exactly like they want them to.

In the following chapters in this section, we'll discuss the various types of calls. None of them is the "best" – and all of them are. If you're wise, you'll carry and become proficient with them all.

Chapter 9

The Box Call

The box-call master at work.

Brad Harris, the vice president of public relations for Outland Sports, gave me the beat-up old box call I referred to in the beginning paragraphs of the preceding chapter. That was in 1991, after the first of what would turn out to be many turkey hunts Brad and I would make together. The call wasn't beat up when he gave it to me; I've taken care of that myself, personally inflicting every nick and ding.

I've also carved every one of the 40-odd notches that march along the corners of the sounding

chamber of that call, one for every gobbler that's died as a result of responding to it. I didn't shoot them all myself, but I brought them all in with that call, and what initially gave me the confidence to use a box that much was hunting with Brad.

At the time of that first hunt, I'd been hunting turkeys for a little over a dozen years and had killed 20 or so gobblers. I was at that cocky stage of partial development where I thought I had things pretty well figured out. I'd killed a few good gobblers, and I was full of myself; I was your typical 20-turkey expert. You know the type. You run into them all the time at turkey banquets, at check stations and in the woods. They're the ones who exude the arrogance, braggadocio and self-confidence of a 2-year-old gobbler on opening day.

In those days, I used diaphragm calls almost exclusively. Since diaphragms were the rage of the age, so did most of the other turkey hunters I ran with. But on that three-day hunt with Brad in 1991, I learned there's more to an effective turkey-call arsenal than metal horseshoes, tape and latex. It was one of the most important things I've learned as a still-developing turkey hunter.

The first morning, both our hunt and our turkey got fouled by a pack of dogs chasing a deer. The second morning, it rained buckets. We hunted hard both days, but couldn't get anything to go our way.

On the final morning, however, we got on a gobbler in a wide-open hardwood valley, where there wasn't so much as a twig to hide our approach. We had to set up almost 400 yards from him, but when Harris started making his box-call music, the gobbler started coming. He marched straight in at a leisurely pace, taking a little less than 10 minutes to get there, and I took him at 28 steps.

What impressed me most about that three-day hunt was that Harris used a box call at least three-quarters of the time. He used a diaphragm, too, and sometimes a slate, but mostly it was the clunky old box. In my ignorance and arrogance, I'd thought until that hunt a box call was a beginner's tool. Experienced 20-turkey experts like me had surely outgrown the need for such an ancient, old-fashioned call.

Boy, was I wrong.

Afterwards, we went to the Lohman factory in Neosho, Mo. Standing beside the assembly line, Harris started picking up box calls and examining their grain. After yelping on a couple, he handed one of them to me.

"Here," he said. "You'll kill some turkeys with this."

Boy, was he right.

You may have more experience in the turkey woods than me. You may have more beards in your cigar box. You may be a better turkey hunter than I am. I wouldn't be a bit surprised; there are lots of people in all those categories. But I'll bet you double or nothing on the cost of this book you don't have more experience or more turkeys than Brad Harris. This guy started hunting turkeys as a teenager in 1971, and he's taken gobblers in more than 20 states so far. Each year, he takes six to a dozen gobblers and guides other hunters to twice as many birds as he tags himself. If you don't want to follow my lead on this subject, then follow his:

"I started using a box call in 1974, more or less for sentimental reasons," Harris says. "It was a scratch box, with a separate striker, that my Grandpa made. I didn't think it was very cool to use a box, because there were these 'new' diaphragms on the market then."

Harris says his success rate began to improve along about then, but he succumbed to a case of 20-turkey expert-itis, too. He was killing more turkeys, but he believed he was doing so because he was becoming a better turkey hunter, and he was killing them not because of the box call but in spite of it. He was only half right.

"It took me several years to figure it out," he says. "I didn't give the box credit. I was giving me credit. I was mistaken."

About six or seven years into his improved success phase, Harris sat on his Grandpa's old scratch box and broke it. By then, his grandfather had

Two scratch boxes, one commercial and one homemade.

died and he couldn't get another one, so Harris retired the call and went back to exclusively using diaphragms. His success rate immediately fell off.

"That's when it hit me that the box call was making me a more effective hunter," he says. "I started realizing you could be creative and do more with a box call, and it was helping me call in more turkeys."

He's been using box calls ever since. His company still makes a scratch box, but Harris's main box call these days is the hinged-paddle style. More specifically, he uses the Gibson-style box call (one solid piece of wood instead of several pieces glued together) his company manufactures. Harris says he likes a Gibson-style box for several reasons:

"First of all, a Gibson-style call is durable. I like the strength of one piece of wood as opposed to several pieces glued together, because I run a call hard and I need it to be tough. Also, the joints and glues used to hold multiple-piece calls together tend to act as a sound dampener, and one of the reasons the box call is effective is that it produces a loud, ringing tone. You have more weather-related problems with a glued-together call, too, because humidity affects the pieces of wood differently, and this can change the call's pitch and tone."

Naturally, Harris uses Lohman box calls, since he'd probably lose his job if anyone caught him using the product of a competing manufacturer. But he's fair-minded, and he readily points out there are many other excellent brands on the market. Since this isn't intended to be an infomercial for Lohman, let me add that I also hunt with other brands of box calls as well – among them Woods Wise, Hunter's Specialties, Quaker Boy, Lynch, Knight & Hale and others. But when the chips are down, I always go back to that sweat-stained, oil-darkened, notched-up old Lohman, because I have confidence in it. I believe I can call in turkeys with it, and so I do.

"Confidence in a call is almost as important as the call itself," Harris says, "and I think it's easier to gain confidence in a box call than any other type of turkey call."

The reason for this, he believes, is because it's easier to become proficient with a box call than calls like slates, diaphragms, tubes and wingbones.

"If I had 15 minutes to teach somebody how to use a turkey call before they had to go out and try to call up a gobbler, I'd grab a hinged-lid box call or one of the new pump-action calls," he says. "Most people can produce realistic turkey sounds almost from the first try. Box calls are excellent beginner calls because they're quick confidence-builders. The mistake many hunters make is thinking they're only beginner-level calls."

A Gibson-style box, center, flanked by two laminated boxes. Note the glued-together pieces of wood on the laminated calls, as opposed to the one-piece construction of the Gibson-style box.

In other words, most hunters make the same mistake both Harris and I initially did. It took both of us quite a few years to learn we were wrong.

"The box call is the most versatile turkey call on the market, even more so than the diaphragm," Harris says. "You can run it soft or loud, and you can make everything with it from an almost inaudible whine to a gobble. There's practically no turkey sound you can't duplicate with a box call."

Not only will the box call make all those sounds, but they also sound more turkey-like.

"I've spent the past 20 or so years hunting around some of the best turkey callers in the nation," Harris says. "And I can almost always tell the difference between these good callers and a real turkey – except when they're using a box call. In the hands of someone who really knows how to run it, the box call makes the most realistic turkey sounds you can make unless you have feathers."

He says a box call has a high pitch and tone that's put it head and shoulders above other types of calls for a long time.

"A good box has a pitch that almost hurts your ears," he says. "The high-frequency calls on the market today aren't anything new. Box-call users have been making high-frequency calls for more than a hundred years, since the box call was invented."

Harris says that's yet another advantage of the box.

"A good box call has more range than other calls. I learned this when I started hunting turkeys in the West and Southwest, where visibility is better and you can see turkeys at farther distances. I'd always hunted the forests of the Ozarks, and most of the time in the woods you're calling to a turkey you can't see. You can hear him gobble, but you really don't know how he's reacting to the call.

"I learned gobblers would come to box calls from long distances, but not only that, I could see how they *reacted* at those distances. With a diaphragm or slate, I could call to a distant but visible gobbler and often he wouldn't react at all. I'd be pretty sure he could hear it, but it was so faint and muffled, and the tone and pitch were so low, it didn't get him excited. But when I'd switch to a box on that same turkey, he'd gobble back and go into strut and start coming."

I remember a windy afternoon when Harris and I were driving around in Missouri, scouting new territory. We were heading down a hill on a gravel road when we saw two black specks in a distant pasture. Through binoculars we made them out as longbeards, and they were a good 900 to 1,000 yards away. They were feeding and paid us no attention because of the extreme range.

A box call makes louder notes and has a "ring" to it. In combination, these two things give box calls more range than most other types of calls and make them a good choice for hunting open country.

One more notch for an already well-notched box.

Harris says most hunters overemphasize the supposed disadvantage of excess movement required for working a box call. The call can be placed on the ground and operated behind your raised leg.

We got out to watch them, partially screened by roadside brush. With a diaphragm, Harris yelped and cutt as loudly as he could. The turkeys made no visible reaction.

Then he brought out a box call and yelped loudly. I was watching the gobblers through the glasses, and seven seconds after he made the call, both of them shot bolt upright and looked sharply our way. One puffed into a half-strut. Harris cutt again on the box, and seven seconds after that, I saw both gobblers run their necks out.

Seven seconds later, we heard the whispery double-gobble, so faint and fragile we'd have never heard it if we hadn't known it was coming. Harris chopped another series of calls out of the box, and sure enough, seven seconds later I saw both heads jerk forward again. Seven seconds after that, we strained our ears and heard the sound.

It was late afternoon and the turkeys were near their roost, so they made no move toward us. But Harris called to them for 10 more minutes, and every time he used the box, the turkeys gobbled back. Every time he used a diaphragm or slate, they either ignored it or failed to hear it. It was dramatic proof of the box call's long-range effectiveness.

Harris doesn't buy into the oft-quoted disadvantages of the box call.

"Lots of hunters claim wet weather is a disadvantage, but it's really not much of a problem. For one thing, there are several call-waterproofing products on the market, and they're all effective when used properly. But you can keep a box call dry with an empty bread sack, and you can run it without taking it out of the sack. It probably muffles a little of that high-pitched ring you want to get out of the call, but it'll work." (At least one manufacturer, Woods Wise, makes a box call with a patent-protected paddle of space-age material that works even when wet.)

Harris also disagrees that the movement required in running a box call is a disadvantage, especially when a turkey is close.

"That's not a disadvantage, it's an excuse," he says. "Sure, there's some movement involved, but once you develop a little experience as a turkey hunter, you begin to learn what you can get away with and what you can't. You can hide the movement behind your raised leg, or whatever. Often, I'll lay the call on the ground beside me and yelp or cluck with it that way."

Box Call Tips from the Box Call Master

Chalk?

"Eliminate it. Chalk is designed to increase friction, but it's not needed on a properly tuned box call. Chalk acts as a sponge in damp weather, absorbing moisture. It gets gummy and dampens the ringing tone of a good box call. You need high-quality wood to start with, but if you have it, the call will sound better without chalk. Also, it's one less thing to deal with."

How do you keep a box call dry?

"It's not hard, unless you fall out of a boat. Carry an empty bread sack. If it starts raining, put the call in it. You can waterproof the call with such products as Box Call Magic, but this sometimes changes the pitch and tone and you'll have to resand and recondition the call. I've done it both ways, but I used box calls for nearly 30 years before waterproofing products came along, and generally managed to keep them dry."

What if your box call gets wet, anyway?

"The best thing is to keep it dry in the first place, but if you do fall in a creek with it, you can still salvage it. I once reconditioned a box call I left under a tree in South Dakota from one turkey season to the next. It weighed about four pounds when I found it, and of course I had access to plenty of new ones. But I reworked it just to see if I could, and got it back sounding pretty good.

"The key is slow, dry heat. Turn the oven to the lowest setting, put the wet call inside and prop the door with a spoon or block of wood so moisture can escape. Leave it for 24 hours or so. If you dry it too fast, you'll split the wood and ruin the call.

"Next, sand and debur the call all over again, because the soaking will have raised the grain and changed the striking surfaces. You may never make it sound like it did before the soaking, but if I can recondition a call that went through a South Dakota winter, you can fix one that got rained on."

Have you ever made your own box call?

"Other than helping work on prototype calls, no. I guess I could, but why bother? There are a hundred good brands out there. It would be like building your own car from scratch – you could do it, but what's the point?"

What turkey sounds do you usually make with a box call?

"I use 'em all, but I especially like a box for excited-type yelps and cutts. The trick is to be versatile, to learn to make the various sounds and know when and how often to use them."

Is the box your favorite call?

"That depends. Sitting here in the office, yeah, my favorite call is the box. It's the call I'd choose if I could only use one call for the rest of my life. But a hunter's versatility should extend to other calls, because there are days and circumstances when box calls just don't work. That's the way turkey hunting is, and on those days I don't hesitate to switch. In the woods, my favorite call is the one that's working."

Any final advice?

"Most hunters don't get their money's worth out of a call, no matter what type it is, because they don't experiment and practice enough. A good hunter takes the time to become proficient with all his calls, and a mediocre hunter doesn't. You get out of a turkey call only what you're willing to put into it, and that goes for diaphragms and slates and tubes as well as boxes. It goes for turkey hunting in general, too, for that matter."

Harris says he always keeps a diaphragm in his mouth, and once the bird is close, he sometimes switches to it for the final work. "Mostly, though, when the turkey is close enough that I feel it's too risky to use the box, somebody ought to be pulling the trigger, anyway. I'll use a diaphragm to cluck or cutt at him to get him to raise his head for the shot, but I could just as well yell 'Hey, turkey!'"

Harris just smiles when he hears some 20-bird expert refer to a box call as a beginner's tool.

"Sure, it's for beginners," he says. "But beginners who go on to become good turkey hunters don't lay the box call down. The reason it's a good beginner's call isn't because it's easy; it's because it works. It's not old-fashioned; it's traditional."

Tradition, in turkey hunting as well as life in general, is a good thing.

A bread sack is just the thing for protecting a box call from moisture if you get caught in the rain.

Plain old vanilla production calls, like this well-used Lynch, sound just as good as custom calls that cost 10 times as much.

Tuning a Box Call

"You can take a new rifle out of the box and use it, but everybody knows better than to do that," says Brad Harris. "You want to clean it and sight it first, and serious shooters may take it to a custom gunsmith to have the barrel floated and the trigger reworked. A box call is the same way. You can take it out of the box and use it, but it'll perform better if it's tuned."

Smoothing the contours and edges of the call is the first step, according to Harris. "I use fine-grit sandpaper to debur a new call inside and out, both in the box chambers and on the striking surfaces. Then I start playing with it, adjusting it until I get it sounding right, looking for the 'sweet spot.' Every call has one."

Then, Harris says, it's just a matter of practice, developing the skill and muscle memory so you can run the call automatically, without thinking.

This fine-tuning, by the way, is a never-ending process.

"The way a box call makes sounds is through friction," Harris explains, "and friction causes wear. Just by using the call, you'll gradually get it out of adjustment, and you need to resand and readjust the call from time to time. Don't worry about it if you make the call sound worse at first; keep on working with it until it sounds good again. The important thing to remember is not to sand it too much. You don't want to change the angles and radius of the striking surfaces; you just want to smooth them."

Think of your box call as a violin. Take it out of the blister pack and go hunting with it, and you'll have a fiddle. Sand it and tune it and learn to find and use the sweet spot, and you'll have a Stradivarius.

To tune a box call, use fine-grit sandpaper only, and be careful. If you remove too much wood from either striker paddle or box, you can't put it back.

Adjust the screw tension, then run the call. If it sounds better, you're getting there. If it sounds worse, don't panic. You'll eventually get what you want out of it.

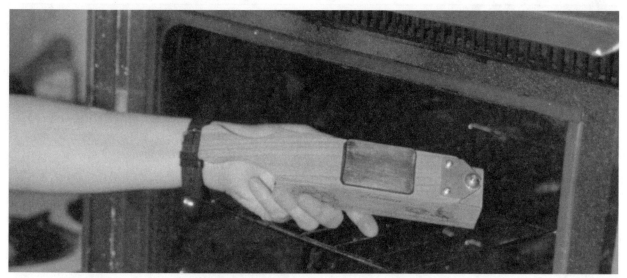

If your call gets wet, you can dry it in the oven. Use the lowest possible setting, prop the door open with a block of wood so moisture can escape, and leave it overnight or longer. It will probably be necessary to re-sand and readjust the call after drying, but you'd have to do all that if you air-dried it as well.

A few boxes from the author's informal collection

Choosing a Box Call

What material makes the best box call? How do you pick out a good one when they're in blister packs and you can't hold one in your hands and run it?

"I think wood creates the best sound in a box call," says Brad Harris, "and hardwood is best. Walnut, maple, cherry, mahogany and other dense woods allow the call to go to a higher level of pitch and tone. Soft woods like cedar make pretty calls, but those calls don't have the range hardwood calls have." Harris says mixing woods between box and paddle can also be effective, such as pairing a maple paddle with a walnut box.

Beyond that, Harris has some tips for choosing a box call off the rack.

"Look for clean, regular, close grain, with no flaws or irregularities," he says. "If the call has a consistent color and grain density, it's probably going to be a pretty good call. Different-colored wood grains running through a call may be pretty, but those different colors have different hardnesses and the call probably won't sound as good."

Harris is unimpressed by expensive calls. "If you like art, fine. Buy one. But a $150 hand-made call isn't going to sound any better than a $15 production call. Money doesn't mean much. Hardness of the wood and consistency of the grain are the keys."

Chapter 10

The Tube Call

Barney LaRue's Gobble Tube is one of the most realistic calls for gobbling on the market. This Arkansas gobbler thought it sounded fine.

It was April 1996, the middle of the turkey season in Arkansas, one of those ho-hum mornings. The weather was nice enough, and there'd been a little gobbling on the roost, but we couldn't get anything going after fly-down. Barney LaRue, owner of B&R Calls, and I were working our way through 2 miles of the north slope of Poteau Mountain. We hunted high and we hunted low, and we finally got a response from a gobbler at 9:30.

Barney and I both called to him, and he answered eagerly enough. But he wouldn't move. The woods were too open and the gobbler too close for us to risk repositioning, and anyway, we had about the best shapes on him we were likely to get. Finally, when it became obvious the gobbler wasn't coming, Barney whispered, "Time for something different."

He pulled out a funny-looking contraption, raised it to his lips, and came out with the most realistic gobble I've ever heard come from a turkey call. The unseen turkey didn't say anything for three minutes, even though he'd been gobbling about every 30 seconds. I cut my eyes over to Barney, who gave me a slight apologetic shrug. His shoulders were still in the upraised position when the turkey gobbled ferociously, just out of sight beyond a honeysuckle thicket. The bird had cut the distance by two-thirds, moving 100 yards closer during his three minutes of silence.

I think the bird must have been in sight when he gobbled and saw me flinch at the sound, because after that, we never heard another peep out of him. An hour later we backed out, eased down the slope to get out of the gobbler's territory, then headed back to camp.

Tube calls are excellent for excited cutting and long-distance locating, but require considerable practice.

Lohman's Tube Yelper, an offshoot of the Pump Action Yelper, is another good cutting/gobbling call.

"OK, what was that thing?" I asked as we walked through the woods.

"A Gobble Tube," Barney answered. "I'm just putting it on the market this year."

"Gimme it," I said, and he did. I started fooling with it as soon as we got back to camp, making awful-sounding noises. In 15 minutes, though, I was making sounds that roughly approximated a turkey's gobble. Barney, being charitable, a nice guy and a good politician to boot, told me I sounded pretty good.

Or maybe he wasn't being so charitable. At 2:30 that afternoon, I slipped back into the area where we'd worked the gobbler that morning, built a little hide near a small natural opening in the woods, and started calling with a diaphragm. The bird answered almost immediately, but hung up on the hen talk like he'd done earlier. I gobbled on the tube, and he went silent the way he'd done that morning.

Three minutes later, though, he gobbled again, so close behind me I could hear the rattle in the bottom of it. Then I could hear him drumming. As he slowly moved into view, I picked my moment and made my move. He was a healthy 2-year-old that pulled the check-station scales to 22 pounds.

That was the second time I'd seen a tube call work when nothing else would. The first time had been on April Fool's Day, 1992, near Pine Mountain, Ga. Realtree president Bill Jordan and I were hunting a gobbler we'd seen strutting in a field just before fly-up time two days straight. We knew the bird had to be roosting nearby because of the late hour when we were seeing him, so we went into the area blind before daylight the next morning.

He gobbled at an owl, and we let him fly down into the pasture before going to work on him. He didn't seem much interested, so finally Bill got out a loud, homemade tube call and started cutting aggressively. We immediately got a hard, no-nonsense response from a gobbler 250 yards in a different direction, and when the bird gobbled again a minute later, he was closer.

Forgetting about the uncooperative strutter in the pasture, we shifted our attention to the new kid in town. He came closer yet, but hung up just out of sight and refused to close the gap any more. While Bill was talking to him with the tube, we heard a telltale crunching in the leaves on the hillside behind us. Then a turkey

Four good commercial tubes, from left: B&R Game Calls, Lohman, Hunter's Specialties, and Primos.

drummed, so close behind me I could feel the vibration of it in my chest.

Pinned down like beetles in a high school bug collection, all we could do was listen and try to crank our eyeballs around to the backs of our heads as the pasture gobbler strutted and drummed within 10 yards of us. Finally we heard him going back down the slope. I twisted around to shoot, but he was already out of sight over the break of the rise. By the time he came into view again, he was 80 yards away. He went back to his strutting zone in the middle of the pasture, and he was still there when we left two hours later. The other bird, of course, never showed up.

I never did kill that pasture strutter, but I did get one more crack at him when he came to the tube call the next day. This time I was by myself on the edge of the pasture, and I managed to pull him within 30 yards by clucking and yelping on a tube call I'd borrowed from another hunter in camp. I could have killed him easily enough, but he had six hens and two jakes with him, and I never had a clear shot at his head without running the risk of killing other birds. Jordan told me later another hunter finally killed him the last week of the season, after all the hens had started nesting. Yes, the hunter used a tube call.

They're not common in the pockets of modern-day turkey hunters, but tube calls are deadly in the hands of someone who can coax the right sounds

out of them. I think the reason most hunters don't use tube calls is because a tube requires a considerable amount of practice. A beginner can pick up a box call and be making acceptable turkey sounds in minutes, but most folks can't do that with a tube.

Maybe this explains the effectiveness of the tube call. Maybe turkeys aren't used to hearing them. Maybe. But my opinion is, most users of tube calls are members of that special, dedicated group of turkey hunters who take the time and effort to become proficient with as many types of calls as possible. If my theory is right, tube calls are made more effective by those who use them, not vice versa.

Whether I'm right or not, the tube call is still a worthwhile addition to your call collection and to your calling repertoire. A tube is versatile in the extreme; in addition to gobbles, cackles, cutts and clucks, a good hand with a tube call can make it purr, fighting purr, whine, kee kee and do almost anything else you've ever heard a turkey do.

Ronnie "Cuz" Strickland, Mossy Oak's media vice president and a raconteur of the turkey woods, loves to use a tube call as a locator. He rarely uses it for close-in work, since he's usually running a video camera and has to use a diaphragm to keep his hands free, but he says a loud, abrupt cutt on a tube call will pull a gobble

73

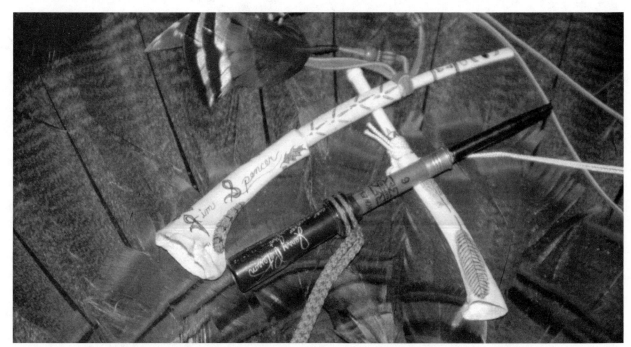

Like tubes, wingbones are specialty calls that require considerable practice to learn, and not many hunters use them. For precisely that reason, this is an excellent call for hunters to master and carry.

out of a dead turkey. Having watched him use tubes to locate gobblers in both Mississippi and Alabama, I can't find it in me to disagree.

Cuz usually makes his own tube calls with a pocketknife and a black plastic 35mm film canister. He cuts the bottom out of the canister itself, cuts off half the snap-on cap, and fits a rubber diaphragm across the opening in the lid. He made me one, once upon a time, sitting at his desk before we left for a hunt, and it took him maybe three minutes. It's the 1990s version of the snuff-can call your granddad made and used 75 years ago, and it'll work every bit as well for you as it did for Granddad. I've taken several gobblers with the one Cuz made me.

Barney LaRue's Gobble Tube is of similar design, although the barrel is configured differently and the call is quite a bit bigger than Strickland's homemade film-canister version. Although you can learn to gobble effectively on both types, I've found it much easier to make decent gobbles with LaRue's commercially made call than on the snuff-box style. (For more information on the Gobble Tube, contact B&R Game Calls, P.O. Box 104, Rudy, AR 72952, phone 479-474-7146.)

There are two areas where anyone using a tube call needs to exercise a little restraint and caution. First is the obvious one: safety. Making the sound

of a turkey gobbler can put a human caller in real danger, especially when hunting on public land. Never gobble on a tube call unless you're in a secure hunting area or are standing in a wide-open area where there's no remote chance you could be mistaken for a turkey.

The other thing that needs a mention here is the tendency of hunters to be too loud when using a tube call. Like Cuz says, a tube might pull a gobble out of a dead turkey, but it might also scare a live one into the next county if you don't tone down the volume when you're trying to call him in. Fortunately, this isn't all that hard to do, once you've mastered the call in the first place. It's just a matter of the amount of air you force through the call.

If you're a typical turkey hunter, you're always on the lookout for a new trick that will give you the edge. Well, the tube call isn't new. But it's unusual enough to give you the edge on a turkey or two, if you take the time to learn how to use it – and then manage to not make all the mistakes I usually make on turkeys.

Chapter 11

The Slate Call

Steve Stoltz is one of the best slate-call users in the woods today.

The Merriam's gobbler seemed content to stay out in the middle of that South Dakota pasture and sing his silly song for the rest of the day ... or for the rest of his life, as far as I could tell. I'd spotted the bird with my binoculars more than two hours earlier, and after a 30-minute roundabout stalk I was at the edge of the brush, but still more than 300 yards from the gobbler. It was as close as I could get without spooking him.

The past 90 minutes I'd invested in calling to this bird from the brushline had accomplished nothing more than frustration on my part ... and possibly a sore throat on his. He gobbled at everything I threw at him, but held his ground in the sunny pasture and stubbornly refused to come my way.

If he'd been an Eastern gobbler in the heavily forested country around my home, I'd have given up on him and gone looking for a more coopera-tive turkey. But he was right out there in plain open sight, you know? Maybe you can walk away from a bird when you can see him out there gob-bling back at you, but I can't.

So I hung in there with him, continuing my end of this protracted conversation, and getting absolutely nowhere ... until I rummaged around in my vest and found a little homemade slate call I'd forgotten I even owned. I sanded it, made a couple of practice imaginary strokes above the slate with the striker, then touched wood to rock and sent forth a short string of yelps.

It had been at least a year since I'd put a peg to that call, and my yelps were ragged and discor-dant. Even so, when the sound reached the gob-bler he popped out of strut like I'd goosed him

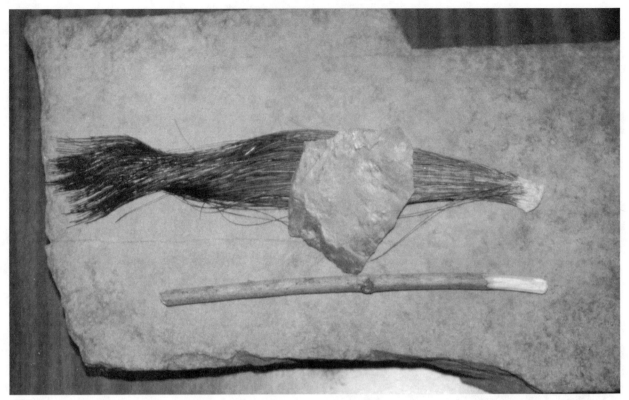

The first slate calls were rudimentary, primitive affairs consisting of no more than a chunk of raw slate and a smoothed, possibly fire-hardened hardwood stick.

with a cattle prod. He craned his neck my way and gobbled with noticeably more enthusiasm than he'd been showing, then went back into strut. But now, instead of continuing to strut around in circles, he started moving my way.

He never got in a big hurry about it, and a couple of times along the way he hung up. Every time he stopped, though, I was able to get him started again with the slate, and nearly 45 minutes later he crossed the invisible 40-yard line that made him killable. He was so deep into the self-hypnosis of his mating dance, I couldn't get him to slick down for the shot. After a half-dozen sharp clucks drew no response except to tuck him even deeper into his display posture, I finally shot him in full strut at less than 20 yards, taking him out but also blowing off a good portion of his already wispy beard.

That gobbler was my first Merriam's. But more important, he was also the first turkey of any subspecies I ever killed using a friction-type turkey call. Like most other hunters who took up this sport in the 1970s or 1980s, I started out with diaphragm calls. After killing a few turkeys with them, I quickly decided diaphragms were the end-

all, be-all turkey call. Go afield with three or four of these babies in different pitches and tones, I told my buddies in the tone of a True Believer, and you didn't need to worry with any of those other bulky, cumbersome, old-fashioned, hand-operated friction calls.

That slate-loving South Dakota gobbler, though, got me thinking otherwise. I continued to rely on a diaphragm for most of my turkey-calling chores, but when I encountered a gobbler that didn't want to play, I'd switch to a slate. A few years later, after a well-known turkey-hunting guru showed me what a good box call could do (see Chapter 9), I started carrying a box as well. Over the years since, I've switched more and more of my allegiance to these "bulky, cumbersome, old-fashioned, hand-operated friction calls." I'm a believer now: Where turkey hunting is concerned, friction is sweet.

According to historians who claim to know such things, the wingbone is the oldest style of turkey call, used by Native Americans long before the first European explorers arrived. Wingbone calls have been found in archaeological digs at sites dating back thousands of years. The earliest

Slates and strikers come in a bewildering variety of styles and materials. Each combination of slate and striker produces a different sound. There are 19 slates and 14 strikers in this photo. You do the math.

hinged-paddle box calls, by comparison, were made in the late 1800s.

Slate calls came along sometime in between, but the first ones were no doubt rudimentary, primitive affairs consisting of no more than a chunk of slate and a smoothed, possibly fire-hardened hardwood stick. These have been found at ancient archaeological sites, too. Evidently the Indians discovered this trick a long time before European settlers came along, the same way they did with wingbones.

Regardless of who first figured out that scraping a stick across a piece of slate sounded a lot like a turkey, he did the rest of us a big, big favor. The pot-and-peg type slate call has been an effective tool in the hands of turkey hunters for more than a century, and it's been responsible for the death of more turkeys than you could fit into Yankee Stadium. And this venerable call may be even more effective today than it was when it was brand new.

Thanks to modern materials, the curiosity and inventiveness of thousands of turkey hunters and the fierce competition between manufacturers, these calls have come a long way from that first

chunk of rock and a fire-hardened hickory twig. There are literally hundreds of pot styles, sizes and shapes, made of everything from molded graphite to coconut hulls to terrapin shells. I once saw a pot made from the headlight housing of an old 1920s touring car – a Packard or something similar. The call was as big as half a honeydew melon and as ugly as a mud turtle, but it sounded like a turkey when I ran the peg across its surface.

Although turkey hunters almost always refer to this style of call as the "slate" call, the sounding surfaces are now being made not only of natural slate, but also copper, Plexiglas, aluminum, acrylic, crystal, Teflon, graphite and a dozen other exotic and esoteric materials. And the strikers used with them are more varied yet.

The result of all this variety in materials, sizes and shapes is an almost infinite range of tones available to the turkey hunter who uses slate calls. There's even more sound range available with slates than with box calls, because of the wider variety of materials used for the striking surfaces in slates.

In addition to the wide range of tones made possible by the various materials, a hunter proficient

Excellent fighting-purr sounds can be made by using two strikers on the same slate. Throw in some excited cutts and yelps with a diaphragm, and one hunter can sound like a whole flock.

with a slate can get a wide variety of pitches and notes out of a single instrument by doing nothing more elaborate than varying the angle and pressure of the striker against the sounding surface.

This takes practice, of course, and that brings us to one of the disadvantages of using a slate call: It's fairly difficult to truly master. Becoming a sure-enough slate-call expert is a task that never really ends, and few hunters ever achieve expert status. It's a worthy goal, though, because a slate call in the hands of a master can effectively produce every turkey sound except the gobble and the spit-and-drum, and I know one hunter who can even drag a passable gobble out of a slate.

The other side of the coin is you don't have to be a slate-call expert to get good results with it. The better you are, the better your results will be, of course, but it only takes a few minutes to learn how to make passable yelps and clucks. With some practice, the purr, cutt and cackle are well within the skill level of most of us who have a moderate degree of hand-eye (hand-ear?) coordi-nation. Also, slates are one of the best tools on the market for producing the aggravated or fighting

purrs that have become popular in recent years. This call, too, is not difficult to learn.

Slate calls are unsurpassed for soft, close-in work, as long as you can make the necessary hand motions without being detected by your gobbler. There's no better type of call for making those soft, contented, almost inaudible clucks, purrs and whines turkey hens make when all is right in their world.

Getting away with the necessary hand motions can be tricky at times, but by laying the call on the ground or cradling it in your lap or the crook of an arm, you can use a slate even when your gun is mounted and the gobbler is in sight. I know this because I've done it. More than once. (Refer to Chapter 9 for Brad Harris' take on this perceived problem with friction calls.)

Another time the slate is an excellent choice is when you're in very tight on a roosted gobbler and you don't want to call loudly. Several times I've moved in too close to a gobbler in the dark, and when daylight came found myself too close to do much besides sit still and hope I didn't get made.

Twice, I've been able to salvage the situation and harvest the gobbler by making the softest

Sandpaper works well on true slate surfaces, but a kitchen scrubbing pad does the job just as acceptably, is more durable and doesn't remove as much material from the surface of the call. Sandpaper will eventually wear a depression in the slate surface and might ruin the tone of the call.

purrs and clucks I could possibly make on a slate, then waiting for the gobbler to fly down and come looking for me. Both times, I was within 30 yards of the tree the gobbler was roosted in, and could have shot both of them off their roost limbs if I'd been so inclined. Both times, the gobblers looked around for a while for the close but unseen hen, then dropped almost straight down from their roost trees and landed practically at my feet.

Slate calls can also be pretty loud, especially those with metal, crystal or acrylic sounding surfaces. They won't match the volume of a good, ringing box call, but they have considerable reach and retain their tone and realistic turkey sounds at these louder volumes. Above a certain level, the notes produced by a box call, tube call or diaphragm call are prone to break or squeal and lose some of their realism, but most slates sound as turkeylike at their loudest as they do at their softest.

It's difficult to give calling lessons in print, but there are a few tricks that can help you become a better caller with the slate.

First, keep the sounding surface roughed up at all times. True slates need no more than extra-fine

sandpaper or even a little square cut from a kitchen scrubby pad, while other surfaces call for harder stuff. But they all need to be kept rough, so they'll create the necessary friction against the striker to make the sounds.

Don't ever, repeat, ever touch the sounding surface or the end of your striker with your fingers or bare hands. Your skin will leave a residue of oil, and this can deaden the sound. Some of the previously mentioned call materials aren't bothered by this, but it's a good habit to form.

Every slate call has a "sweet spot," and it's up to you to find it. Once you find it, mark it in some way so you can find it again, preferably without looking at the call. I prefer to cut or file a small notch on the rim of the call where the knuckle of my right pinkie finger rests against the edge of the pot when I'm holding the striker and getting ready to use the call. When I grab the call, all I have to do is spin it with my left hand until the notch hits my knuckle, and I know the striker is over the sweet spot. With the notch, I can position my slates properly with my eyes closed. You may well develop a different method, and that's

It's easy to mark the "sweet spot" on a slate. First, determine where the spot is, and then cut a notch or rough up the rim of the call at the precise spot your thumb, knuckle or whatever part of your hand you prefer touches when you're holding the call. Then, always grasp the call so that your knuckle and the mark line up, and you'll be on the sweet spot.

Turkeys like slate calls.

fine; just be sure you know where the sweet spot is, and be sure you can find it quickly every time, without having to stroke the call to do it. When you're in tight on a gobbling turkey is no time for experimentation.

There are two "best" ways to hold the pot of a slate call. One is to "fingertip" it, holding it in all five fingers with the pot suspended over your palm. The other is to use your thumb and index or middle finger to encircle the call, leaving the bottom of the pot open and unblocked. Both methods allow the sound to escape unhindered and unaltered. Use whichever feels more comfortable and results in the best sounds for you. Some slates seem to run better with one grip or the other.

With either grip, hold the call fairly loosely. Gripping it too tightly causes several problems, among them hand fatigue, inconsistency of grip

81

When running a slate call, hold it in such a way that the sound isn't muffled and can escape. The two most popular grips are by cupping the call in your fingers and by grasping the rim of the call. The former grip is usually better for close-in work, because you can muffle the sounds by palming the call rather than cupping it. Holding the call by the rim is better if you're calling to a long-distance bird or using the slate as a locator call, since this grip lets the sound out better.

and possible deadening or inconsistency of the sound.

Speaking of consistency, it's important when you use a slate. Figure out what calling position of body, arms, hands and fingers is most comfortable and produces the best sounds for you, and then stick with it. Be consistent with everything when you stroke the call – body position, arm position, hand position, grip, angle of both the striker and the slate. This helps you develop muscle memory, and it will make you a better, more consistent caller. This is why I like to rest my pinkie knuckle against the edge of the pot. It makes my hands steadier, and it's easier for me to maintain the proper relationship of striker to sounding surface.

Finally, practice. Remember, it's easy to achieve mediocrity and even so-so competence with a slate call, but it's much harder to become a master. And the better you are, the deadlier you'll be.

One final advantage of using a slate call is that turkeys don't hear them as often as diaphragms. Everybody these days carries a slate or two, it seems, but few of us ever take the things out of our hunting vests and actually *use* them. It's been my experience that you'll hear slate calls in the turkey woods even less often than box calls.

I consider that as in-the-field proof of faulty thinking on the part of most turkey hunters. Don't be part of it.

Chapter 12

The Diaphragm Call

By far the most popular calls on the market today, diaphragms are inexpensive and easy to carry. This sometimes makes them less effective for most hunters of average skill, because the turkeys have heard so many of them.

It's past the halfway mark of the spring turkey season, and you're trying to find a workable turkey on public land that's been hunted heavily since the season opened – and probably for a week or two before that, as well. While there are still quite a few gobblers around, the survivors have been yelped at for more than two weeks by an army of hunters whose skill levels varied from near-expert to way past awful. Consequently, the remaining gobblers all have graduate degrees, and they're even more skittish than normal.

However, by virtue of your skill, ability and stick-to-it-iveness (not to mention a generous dose of luck), you've located a gobbler still willing to play. The only problem is, he's being oh-so-coy about coming to the call. You raised him with a crow call at midmorning, then slipped into good calling position and started working on him with a pared-down assortment of callers you're fairly sure he hasn't heard much. Your selection includes a homemade slate call that produces a peculiar note that's both raspy and high-pitched, a custom-made wingbone and a tube call you made yourself from a 35mm film canister and a non-lubricated Trojan.

The gobbler liked the slate, but wouldn't commit to it. But once you took rounders on him and started using the wingbone and the tube interchangeably from a different calling position, he started moving slowly your way. Now, 45 minutes later, he's in easy gun range and you can see him. You could kill him where he stands, except that the only part of him in sight is the tip of his tail fan as he struts just under the lip of the hill on which you're sitting.

The gobbler moves back and forth along a tight little track, never dropping fully below the rise but never cresting it, either. He's quit gobbling now, but he's so close you can feel the low pulse of his drumming as he struts just below the break of the hill. Your hands are on your gun, and both the tube call and the wingbone that brought him to you are dangling from their cords around your neck. They're only inches from your hands, but you don't want to risk the movement required to bring either of them to your mouth.

Ten minutes later, you can't stand it any longer. You ease your trigger hand away from the gun and slowly fumble the wingbone into position, hoping you can get away with making a soft yelp and getting your hand back to the trigger before he sticks his head up.

It almost works, too. Almost. Your dry lips kiss the bone and an almost passable yelp emerges. You drop the call and reach for the trigger guard. But the call knocks against the receiver of your shotgun with an unnatural *click!* and things happen very fast after that.

The gobbler runs his head up at the yelp, jerks it back down at the click and before you can react launches himself off the backside of the hill. You hear him go, you observe the whirlwind of leaves his powerful wings kick up from the forest floor, but you never see so much as a feather of him when he departs. By the time you stagger to your feet and run the 25 steps to the crest of the hill, he's vanished from your life forever.

You've just had a ringside seat for an excellent example of why a turkey hunter should always have a diaphragm call in his or her mouth. And lest you think it was a made-up example, let me confess: The hunter who dropped the wingbone on top of his shotgun was me. It happened in the Hanging Bog Wildlife Management Area in western New York in 1990, and I haven't been on a turkey hunt since without having a diaphragm call tucked into my cheek, ready against the chance I might need it.

From its crude beginnings in the '40s and '50s, when a handful of dedicated hunters made their own diaphragms from plumber's lead, condoms and (maybe) first-aid tape, the diaphragm has become the most widely used type of call in turkey hunting today. You'd be hard-pressed to find a hunter in the woods who doesn't have a diaphragm call in his or her pocket, and most

Diaphragms are invaluable when a bird is too close to move your hands, and you need him to raise his head for the shot.

85

Roger Hook is an example of a successful competition caller who is also an excellent turkey hunter. He uses a diaphragm in most hunting situations, and he's successful with it because he's reached that level of expertise with a diaphragm that few of us will ever attain.

fessionals on the calling-contest circuit and on the plethora of turkey hunting videos on the market today. That's five. The sixth reason, and the most important of all, is elemental: They work.

They don't work as well as they used to, though, and the reason for that is the extreme popularity of diaphragms we just talked about. My turkey hunting career spans only a quarter-century, but I've watched the evolution of diaphragm calls and diaphragm calling grow until it's reached the point of diminishing returns. There are literally hundreds of brands and styles of diaphragms on the market today. Probably thousands. As if that weren't enough, if you don't like any of the commercial models, you can buy the materials and custom-make your own. They even sell kits.

It's a fact sad but true: When everybody in the woods is using the same type of call, turkeys quickly get wise to it. And that's what's happened with diaphragms in many areas, especially on public land where turkeys are hunted hard.

Even so, that's no reason to throw away your diaphragm call case. If for no other reason, you should always carry a diaphragm just for close-in work, when the bird is in sight or imminently so and it's too risky to use a call that requires hand movement. My blown chance at the Hanging Bog gobbler illustrates the huge value of that. If I'd had a diaphragm in my mouth, I could have made that soft cluck I needed while keeping both hands on the gun. When that bird stuck his head over the hill, I could have punched a dozen or so No. 5-size holes in it, instead of blowing the hunt by not being ready for the split-second opportunity that presented itself.

However, a diaphragm is good for much more than that, when it's in the hands (or rather, in the mouth) of someone who really knows how to use it. That's the key to effectively using a diaphragm: You need to be good with it. Very good. Almost anybody can stick a tape-covered horseshoe of aluminum in his mouth and, after overcoming the gag reflex and learning how to force air over the reeds, make vaguely turkeylike sounds with it. But turning those sounds into real turkey talk requires quite a bit of practice. Fortunately, practicing with a diaphragm turkey call is something you can do while driving in your car, which at least partly explains the folks you see sitting alone in cars at traffic lights in February and March making weird mouth movements.

hunters carry several – thick reed, thin reed, single reed, double, triple, quadruple, stacked, cutter, raspy, high-pitched, loud, soft. And yes, homemade.

The reasons for this almost universal popularity are six: diaphragms are cheap; they're easy to carry; they're a no-hands call; they're not all that hard to master; they're used and touted by the pro-

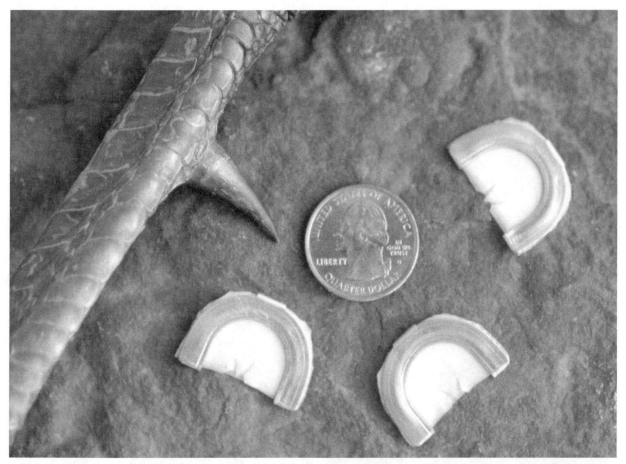

Like many contest-level callers, Roger Hook prefers his diaphragm calls without tape. For the accomplished caller, these stripped-down models are easier to control, but there are disadvantages as well. If you have fillings or metal crowns, touching one of these calls to a tooth can feel like an electric shock. Also, these small calls are much easier to swallow, so extra care is needed when you're using one.

Being good with a call, really good, is more important than most turkey hunters believe. Most writers of turkey hunting articles, judging from what I've been reading for years, also underestimate the importance of calling. Almost every turkey hunter you'll ever run into has a tale or two about how their great-aunt called a gobbler into the back yard by scraping a stick against a paint can lid, or about how they themselves once called in a longbeard with a call that sounded like somebody knocking two pebbles together. You probably have a similar tale or two. I know I do.

True story: I once called up and killed a fine, hook-spurred Rio Grande gobbler by pulling a strand of barbed wire back and forth through a loose fence staple. It sounded awful, but the turkey gobbled at the squeaky sound when I crawled through the fence to set up on him. Just to see what would happen, I set up against the fence post and "yelped" three times with the wire. The turkey triple-gobbled in response and came run-ning at me like his tail feathers were on fire. I shot him at 10 steps, more or less in self-defense, and nobody back at camp believed it. You don't have to believe it, either, but that's the way it happened.

Of course, that's not the way to bet. Nor is it the way to call. The thing is, you can't depend on finding one of those gullible, non-discriminating gobblers every time out. You can't even depend on it once in every season. If you do find one, it's most likely to be an opening-day turkey, a 2-year-old with an underdeveloped sense of self-preservation. Fine, I'll take those easy opening-day gobblers, too, and be thankful for 'em, but what about the fourth day of the season? Or the fourth week of it?

The nationwide turkey population is in good shape and still growing, but growing, too, are the legions of hunters in the woods after them. Both are good things, but they create problems by creating call-wise gobblers. Being a good woodsman, knowing your hunting territory, understanding

good enough. The truth is, being "good enough" often isn't.

This is true with any type of turkey call, naturally, but I think it's especially the case when the call in question is a diaphragm. The reason for that is the diaphragm's versatility. Used by someone who has really practiced with it and mastered it, a diaphragm is an excellent choice for making the widest variety of turkey sounds, from soft clucks, whines and purrs to louder yelps, cutts and cackles and even gobbles. To take full advantage of this wide range of sounds, though, expertise is required.

Most hunters either don't have the ability to become that good with a diaphragm, or (more likely) don't have the time or willpower to practice diligently enough to get there. I know personally and have hunted with a half-dozen or so Grand National calling champions, and another dozen or more winners of various regional, state and world contests. And I promise you, not a week goes by throughout the year that these hunters aren't practicing their calling. Most of them do it every day, all the way around the calendar, sometimes for hours at a stretch.

These folks are the elite, the best of the best of the best. Their regimen of regular, relentless practice gives you some idea of the direction you need to be heading if you want to achieve expert status with a diaphragm. You don't have to be as devoted as these champions are in order to become more than proficient with a diaphragm, but neither can you expect to get anywhere near their skill level by sticking a call in your mouth two days before the season opens and throwing it away on the day the season closes.

And though it's not necessary to become Grand National material to become super-proficient with a diaphragm, the closer you can get to that benchmark, the better your success rate is going to be. Practice a little, and you'll sound like all the other mediocre to so-so to pretty good callers out there. Practice a lot, and you'll be head and shoulders above them. With practice, you can not only make the entire repertoire of turkey calls with a diaphragm, but you can also vary the air flow and tongue pressure to change the pitch and make the same call sound like several different hens.

Another advantage of using a diaphragm is that you can use it while simultaneously running a friction call such as a slate or box. This opens up a

It's not necessary to become a championship caller to effectively use a diaphragm, but the better you are, the higher your success rate will be.

turkey behavior, having effective camouflage and being able to sit still are probably more important than being an expert turkey caller, all things considered ... but there's another verse to that song. All those other things being equal, the hunter who is the better caller will tag more gobblers than the one who thinks sounding vaguely turkeylike is

There are literally thousands of diaphragm styles and brands.

whole new realm of calling possibilities, from carrying on a calm, low-key conversation between two or more hens, to engaging in a mad hen cutting contest, to staging a gobbler fight with two push-button calls and simulating the excited yelping, cutting and cackling of a group of onlooking hens and jakes.

I often use a diaphragm call to locate turkeys, both at daylight and well into the day, because I've learned I can create excited cackling and cutting more realistically with a diaphragm than with other types of calls. Then, when I move in closer to work the gobbler, I'll switch to a slate, box, tube or wingbone. Or, sometimes, if the gobbler is responding well, I'll stick with the diaphragm for the entire encounter. This works more often early in the season, before the turkeys have heard every brand of diaphragm call on the market.

Even on the last day of the season, though, if you run into me in the turkey woods, you'll notice I'll be talking a little funny, like someone who's worked hard to overcome a speech impediment. That's because I'll have a diaphragm tucked, like Walt Garrison's pinch of snuff, "between cheek and gum." I might not make a call with it all day long, but it'll always be there.

Sooner or later, it'll come in handy.

Section 4

Tricks, Tactics and Techniques

Chapter 13

Long-Distance Scouting

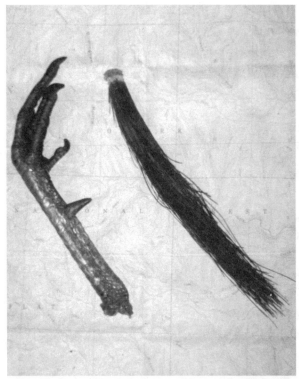

Every experienced hunter has a few favorite spots, but by using topo maps, you can find a lot more of them over time.

Like most other turkey hunters, I have some favorite "honey holes." I go back and hunt these places often. They're favorites for various reasons: I've had exciting hunts in some, and I've killed exceptional trophy gobblers in others. I've called up turkeys for other hunters in still others. I've been consistently beaten by gobblers in others yet.

I like some of my honey holes because they're scenic. Some I like because they're hard to reach, and some I like for exactly the opposite reason – because they're easy to reach. (Sometimes, during

a particularly wearing season, I need an easy place to hunt every once in a while.)

Because I've hunted these favorite places often, I know them well – not as well as the turkeys that live in these places know them, admittedly, but pretty well. It's a big advantage, too, when you're trying to work a gobbler. If you know where the ravines and fences and other potential hang-up obstacles are, in many cases you can take these obstacles out of play before starting to work on a gobbler. Even when you can't get around an obstacle, if you know it's there you can adjust your hunting tactics accordingly.

However, as comforting and advantageous as it is to make tracks in these familiar territories, I suspect I wouldn't hunt turkeys nearly as often (or as hard) if I had to go back to those same spots every time. I know quite a few hunters who hunt the same two or three properties exclusively, year after year. I know one or two who do every bit of their turkey hunting on just a single hunting area. One guy I know spends his entire turkey season on a 160-acre patch of woods owned by his family. He hunts this little place eight or 10 days every spring, and kills a turkey or two in there every year. But I can no more confine myself to that small a chunk of the world than I can grow fins and become a catfish.

The world is too big a place, and there are turkeys in too much of it, for me to limit myself that way. Turkeys are present and are legal game in every state except Alaska, not to mention Canada, Mexico and New Zealand.

That fact haunts people like me. Even when we're surrounded by gobblers on familiar ground, in the back of our minds is the knowledge that somewhere far away, other turkeys are also gobbling … and we're not there to hear them. And we can hardly wait to leave these familiar surroundings and depart on our next trip.

Of course, this itchy-footedness has its disadvantages. One of those disadvantages is the very thing that makes traveling to hunt so attractive in the first place: On new ground, you're unfamiliar with both the landscape and with the habits of the critters living there.

Up to a point, there's nothing you can do to change that situation. Aside from hiring a local guide (there's nothing wrong with this, either, but it adds enormously to the expense), you just have to get out there and learn the territory on your own. Furthermore, you have to do it pretty fast, because you're probably not going to be there long.

But there are things you can do to help yourself along in this process. And you should do most of them well in advance of the season.

First, talk to people who live in the area you're planning to hunt, or to people who have traveled to hunt there before you. Turkey hunters, by and large, are a bunch of gypsies. While we're secretive in the extreme about the specific whereabouts of a nearby gobbling tom in April, most of us are perfectly willing to share our knowledge about conditions in faraway places, especially in general terms. If you're planning a hunt in Missouri or Georgia, say, put the word out among your friends. Chances are, somebody in your circle of acquaintances has hunted there, or knows someone who has, or has knowledge of the area through some other avenue.

Of course, planning a hunt in "Georgia" is painting with a broad brush. Georgia has everything from coastal lowlands to mile-high mountains, and that's the case most other states as well. Narrow the focus of your research, and do it early in the process so you don't waste time and energy gathering information you don't need.

Usually, the easiest way to both narrow the focus and start the information-gathering process is to call your target state's wildlife resources agency. Sometimes you'll be in for a frustrating, hair-pulling experience wading through the "I don't knows" and "Let me transfer yous" of a state agency before you get to the person you need to talk to, but it's worth the effort. To streamline the process a little, look in a recent copy of *Turkey Call* magazine and find the list of NWTF

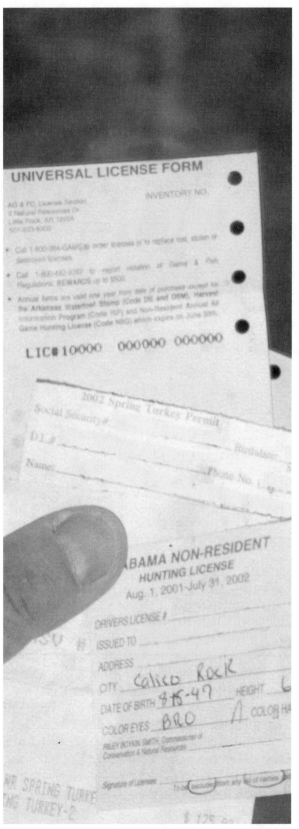

Turkey hunters have itchy feet. Many of us hunt several states each spring, and this often puts us in the position of hunting on unfamiliar ground.

"Telephone scouting" is a productive way to gather a lot of information in a short time, but be ready before you make the call. Have maps and notebook ready.

Technical Committee members. Then when you call the state agency, ask specifically for that person. More than likely, this will be the person most knowledgeable about the whereabouts and status of turkey populations. More to the point, it's part of that person's job to talk to you as a potential visiting hunter/license buyer.

When you make the call, have a state highway map opened and ready, along with a pen and notebook. Write your questions down beforehand, so you won't forget any of them. Keep your questions general at first, unless you've already decided on the specific area you want to hunt (in which case, you'll want to have maps of that area on hand as well as the state highway map). Ask about recent hatches. The hatch you're most interested in is

spring before last, since it's the one that determines the number of 2-year-olds in the population. Ask about hunting pressure in various parts of the state. Ask about the availability of public land, and campsites, motels or whatever other accommodations you want. Ask for a copy of the most recent harvest records; most states compile these annually, listing harvest by county or zone. Ask for the current hunting regulations, so you can stay legal. Ask if the agency has free or for-purchase maps of the areas you want to hunt, and ask how to obtain them. And by all means, ask: "If you were me, where would you go hunting next spring?" You'll be surprised how much most of these folks will tell you. They're not going to draw you a map to their favorite listening spot, but they'll give you plenty of information to enable you to find a good one of your own.

Another good bet is to call the NWTF State Chapter president of your chosen state (these folks are also listed in *Turkey Call*). But remember, this person, unlike the professional turkey biologist, is a volunteer. Feeding you information about turkeys in his or her home state is not a part of his or her job. Even so, these people are avid turkey hunters themselves, and most are willing to help a fellow addict. It's also a good idea to ask these chapter officers if they know other hunters who might be willing to talk to you. Chances are, they do.

After you've narrowed your search through your telephone conversations, you'll need maps. Even if you get maps from the state wildlife agency, you'll still need maps with more detail. There are numerous internet map resources available, but most of us are more familiar with the topographical maps produced by the U.S. Geological Survey (which are also available online at www.usgs.gov.) These are still the best all-around maps you can have. Combined with a county atlas or a WMA or U.S. Forest Service map, a topo can help you select a good hunting area better than any other single tool. Road networks, saddles, creeks, trails, valleys and ridges, fields, ponds and a multitude of other terrain features show up on these maps, and you can familiarize yourself with more strange country in an hour with a topo map than you can in a month of prowling the landscape.

If you want to get away from the crowds, look for rough chunks of country that are a mile or more from roads. Few hunters will penetrate that far. If you want to drive the roads and prospect for gobbling turkeys until you learn a little bit about the territory, look for a series of connecting roads that stick mostly to high ground, because you can hear farther when you're up high. Use the maps to cut down on the amount of exploring you have to do when you reach your hunting ground. With a little practice and experience, you can have a hundred potential hot spots marked on your maps before you ever leave your living room.

Which brings up an important point: Be sure to armchair-scout at least three times as many potential hunting spots as you'll have time to visit. Remember, you're doing all this work at long-distance, and you never know what might be going on when you get there. New roads get built into areas that show up as near-wilderness on the map. An area may be wall-to-wall with other hunters. Another potential hot spot might have been clearcut or tornado-struck last season. If you have enough areas marked, though, some of them will pan out.

Another important thing when you're planning a hunt in new territory is to carry everything you think you might need. I know that sounds impractical, and it's hard to do if you're flying. But you never know what's going to come up on a trip, and in many cases you're going to be a long way from the nearest Wal-Mart. In my first years of traveling for turkeys, I came up short-handed time after time, finding myself needing this or that. It was usually some small, inexpensive thing – a pair of scissors for trimming the tape on a diaphragm call, maybe, or a 3-foot piece of rope, but I always seemed to need it very badly.

So I started carrying an old suitcase as a standard part of my turkey hunting gear. It's a rigid three-suiter, and I ripped the guts out of it and made it into one big compartment. I've still got that old thing, and it lives in my truck the entire turkey season. I root around in it pretty often. I've got more stuff in there than you could imagine, from needle and thread (ever popped the button off your camo pants?) to an assortment of spare turkey calls, to shoelaces to an extra compass to a pair of $20 bills in a film canister. Every time I think of something I might need someday, or every time I find myself needing something I don't have in the suitcase (these times don't hap-

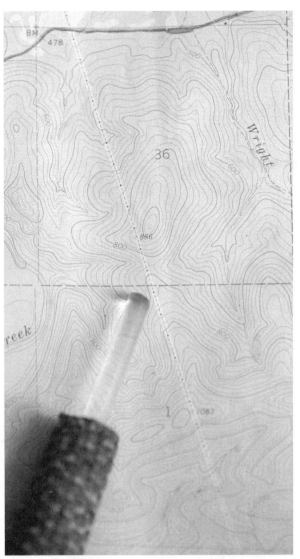

Topo maps are excellent tools for armchair scouting. Terrain features like saddles are easy to find on good topos, and these make excellent starting places for hunts in new territory.

pen often anymore), I add it at the first opportunity. Everything's in a big jumble in there, and it may take me 10 minutes to find what I need, but if you're ever on a turkey trip with me and you need some small item, I'll bet a custom-made box call against an empty shotgun hull I'll have it.

Long-distance scouting – long-distance hunting, for that matter – isn't the easiest thing in the world. Nor is it the right choice for every hunter. But with turkey populations flourishing all over the United States and beyond, every hunter owes it to himself to give it a try. There's nothing wrong with hunting those local birds, but there's a lot more to this grand sport than a single state or geographical area can offer.

Chapter 14

The Home Field Advantage

Snowbirds from Northern states come south in March; Southerners go north in May. We all like to stretch our season, and the best way to do that is by traveling.

Modern-day turkey hunters are an itchy-footed bunch. If you don't believe it, check out the license plates on the vehicles parked along the roads during turkey season in any national forest with a decent turkey population. Likely as not, you'll see as many out-of-state tags as local ones.

It works in all directions. Snowbirds from the Northern states, sick of winter and giddy with cabin fever, flock southward to take advantage of the earlier seasons in the South. Later in the spring, the migration pattern reverses, as the good ol' boys visit their Yankee friends and keep their hunting season going just a little longer. Eastern hunters go west to try their luck at Merriam's or Rio Grande gobblers in the arid, open country. Western hunters go east to experience the claustrophobic thrill of hunting turkeys in the Big Woods. Turkey hunters from everywhere else descend on Florida like locusts on a Mormon wheat crop, searching for an Osceola to round out their Grand Slams.

There's absolutely nothing wrong with this annual population shift, except maybe it tends to crowd the woods a little too much on opening day in the Southeastern states. Traveling to hunt turkeys in new areas far from home is one of the most enjoyable aspects of the sport, and it puts more money in the budgets of state wildlife agencies so they can make things better for turkeys and other critters. Most turkey hunters eventually get around to doing some long-distance turkey hunting. Many of us make it a way of life.

There are two problems, though, with lengthy out-of-state expeditions. First, they cost more money than hunting locally. Second is the time requirement. You can't drive from Ohio to

Mississippi for a two-hour hunt before work on Tuesday morning.

But you can pull off a two-hour hunt for those birds that live in your back yard.

With today's greatly expanded turkey ranges and turkey flocks, most of us live within an hour or less of a huntable population of turkeys. Sometimes much less. Where I live, for example, I can walk out the back door, take exactly 17 normal walking steps, and be standing on Forest Service property in a 150,000-acre chunk of prime turkey territory. Last fall, I killed a long-beard within shouting distance of the house. Last week, I watched a hook-spurred old gobbler eat sunflower seeds underneath the bird feeder in the back yard. Most hunters don't have it quite that convenient, of course, but you get the idea.

These close-to-home hunting areas, though they don't provide the romance and sense of adventure that come with a thousand-mile road trip across three dozen area codes, nevertheless allow a dedicated turkey hunter to get into the woods more often without running too much risk of losing friends, family and job.

There's another obvious benefit. By concentrating your hunting efforts on one or two close-to-home areas, you can learn the lay of the land much more thoroughly than you'll ever get to know those distant hunting spots you may visit only once or twice in your lifetime. And, as any experienced turkey hunter knows, having an intimate knowledge of the territory is a distinct advantage.

If you don't live in a rural area or don't have nearby public land to hunt, finding a home field flock on someone else's land and getting permission to hunt there is always a possibility. It may not be the easiest thing to do, but it's worth the effort. I've gotten permission on several such properties over the years by doing no more than showing up at an appropriate time and asking.

Note the word "appropriate" in that last sentence. Farmers and landowners don't need or want company when they're driving a tractor or baling hay, or when they're sitting down to supper. They also generally don't appreciate it if someone shows up wearing camo and carrying a shotgun, asking permission to go hunting right then. Pick your time, and do it during the off-season when the landowner isn't busy.

Many landowners aren't interested in turkey hunting, and they may give you permission if

Not everybody lives in a place that has turkey hunting opportunities right out the back door. Most of us have to travel, at least a little way.

you're polite and not pushy. Even with harder cases, offering to take the landowner or a member of his or her family on a turkey hunt – or offering the bird to them should you take one – may help you get your foot in the door. Leasing turkey hunting rights (even if they're non-exclusive) is another option, and it's often surprisingly inexpensive.

Once you secure permission to hunt and establish a relationship with the landowner, you might be able to get his OK to make minor habitat improvements and create a more attractive environment for turkeys on the property. You probably won't be able to make large-scale changes, but planting a few green food plots, chufa or clover patches, or whatever is appropriate for your locality, might be acceptable. It'll pay off during hunting season.

It's also not a bad idea to invest a little woods time to improve a few potential setup places around your home field, so you'll have a leg up when hunting season comes. There's no need to spend hours constructing elaborate log-and-brush ground blinds, but positioning a few dead limbs and sticking a bush here and there around suitable setup trees on likely approaches, travelways or strutting areas can be of tremendous help later, when a gobbler is approaching fast.

Don't, however, limit your home field efforts to the activities discussed above. Get out there and simply prowl the landscape several times during the off-season, especially in winter when visibility is better. In addition to learning every fold and detail of the landscape, year-round scouting lets you keep a close eye on the habits and condition of the home field turkey flock. It also provides the birds with more protection from poaching, since your regular presence will discourage illegal activity on the property.

During the last few weeks before the season, get out to the home field as often as possible to listen for gobbling activity. It's much easier to pattern those home field birds than more-distant turkeys as the season draws near, since going out to listen at first light doesn't require a big investment of time.

One year not too long ago, after a move to a different town, I started a campaign to learn a new home field not far off my regular route to work – a 25,000-acre wildlife management area

Gaining permission to hunt on private land is getting harder, but it's well worth the effort.

with a good turkey population. My turkey log-book shows I started listening for gobblers in late February, and by the time the season opened in early April, I had made 22 pre-work listening trips. In that time, I'd located more than 30 actively gobbling turkeys and had thoroughly patterned nearly a dozen of them. By 8 a.m. opening morning, I'd called in mature home field gobblers for two other hunters, and I killed a gobbler myself early on the second morning.

That was an unusual situation, and most home field hunting areas aren't that big or that target-rich. But it gives you an idea of the potential involved here.

On these frequent pre-season listening trips, don't make the mistake of trying to locate turkeys by calling to them. Most hunters know it's a bad idea to call in – or even call to – pre-season gobblers with turkey calls, but this pre-season taboo also extends to locator calls as well. I don't know whether turkeys actually wise up to crow-, owl- and coyote locator calling, but they certainly acclimate to it, and the more they hear them, the less likely they are to gobble at them.

Save those locators for use during the season, and let the turkeys sound off on their own when you're scouting. There's little to be gained in making a chronically shut-mouthed old hermit gobble in spite of himself, especially when every time you do it you're increasing the chances you won't be able to get him to do it when you can hunt him. Your objective is to locate the turkeys most likely to gobble on their own, anyway, and further, to learn where they like to roost and which direction they usually travel after fly-down.

If you go out to listen to your home field turkeys as often as you should, you'll hear more than enough gobbling to accomplish those goals, and all without the turkeys ever becoming aware of your presence.

There can also be disadvantages and pitfalls to concentrating most of your hunting efforts in one area. Among them is the almost inevitable boredom and sloppiness that generally result from repetition. Even in a sport as inherently exciting as turkey hunting, hunting the same ground morning after morning is eventually going to lose its thrill for most of us. Some hunters can spend their whole

If you hunt a place regularly through the season, spending a day constructing semi-permanent blinds in good calling/strutting areas can be a valuable investment of your time.

Finding fresh turkey sign in January or February may or may not be useful information, but finding fresh sign a week before the season opens is.

turkey hunting careers on the same patch of real estate and be content, but I'm not one of them. I have to avoid hunting the same territory too often, or I find myself getting careless. Careless hunters kill few turkeys. Luckily, since my home field is that 150,000-acre national forest I mentioned earlier, this isn't much of a hardship. If your home field is a small area, though, it might be a good idea to try to develop two or three alternates.

Turkeys can also become pretty much immune to your calling and hunting techniques if they get to know you too well. A bird that hears your calling morning after morning from the same spot on the property will quickly wise up. Once that happens, you're dead in the water with that bird from that calling position. If you hunt the same area repeatedly, try to vary things as much as you can. If there are several accesses to the property, rotate your hunts so you come in a different way each time. This can be especially important if you find yourself in a prolonged several-day duel with a particular gobbler. Hit him from different directions and keep him off balance. Don't let him pattern you.

Turkeys can also become familiar with a hunter's favorite calls and calling styles. To mini-

mize this, switch calls on a regular basis. I'm sure you have a favorite call or two, as I do, but using those favorites day after day on the home field is a bad idea. Although it can be difficult, try also to vary your calling rhythm and pattern. Most of us have consistent ways we run our calls – the cadence and number of notes in a run of yelps, or a particular calling sequence – and whether we recognize it or not, the turkeys quickly will. Make a conscious effort to mix it up.

If you have the option, mix up your hunting times as well. Most of your hunts on home fields are going to (of necessity) be early-morning, before-work affairs, but if you can swing it, try a midday or afternoon hunt. Simply changing the timing can defuse much of a home field gobbler's suspicion. If he's accustomed to having the woods all to himself after 8 a.m., slip in there and try him at 11:30 some morning and see what happens. I've taken several gobblers on the way home from unsuccessful hunts by simply driving by the home field, stopping and making an exploratory call or two.

No matter how much you feel the need to brag about your successes or commiserate about your

Many hunters use locator calls for pre-season scouting, but it's better to let the turkeys sound off on their own. Gobblers can get wise, to owl-, crow-, hawk- and coyote locator calls the same way they can get wise to hen calls.

failures, never give away too much information about the location of your home field. If it's close enough for you to hunt it before work, there are plenty of other hunters in range of it, too. I don't even tell my close turkey hunting buddies about my favorite home fields. I don't have any fear of them horning in on the action, but turkey hunters like to talk, and they might let the information slip. Loose lips sink more than ships; they can also torpedo a perfectly suitable home field as well.

If I had to give up either home field hunting or the expeditions I make each spring to distant locations, it would be no contest. I'd quit hunting the home fields because I love to make tracks in new territory. But I don't have to make that choice, so I'm going to keep hunting both. Developing an intimate knowledge of a few close-in hunting spots has added a lot of woods time to my life, and it's going to add a lot more before my ride to the boneyard.

Life is short, and turkey seasons are even shorter. Maybe it's time you started cultivating a few home fields of your own.

To keep turkeys from learning your calling styles and cadences on your home turf, try to vary your methods as much as possible. Change calls. Vary your cadence or the number of notes. One simple way to make a slight change in the way you sound when using a box call is to change the way you normally hold it. If you've been using it by holding the box stationary and moving the lid, reverse it and strike the box against the paddle. With practice, it'll still sound good to the turkeys, but it won't sound like the same caller.

Chapter 15

First Contact

Owling at first light – the standard opening ploy for the turkey hunter.

Turkey hunters are fanatics about getting to the woods early, but this time we pushed it almost to the point of silliness. When we pulled off the road into the little turnout, it was at least 45 minutes before the normal starting time for a hunt.

It was a necessary strategy, I thought. Although I hadn't put this turkey to bed the evening before, I'd heard him the previous morning. If he was roosting in the same place, we'd have to park practically underneath him in order to hunt him. The road, a narrow two-track Forest Service dead-ender, had no pull-offs for a half-mile either way except this one, and logging traffic from a timber sale at the end of the road made it imperative that we get completely off the right-of-way.

Because we had to either park underneath him or walk a half-mile and risk missing the dim, seldom-used pullout in the dark, we needed to get there early enough to give the bird time to settle down. So there we were, Bill White and I, standing by the truck almost an hour before the crack of dawn. We occupied ourselves at first by quietly going through our gear and making sure everything was where it was supposed to be, but it was opening day and our turkey vests were pristine. Everything was functional and still in place, because none of it had seen battle yet. We were at peak organizational status, and so the job took less than five minutes. Then we found ourselves leaning against the warm hood of my ticking, slowly cooling pickup, surrounded by the cool, black night.

We could have gotten back in the cab and tried to catch a catnap, but, you know, it was opening day. We were stoked on caffeine and pre-hunt adrenaline, and sleeping was out of the question.

We'd been leaning there five minutes without speaking when a barred owl hooted from a tree almost directly above us, and the gobbler racked off an immediate, angry response from his tree less than 150 yards from the truck. An invisible fist punched me in the shoulder as Bill shared his excitement. He nearly knocked me off the truck.

We donned our gear and moved slowly toward the bird, feeling our way through the inky woods. After we set up and first light finally came, the turkey gobbled three more times at widely spaced intervals, then flew down into a little bowl below us, and shut up. We couldn't see him, but we knew he was still in there because we could see all the exits and he hadn't used any of them. Nothing else was gobbling within hearing range, so we just sat there on the edge of the bowl above him, making soft, contented hen sounds every 10 minutes or so.

Intermittently, one or the other of us thought we heard drumming, but since it was windy that morning and drumming is more a vibration than a sound, neither of us was sure. Finally, though, I definitely heard it, and moments later the gobbler just materialized out of the ether, the way they do. When I saw him, he was straight in front of Bill but screened from him by a thin stand of black-berry canes. Bill picked him out about the same time, and when the bird strutted behind a tree, he raised his gun.

This old boy was in no hurry. He stood behind that tree for what seemed like an hour and was probably an honest 20 minutes, alternately swelling into strut and then slicking down to survey the landscape. I had him in full sight the whole time, but my gun was still in my lap. All Bill could see of him was the tips of his tail feathers when he went into strut. At last he waddled out from behind the tree, and nearly four hours after he gobbled at the owl, less than the length of a football field from where we'd parked and half that distance from the roost tree, Bill pulled the trigger on that 3-year-old, 22-pound gobbler.

There's a lesson in that hunt, and the lesson is as simple to tell as it is difficult to carry out when you're hunting: When you make contact with a gobbler, don't get in too big a hurry and screw it up. Think before you act. Many turkey hunters, especially those relatively new to the game, tend to rush things when they make initial contact with a turkey. Usually, that's unwise.

Bill White with the slowpoke gobbler, taken after four hours in the same setup spot.

Both commercial hooters and natural voice owling are effective techniques for making first contact.

Sometimes, after making contact, the best thing to do is just sit quietly and see what happens.

The decisions you make in the first few minutes after establishing contact with a gobbling turkey can make or break your chances to shoot that given bird on that given day. Everyone who's ever blown a chance at a gobbler knows this. Your initial decisions set the ball rolling in one direction or the other – in the direction that will eventually allow you to tag that bird, or in the direction that will eventually allow him to survive. Sometimes you can recover from a first-contact mistake and still kill the bird, but your odds of success are always much better if you can get off on the right foot when you hear his first gobble.

Sometimes you have to come back the next day (or even the next or the next) to rectify a first-contact mistake. One time a few springs ago, I hunted a turkey-rich bottomland area where I had the unprecedented luxury of three consecutive days to scout immediately before the season. On each of those three days, I heard the same gobbler sounding off from the same place at daylight. Each day, I stood on a gravel road a quarter-mile away and listened to him gobble several times, then set off to locate other turkeys during the pre-flydown gobbling time.

On the third day, the day before the season opened, I went into the area at noon and scoped out the roost. It was a small cypress pond surrounded by bottomland forest, and I figured the turkey was roosting over the water and flying down on the dry land. Circling the pond, I located a flat, relatively open area with a clear flight line to several large cypresses in the pond. Bisecting the opening was a smooth woods road that half-circled the wet area and then led back into an expanse of hardwoods on the opposite side of the pond. The road was full of turkey sign – droppings, tracks, feathers, scratching.

Aha! I thought. *Here's his landing zone, and he's drifting back into the big woods to spend the day.* It was a textbook situation, and I found a good setup tree within easy shotgun range of the opening and stuck a few bushes in strategic places to break up my outline. I went to bed that night with as big a case of misplaced confidence as I've ever had.

On opening day, I was sitting in my crude little blind 20 minutes before first light, with a hen decoy in place on the edge of the road. Daybreak came and with it the owl, and the first hoot triggered the thundering full-roll gobble of a very nearby gobbler. When the light grew a little more, I could see him out there over the pond, restlessly pacing up and down a waist-thick cypress limb, breaking occasionally into a full-blown strut. When I softly tree-yelped to get his attention, he spun around on the limb so fast, he almost fell off. He gobbled immediately, straight at the decoy and me.

Textbook stuff so far. But then the hens that were roosting on the other end of the pond started their usual early-morning chatter – hens I didn't know about until that very second – and my textbook hunt began to unravel. The gobbler promptly forgot all about me, spun back around on his limb and started gobbling back at the hens. I tried to compensate by calling to him, but that only stirred up the hens even more. Soon, they flew down on the opposite side of the pond. Predictably, the gobbler followed them, and I was left to contemplate the beautiful spring morning, a lonely hen turkey decoy and the fate of overconfident turkey hunters.

The next morning, I was back in the same spot. This time, I had two hens and a jake in the road – which, by the way, had more fresh sign in it. I waited for him to gobble, and when he did I tried to outcall the real hens by using several calls at once. It didn't work. For the second time, the hens flew out the other way and led the gobbler to safety.

I am not a particularly good turkey hunter, but by God I am a persistent one. On morning three I was back in the same spot, but this time I left the decoys in my truck and the calls in my vest. I let him start gobbling on his own, resolutely suppressed an almost overwhelming urge to call to him or to the hens when they started yelping, and listened quietly to their back-and-forth calling for half an hour that seemed like half a month. But this time the hens weren't bothered by the possibility of a stranger joining their harem, and so they flew down in their normal landing spot – right into my little opening. I saw the gobbler pitch off his limb 10 seconds later and heard him land heavily on the edge of the pond 75 yards from the hens. Two minutes later he was there, strutting into the opening and into the presence of his ladies. I clucked once to make him raise his head, and a few minutes later my little pocket tape revealed his sharp spurs were 1 1/4 inches long.

I'd have taken that gobbler the first morning if I'd made the right decision and kept mum when I heard the hens start calling, but I think I can be excused for that one. You just never know in a situation like that whether it's a good idea or a bad

Learn as much as you can about the habits and movements of a turkey you're trying to pattern.

The first few minutes after making contact are crucial. How close should you get? Where do you sit? What calls do you use? Decisions, decisions.

one to call to a gobbler's flock of hens. I learned that first morning it was the latter.

That's why I still to this day feel like I ought to have my butt kicked for making the same mistake again the next morning. I was almost certain from the amount of sign on the road and in the opening that it was the usual fly-down spot – or, at least, the usual staging spot – for this particular bunch of turkeys. Even so, I let my eagerness get the best of me and tried to bend the turkeys to my will, a tactic that almost never works.

Fool me once, shame on you; fool me twice, shame on me. That third morning, I made the proper decision at first contact – which was to not call at all until the turkeys were on the ground. That time, the gobbler got a ride in my truck.

If you want to know the truth about it, I'd already made a bad decision on that particular turkey even before the season opened. For three straight mornings I left him before finding out anything about his normal behavior pattern after he flew down, and I didn't even know the hens were there until the first morning of the season. Already I was at a disadvantage. If I had just stuck around a little while, I'd have known about the hens and maybe it wouldn't have taken me three mornings to get the gobbler off the bead of my shotgun.

Most first contacts with gobblers, though, don't have such a lengthy gestation period. Typically, a hunter goes out, listens for gobbling and when he hears a turkey, starts formulating a plan to hunt that bird. He's already got a basic game plan in mind, of course: Call the bird in and shoot it in the head. But turkey hunt plans are fluid, flexible things – or, at least they'd better be if you expect to be successful. If you're not flexible and willing to alter or even abandon your original game plan, you're not going to tag many gobblers.

Every single thing that happens in the first few minutes after you make contact with a turkey demands a rapid-fire set of decisions. Then, every decision you make demands another set of decisions behind that. How close do you get? What calls do you use? How much do you call? How loud? You can make mistakes on any of these decisions and still recover and get the bird, but only if you're able to recognize you've made a mistake and take immediate steps to correct it.

Knowing what lies between you and a gobbling turkey is important if you're going to make the correct string of decisions at first contact. It's usually a smart move to get in the best possible calling position relative to the gobbler before making

While a dry wash like this one constitutes no real obstacle to a gobbler, the savvy hunter will make every effort to make sure any turkey he tries to call doesn't have any such barriers to use as an excuse to hang up.

your first call. That means, in most cases, cutting the distance. The closer you are, the less chance you have of an obstacle being between you and the bird.

Of course, this in itself is a tough decision. What's the best calling position relative to the gobbler's present location? Is he stationary or moving? How close is close enough? How close is too close?

Often, the only way to learn the answer to that question is to give it a try. Get as close as you possibly can, then try to get just one tree closer. "The difference between being close enough to a gobbler and being too close to him is one step," an experienced turkey hunter once told me. "You're not close enough if you think you can get closer without spooking him. You're close enough if you think you can't."

Is there a creek, thicket, fence or other obstacle between you and the bird? If so, better try to get across it or around it. Is the gobbler on a forest trail or logging road? If so, better try to get to the trail and then try to call the bird along it. Is there a good strutting area between you and the gobbler? If so, better try to beat him to it if you can.

Being intimately familiar with your hunting territory is the best way to know the answers to these questions. However, most of us don't hunt the same chunk of territory all the time; we often find ourselves listening to a gobbler in a place we've never hunted before.

Don't forget about the possibility that you can use obstacles to your advantage. If a gobbler is on a ridgeline and you know there's a briar thicket on one side of him, then by all means set up on the side opposite the thicket. It increases the odds of him coming your way. Ditto with water, well-traveled roads, steep drop-offs and a thousand other things.

Does your gobbler have hens? Whether he does or not determines yet another series of first-contact decision-making: If he has female company, do you want to try to call him away from them or challenge them and try to call them in? Or do you want to back off, leave him alone for a few hours, and then try to raise him again after the hens have had time to leave him for the day?

That's a tactic that's worked for me on several occasions. A gobbler that's absolutely uncallable at sunrise can be a pushover at 11 a.m., when his hens are gone and he's lonesome again. There's an obvious downside to leaving a gobbler, though. You might not find him again, or some other hunter might get to him first.

Keep in mind something that was said earlier in this chapter: A turkey hunt plan must be flexible. Take your cues from the gobbler. If he likes a call you're making, then by all means keep on making it. If he loses interest, change calls and see what happens.

Or change calling positions. This is a first-contact decision many inexperienced turkey hunters seem reluctant to change, once they've set up on a gobbler and started calling to him. But if he seems reluctant to approach a given calling position, something's wrong. Drop back and circle around to a new position, then try him again.

Which brings up still another thing: Don't spend too much time on an unproductive tactic. A turkey only has so many gobbles in him on any given morning, and at some point during the day he's almost certain to dummy up. Give him a reasonable time to do what you're asking him to do, and if he doesn't, modify your plan and try something else.

On the other hand, don't get in a big hurry and abandon a tactic too soon. Likewise, don't rush things when you're analyzing the situation and getting into the best calling position during those moments of first contact. Being too slow can cost you some gobblers, but you'll blow a lot more opportunities by rushing things. You usually have more time than you think.

Turkey hunting has no absolutes. There are no hard-and-fast rules, and that's what makes it so interesting. Every time you make contact with a turkey, it's a brand new game. You rely on clues and gut instinct, on past experience and what you've learned from other turkeys. You'll make mistakes, but don't let that knowledge paralyze you. The difference between an ineffective turkey hunter and an effective one is that the ineffective one is scared he's going to make mistakes, while the effective hunter knows he's going to. It's all a process of experimentation and elimination, and one of the most crucial challenges of the hunt is figuring out, once you find a gobbler, what to do next.

On second thought, there is one hard-and-fast rule that should guide you during those fleeting moments of first contact:

Think before you act.

You can also use obstacles to your advantage. Setting up with your back to a creek or ledge removes the possibility that your gobbler will circle and come in behind you.

Turkey hunting has no absolutes. From time to time, no matter what, you're going to get beat.

Chapter 16

Sit Down Right for Success

Sitting down wrong is easy to do. This hunter didn't.

"Well, the first thing was, I sat down wrong," said the gray-whiskered old man, spitting a brown stream of tobacco juice into the dusty gravel.

We were standing on the weathered front porch of a mom-and-pop grocery store in the rural South, and the old man was explaining to a half-dozen other camo-clad hunters how and why he'd been beaten by the gobbler he'd worked that morning. It was midday rehash time, when hunters gather in back-roads stores through-out turkey country and gloat over their successes and share their tales of woe. I'd only been hunting turkeys a few years at the time, and I was full of

the arrogance that comes with youth, inexperience and a half-dozen kills. The basic reason the old gentleman had been beaten by his gobbler, it turned out, was that he'd chosen a setup that didn't work. I remember thinking, *Well, you silly old coot, how come you sat down wrong?*

The next morning, I received an object lesson on the topic.

It was that time of the morning when all the turkeys seem to have crawled into armadillo holes, and I was covering ground, looking for action. I wasn't really expecting to find any, though, and I was ambling along a ridgeline with only about half my mind in the game when a close-by turkey gobbled at the sound of my footsteps in the leaves.

While you don't have time to dawdle, you usually have more time than you think to choose an effective setup spot. Take a few seconds to ponder the situation, because where you sit is a crucial part of your strategy.

He was less than 75 yards down the slope – considerably less, it sounded like – and I went immediately into a state of reactionary panic.

If he'd gobbled earlier, when I was farther away – or even if he hadn't gobbled at all – I'd have been better off. As it was, the gobbler startled me into taking action without thinking it through, and I doomed my chances from the start. I was in a thicket of waist-high blackjack oak saplings when he gobbled, and instead of taking my time and easing on through the thicket or backing out of it to find a better setup location, I dove for the nearest tree trunk, yanked my head net into place, and yelped an answer.

Only then did I recognize my mistake. Standing up, I could see over and down into the closely spaced young blackjacks out to a distance of maybe 30 yards. Sitting, I couldn't see more than 15 feet in any direction. Sometimes it's best to stand to a turkey rather than sit to him, and this was one of those times. But I was too green a turkey hunter to have made that discovery yet; I thought it was written in stone you had to sit, so I did. And when I sat, the leathery, hand-sized leaves of those young oaks walled me in as effectively as if I'd been in a closet. By the time I figured that out, it was too late. The turkey hammered back at my first yelp, and when he gobbled again a half-minute later, he was right on top of me.

That turkey stayed right in there with me for the next 45 minutes, gobbling and strutting and drumming for all he was worth. I could have killed him anytime I wanted, except for one little detail: I couldn't see him. Every once in a while I'd notice a sapling shake as the gobbler brushed against it, but I never saw a feather on the bird itself. Finally he got tired of the whole thing and left.

Just like the gray-whiskered old coot at the grocery store, I'd sat down wrong, and it put me in a hole from which I couldn't recover. I beat myself from the start.

Sitting down wrong. It's easy to do. Anyone who's been hunting turkeys for any length of time has been painfully reminded, many times, of the importance of setting up properly. That morning was only one of the numerous reminders I've had over the years. And it'll happen again, I'm sure, when other gobblers in my future scare me into doing something without stopping to think it through, or when I neglect to consider one or more of the factors we're going to discuss here in a minute.

This hunter's visibility is excellent at this setup. Unfortunately, so is the turkey's when it approaches.

That's the key to the whole business of turkey hunting, anyway: thinking things through. That was covered in the previous chapter, I know, but it's important. It bears repeating. And when it comes to choosing a proper setup, thinking things through is even more important. Blow this part of the hunt and it doesn't matter how well you know the lay of the land or how good a caller you are, or how well you're camouflaged, or how tight a pattern your shotgun throws. Sit down wrong and you're beat.

First of all, don't ever make a call until you set up, or at least until you look around and pick out a good spot you can get to very quickly if need be. If a turkey gobbles right back at you from close range when you make a call, you'd better already have this part of the decision-making process out of the way. The nerve-jangling situation that blossoms around you when a turkey gobbles at close range is not conducive to the analytical thought process that goes into making a good setup. Reread the beginning paragraphs of this chapter if you don't believe it.

It's not a bad idea to pick out a never-ending series of setup locations as you move through the woods, just in case something happens unexpect-edly – even when you're just walking through the woods and not calling. Had I been doing that when the turkey gobbled at the sound of my feet in the leaves that long-ago morning, his spurs and beard would be in my collection right now. More or less the same thing has happened to me six or seven times in the years since, and after blowing another couple of chances at these birds by setting up too hastily in a gobble-induced state of panic, I've learned to keep myself aware of nearby setup possibilities as I move through the woods. Now I do it almost without thinking about it, and I've tagged three of the last four birds that gobbled at the sound of my footsteps.

When you're picking out a spot, regardless of the circumstances, don't get in too much of a hurry. Think each location through. If you're not in contact with a turkey and are just prospecting and trying to raise one, you have plenty of time to consider the pros and cons of various setups and choose the one you think is best before making a call.

If you've been working a turkey and decide to move to a new location, though, the tendency is to rush things when you get to your new setup. Resist that tendency. Take a few extra seconds and make a wise choice. It's a good investment of your

Swing your gun barrel to make sure you have clearance. A sapling like this can cost you your gobbler.

time, because you're liable to have to live with it for the next hour or so.

Even when a gobbler surprises you at close range – the way the bird did me that morning – you probably have more time than you think to make a decision about where to sit. The reason the turkey gobbled at you was because he thinks you're either a hen or another gobbler. Either way, he's not likely to move toward you before you answer him with a call of your own. Not very rapidly, anyway. So take a deep breath and give a little thought to it before you sit. Obviously, you don't have all day to stand there and mull over the choice between this tree and that one, but you don't have to just plop down in a blackjack thicket, either.

There are several factors involved in choosing an effective setup. Two of the most important are the range between your current position and the turkey you want to call to, and what's between you and the bird. If you're not familiar with the lay of the land, you'll probably have to make an educated guess. But in almost every case, you want to get as close as possible to the turkey before sitting down. Not only does this help minimize the chance there will be an obstacle between you and the bird, but it also reduces the amount of ground

the turkey has to cover before he's within gun range. Both of those are good things.

Visibility is another key factor to consider when deciding where to sit. Remember, there can be too much visibility as well as too little of it. I needed a little more visibility that day I was in the blackjack thicket, but I remember other times when I had way more than I needed.

One such time was the morning in Kansas when I got on a gobbler on a wooded ridge in the Chautauqua Hills. The woods had burned the previous winter, and spring green-up hadn't yet caught up. It was as black and bare as an empty coal bin.

I went to the gobbler from a considerable distance and took my time finding a nice tree to sit against. When I called, the turkey gobbled from 250 yards away. He closed the gap to 100 yards, and by then I could see him down through the blackened forest. At that point, he hung up and refused to come one step closer.

For the next two hours, he strutted back and forth on a level spot the size of a tennis court, gobbling every so often and showing off his mating duds. But the woods were so open, the turkey figured he ought to be able to see any hen calling to him, and he wasn't about to budge until he saw one.

I chose that spot precisely because it gave me excellent visibility, and it was precisely that excellent visibility which kept the gobbler from coming in. Live and learn. There are times when I still have to make my set in wide-open places, but nowadays I use a decoy or two in these cases so there'll be something to draw the turkey closer.

The ideal setup, in my mind, is a place where the gobbler will be out of sight until he's within shotgun range. If a turkey is on the other side of a ridge, I like to position myself just under the crest. That way, when he tops the ridge and comes into sight, he'll be 30 yards away and in big, big trouble.

Another factor to keep in mind when choosing a setup is your effective field of fire. If a setup only gives you a gap of 15 degrees in which to find your target and make the shot, it's not a very good place to be. Usually, the reason some setup spots afford a restricted field of fire is because many hunters tend to hide too well when they sit down to a turkey. I've seen hunters who blinded up so well in a brushpile that when the gobbler came in, they couldn't see it well enough to shoot it.

Instead, sit in the bare open, with your back against a tree or other obstruction that will break your outline. If you feel you must, stick a few twigs or leafy saplings in the ground in front of you, but don't overdo it. You need good visibility.

Along those same lines, it's important to remove any and all barrel obstructions when you first set up. If there are any twigs or saplings close in front of me, I make a test swing of my gun to see if the barrel will clear the obstructions. If it won't, I clip off the offending twigs and saplings with the pair of heavy-duty garden clippers that are always in my turkey vest.

Consider shade availability and sun direction when choosing a setup. It's always preferable to sit in the shade if at all possible, because of the obvious: It's easier for a turkey to pick you out if you're in the sun. If it's early or late in the day and the sun is slanting in low, put yourself between the turkey and the sun if you can. You want the sun in his eyes, not yours, so you can see better and he can't. He'll still be able to see better than you, but this will even it up some.

And by all means, choose a comfortable setup. You may well be there for the next several hours, unable to move, and if you're not as comfortable as possible from the start, you're going to be in for a rough time. There is no faster-growing thing on the face of the earth than a marble-sized pebble under the cheek of your butt. It feels insignificant when you first sit on it, but it'll grow to the size of a cantaloupe in 30 minutes. Get rid of all such pebbles before you start calling, and do everything else you can think of to make your potential stay in that spot as bearable as you can. Smooth any burrs off the trunk of the tree as best you can, so they won't dig into your back. Make a comfortable, level spot for your feet. Use a seat cushion. Lay your water bottle, calls and anything else you think you'll need close to hand, so you can reach them with a minimum of movement.

No matter how much thought you put into choosing an effective setup, though, there are going to be times when it all goes awry anyway. The gobbler will circle around and come in right behind you, or something else will happen that blows it for you.

But if you'll take a few seconds to think it through every single time you sit down to a turkey, it'll pay off in the long run. And you won't have to start as many of your late-morning recap stories with "Well, the first thing was, I sat down wrong."

This hunter's setup is nearly ideal – decoys in the sun, hunter in the shade, with a wide tree for a rest, and a log to further break up his outline and help him get away with movement. Of course, the gobbler could always circle around and come in behind that log.

Get comfortable when you set up. You may be there for a long time.

Chapter 17

The Old Versus the New

Decoys are a relatively new concept in turkey hunting, and in certain situations they help immensely. This gobbler is hypnotized, and the hunter can get away with a lot more movement than if there was no decoy present to occupy the bird's attention.

He was ancient and feeble, sitting in the warm spring sunshine on the rickety porch of the country store. The wicker rocker that cradled his spindly old body looked as old as he was. There was a rattan cane parked beside his knee, its crook worn to a honey-blonde sheen from long years of use. He was the prototype geezer, the one you still occasionally see on small-town Southern courthouse squares during warm weather, spitting and whittling.

Geezer or not, though, his eyes lit up like a teen-ager's when we parked and started up the steps. It was 1981, maybe '82, early April, and we were dressed head-to-toe in dirty, barbed-wire-torn camouflage. You didn't need to be a Harvard professor of logic to figure out we were turkey hunters.

"Ye'uns doin' any good?" the old man asked, peering at us from under the brim of a greasy John Deere cap.

"Some," we answered in typical close-mouthed turkey-hunter fashion. "Not much."

With no prompting at all, the old man launched into a hoarse, crackly monologue about his own now-extinct turkey hunting career, which he said had started about the turn of the century when he was still a shirttail boy. "Kilt my first one in ought-one," he said. I hadn't been listening very close, just being polite, you know, and waiting for the old man to wind down so we could get our pop and pork and beans, and get back to the woods. But when he said "ought-one," I sat down on the edge of the porch and started listening closer.

Turkeys were already scarce or wiped out by the turn of the last century in the more settled parts of the South, but in the rugged and sparsely populat-

114

ed Ouachitas where we were hunting that day, they were still present in decent numbers. Times were hard, made harder by the effort of scratching a subsistence living out of the rocky, droughty, infertile soil, and the wild turkey was viewed as a handy food source. Hunted year-round, the birds eventually bowed to the unrelenting pressure and dwindled in the Ouachitas as well.

But for a couple of decades during the old man's youth, he said, turkeys were still "thick as seed ticks on a black-an'-tan's ear," and although he hunted them year-round for food, he also hunted them in the spring for fun. "I expect I've killed a couple hunnerd gobblers in dogwood time," he said offhandedly. "Still got the beards. They's three cigar boxes plumb full."

No turkey hunter can resist talking turkey, and it didn't take me long to start picking the old man's brains. He'd lived across the hiatus, from the time of plenty of turkeys through the time of almost no turkeys and back to a time of plenty. He'd hunted them all through the lean years, he said, when just hearing a turkey gobble constituted a good season, and he'd stayed after them well into the 1970s, when failing health and eyesight finally forced him to quit. But still he loved it, and still his passion showed.

Our conversation bounced around, as conversations of this type do, and eventually we drifted into a discussion of the evolution in hunting technique and equipment the old man had witnessed in nearly eight decades of turkey hunting – smokeless powder, hardened and buffered and collared shot, magnum shells, screw-in choke tubes, space-age materials in turkey calls, camouflage clothing.

"Don't you wish you had stuff like this to wear back then?" I asked, fingering the camo material of my shirt. Jim Crumley's original Trebark pattern, I think it was; this was the early '80s, remember, and the designer camo boom was still in its birthing stages. "Camouflage clothes would have made it a lot easier to kill a bird, wouldn't it?"

The old man looked at me like I was the village idiot and had just taken a leak on his leg. "Hell, boy," he said, clamping both arms to his sides to demonstrate motionlessness, "if ye can sit still, ye don't need a shirt that looks like a tree. We nearly wiped 'em off the face of the earth wearin' blue bib overhauls."

Who knows how many camouflage patterns are on the market today? Certainly dozens, probably more than a hundred. But our forefathers didn't need such clothing; they knew the value of sitting still.

Hunters call more these days than our grandfathers did. We have a luxury they didn't: a reasonable chance of finding another gobbler to play with if we screw up the one we're working with.

Another reason we call more than our grandfathers did is because if we don't, we're more than likely going to get outcalled by a real hen. There are more of them out there too, you know.

Back From the Brink

But the old man and his "overhaul"-wearing contemporaries didn't quite manage to wipe turkeys out altogether. In meager, stubborn little flocks they survived – in the Florida parishes of southeastern Louisiana; in the wildest and most remote sections of the lower Mississippi River bottoms; in the vastness of the big hardwood swamps of southern Alabama and Georgia; on the large delta plantations of the South Carolina Low Country. A pitiful few birds even managed to hang on right there in the very area we were hunting the day I talked to the old man in the John Deere cap – in the rugged, remote valleys of the central Ouachita Mountains.

These few surviving pockets of birds managed to persist because of two things: They lived in the most inaccessible places, and they were the most wary individuals of their species. The more accessible and less-wary birds fell to the relentless guns of the old man and his contemporaries, leaving behind the most reclusive of their cousins in the remotest hills and hollows and the most impenetrable river swamps. And it came to pass, eventually, that these few – these paranoid, spooky, hard-to-reach few – furnished the seed stock for the

great comeback of the wild turkey. There may be other factors, but that one is the biggest reason the bird we hunt today is a much different creature than the one adolescent boys routinely shot for the supper table before the Civil War.

Because we hunt a different bird today, we have by necessity developed a different set of hunting techniques. Or, more accurately, we have modified and built upon the old ones in use 150 years ago. During the dark days of the 1930s, 1940s and 1950s, it was a remarkable event just to hear a turkey gobble.

If you were a turkey hunter in those decades, you were truly a member of the minority. You conducted your operations more from a sense of tradition and unreasoning faith than from any reasonable expectation of actually killing a turkey, and it was not at all unusual for the brief spring season to come and go without your ever hearing or seeing a bird. If you did get lucky enough to hear a gobbler, you'd stick with him and do everything in your power to not make a mistake. It might well be your only chance of the season.

Old Calling vs. New

These desperate circumstances created the climate that gave rise to the old style of calling,

Trying to find gobbling turkeys from roads — staying close to the vehicle until a bird is located – is a popular and still-effective technique for covering a lot of ground in a short time, but many gobblers refuse to respond to this tactic because it's used so often.

which basically was to sit down to the turkey at the paranoid distance of 300 to 400 yards, yelp softly about three or four times, then wait for 30 minutes or more before making three or four more soft yelps. If the gobbler ever answered your call, the conventional thing to do was absolutely nothing. That was the time to get your gun up, not call any more, not move another muscle and wait, watching the woods for movement ... until sundown or until the gobbler showed up, whichever came first. The conventional wisdom was that if the gobbler ever answered you, he'd eventually come looking for you.

Things being as they were, it wasn't a bad game plan. There were very few gobblers, but that also meant there were very few hens. It was unlikely a real hen would come along to bollix your hunt. It was also unlikely another hunter would interfere, since, as we've already mentioned, the scarcity of turkeys caused all but the dedicated, stubborn few to despair and quit. If you did hear a turkey in those days, you could be almost certain you were the only hunter hearing it.

That's no longer the case. Turkey populations are at saturation levels in much of today's turkey range, and that means there are lots of turkey hens

out there willing and able to steal your gobbler. The great turkey comeback has also resulted in a resurgence of interest in this grand spring sport, and there are more turkey hunters today than at any point in history. Unless you're deep within a wilderness area or on a secure plot of private land, it's best to operate on the assumption you're not the only hunter listening to your gobbler. More often than not, you'll be correct.

So calling techniques changed to meet these new conditions. Today's hunter is a more aggressive caller than his great-grandpa was. I'm pretty sure I call more in one day than the old man in the John Deere cap did in two seasons – and I consider myself a pretty conservative caller. I don't call nearly as much as some of the top-flight hunters with whom I've shared spring mornings.

We call more aggressively these days for four basic reasons. First, there are more turkeys around. If we don't call more aggressively, we're going to get outcompeted by real hens, which will either go to our gobbler or will call the gobbler to them while we're being coy and playing hard-to-get, fooling around with that yelp-three-times-and-wait-till-moss-grows-on-the-call business. Second, there are also many more turkey hunters around

117

Today, we have a staggering number of choices in turkey loads and turkey guns.

these days, and if we dawdle around and play it too cute with a gobbler, they'll outcompete us as well.

The third reason we call more aggressively these days is because we can afford to. If we get too loud or too eager and run this bird off, we have an excellent chance of raising another gobbler to play with. If not today, then tomorrow … and hot gobblers are a lot more fun than cold ones.

The fourth reason got mentioned at the tail of that last sentence. Aggressive calling is sexy and cool and effective and exciting. It often produces spectacular, thrilling results, with a turkey gobbling a hundred or more times as he comes to the call and putting on a show like nobody's business. It's the stuff of which turkey videos and adrenaline rushes are made.

But the fact is, our collective habit of calling like maniacs is creating a breed of savvy turkeys that stand out there and gobble their heads off, but refuse to come to the call. Their frequent gobbling reinforces our efforts and encourages us to redouble the intensity of our calling, and the turkey gobbles more, and we call more, and … well, you see where this is going.

The pendulum, though, seems to be swinging back the other way. Aggressive calling still works, but more and more often it doesn't. And instead of shifting to a more conservative calling style and

trying some soft, seductive stuff, most hunters simply go look for another gobbler.

The New Style of Hunting

Which brings us to another considerable change in this grand spring sport – the actual techniques of the hunt. We not only call more aggressively, we also search more aggressively for turkeys.

The old man in the John Deere cap lived in the turkey woods year-round, as did most of the turkey hunters of that era. Consequently, he had an intimate knowledge of the home ranges of most of the turkeys in his neighborhood. He didn't need to cover a lot of ground in an attempt to find one. His hunting technique was as simple and laid-back as his calling: He slipped slowly through the woods within the known home range of a gobbler, calling sparingly and not covering much ground. Or, just as likely, he slipped into the woods in the dark and made a blind in a favored travel or feeding area and spent the day there.

Some people still hunt this way, especially in situations where they're restricted by the boundaries of a small hunting lease or the presence of other hunters. But by and large, the 21st century turkey hunter is a traveler, both in the woods and on the road. We hunt in numerous places instead of just in the township where we were born. We travel from

Modern turkey guns shoot like rifles, delivering dense swarms of shot at impressive ranges.

state to state, even from country to country, hunting today's abundant turkeys.

Because we travel so much, we often find ourselves hunting unfamiliar territory. We don't know what's over the next ridge because we've never been within 100 miles of it. Likewise, we don't know the ranges or habits of any of the area's gobblers.

So we compensate by covering a lot of ground in an attempt to find a cooperative gobbler. Some of us do this on foot, walking ridges, creek bottoms and logging roads, and calling frequently to stimulate a response. Some do it by vehicle, driving back roads or boating along a lake or river, stopping often to call and listen for turkeys. Many of us also use topographical maps to locate promising-looking places to look for turkeys, substituting armchair scouting for on-the-ground reconnaissance.

Space-Age Technology

Hunting techniques and turkey numbers aren't the only things that have changed, of course. The old man in the John Deere cap hunted turkeys for three times as many years as I have so far, but in my relatively short span as a turkey hunter I've seen much more evolution in equipment and techniques than the old man saw in his entire career.

Take shotgun shells, for instance. In a few short years, we've gone from soft-lead, standard loads to high-velocity loads, hardened and coated shot, protective shot collars, cushioned wads, powdered polymer buffers, increased payload, and other improvements I'm either forgetting or don't have the smarts to understand. We even have shot that's heavier than lead. At the same time, shotgun manufacturers and ballistics experts have combined their talents to produce a whole new arsenal of turkey guns with special sighting devices, super-tight chokes, ported barrels – even telescopic sights.

The result of these improvements is a whole selection of shotguns that shoot like rifles, delivering dense swarms of shot at impressive ranges. Today, I own six tweaked and fine-tuned turkey guns that consistently punch 90 percent patterns at 40 yards – two Remingtons, two Mossbergs, two Berettas. And I've got my eye on a Benelli.

Turkey calls have also vastly changed from the homemade slate, wingbone or box call the old man in the John Deere cap used. I couldn't begin to guess how many call choices today's turkey hunter has, but I bet you couldn't put one of each in a boxcar and get the doors closed. There still are boxes and wingbones and slate calls, of course, but today's added starters include pump calls, push-button calls, pull-string calls, diaphragms of various kinds and configurations,

Slates, diaphragms, push-buttons, boxes – the choice of calls is staggering these days.

tube calls and a whole host of combinations and variations that don't fall into any of those categories. Some of them work. Others are gimmicks.

And within those categories, there are thousands of variations. Slate calls aren't just made of slate anymore; in fact, it's becoming unusual to find one that is. Crystal, acrylic, porcelain, aluminum, copper, hard rubber, brass, on and on and on. You name it, and somebody uses it to make a "slate" call. And let's not even get started talking about the many types of diaphragm calls or the more than 100 camouflage patterns available today.

Some Things are Still the Same

Yep, no doubt about it: Where turkeys and turkey hunting are concerned, things changed a lot during the century we just left behind. But most of those changes have been for the better – particularly in the last half of that century.

Our equipment is vastly improved and more varied, and information for beginners, intermediates and experts alike is everywhere, in the form of books, videos, magazine articles, guided hunts and seminars. Turkeys have rebounded, from a low of as few as 30,000 birds in the 1920s to something

like 5.6 million today, and the number is still growing. We can hunt turkeys now in 49 states, plus Mexico, Canada and New Zealand, and maybe some other countries I haven't heard about.

The old man in the John Deere cap is in his grave now. But if he could come back and hunt in this day and time, he'd no doubt be amazed at the changes he'd find.

But two things remain unchanged, from the day the old man killed his first one in 1901 to the next one you or I kill next spring. One of those things is the fact that hearing the gobble of a wild turkey is still one of the most thrilling experiences in the universe. The other is what the old man said, and I can't say it any better so I'll just quote it again: "If ye can sit still, ye don't need a shirt that looks like a tree."

Even so, I still don't think I'm quite ready to go out there wearing blue bib overhauls.

Chapter 18

Taking the Game to the Gobbler

It's hard to compete with the real thing, but there are ways to do it.

The first time he gobbled, he surprised me with it. He was roosted near the bottom of the south slope of a feeder ridge coming off Blowout Mountain. I'd walked past him in the dark, climbing the ridge to listen into the remote country beyond it. But the turkey was below and behind me, barely 200 yards from where I'd parked the truck. I'm certain my headlights hit him when I'd pulled in.

He didn't gobble much, but it was enough. I was fairly close to him when he started, and it was still early enough that I had time to lose altitude and set up before fly-down time.

He was roosted in the edge of a shortleaf pine stand that had received a well-executed prescribed burn two months earlier. The forest floor was as bare and black as the bottom of a Dutch oven. Because of the darkness, though, I was able to get in fairly tight on him, in what I thought was a decent position – 90 yards from the roost tree, with a low ridge between us with a skidder road and an old log yard. The ridge was a perfect fly-down and strutting area, and I was within shotgun

Hunting with a partner is more difficult in some ways, but it also opens options that aren't available to the solitary hunter. One hunter can stay put while the other fades back and calls, or both hunters can get into a turkey "conversation" that sounds much more realistic than a single hunter trying to do it.

range of most of it. All I had to do was let the turkey know I was there, then wait him out while trying not to let my smugness completely overcome me.

It was a good plan. Don't ask me why it didn't work. When I judged the light intensity to be about right, I waited until he gobbled again, then sent out the softest run of tree yelps any turkey ever uttered.

He answered so fast and hard, it was startling. While I was trying to decide whether to answer him or not, he gobbled again, then again, then again and again and again. Whatever I'd said, it tripped his trigger, and now he didn't seem to be able to shut up.

Smiling through my face paint, I rested the shotgun on my knees and settled in to wait. According to the book, this was the part where I dummied up until the gobbler was on the ground, so as not to cause him to hang up in the tree.

Trouble was, the book hadn't mentioned the possibility of a real hen butting in. I heard this one yelping behind me a minute or two before I saw her. The talkative gobbler heard her, too, and he redoubled the intensity and frequency of his gobbling. The hen marched past me, clucking and yelping, heading for the gobbler. Pretty soon I heard him fly down, and then things got quiet. I belatedly started calling, but it was too little, too late. He gobbled eight more times in the next 30 minutes, each time farther away, and then he was gone. I was left there by myself in the burned-over woods, soot on my butt and egg on my face.

Infrequent, low-key calling was probably the right tactic to use in that situation, until the hen showed. It seemed to be working, anyway, and it's worked for me on similar hunts before and since. But when the hen arrived, the rules changed. I lost the gobbler because I failed to change my game plan.

Off the top of my head, I can think of at least three different strategies I could have brought into play to counter the hen's influence.

First, I could have simply scared her away by moving enough to let her pick me out as she came by me. Given that particular setup, it would have worked. I had a ridge on the gobbler, and my movements and those of the hen would have been hidden. All I had to do was wave an arm at her or wiggle a little bit as she walked by at 15 yards. She'd no doubt have set up a racket as she left, but I've reassured gobblers more than once in similar situations when hens started putting by mimicking the hen as she left, then slowly calming my calling down and finishing off with a series of contented yelps. I could have probably pulled it off that time, too.

Second, instead of chasing the hen away, I could have let her to go the gobbler and started calling sooner, in an attempt to call both birds back to me. That's a much-lower percentage play, but it works just often enough to keep it in mind when things start to go sour. If you try this, mimic the hen's calling if she's doing any, and try your best to match her note for note. If she's not calling, one option is to get aggressive, trying either to challenge her into coming over to show you who's boss or to pull the gobbler away from her. However, I've had mixed results with this technique, and often what happens is the hen or hens will lead the gobbler away from the aggressive calling. Sometimes soft calling, with some kee-kees thrown in, works in this instance. The thing is, you just never know.

The third strategy that might have worked would have been to wait until I learned which direction the hen and gobbler were headed, then try to get ahead of them and set up in a calling/ambush position along their likely travel-way. That would have been relatively easy in this case, since the turkeys moved along just under the ridgeline all the way out of hearing. The gobbler was talkative enough for me to easily keep track of him, and I expect he'd have gobbled even more if I'd moved between calls instead of sitting there like a stump and letting him walk away from me.

Of course, there's no guarantee I'd have tagged that gobbler, no matter what. But at least if I'd attempted one of those other tactics, I'd have still been in there swinging and I still would have had a chance. Like the big boys say in high-stakes poker, "You can't win it if you're not in it." After the hen showed up that morning, I was no longer in it.

Another time in another spring, I was hunting the ridges and hollows of southwest Mississippi. My partner and I hunted the first half of the morning without hearing a single gobble. We were still going through the motions, but mentally we'd already given up, which is bad business for a turkey hunter. We were sitting against opposite sides of the same huge loblolly pine at a pre-

"Firing one up" is exciting, but it's getting harder and harder to do with the increasing hunting pressure.

arranged spot in the woods, waiting for the third member of our hunting party, an hour earlier than our stated meeting time. My buddy was asleep (I know he was because I could hear the gentle bubble of his snores), and I almost was. I was calling desultorily, more from boredom than from hope, when I saw on an adjacent ridge what I first thought was a black-and-white hound.

But the hound turned out to be a strutting gobbler, alone, moving rapidly and angling closer as he followed the narrow spine of the ridge. The hollow between us was too wide for him to be in gun range when he went by, but I could still see him through the early-spring woods when he stopped on a flat 125 yards away. He was soon joined by two other strutters and a whole mess of hens, and they stayed there for the next 30 minutes.

Leaving my partner asleep on his side of the tree, I ooched forward along the ground until I gained the cover of the hogback, then scooted across the hollow and eased up to the ridgeline,

Switching calls from the same setup spot is one easy way to pick up the tempo when a gobbler doesn't want to come. Sometimes just changing calls is all it takes.

using a tree for cover as I peeked over the top. The turkeys were still strutting, chasing each other around and generally having a good time, about 75 yards away. I belly-crawled around to the front of the tree and set up, then started calling softly.

They ignored me until I started really leaning into it, at which time the hens started yelping and cutting back at me. The gobblers, meanwhile, strutted silently around on the little flat. Ten minutes later, though, it appeared the whole flock was gradually edging closer. I kept calling, and in another five minutes the narrowing of the gap was obvious. Somewhere along the way, two of the gobblers peeled off and disappeared. When the hens arrived, they had only one tom in tow. He trailed them by 15 yards and never broke out of strut, even when I putted at him to get him to raise his head. Finally one of the hens picked me out, and I shot the gobbler in strut. He never knew what hit him.

Not one of those three gobblers ever uttered a sound that I could hear. The one I shot wasn't even drumming as he followed the hens. I'm convinced none of those turkeys would have come to the call if the hens hadn't led them there.

The only real difference between the two hunts I've just described is that I kept myself in the game in the second one. More and more in today's turkey woods, the prize goes to the hunter who refuses to take no for an answer. These successful hunters have learned that in most cases, indecisiveness on a turkey hunt is an excellent way to save your tag for another day. When Plan A isn't working or when something happens to alter the situation – the unexpected arrival of a hen, say – they switch immediately and without hesitation to Plan B. And the successful turkey hunter always has a Plan B, even if he has to make it up on the spot.

I'm not really talking here about the aggressive, run-and-gun hunting style that's been popularized in the last 15 years or so on TV shows and videos by the professional turkey hunters and call makers. These high-profile hunters have developed this hunting style partly because it's often effective (particularly on early-season or lightly pressured 2-year-old gobblers), but mostly because their livelihood depends in large part not only on how many turkeys they kill, but also on how flashily they kill them. A hunt needs to be full of loud calling and hot gobbling for the camera, or else it'll put the viewers to sleep as soundly as my hunting buddy was when I dropped the hammer on that Mississippi longbeard.

Run-and-gun hunting is, of course, one of the ways to take the game to the gobbler. Furthermore, it's a heck of a lot of fun when you find the right bird. But it's certainly not a cure-all and shouldn't be viewed as such.

More than 20 springs ago, when I was still new to turkey hunting and easy to impress, I shared a three-day Oklahoma turkey hunt with one of the famous hunters/call makers of the 1970s and 1980s. I went to the hunt all goggle-eyed and in awe of the Famous Turkey Hunter, but I left with a healthy dose of disillusionment. During that three days, the FTH showed me he wasn't such a hot-shot after all. All he knew how to do was (to use his term) "fire one up."

Oh, he was a whiz with a mouth call, no question about it. I've hunted with a bunch of state, world and Grand National champions since, and none of them was appreciably better than this old boy. He had a repertoire of cutts and cackles and hot hen yelps that could have pulled a gobble out of a buzzard, but if he got out there and was unable to find one of those super-hot toms that like that kind of stuff – one of those easy birds, in other words, that come along once or twice in a season and make us all feel like world-class turkey hunters – he was out of business. He didn't have a clue. His success depended on volume and on the law of averages; he was able to hunt 40 to 50 days every spring, and he stuck to the roads and zoomed from one calling spot to the next. Giving up easily wasn't one of his weaknesses, and he'd do this from first light to noon every day, day after day. In a typical morning, he might make 100 stops and cover nearly that many miles.

Sure, he killed turkeys. When you have 50 days to do it in, you can kill turkeys no matter what tactics you use. But not many of us have the time to hunt 50 days a year, and not many of us would do so if we did have time, so we can't depend solely on the low-percentage, high-volume tactics the Famous Turkey Hunter used. We need to make a better showing on the more limited number of turkeys we come in contact with, and we must do that by playing the hand we're dealt, each and every time. We can't afford to give up on a bird because he's not out there jumping up and down.

If you're hunting in unfamiliar territory, it's easy to set up with a barricade between you and the gobbler you're working. Knowing the terrain can help in this regard.

Moving to a different setup spot, even if you don't move any closer to the turkey, can sometimes induce a gobbler to come in.

The hallmark of a truly good turkey hunter is flexibility. We all like to find those hot gobblers, but we all know they're scarce – especially after the first few days of the season, when that year's crop of extremely cooperative birds have either been educated or executed.

However, even if a turkey doesn't want to get "fired up," that doesn't mean you can't hunt aggressively. There's a lot more to this business of taking the game to the gobbler than just calling hot and often.

The simplest, easiest way to hunt aggressively is simply to switch calls on a gobbler that doesn't respond to your first offerings. Every experienced hunter has known tons of gobblers that wouldn't budge for a diaphragm call, but worked into range after hearing a slate, box or tube, or any combination of those calls. Changing from soft yelps and clucks to hard, aggressive calling will sometimes break a gobbler loose and bring him in, but so, occasionally, will toning down from aggressive calling to soft, contented stuff. You just never know what's going to churn a gob-

bler's butter, so it makes sense to try the easiest option first.

If switching calls and/or tempo doesn't work, though, changing calling positions is in order, and that's when things start to get a little risky. When you move, you always run the risk of being spotted by your gobbler, or bumping other turkeys you don't know are in the neighborhood, or running a pesky deer over the top of your gobbler, or whatever.

Despite the risk, moving on a reluctant gobbler is a good tactic. Elsewhere in this book, considerable attention is devoted to the importance and value of learning as much about your hunting territory as possible, to minimize the possibility of setting up where there's an obstacle between you and the bird you're trying to work. The trouble is, you never know what constitutes an "obstacle" in the mind of that pea-brained bird standing out there gobbling at you.

We're all aware that a river or the arm of a lake or a hog-wire fence are bona fide obstacles, but over the years I've had gobblers hang up at things that couldn't possibly have hindered them.

Gobblers have hung up on me because they couldn't see into the thicket I was hiding in, and they've hung up on me because they were in a thicket themselves and didn't want to come out into the open woods. I've had them hang up on the other side of power line rights-of-way and seldom-used, blocked-off woods roads literally trampled with fresh turkey tracks. I've had them hang up because they were in fields and didn't want to enter the surrounding woods, and I've had them hang up because they were in the woods and didn't want to come into a field. I've had them hang up, as near as I could tell, because they didn't want to approach eastward into a rising sun, or westward into a setting one.

True story: I once had two gobblers refuse to come to the gun because there was a limb the size of my forearm lying flat on the ground on the old logging trace the birds were using as an approach route, and they stubbornly refused to step over it. They came from more than a quarter-mile away, not super-fast but fast enough, until they hit that stick of stovewood, and it stopped them as surely as if it had been putting out a force field. I watched them approach along the trail, gobbling and strutting, and then they stopped at the limb and craned their necks out over it as they gobbled at my calling. They obviously wanted me, but three times they refused to cross that dinky little stick. I finally killed one of them by letting them fade out of sight after the third refusal, then scooting forward and removing the stick from the trail. When I called them back the fourth time, they strutted right into my lap, and I shot the biggest one at something like 15 yards. Go figure.

Sometimes there's no obstacle involved, not even a stick of stovewood, but a turkey will still refuse to come to your stationary calling. For a hen to call in a gobbler is an unnatural act in the scheme of nature. The reason gobblers gobble is to let hens know where they are, but it also alerts predators to their whereabouts, and that's never a good thing. Everything likes to eat turkeys. If the survival advantages of gobbling (i.e., providing for a more efficient mating system) didn't outweigh the disadvantages of letting every coyote, bobcat and fox in the neighborhood know where they are, Darwinian forces would take over. In a dozen generations, turkey gobblers would become as silent as the Sphinx.

One of the most frustrating types of turkeys is the one that answers your calls but steadily moves away. If you can keep up with the bird until he gets to where he's going, it's occasionally possible to work him after he stops. The trouble is, it's hard to maintain contact without getting busted.

127

So, already, we're fighting against a turkey's nature when we try to call him in at all. When we compound that by doing all of our calling from one place, like a hen turkey with her foot caught in a knothole, the wonder isn't that turkeys sometimes hang up for no apparent reason; the wonder is that we ever call one in at all.

Changing calling positions takes a little bit of that unnaturalness away. It still might not bring him to the gun, but often it helps.

One thing to keep in mind is that it's vital to know the turkey's exact whereabouts before making a move. If the bird has gone silent, stay put for a while. He may be sneaking in, or he may be standing out there at the limit of your vision peering down through the woods trying to catch a glimpse of that elusive hen. Change calling positions at this point and you're toast. The safest time to move is immediately after he's gobbled, so you can be sure of his position.

Another thing: If the turkey is still gobbling at you, he's not suspicious. A suspicious turkey doesn't continue to gobble, no matter how far away he is. He shuts up and leaves. The lesson here is to never give up on a bird as long as he responds to your calling, or as long as he's gobbling on his own. He doesn't smell a rat; he's just reluctant to come for one reason or another, and changing positions is a good way to remove whatever reason it is.

Moving straight toward a bird is rarely a good idea. It's a fine way to get spotted, for one thing. For another, it seems to give a gobbler the idea that his hen is finally coming to him, and it reinforces his decision to stand pat and let nature take its course. It's been my experience that a gobbler will rarely meet you halfway if you go straight at him. Instead, cut the angle on him, and move to a position that's different, but not necessarily closer.

Occasionally, taking the game to the gobbler involves more than just getting to the right calling location. Sometimes, it involves chase. We've all come across those itchy-footed gobblers that talk a lot, but move steadily away. These traveling salesmen can be frustrating, but sometimes it's possible to get around in front of one and set up along his line of travel, and either call to him from a direction he obviously wants to go in or simply sit there and bushwhack him when he comes by.

Occasionally, the best way to take the game to the gobbler is by making him think you're taking it away from him. If you've tried the things discussed so far in this chapter and nothing has worked, maybe it's time to try losing interest in him. Call at the gobbler one final time from your position, and whether he answers or not, get up and move quickly back 50 to 100 feet or so and call to him again. If he answers, all the better, but regardless, move another similar distance after calling and then call again.

Two or three calls given during a retreat like this will sometimes break a hung-up gobbler loose, and sometimes he'll come so fast you have to hurry to get ready. I actually had one such gobbler fly to me when I tried this, and he made a clean getaway because I was still in the process of sitting down when he came gliding in like some pot-bellied cropduster. He picked me out while he was still airborne, veered away, and sailed off the ridge and out of my life forever.

I suppose the point of this chapter is the basic premise of this whole book: When you make contact with a gobbler, you never know what's going to happen next or how the turkey will react to your strategies. That's why it's usually a good idea to start off with conservative tactics and forget all that aggressive stuff at first. The turkey you're dueling with may not need you to take the game to him, and conservative tactics are often just the ticket. And even if it's not, starting off conservatively usually won't hurt your chances if you decide to try something else. Start off too aggressively with an already spooky gobbler, and you may botch the opportunity.

Give the conservative approach a chance to work; it's been a proven hunting technique for more than a century. But don't hesitate to shift gears if it doesn't seem to be working. After all, you're playing on the gobbler's home court, and he has the advantage in that respect. If he doesn't want to play your game, you have to try to play his.

The Catch-22, of course, is the turkey won't tell you what his game is; you have to figure it out on your own. That's the most appealing and also the most aggravating thing about this whole business. You have to figure out a new game every time you make contact with a turkey.

It's not easy. But then, if it were, there'd be a whole lot more people out there doing it.

Even with the aid of maps, a hunter doesn't know the territory as well as the turkeys do. Right away, we're operating at a disadvantage.

Chapter 19

When to Shout, When to Whisper

The ones that get away are every bit as memorable as the ones we tag.

It's a simple truth, and every turkey hunter knows it: The ones that get away are as unforgettable as the ones whose beards and spurs hang in the den. Maybe even more so. So it is with the bird of Black Mountain …

The first morning of the hunt, he started gobbling while it was still pitch-dark. He wasn't far away, just 300 to 400 yards across the valley. But what a valley it was. Getting to him meant losing a thousand feet of altitude over ankle-turning, head-sized rocks down to the valley floor, crossing an icy, slick-bottomed, waist-deep creek, then climbing over more head-sized rocks that same thousand feet back up to his level. It was bad enough crossing the valley in full daylight, but in the dark, it would be awful. So I resisted the impulse, stayed on my side of the valley and listened to him gobble nonstop over there until 11 a.m., while I vainly searched for a turkey on my side.

The next morning he started gobbling again in the dark, and this time I went to him. But by the time I slipped and stumbled across the horrible terrain of the valley and clawed my way up the imposing face of Black Mountain, he had either shut up or moved out of hearing range, and I failed to raise him.

The third morning he was still gobbling over there, and he pulled me across once more. After another brutal, futile trip across the valley, I decided that in the future, he'd have to come to me.

I knew trying to call him across that canyon held about the same chance of success as calling him off the dark side of the moon, but I figured at least I'd run less risk of breaking my neck than if I kept letting him lure me across that horrible hole every morning. My current tactics weren't working so hot, anyway.

130

So on the fourth day, when the gobbler once again opened for business from the same narrow bench on Black Mountain, I was standing straight across from him, prepared to engage him in long-range conversation. I started calling when he made the first gobble, and for the next 45 minutes I never shut up for more than five to 10 seconds. Diaphragm, slate, box, tube – every call in my vest got a good workout. I more than likely called more in that three-quarters of an hour than I did the rest of the turkey season put together.

During my calling marathon, the Black Mountain gobbler nearly gave himself a stroke. He gobbled almost as much as I called, and once, when I paused to rest my hand and switch from a box to a slate, he sounded off five times in a 10-second period.

At the end of the 45 minutes, I still didn't seem to be any closer to getting that gobbler than I had been all week, but at least the interlude had been enjoyable. I stopped calling to rest, think things over and decide what I wanted to do. While I rested, the turkey kept gobbling.

He almost pulled me down into the hole again, too, but finally I decided to quit fooling with him. So I started walking along my rim of the valley, determined to leave the gobbler for that day and forever.

But I couldn't resist taunting him one last time. After walking 150 yards, I stopped and gave out with a series of three or four excited cutts, smiled as the gobbler eagerly responded, then holstered the box call and kept walking away from the Black Mountain gobbler, calling occasionally as I went in an attempt to get something going on my own mountain.

It was then that I realized the turkey was paralleling my line of travel along the other side of the valley, matching me step for step. I stopped and called to him again, then picked up the pace.

Soon I was trotting along the edge on my side, and the gobbler across the way was staying right with me. I came to a narrow hollow that branched off the main valley and barred my path. When I turned to go around it, I moved away from the gobbler, still calling as I went just to torment him some more. Skirting the head of the hollow, I headed back toward the main valley … and ran head-on into the Black Mountain gobbler. He'd evidently panicked when he heard me leaving him and had flown across the quarter-mile-wide valley

Hunting in mountainous territory gives a hunter the chance to "shout" to a lot of distant turkeys … but they may be on the other side of a canyon.

Turkeys, unlike turkey hunters, don't have to respect posted signs.

in pursuit. He was running toward me along the lip of the side hollow when we almost collided.

You know the rest of the story. He went ballistic and I went spastic, and before I could get my gun unslung and to my shoulder, he was flying back across the hole to the hulking safety of Black Mountain. In half a second, I screwed up a battle of wills that had festered for four mornings before coming to a head.

I never saw or heard from that gobbler again, which is probably just as well. But I'll never forget him, and I've since used what he taught me on several other hard-to-reach gobblers. I've called two of those birds across valleys, one across a sizable river, one across an arm of a big lake, and one out of posted property and across a paved road onto the public land I was hunting.

When to "Shout"

Those situations mentioned in the last paragraph are classic examples of when to "shout" to a turkey. I believe the tactic is sometimes effective because it gets the bird – the right bird, anyway – so fired up he loses all sense of propriety and protocol. In nature, the hen almost always goes to the gobbler, but if you, the hen, can't go to the bird – because of a natural barrier, say, or an unfriendly string of posted signs – you still have a chance if

you can get the unreachable gobbler so worked up he can't stand it.

Call a lot to such a gobbler. He's completely out of your reach, anyway, so you have nothing at risk. If you run him off or shut him up, so what?

Often, of course, that's exactly what will happen. But if you do succeed in firing him up, getting him gobbling wildly at every call you make, it's time for phase two of this shouting strategy: leave him.

It seems like exactly the wrong thing to do, but experience and experimentation have taught me that leaving is a critical part of this unorthodox hunting strategy, and the one option that gives you the best chance at such a turkey. The excited bird must be duped into thinking he's about to lose contact with this ardent hen he's been wooing via long-distance.

For safety's sake, it's best not to call while you're actually in motion. Instead, move 50 to 100 yards away from the gobbler, stop in an open area and call lustily to the gobbler, wait for his response, then repeat the process as you continue to put distance between you and the bird.

During this stage of the game, be alert for any change in the gobbler's position and keep picking out good setup spots as you retreat. You need to be ready; you may have to set up fast. It's been my experience that when one of these gobblers decides to chase you down, he'll come quickly. The Black Mountain gobbler isn't the only bird that's caught up to me before I was ready for him in situations like this.

It's also been my experience that pursuing gobblers will often come at you silently, at least at first. The turkey's first order of business seems to be to close the ominous gap that's suddenly widened between him and his prospective lady love, and he'll often do it by flying at least part of the distance, particularly if there's a valley or waterway between you. Be alert for this possibility if the gobbler suddenly goes quiet after gobbling his head off. Either he's given up on you, or he's rapidly closing the distance. You won't know which is happening, so if he shuts up, sit down and get ready. When the turkey nears your last calling position, he'll sometimes begin gobbling again, but sometimes he'll just keep charging ahead until he runs you down.

Another time "shouting" at a turkey can be effective is when you're more or less equidistant between two vocal but nailed-down gobblers that seem hesitant to leave their respective strutting areas. These gobblers will respond politely to conservative calling, but they'll seldom break out of their pattern and come all the way in.

The trick here is to make one of the birds think the other one is about to walk away with the prize. The first step in this strategy is to pick up the tempo and excitement of your calling, as in the preceding strategy. You want to try to fire one or both of them up.

If you succeed in doing that, try to determine which of the birds seems hotter. If you can make this determination, pick up your stuff and move away from the hot gobbler and closer to the less-hot one. Time your calling so that you're responding to the cooler bird, and resist the urge to call to the hotter one. It sounds like a backwards strategy, but my theory is that the hotter gobbler is the one most likely to come in, and you need to give him a little nudge. Ignoring him in favor of the other gobbler, therefore, would be more likely to break him loose than would calling to him and giving him the impression he's about to win.

Sometimes moving noticeably toward the cooler bird and concentrating your calling on him will

You can create the illusion of a departing hen by directing your calls away from the gobbler and reducing the volume. This is easier to do with mouth-operated calls such as diaphragms and tubes.

133

The plethora of turkey videos on the market today lead many inexperienced hunters to believe "shouting" is the only way to interest a turkey. Don't be misled. Most gobblers want something a little less demanding than the typical calling you hear on a video.

get him more fired up, and sometimes it even induces him to meet you halfway. Other times, this tactic generates enough angst in the ignored turkey that he'll abandon his strutting area and pursue you. And then again, of course, sometimes neither of those things happens.

Maybe I'm giving turkeys too much credit for reasoning things out, but this strategy works for me.

Aggressive calling can also be just the ticket when you make contact with a gobbler that has already gathered a harem. You have little chance of calling the gobbler away from his hens, so what you want to do here is work on the hens instead. If they come, the lord and master is sure to come tootling along behind, strutting his stuff.

In this scenario, aggressive calling isn't the way to start. Even in spring before they begin egg-laying, hen turkeys still have a strong maternal instinct. A fall calling style, laced heavily with whines, clucks and kee-kees, will often bring in

the hens. But if it doesn't work – and it won't take long to make that determination – it's once again make-it-or-break-it time. Try to challenge the dominant hen in the flock. There always will be one, and if you can get her "trash talking" back to you, she'll sometimes come in to settle your hash, dragging the gobbler along behind. Mimic every sound she makes, except more aggressively. If she starts cutting back at you, you're making progress.

As with the two previous strategies, this one often results in shutting the game down, since sometimes then hens, instead of coming to mother you or beat you up, will lead the gobbler off in another direction. But again, you have little at stake here, because it's a cinch you're not going to call the gobbler away from his hens.

When to "Whisper"

There are plenty of other turkey hunting situations where "shouting" at a gobbler is the right thing to do. And a good thing it is, too, because

Sometimes an approaching turkey will gobble quite a bit. Just as often (perhaps more often), they won't.

it's a fun, exciting way to hunt when it works, and it makes turkey videos a lot more fun to watch as well. But as more and more hunters take up turkey hunting and hunting pressure increases, there are more and more times when a delicate touch is the answer.

Don't be misled by all those turkey videos. The typical video star turkey is a hot, agitated gobbler, usually a 2-year-old, responding to a whole bunch of frenzied calling by the hunter. The reason for this is simple: Low-key calling and slow-gobbling, slow-coming turkeys make for boring TV. We want Rambo, not Sir John Gielgud.

Sad to say, though, most gobblers are of the Gielgud type. On public land and private land alike, turkeys often hear so much loud, aggressive calling the survivors quickly wise up to it. This is the time to "whisper."

As a very general rule of thumb (which, if you haven't figured it out by now, is the standard, understood preface for discussing any facet of

turkeys or turkey hunting), it's better to begin an encounter with a gobbler on the conservative side. You can always pick up the pace and get more aggressive and demanding with your calling if the cautious approach doesn't seem to be working, and it's a lot easier to work up the scale than to try to back off and tone it down if you start off too strong. You may not be able to undo the damage.

Hunting reluctant gobblers is the supreme challenge of turkey hunting, and several other chapters of this book go into greater detail on various strategies for dealing with these birds. The reason there are several other chapters devoted to different facets of the challenge is because dealing with these toms is tough, demanding, tedious and frustrating. Sometimes they'll gobble quite a bit, but usually they won't. And if they come at all, they'll do it slowly. It's a real test of a hunter's patience and willpower to hang in there with one of these reluctant birds. The temptation is strong to look for greener pastures.

When you're in a turkey-rich environment on what you think is probably a good gobbling day, that's often the best strategy for dealing with a reluctant turkey. Bid him good-bye and go find a friendlier game. But on those all-too-frequent mornings when the world is silent, even a reluctant gobbler offers you a better chance than blind-calling to the trees. At least you know where the bird is.

So whisper. Move in as close as you can without bumping the bird. Pick out a comfortable setup spot and test it for butt-worthiness before you ever make a call, because you're probably going to be there a long time. Take a drink out of your canteen. If you smoke, go ahead and have one. Once you make that first call, all that stuff is going to be behind you for a while.

Resist the urge to call much, even if your reluctant gobbler is answering you fairly well. You're not going to overpower this gobbler with your calling; all you'll do is run him off. Remember, aggressive calling is probably what made him reluctant in the first place. Instead, try to sound like a small group of hens talking among themselves. Use two or more calls you can run simultaneously, such as a diaphragm and a slate or box, and create a soft, contented hen dialogue of clucks and purrs and whines and soft yelps. Scratch in the leaves with your hand or with a stick.

If the gobbler answers this, try to keep from changing the level or excitement of your calling.

The overriding premise of this whole book is that turkey hunting requires you to keep your head in the game, but this kind of hunting demands it even more. Often, a reluctant gobbler will ghost in as silently as frost forming on a blade of grass, and just about as slowly, too. If you're doing any moving at all, you may never even know he was there. Stay alert. The silence common to this hunting strategy often lulls even experienced hunters into thinking the gobbler has lost interest and left the area, but he may be sneaking in to have a look. Sometimes you'll hear him drumming as he approaches, but often he'll just show up. If he does, you need to be ready.

In the end, there are no surefire strategies for taking either excited or unresponsive gobblers – or any gobblers in between, for that matter. That's no news flash; some days, nothing you try will work, and other days you could call one in by rubbing two sticks together. But rather than writing that

fact down in the negative column, most of the turkey hunters I know consider it a big part of the appeal of turkey hunting.

One spring morning in Alabama, Mossy Oak originator and president Toxey Haas and I set up on a bird that gobbled a lot on the roost, then shut up shortly after he flew down. Toxey played his part well, first "shouting" to the aggressive gobbler, then taking his cue from the now-silent bird and "whispering" until he showed up. But when he came, he'd taken rounders on us and came in from an unexpected direction.

I had my gun up, but he was more than 90 degrees off the barrel toward my wrong-side swing, and I was effectively handcuffed in the open woods. I watched him out of the corner of one eye, and when I thought he was behind a tree, I made my move.

He saw me, though, and put on a burst of that ground speed that always surprises me, his bushy beard swinging like a bell rope as he sprinted through the trees. I let him go, not wanting to take a risky shot.

Toxey had seen the bird coming quite a while before I had, but we were too far apart for conversation and he couldn't get my attention. He caught the whole thing on video: the gobbler working in close, then panicking and escaping; me with gun raised and egg on my face mask. A few minutes later, we sat in the greening woods and watched the instant replay through the tiny in-camera monitor, chuckling and shaking our heads.

"Look at that!" I said. "He was right there on top of us, and I still let him beat me."

Toxey tilted his cap back and put on one of his patented grins, grinning not so much at me but at the woods and the world in general.

"Yeah, he did," he said. "Ain't it wonderful?"

Scratching in the leaves with your hand to imitate the sound of a turkey walking or feeding is an effective way to entice a reluctant gobbler those last few steps that will bring him into sight or into gun range.

137

Chapter 20

Getting the Go-Away Gobbler

Turkeys can make tracks faster than turkey hunters can. Because of this, go-away gobblers are tough customers.

The dusty, sandy, hot, cactus and mesquite country of south Texas isn't particularly conducive to walking long distances, but that's what I found myself doing on that hot spring morning. I'd gotten on a group of Rio Grande gobblers in a live oak roost at daybreak, but they'd flown down and headed the other way. They weren't exactly running, but they were moving along considerably faster than I wanted to trudge through the deep sand after them. They'd gobble at every type of call I threw at them, but they were gobbling over their shoulders as they moved steadily away. As far as I could tell, they never took a single step in my direction. But nothing else was talking in that neighborhood that morning, so I gave chase.

Now it was past 10 a.m., and I was sweaty, hungry, thirsty, tired and 3 miles from the truck. And I was no closer to tagging one of those gobblers than I'd been when I heard them on the roost at first light, more than 4 hours earlier. Finally, they crossed the fence that marked the property line of the ranch I was hunting, and they went out of hearing still gobbling lustily. I leaned against a fence post on the property line and listened to them go. If you want to know the truth, I was glad to be rid of them.

There's a thing about Rio Grande turkeys over most of their range, though, and that thing is, they almost always roost in pretty much the same place every night. The next morning, I put an extra water bottle and a couple of candy bars in my vest and went back to those same birds. Sure enough, they were there. And sure enough, they did me the same way, following a different route this time but going in the same general direction. They crossed the

Realtree founder Bill Jordan and outdoor writer Nick Sisley inspect the beard and spurs of the go-away gobbler Jim Spencer finally killed after three frustrating days.

fence and left the property at the same place, where a graveled ranch road went through a cattle gap.

The third day, I decided not to set up on those hike-happy birds at the roost. Instead, I hunted elsewhere for a couple of hours, and when I couldn't get anything going with other turkeys, I drove to the cattle gap on the property line. I hid my truck behind a mesquite clump a quarter-mile down the road, settled into a mesquite thicket 30 yards from the crossing, and commenced to wait. At 9:30, I heard them coming. They were traveling more or less the same general route they'd led me on the two previous days. They were a long way off, but every few minutes one or more of them would gobble. Each time, they were closer.

The four gobblers came onto the road 500 yards away, and I had a momentary sinking feeling because they were on the far side of where I'd parked. No worry, though; they walked past that red vehicle with no more concern than if it had been a dead horse. When they were still 300 yards out, I made one call to them, just so I could say later I called them in. The call neither helped nor hurt the cause, but all four turkeys gobbled at it

and legitimized the lie I'd soon be telling back at camp. They came abreast of my hiding spot, walking broadside and single file. I had more than enough time to evaluate them and pick the bird with the longest beard. I even had time to double-check and make sure the one I picked out had a decent set of spurs as well. When I'd made my choice, I clucked once on a diaphragm to stop them, and that night only three gobblers went back to the distant live oak roost.

I've hunted other gobblers longer and chased them farther, and failed to tag them at the end of the hunt, to boot. These go-away gobblers – those birds that gobble enthusiastically at everything you throw at them, but move steadily away from your calling position all the while – are the most frustrating and aggravating turkeys on earth, and if you're a turkey hunter you know that's saying something. For me, at least, these road-running gobblers are even more frustrating than those silent birds that never gobble at all. If they'd just shut up and leave, you could go off somewhere else and start looking for another bird. But no, they stroll around out there, tantalizing you with

Sometimes the hunter can win by figuring out where the turkey is headed, then beating him to that spot and setting up an ambush. It helps immensely if you're familiar with the hunting area.

their eager-sounding responses. And all the while, they're doing a number on you.

Open-land gobblers, especially those of the Rio Grande, Osceola and Merriam's subspecies, are more likely to have itchy feet than Easterns. But even in the heavy hardwood forests of the East, a good portion of the gobbler population seems to like to travel and sing. Regardless of their subspecies and their habitat, go-away gobblers are tough to kill, even for the pros.

"Bushwhack 'em."

"Ambush 'em."

Those were the immediate knee-jerk responses of veteran turkey hunters David Blanton and Glenn Garner, when I asked them what advice they had for dealing with these itchy-footed turkeys. Both men laughed when they answered,

but just the same, it was obvious they meant what they were saying.

"I'm serious," Blanton assured me about his advice to bushwhack a go-away gobbler. "That's the best way to kill them." Blanton oversees video production for Bill Jordan's Realtree/Advantage camouflage company, and in the course of gathering footage for the company's videos, he spends an awful lot of time in the spring woods. He's dealt with his share of go-away gobblers.

"Keep the turkey gobbling any way you can," he advises. "Try to figure out where he's going, and then get around in front of him and wait for him. Sometimes you can make a gobbler veer from his intended course if you get in front of him and misjudge his path a little bit, but usually you're going to have to be right on the mark when you get ahead of him and set up."

Glenn Garner, a former Realtree staffer, agrees, but with a kicker: "Double-teaming often works on these traveling birds. One hunter can hang back and keep calling to the turkey to keep him gobbling, using a crow call or whatever, while the other circles around and sets up the ambush."

The problem with this strategy, of course, is that only one member of the team is going to be in on the action. The poor sap who has to sit tight and do the calling is on the sidelines and out of the game. It takes a generous hunting buddy to follow along and keep the turkey gobbling while you ease into bushwhack position and kill it.

If you can't manage to or simply don't want to ambush a traveling tom, another technique that's sometimes effective is to simply tag along behind the gobbler, maintaining contact and biding your time until the turkey stops moving. In some cases, traveling gobblers never stop, but usually a bird like this has a destination in mind – a favored strutting area, usually – and eventually he'll quit galloping through the woods and settle into one spot. Once he does, you can ease in close and work him just like you'd work any other turkey – trying different calls and techniques until you either win or lose.

If you decide to follow a go-away gobbler to his destination, don't call to the turkey at all if he's making enough racket to let you keep tabs on him. Your hen calls might slow him down or make him alter his course. If he's not gobbling enough to let you maintain contact, try locator calls at first and hen calls only as a last resort. You don't want to slow a traveling turkey down, because it's only

Two hunters creating a calling "frenzy" with push-buttons and box calls, while simultaneously calling with diaphragms, can make more racket than a turkey farm with a bobcat in the middle of it. This is a last-ditch effort on the average hunt, but it sometimes yields spectacular results.

when he stops at his intended destination that you can finally go to work on him with any decent chance of success.

I once followed one of these on-the-move gobblers for a measured 4 miles through the Arkansas Ozarks, listening from his back trail as he got into a fight, mated with at least one hen, and got chased by a coyote. (I know because I saw the coyote.) I tagged along behind, calling to him with crow calls and turkey calls when I needed to get a fix on his current position, but mostly just following – until he finally stopped in a shady little bottom between two steep-sided ridges. I didn't kill that bird, but it was my own stupid mistake that kept me from it. When he stopped and I caught up to him, I short-sightedly set up to call to him from up on the side of one of the ridges, instead of getting down in the bottom with the turkey like any sane hunter would have done. He came into view still well out of range, and I was pinned down like a soldier in a foxhole on the side of that sun-drenched hill. He strutted around down there below me for a while, finally picked me out and ran away.

The point is, though, I beat that gobbler by hanging in there with him until he got to where he was going. It was my own poor judgment in choosing a final calling position that kept me from taking him home.

In this scenario of following a bird until he stops, the best strategy I've discovered is to get as tight on him as possible, so I won't have to pull him far. I've had more luck with aggressive calling than by being timid in these situations, but despite that, I feel it's always best to start by trying some soft stuff. Remember, you're right on top of the turkey at this point, and you might blast him off the strutting ground if you start too strong. Sometimes, a soft cluck or a gentle run of yelps is all it takes.

I've brought a few birds to the gun in similar situations by doing no more than scratching in the leaves. Spitting and drumming at a gobbler from close range like this is also sometimes an effective technique, especially when coupled with leaf-scratching and soft hen yelps and clucks. Several companies manufacture spit-and-drum calls, but that's just one more thing to carry. Most hunters, with a little practice, are able to spit and drum as well with their natural voice as with a commercially made call.

If the soft stuff doesn't work, the highest-percentage play is to change calling locations and try soft stuff one last time, to reduce the chances that an obstruction between you and the gobbler is what's keeping him from coming in. If you know that's not the case, or if your soft, low-key calling

141

If you lose the race with a go-away gobbler and make contact with that same bird the next day, setting up along the route he followed the day before can be a deadly tactic. Set up in a bottleneck if possible – use a road leading through a thicket, a saddle or whatever natural features are present that would tend to narrow the gobbler's path.

doesn't get any results at the second setup, it's make-it-or-break-it time. This is when I pull out all the stops. First, I lay out all my calls – a box, two slates, several diaphragms, maybe a push-button call or two. If a sudden burst of excited cutting and yelping doesn't get the gobbler headed my way, I stage a turkey fight, making as much racket as possible. I use aggressive purring, loud cutting and yelping, excited clucks. I slap my cap against my pants leg and flail at the leaves with my hands and feet. In short, I try to sound like an entire flock of turkeys has suddenly gone berserk and started attacking one another.

When this technique works, it usually works very quickly. Be ready.

If it doesn't work, it's time to lob a few hand grenades.

Seriously, if that fails, you might as well quit calling altogether. But unless you think you know where you can strike another gobbler, your best option is to just sit tight. Stay in the neighborhood

with your traveling gobbler – all day, if you're hunting in a state that allows all-day hunting and you can stand to hang around there that long. Often a gobbler that shut up and disappeared when the "turkey fight" started is still in the immediate neighborhood, and a good part of the time he'll either start gobbling again nearby or he'll come sneaking in some time later to investigate. Also, it often happens that a gobbler you followed all morning will begin to work his way back along his original path as the shadows grow long. Though they generally gobble much less on this return path, they'll still gobble, and you can still pattern them and kill them.

If you go through all the above stuff with a go-away gobbler and still nothing works, try going back to that gobbler the next day and setting up either on the strutting area he used the day before or somewhere along the route he took, the way I did with the Texas birds at the beginning of this chapter. Gentle calling is OK and may help coax

Never forget safety. No turkey is worth the risk of an accident.

the gobbler to come in, but I've also spooked these birds or hung them up by calling. It's probably best to say nothing unless it appears the gobbler is going to miss your position as he goes by.

Choose a bottleneck location, if possible – a gap in a fence like the one I used on the Rio Grande longbeard, a logging road through thick brush, a narrow ridgeline. Many times, these traveling gobblers are creatures of habit. More often than not, they'll roost in the same general area and use the same general route to reach their favored day-use area. Why these turkeys don't simply roost closer to where they want to spend the daylight hours and save themselves all that wear and tear on the pads of their feet has always been a puzzler to me, but they don't, and turkey hunters have to deal with them. However, the very fact that they move from one area to another gives a thinking turkey hunter the opportunity to plot a hunting strategy that will cure the gobbler's wanderlust in a permanent, convincing way.

In all of the above tactics of trickery, never forget safety. Turkey hunting is safer than driving a car, but it still carries the worst statistics, percentage-wise, of any type of hunting. And moving through the woods in the vicinity of a gobbling turkey can lead to disaster if you're unlucky or incautious. Any time you're on the move in a situation like this, wear an orange hat, vest, or both. You're not in sight of the turkey, but you may well be in sight of another turkey hunter. Do what you can to make sure that hunter sees you for what you are. You'll have plenty of time to remove the orange and become invisible again once you reach a setup location.

Dealing with these sightseeing gobblers isn't the game for a hunter who doesn't like to or isn't able to travel long distances on foot. Nor is it a viable tactic when your hunting area is limited, because the gobbler you're chasing will usually go onto another property before you can close with him. But if you've got the legs for it and enough hunting area to work with, killing one of these go-away gobblers can be just like a walk in the park.

A big, big park.

143

Chapter 21

Dealing With Talkative Turkeys

Sometimes turkeys gobble too much. It's enjoyable to hear, but at some point the gobbling becomes not as much enjoyable as nerve-wracking and aggravating.

If turkeys didn't gobble, few of us would hunt them. Spring turkey hunting involves a lot of bother and no inconsiderable expense, and without the gobble, it would be far less exciting. And I don't even want to think about the frustration factor.

If you need proof it's the gobble that draws us out there, look no further than the relative popularity of spring versus fall turkey hunting. They gobble a lot in the spring, they don't gobble much in the fall, and the number of hunters who go after fall turkeys in states that offer a season are a pitiful fraction of the camouflage-clad army that invades the spring woods. There are a few states, like Virginia and New York, where the fall turkey hunting tradition is deep-rooted and well established. There are more fall turkey hunters in these states than elsewhere, but even in these states, spring hunting is vastly more popular than fall hunting.

Yep, it's the gobble (and its associated mating behavior, of course) that makes the difference. Ask 10 turkey hunters to name the single most enjoyable aspect of this grand spring game, and if nine of them don't answer you with some version of "I just like to hear 'em," I'll eat a box call. With no mustard.

But sometimes turkeys gobble too much. It's enjoyable to hear, but at some point the gobbling becomes not so much enjoyable as nerve-wracking and aggravating. Listening to a turkey sound off is vastly preferable to a hunt in which you fail to hear a gobble, no question. But don't lose sight of the central fact that the object of turkey hunting is to kill one, not give your eardrums a workout. Sure, it makes for an exciting morning when you get on a bird that gobbles a couple hundred times, but all too often these talkative gobblers live to gobble another day.

You'd think it would be enjoyable to hear two gobblers in different directions gobble 300 times each, but the gobbling of an uncooperative turkey is more bothersome than enjoyable.

Not always, though …

On the sixth morning of a turkey season quite a few springs ago, the two Missouri longbeards across the wooded bowl were showing every indication of getting bored with the conversation we'd been having with them for the past two hours. They were chorus-gobbling every 20 to 30 seconds, as they'd been doing since we got on them, but they were beginning to drift away. Things looked discouraging. Again.

I was the only one carrying a shotgun. Jody Hugill was the guide/caller, David Billman was lugging a video camera, and I was the designated shooter. We were trying to capture the hunt on film for one of Lohman Game Calls' earliest turkey hunting videos, but the way the hunt was playing out, it didn't seem as though the executioner would have the opportunity to play his part.

We got on these birds pretty early, and though they were already on the ground when we heard them, we thought we had a pretty good setup. They were below us on the side of a big ridge that bordered a large reservoir, and they were crabbing along the side of the ridge and gradually gaining altitude as they came, angling toward a ridgetop pasture not too far away. It looked like all we had to do was stay above and ahead of them, and eventually we'd run together.

It didn't work. They never quite topped out, and we wound up on the opposite side of this little hollow just off the crest of the main ridge, arguing back and forth about just who was supposed to come to who. The gobblers refused to cross the hollow, and the distance was too short and the woods still too sparsely vegetated for us to risk

another move. So there we were, trapped like possums in a chicken house. Two hours and 200 gobbles after this encounter started, we were no closer to killing one of these birds than when we got out of the truck at dawn.

Finally, frustrated, Jody quit calling. The turkeys stood out there gobbling lustily for another 20 minutes, then started slowly drifting away. I cut my eyes over at Jody. "We need to let 'em go on to wherever they were headed," he whispered. "They're eventually going to quit gobbling, and we need to get to a good setup before they do. This one sucks."

The birds moved slowly but steadily away, eventually working their way to the top of the ridge. We moseyed along behind and kept mum. They entered the pasture at an unlikely place we'd never have chosen for a setup, a neglected corner where oak saplings were busily reclaiming the ground. The head-high trees were thick as dog's hair, and though the gobblers were only 60 or 70 yards into the pasture, we couldn't see them through the vegetation. We eased carefully through the fence, scrooched back against a couple of large fencerow oaks, and got ready for action.

It wasn't long in coming. At Jody's first run of yelps the turkeys double-gobbled in unison, then followed with a cacophony of gobbles as they came, slowly but surely, through the oak thicket. I tracked the near-continuous sound with my gun barrel, prepared to clinch a starring role in next year's turkey video.

They were well within range when I first saw them, but there was a hitch: The gobbler's heads were only inches apart. At the 30-yard range, I'd have killed them both. Missouri frowns on that, so

145

I held off. I knew the gobblers would eventually separate far enough for me to shoot.

They didn't, though. After a few minutes of peering through the oak scrub for the elusive hen, they faded back into the thicket and then moved off down the pasture, still gobbling. We let them go, then pulled a rounder and looped out ahead of them again. Once more they came marching in at Jody's call, and this time they were far enough apart. The one I shot weighed 21 pounds. His running buddy looked considerably bigger.

It was 10:30 when I pulled the trigger on that gobbler, and we'd been after him and his companion for nearly four hours. In the process, we covered more than a mile of that long ridgeline above the lake, and if those two turkeys gobbled once, they gobbled 500 times. That's well above the norm, certainly, but not unheard of when a pair of longbeards are in the mood for conversation.

We tagged a bird that morning because we were able to stay with the pair until they got where they wanted to go, then slipped into position and did our calling from close by. But that tactic doesn't always work on a talkative turkey.

The next day, Jody went back to the same ridge. However, this hunt shook out quite a bit differently. The survivor was just as talky as he'd been the day before, but he refused to fall for the tactics that had done his buddy in.

Jody started his hunt that morning at the oak-thickety pasture, heard the gobbler down the ridge and just sat tight and waited for him to show up on top. The bird entered the oak saplings and gobbled, according to the previous day's script, but this time he wouldn't come to conventional calling. After trying three or four setups around the thicket without success, Jody fell back to a part of the pasture that didn't have as many oak sprouts and provided better visibility. He put out a jake and two hen decoys, then staged a mock turkey fight by alternately running a box call and a slate call while yelping and cutting nonstop on a diaphragm.

In the oak thicket 250 yards away, the gobbler went crazy, and then went silent. Jody quit calling and got ready, but nothing happened for a long time. He was about to decide he'd chased the turkey away with his frantic calling when all of a sudden the bird was there, standing in the woods at the fringe of the pasture and staring suspiciously at the decoy group. He hadn't made a peep in 45 minutes. Later that morning at the check station, the scales confirmed he was the heavier bird – 24 pounds.

A talkative gobbler offers the hunter one spectacular advantage over a turkey that isn't so fond of his own voice, and that advantage is pretty obvious: You have no trouble keeping track of him. That old, familiar "Where in the heck is that turkey?" feeling is held at bay. You have a clearer idea of the range to the bird, which direction he's heading, and even how he's reacting to various calling strategies. If he cuts you off when you hit him with a slate call but ignores the sound of a diaphragm or box, that's your cue to keep using the slate. Of course, just because he gobbles at it doesn't mean he's going to come to it, but it does give you a good indication of the gobbler's preferences that day. Communicating with the gobbler is very important to the success or failure of most turkey hunts. As long as he's talking, you can keep experimenting, trying to find the right combination of calling sequence and location that might enable you to tag the bird.

The downside of a turkey's frequent gobbling has at least three faces. One possibility is that he'll call up a hen or two. While your hunt isn't exactly ruined if that happens, you can safely bet the degree of difficulty is going to double or triple.

Another possibility is that an overly gabby gobbler will call in a predator such as a coyote or bobcat. There's little danger of one of these predators actually catching the bird, but they'll definitely shut him up and disrupt your hunt – at least for a while.

This, incidentally, probably happens more often than most turkey hunters think. I've done eight or 10 times as much of my turkey hunting in heavily forested cover as I have in the more open country of Florida and the West, but judging from my (relatively) few experiences in hunting open areas, I'm convinced it's a common occurrence. I've observed three incidences of predators trying to catch a turkey I was working, and in every case it was one of these loudmouth gobblers. I've also worked talky birds that were out of sight and heard them suddenly putt and run or putt and fly. Although I couldn't prove it, I'm almost certain predators crashed the party in many of these instances, too. Coyotes were the culprit in the three cases I've witnessed, but I'm sure bobcats and possibly gray and red foxes might also make the attempt from time to time.

I'll bet this same thing has happened to you, although you may not have actually seen the event take place unless you hunt open country a lot. But think back: How many times have you been dealing with a talkative turkey that suddenly and inexplicably goes mum? I'll bet you can remember several times.

Of course, it isn't always a predator that causes a formerly loquacious gobbler to dummy up. Sometimes these birds hush because they've decided to investigate your calling and are sneaking in to do so. Remember Jody Hugill's hunt earlier in this chapter. Therefore, the best thing to do when a gobbler shushes is to do nothing at all, except watch closely for the movement of a quietly approaching bird. But often the turkey just goes silent and you never hear him or see him again, and you're left in the quiet woods to ponder your navel and smell the staleness of your head net.

The third undesirable thing that might happen when a turkey gobbles too much and too long is that he'll call up another hunter. This is especially likely on public land. The ethics of the situation demand that the second hunter, upon realizing that he's intruding on your hunt, back off and look for another bird. Fifteen years ago, you could pretty much depend on that happening.

But turkey hunting has become a glamour sport, and today's turkey woods are crammed with hunters who don't give a yelp about that kind of ethics. There are still a lot of fine, honorable turkey hunters out there, but there are also a bunch of jerks who will horn in on your bird in a minute, and this creates a dangerous situation. When I'm working a gobbler and detect the presence of another hunter working that bird (usually by sound, but occasionally by sight), I give the other hunter that bird right then and there, and waste no time getting well away from that area. I don't care whether the other hunter is one of the good guys who honestly hasn't heard me calling to the bird or whether he's one of the lowlifes who deliberately move in on another hunter's bird. I give him the turkey either way. A turkey is a valuable thing, but not valuable enough to risk getting shot for.

OK, let's backtrack a little. If the gobbler you've been working suddenly goes silent, how do you know which of those above things has happened? It can be important to determine this, because there are instances when you can still successfully hunt a gobbler that's dummied up.

First off, keep in mind that maybe none of those three things we just talked about has happened. A turkey only has so many gobbles in him

Sometimes talkative gobblers suddenly go silent. Sometimes they show up a little while later; sometimes they don't. When they don't, it's an aggravating thing.

on a given day, and no matter how talky he's been, he's eventually going to quit gobbling. But usually when this happens, there's a noticeable period of diminished frequency and intensity of gobbling, as the turkey slowly changes moods. When a gobbler cools off, it's almost always gradual, not abrupt. When a turkey shuts up simply because he's lost interest, it's almost always pretty easy to tell what has happened, and you can go off and try to find another gobbler because your chances of tagging this one just went almost to zero.

It's when the cessation of gobbling is abrupt that the question needs to be answered. Unless your bird is in sight and you can see what happened, your ears are going to have to do the job for you.

If a hen comes in, often she'll do some yelping and clucking to the gobbler, but not always. Sometimes hens come in quiet, the same way gobblers do. You can still be fairly confident a hen is the problem, though, if you're close enough to the gobbler to hear whether he's drumming or not. Gobblers usually switch from gobbling to drumming in the immediate presence of hens, because the primary purpose of gobbling is to attract hens. Once a hen is present, gobbling becomes more of

When a gobbler stops talking, it could be because a hen has showed up. When this happens, a gobbler's normal response is to hush and start strutting nonstop, and if you're not close enough to see him or hear him drumming, you may never know what happened.

a risk than a survival advantage to turkeys, so most gobblers switch over to strutting and drumming once they've attracted female companionship.

If the arrival of a four-footed or two-footed predator is what shut the bird up, there may be auditory clues that will help you figure out what happened. If you hear another hunter calling, that's a dead give-away and you can make up your mind what to do about it – stay and compete or relinquish the field to the other hunter. My advice is to give the turkey to the other guy and get out of there, but that's fodder for a later chapter.

Sometimes when a predator tries to catch a turkey, the predator sneaks in as close as possible and attacks just as the bird begins a gobble. In two of the attempted coyote attacks I've witnessed, that's what happened, and in both cases the turkeys stopped their gobbles in midstream and made safe if undignified escapes. I suppose by attacking a turkey during the act of gobbling, the predator is trying to take advantage of the gobbler's head movement, concentration level and shift of attention during that instant to tilt the odds a little more in his favor. Or maybe it's something else entirely.

In any case, I believe that's when a high percentage of predator attacks on gobbling turkeys occur – during the turkey's act of gobbling.

And sometimes that can give you a clue as to what happened to your turkey. Both before and since witnessing those attempted coyote predations, I've heard actively gobbling turkeys begin a gobble but abruptly cut it off in midsyllable. Those turkeys sounded exactly like the two gobblers I watched. If a gobbler you're working comes out with one of those chopped-off gobbles that doesn't seem to quite get finished, and then he quits gobbling, I'd say there's a good chance he's been rushed by a predator. If the aborted gobble is closely followed by the sound of wingbeats or alarm putts or clucks, you can just about bet the farm on it.

OK, you're now thinking, *so what? How does knowing what screwed up my hunt help me?*

First, don't jump to conclusions about your hunt being botched. That may not be the case at all. Turkeys don't stay spooked forever, not even hook-spurred old settlers with several breeding seasons behind them. The spring mating time is brief, and the survival of the species depends on the birds getting together and getting things done. They don't have the luxury of staying spooked too long after something traumatic happens.

I could give you a hundred personal and secondhand examples of proof, but a couple will suffice: Several years ago, a friend of mine called up and killed a big Wisconsin gobbler less than two hours after his hunting buddy called in and missed the same bird. The identity of the bird in both cases was unquestionable, since he was missing two feathers from the middle of his fan.

And late last season, on heavily hunted public land, I blundered into a flock of hens being shared by two big gobblers. I was more or less in the middle of them before they knew I was around, and it was like flushing a covey of giant quail. The gobblers were less than 20 yards from me when they flew, and there was no question both longbeards saw me and identified me as a human. Less than 60 minutes later, I was looking down my gun barrel at one of those gobblers. I didn't kill him, but that's another story. I called him in, though, very soon after I'd terrified him, and that's what's important to the point.

So we get back to it: When your hunt for a talkative gobbler gets interrupted by hens, coyotes or another hunter – or even by your own clumsiness or greenhorn mistake – you don't necessarily have to give up on that turkey. He may well be workable a little later on. The tactics we're about to discuss here also work on less-talkative gobblers, but the difference is, a bird that was gobbling a lot before being spooked is much more likely to resume gobbling after he settles down than one that wasn't saying much. The less-talkative bird will settle down, too, but he'll be harder to find later in the day when you try to make contact again.

If it's still fairly early in the day when your bird hushes – before 9 a.m., say – go somewhere else and hunt for a couple of hours if you have the option. It's going to be a while before your gobbler settles down, and you might as well put that time to productive use. If you're on a small hunting area or don't feel you can get anything else going elsewhere, take a nap. You probably need one, anyway.

If it's early in the spring breeding cycle and your gobbler has gotten henny, you're probably out of luck for that day with that bird. But if it's later in the season, the hens are going to drift away from the gobbler toward midday, to sneak away to their nests and lay eggs. They won't return to the gobbler that day, and often by noon a gobbler that was wattle-deep in hens at 8 o'clock is as lonely as the Maytag repairman. This type of gobbler can be a pushover, but these are almost always midday or afternoon birds, so in morning-only states you may run out of time before the gobbler gets right.

Just as he'll start up again after his hens bail out, a gobbler will get back to business after a predator attack. Often, the gobbler will simply fly up into a tree and wait for the critter to leave, then drop back to earth, stand around for a while being nervous, then resume his gobbling from the same area he was in before the upset occurred. He'll be no harder to work after the predator incident than before.

If another hunter caused the disturbance, more patience and caution are probably called for. Most of the turkey hunters in the woods today don't have the savvy, experience and patience required to deal with a gobbler after it's been spooked. Nine times out of 10, a hunter who moves in and disturbs a gobbler you've been working isn't going to stick around. He'll go elsewhere, looking for another gobbling turkey to booger up.

Despite my Wisconsin friend's experience, a gobbler is usually a little slower to get back to normal after being spooked by a hunter. A two-footed predator seems to put a gobbler in a higher state of panic than a four-footed one. Maybe that's

Coyotes and other predators may shut a gobbler up more often than we realize. They don't often catch mature gobblers, but they can sure spook them.

because turkey hunters are only out there a little while, but predators are in the woods every day of a turkey's life. Maybe it's because we're a lot scarier than coyotes and bobcats. I don't know. I don't care, either, as long as I keep in mind that a human-spooked gobbler is probably a target for the next day's hunt. In most cases, you're probably better off going elsewhere and trying the spooked bird again the next day.

Finally, in the case of the talkative gobbler that didn't get spooked but just lost interest, you need to do some thinking and analyzing. If you elect to try the turkey again the next day, change tactics, calls, locations, whatever. If you used decoys the day before, don't use them this time. If you didn't, do. Try something different, because what you tried before obviously didn't work.

That last sentence could stand alone as the shortest seminar in the history of turkey hunting, appropriate for many more situations than the one that's the subject of this chapter. Tattoo it into your subconscious, for those times when things get difficult:

Try something different. What you tried before didn't work.

Chapter 22

How to Silence a Silent Turkey

What does he need to gobble for?

Turkey hunters like to hear 'em gobble. Unfortunately, they don't gobble every day.

Sometimes the dearth of gobbling activity is understandable, when the weather is cold, windy, rainy or generally poor in some other way, but sometimes turkeys gobble their heads off in that kind of weather, anyway. But then there are days letter-perfect: calm, crisp and sharp at first light, with the certainty of becoming shirt-sleeve weather by midmorning. Cardinals sing, owls hoot, crows go at it with each other … and the turkeys are as silent as the limbs on which they're roosting.

These gobbleless mornings happen a few times a season, even during the two peaks of gobbling that bracket the primary breeding time. But it's during that peak breeding period we've learned to expect them.

All experienced turkey hunters know about the dreaded gobbling lull. It comes along every spring. It happened last year and the year before. It's going to happen this year. Sure as death and taxes, there'll come a week or more this spring when the woods are as quiet as the inside of a just-laid turkey egg.

This gobbling slowdown is normal. It's the proper sequence of events, and although we dread it and hate it while it's happening, it's the hook on which hangs our future turkey hunting success. The lull is the result of "henny" gobblers, birds that have gathered harems of hens and have no further need to gobble. They'll usually sound off a time or two from the roost, but after the hens gather and they hit the ground, they dummy up and spend the rest of the day strutting, looking pretty for their girlfriends, doing a lot of drumming and breeding the occasional hen. This quiet period lasts for a week to 10 days in most years and in most locales, and it's preceded by a progressive and fairly abrupt decrease in gobbling as the hens become receptive and gravitate to the gobblers.

Conversely, the lull is almost always followed by a gradual increase in gobbling when the hens begin to leave the gobblers each day to lay eggs. The hens stretch the duration of their absences each day over a period of a few days to a week, until finally they abandon the gobbler altogether and begin the 27-day process of incubation. One fateful morning, a gobbler that's been wading around up to the roots of his beard in hens suddenly wakes up alone, abandoned by his recently departed girlfriends. This induces a state of desperation in the surviving longbeard population, and they crank up the gobbling again in a mostly futile effort to attract more hens.

You can hear the desperation in their voices. They start on the roost while it's still dark, and in some instances they gobble all day long. Gobbling during the second peak is often even more common (to say nothing of more insistent, lusty and desperate) than before they all got with the girls and hushed up.

If I could only hunt one side or other of the primary breeding time, I'd hunt the second peak of gobbling, when the breeding is mostly over. Turkeys are generally easier to work then, and they're more likely to be hook-spurred old boys because most of the cooperative 2-year-olds died during the first peak of gobbling that happened before the lull.

Still, knowing things will improve next week doesn't help when today is the day you're hunting, and it's smack in the middle of the lull. I know quite a few hunters who don't seem to feel much

During the second peak, the turkey you hear gobbling is more likely to be a hook-spurred old-timer.

The midday hours are prime time for hunting toward the end of the lull, because hens are beginning to lay and are leaving the gobblers after the first few hours of the day.

pressure to hunt during that inevitable week or 10 days of the season when the gobblers are with hens and aren't saying much, but for the life of me I can't understand that mindset. Those guys evidently don't love it as much as I do.

Sure, gobblers are more difficult to deal with when they're henny and aren't talking, but the spring turkey season is too brief and precious to squander it waiting for gobbling activity to increase. So I suck it up and hunt anyway, as do many other turkey hunters. The thing is, though, most hunters don't make adjustments in their hunting plans and tactics to deal with this reluctance of the gobbler population to do any gobbling. They hunt the same way they do when the turkeys are gobbling well, and guess what? It doesn't work so hot.

Most hunters just keep on plugging away, using the same tactics they've employed all season, and pretty soon the lull passes and the turkeys start gobbling again. Once more the rigid, unchanging hunting tactics of these inflexible hunters become appropriate, and they're back to dealing with turkeys that sometimes come and sometimes don't, but will at least, for Pete's sake, *gobble.*

It seems like, after a few years of suffering through this predictable week and a half of consistent failure, these hunters would learn to modify their tactics during the lull. During that annual period of silence, though, most hunters don't learn a thing, and they go into next spring's lull using the same old unproductive tactics, as single-minded as a dog sniffing a fireplug and as lost as a goose in a snowstorm.

No question about it, hunting the lull is tough duty. When turkeys aren't gobbling, the degree of difficulty increases exponentially. Show me somebody who says they don't have trouble dealing with quiet gobblers, and I'll show you either a liar or somebody who has enough restraint to not hunt them.

Because I have a lot of trouble with these quiet birds myself and really didn't feel qualified to write this chapter without help, I went to the pros. To a man, they admitted having trouble with non-gobbling, henny turkeys, too. Brad Harris, one of the most accomplished hunters in the country and from whom I've learned a great deal about turkeys and turkey hunting, says he's never found a surefire way of dealing with these between-the-peaks birds.

Road scouting is fine if there's lots of gobbling activity, but during the lull, it's a waste of time.

Still, part of Harris' job is to take a procession of writers, sales representatives, product buyers and VIPs turkey hunting every spring, and he doesn't have the luxury of taking a week off in the middle of the lull. He has to go turkey hunting anyway, and furthermore, he has to produce opportunities to harvest gobblers for the people he takes. Although his success ratio is decidedly lower during the lull than when they're gobbling well, Harris still has an impressive track record with these silent gobblers.

"My usual tactic when turkeys aren't gobbling is to just stay out there trying, and I just keep blundering around until something happens," he says.

Harris is being modest here, of course. I've shared many hunts with him, and one thing he doesn't do when he's in the turkey woods is blunder. But his point is valid: In order to kill a non-gobbling turkey, you have to be out there with him. This means, above all, keeping a positive attitude and not giving up in disgust because you're not hearing any turkeys. It also means hunting longer hours – all day, if the state in

which you're hunting allows it and you can spare the time. This is a particularly promising ploy toward the end of the lull, when the hens are sneaking off to lay their daily eggs but haven't begun incubation yet. A gobbler may not be alone until noon or later, but then he becomes vulnerable to calling and may well come marching in.

Even during the morning hours, though, it's sometimes possible to get a response and do something with a gobbler. That's why it's important to stay out there.

"You never know what might work or when," Harris says. "Try anything and everything. What have you got to lose?"

When Harris says "try everything," he means just that – extremely aggressive calling, cluck-purr-and-wait-forever and everything in between. I've hunted with him during the lull in South Dakota, Missouri and Arkansas. He's tireless, stubborn and relentless, and eventually he makes things happen.

"Don't rule out anything," he says. "Sometimes you can fire up a bird when he doesn't really want

Spending several hours at the edge of a likely feeding/strutting area with a decoy in place is a good technique for the quiet times, provided you have the patience to do it. A good book helps.

what's going on where you're going to hunt, you have to get out there and look around a few times. These road scouters will kill a few birds when they're gobbling, but when the lull comes, they're lost. They just don't know where the turkeys are."

Knowing the land and the movement patterns of the turkeys across it gives you several advantages. If you're familiar with the territory, you can concentrate your efforts on areas that provide better visibility – fields, pastures and long expanses of open woods, for example – thus substituting eyesight for hearing. Turkeys may button up, but they can't make themselves invisible, and by playing your hunting area properly you can shift the odds toward your side. By easing into these high-visibility areas slowly and cautiously, from the direction that provides the best visibility and concealment, a careful hunter can often spot turkeys before they spot him. Once you know where they are, you can plan a stalk, get in front of them and set up an ambush, or move to the most strategic calling position and set up on them. (Those first two tactics, by the way, are not unethical turkey hunting techniques. Due to the safety factor, stalking a turkey isn't a good idea on public ground or where other hunters are likely to be, but when you're certain you're in an area by yourself, it's a challenging and satisfying way to kill a longbeard.)

Building a blind at the edge of one of these high-visibility areas and setting up for long periods of time is another effective way of hunting quiet, henny gobblers, if you're the type of hunter who can muster that much patience. Some days I can pull it off; some days I can't. But when I've managed to sit still for long enough, it's been an effective hunting technique for me during the quiet times. Decoys are usually invaluable in these high-visibility, wait-'em-out situations.

Harris says the tactic of calling to the hens rather than the gobbler (discussed in Chapter 19) is also something to keep in mind. "It's a tricky thing, though," he says. "Sometimes it backfires and the hen or hens either resent the intrusion or are afraid of the competition and take the gobbler in the opposite direction."

Harris rarely starts a calling sequence with the object of calling in the hens. But if he's calling to an uninterested gobbler and gets a response from

to be fired up, and sometimes you can call conservatively and coax one in that isn't really in the mood to be coaxed."

Knowing the territory is important in any hunting situation, but when the gobblers are henny it's even more important. You should make every effort to know not only the lay of the land, but also how the turkeys have been relating to it. Refer to the chapter on scouting for more on this subject.

"Everybody talks about scouting, but not many hunters get out there before the season and actually do much of it," Harris says. "They'll listen from the roads a time or two before the season, but that's not scouting. If you want to know

154

Spooking a flock of turkeys sounds like a poor way to hunt them, but it works in the fall and can also work in the spring, provided that when you rush the birds to spook them, you're able to separate the gobbler from his hens.

one of the hens, he mimics her calls right back to her. "Sometimes this will bring her in, dragging the gobbler behind, but other times it will cause her to lead him away from the competition. One way you win, and the other way you're no worse off than you were."

One final trick that occasionally works on a henned-up gobbler is to adopt a chapter from the fall turkey hunter's handbook and scatter the flock. Then, after a settling-down period of an hour or two, you might be able to call the gobbler in while he's separated from his hens.

This radical tactic, naturally, requires getting very close to the birds before they know you're around. Sometimes you can use dense vegetation or the roll and break of the landscape to get in close. On occasion, you can bust up a flock when they're in the open, if you wait until the tom is far enough from his hens that you can get between them when you rush the flock.

Regardless of the situation, you're probably going to have to be pretty close when you attempt the scatter. If the turkeys see you when you're too far away, they'll all flush or run in the same direction. All you'll have accomplished is to further screw up an already difficult hunt.

In the ideal situation, you'd scatter the flock at sundown, before or after the birds have flown up. But in order for this to do you any good, of course, you have to be able to hunt the next morning. If you scatter a flock, it's important to carefully note the direction in which the gobbler flies. After he's spent the night alone, if you can position yourself between him and the majority of his hens, you have a decent chance of calling him in soon after he flies down. Scattering a flock off the roost at first light can also work, but it usually takes a couple of hours for the gobbler to settle down enough to respond to your calling. Scattering a flock at any other time of day, in my experience, is largely a waste of valuable hunting time.

Any way you cut it, hunting the quiet time is a tough assignment. But those turkeys are still out there, and you can call them and kill them. But not unless you're out there, "blundering around until something happens."

155

Chapter 23

Late-Season Turkeys

Hook-spurred old gobblers are nobody's pushovers, but they're more susceptible during "the second season."

Where'd they all go?"

It's a common question, and most turkey hunters ask it sometime during every spring turkey season, during those aggravating stretches of two or three or 10 mornings in a row when the dawn woods are silent. The gobblers aren't gone, of course; they're just wattle-deep in hens and don't have any incentive to gobble. (See the previous chapter for a discussion on how to deal with them.)

Fortunately, that phase passes. As the hens begin to incubate, the gobblers become vocal again. Waking up alone on a spring morning makes a gobbler anxious, and he starts gobbling again in an attempt to correct the situation.

This brings on the second peak of gobbling, the post-breeding time of year some hunters refer to as the "second season." It's a fine time to hunt. The gobblers are workable, and hunting pressure is lighter than early in the season. That's because the less-than-serious have quit hunting, and the successful have tagged out. True, gobblers aren't as plentiful as they were on opening day, but when you find one, you're more likely to have him to yourself. He's more apt to be a hook-spurred trophy, too, because the inexperienced 2-year-olds that gobble and respond best get shot the first week.

On the other hand, those hook-spurred survivors whose hens have left and that are still out there during the second season are nobody's pushovers. Remember, they've survived not only the first half of the current season, but two or more past seasons as well. They may do a lot of gobbling, but they're still not likely to throw caution to the wind and come running to your calls.

Matching your camo pattern to the green conditions is helpful in late-season hunting. Everything is greener, so your camo should be, too.

This is the second season, and it calls for second-season tactics.

Woods conditions are considerably different now. Things change rapidly in spring, and vegetation is much thicker because of the lush, fresh leaf growth. This dictates a change of camouflage, from the predominantly gray or brown that's appropriate early in the season to greener patterns, to enable you to blend in better with the green woods.

But camo is a minor consideration and easily dealt with. What isn't so easy is coping with the sound-muffling properties of that dense new vegetation. First, a hunter must adjust his thinking about distances. A gobbler in a tree will sound much the same early or late, but once he's on the ground, the sound of his gobbling will be much more muffled because it has to penetrate all that foliage. It's very easy to overestimate the distance

between you and a late-season turkey, and most of us overrun a gobbler or two before we figure out we must compensate.

It's a delicate balance. On the one hand, you want to get as close to the gobbler as possible, and heavier foliage helps you do that. At the same time, if you've overestimated the distance to the bird, you might bump him. Caution is necessary, maybe more so now than in early-season hunting, when winterlike conditions still exist in the woods. When the woods are open and free of spring greenery, it's easy to remember you can be easily spotted. Therefore you're careful not to get burned by a sharp-eyed gobbler. But sometimes hunters get careless late in the season, because they think the lush foliage will hide their movements. It will, of course, but only to a point. These are still turkeys we're talking about here. Don't let the

157

Early-season hunting means open woods and long sight distances. Not so in late season.

thick greenery lull you into becoming too bold when you approach a late-season bird.

However, you don't want to be too timid, either. Even though most of the hens have left to begin laying and/or incubating, there are always going to be some receptive hens around during the second season. Some are merely running behind schedule, and others have lost their nests to predation and are attempting to breed again before renesting. So if you dawdle around in your approach and stay too far from a gobbling turkey for too long, you risk having a real hen steal him away.

Patterning a second-season gobbler can be more difficult, too. You might be able to pull it off in a small woodlot, but in the big woods where so many of us do our hunting, getting a firm handle on a late-season gobbler's habits can be impossible. A second-season gobbler whose hens have all vanished is likely to abandon his favored early-season strutting zones and take to the road like a traveling salesman with a quota to fill. He's looking for girls, and since girls are in short supply, he's likely to travel several miles in a day. You might run into one of these traveling gobblers at any stage of the spring mating season, but they're much more common late in the cycle.

I once fell in behind one of these itchy-footed birds on the last day of a 28-day turkey season. I was hunting heavily pressured public ground, and this bird had no doubt been hunted hard; there were signs of turkey hunters everywhere I looked. I'd hunted him several days that season myself, but hadn't been able to do anything with him.

On this final day of the season, he started gobbling from the ridge where he'd been living for more than a month. I was running late that morning, and by the time I got on top of the ridge with him, he was already on the ground and on the move. I set up and called from what I thought was a good location, but he didn't want to come. He moved back and forth along the ridge, sometimes nearer and sometimes farther. He gobbled enthusiastically at everything I did, but after a half-hour of conversation, it was obvious he was drifting away. I got up and followed him off that ridge, across a wide valley, onto another ridge and across it to another valley. Then the turkey did a left-wing 90 up the bottom of the valley and led me on a forced march for well over an hour. He walked out into a fresh clear-cut at the head of the hollow, onto open ground where I

A decoy can be a big help even on a close-up gobbler, as the author learned with a particular hard-hunted gobbler several years ago. The trick is getting the decoy out without getting burned.

couldn't follow without being seen, and there he set up shop.

I peeked at him from the edge of the clearing for 20 minutes. When it seemed fairly certain he was going to stay there a while, I belly-crawled 10 yards into the edge of the clearing and set up my only decoy while he strutted and gobbled behind a slash pile. He stayed out there for another two hours, gobbling back at my low-key calling. Eventually, though, he started moseying toward the decoy. I finally got him close enough for the shot, and he went down in a heap. While I stood on his head, I looked at my watch: It was 12 noon,

more than six hours after I'd made my first call to him. I later determined, from looking at a topo map, I'd followed that gobbler more than 5 miles before he found a place where he felt comfortable and where he thought he might call up a hen.

If you know the lay of the land, it's sometimes possible to get in front of one of these itchy-footed gobblers, as discussed elsewhere in this book. But it's not easy, because most of them cover ground pretty fast. Usually, the best you can hope for is to maintain contact until the bird gets to wherever he's going, then try to formulate a battle plan.

Calling is another challenge during second-season hunting. The thicker vegetation makes it necessary to call louder, but the battle-wariness of the surviving gobblers makes loud calling risky because you might spook the bird. A compromise is in order. Loud, aggressive calling is the ticket for cutting through the greenery and pulling a response out of a gobbler, but once you've got him located, softer, more subtle tactics are needed. In order for this softer calling to work, you usually have to cut the distance, and that's when you run up against the problem we discussed a few paragraphs ago: You have to get close enough for him to hear your softer calling, but not so close you bump him.

Creep in as tight as you dare on a late-season bird. If you think you can get to the next tree, then you're too far away from the bird. If you don't think you can, then you're probably about right.

The farther you are from a bird before you call to him, the greater the chances something will go wrong – a predator, a real hen, another hunter, an obstacle you don't know about. This is especially true in late-season hunting, when hard-pressured gobblers are reluctant because they've been spooked several times already that season. Maybe shot at as well. I've killed several gobblers that were carrying pellets from other hunters.

So get as close as you think you can, then get one tree closer. Next, resort to soft calling, clucks, purrs and soft yelps, and you'll be in good shape for most late-season situations.

Non-vocal turkey sounds are also highly effective for late-season hunting. I've had quite a few turkeys gobble at the sound of my footsteps in the leaves over the years, but I don't recall that ever happening when the woods were bare and open. It always occurs late in the season, when things are thick and you can accidentally walk up on a gobbler without spooking him.

It took a while, but eventually I figured out I could use that leaf-crunching sound to entice close-in gobblers to commit to those last few yards that brings them either into sight or into gun range. Over the last few seasons, I've taken several fine late-season gobblers by scratching in the leaves with my hand or imitating the sound of footsteps by crunching handfuls of leaves in the cadence of a turkey walking.

Decoys can be effective at any time (see Chapter 37 for more on this subject), but they're especially helpful in late-season hunting. Remember, your gobbler's hens have left him, and he's anxious to re-establish a relationship. Give a last-week-of-the-season longbeard a hen to look at – and maybe a jake to challenge his dominance – and you've gone a long way toward hanging a tag on that bird.

The bottom line is, don't give up in disgust when the turkeys enter that aggravating midseason lull. Just wait 'em out. They'll eventually start gobbling again, and by then, many of the less-dedicated hunters will have given up and gone fishing. That's when you can get out there and reap the rewards of the second season.

While a gobbler may or may not have a beard to match his age, spurs don't lie. Only old gobbers, 3 years old or more, have hooks like this one.

The author with a November South Dakota longbeard.

Abandoned home places are always interesting, and they sometimes also provide habitat diversity such as old field sites.

Hunting turkeys gives us a fine excuse to get "out there" and away from it all.

Typical Merriam's turkey habitat – brushy coniferous forest interspersed with wide, open country.

A barrel-mounted push-button call can be handy for close-in work.

A smoked wild gobbler, ready for the carving board.

Jim Spencer and Jill Easton with a pair of Kansas gobblers.

Jim Spencer took this fall gobbler by breaking up a flock of gobblers late one afternoon, then setting up and calling in one of the scattered flock early the next morning.

Vanity license plates all over the country attest to the passion of turkey hunters. This one, on the back of Brad Harris' Realtree-cloaked Suburban, reads "BLND-IN" – good advice for any turkey hunter.

The breakage pattern of turkey eggshells can tell you whether the eggs hatched successfully or were eaten by predators. When a hatching turkey pips the egg, it cuts a neat line around the shell, as is evident on the shells in the above left photo. The eggs in the right photo were broken by a predator. Note the irregular and random breakage pattern. In this case, the culprit was probably a crow.

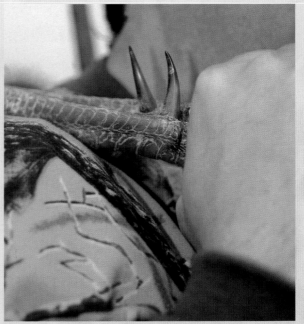

The old mining ghost town of Rush, on the Buffalo National River in Arkansas, is one of many places across the country where history and turkey hunting collide.

Rio Grande gobblers in the Texas Hill Country and the Flint Hills and Chautauqua Hills of Kansas often have blunt, broken spurs due to the rocky terrain. But elsewhere, Rios often develop impressive hooks. This bird was taken in the sandy, mesquite country of south Texas, not far from the Rio Grande itself.

Big lakes aren't the only types of water that provide access to good turkey hunting. A canoe or johnboat on a small stream can put a hunter into some pretty remote country.

The kind of turkey sign we like to find.

Nature has no redder red.

Ammunition manufacturers have made huge strides in developing efficient and deadly turkey loads over the past few years, with high-velocity and/or heavier-than-lead loads delivering extra knockdown power at longer ranges.

Decoys offer certain advantages, but the hunter who uses them must realize it's going to take him longer to set up (or change locations) on a turkey than the hunter who doesn't use decoys.

Be sure you have plenty of room in front of your setup to swing your gun freely. This sapling could cost this hunter a bird if it comes up too far to the right.

Whether you're planning to be there for 10 minutes or 10 hours, take a few seconds to move limbs and sticks out of the way of your butt and legs before you set up. You'll be more comfortable, and that means you'll be able to sit there longer without moving.

Turkey hunting is usually thought of as a solitary sport, but two hunters working together are often more effective than one.

Setting out a decoy or two and spending the midday hours on a known strutting or loafing area is a productive technique on those frustrating days when they're not gobbling.

Hay bales, either small and square or large and round, make serviceable makeshift blinds for open-land hunting.

A Rio Grande hen drinks from a "tank" in south Texas.

Concentrating your efforts near travelway bottlenecks like saddles, fencelines and woods roads through thick cover is good strategy when turkeys aren't gobbling.

Specialty turkey shotguns should deliver dense, even patterns at long range. Extended choke tubes, angle-ported barrels, lengthened forcing cones and other aftermarket items and modifications can improve the pattern of almost any gun.

A camera should be part of every serious hunter's turkey hunting equipment.

Camping in the turkey woods – whether you're a hunter or not, it's an enjoyable way to spend some time in the spring of the year.

The remains of an old wagon in the north Missouri prairie country. Few people besides turkey hunters see old artifacts like this.

A nest broken up by a predator. The breakage pattern here suggests a mammal – skunk or raccoon would be a good bet.

Late in the morning, a crow call is better than owling for eliciting shock gobbles.

Just checking. The author often hopscotches from one small public area to the other during mid- to late morning, trying to find a workable gobbler by using locator calls and covering as much ground as possible.

You don't need a lot of money to be rich.

Decoys, legal in every state except Alabama, are effective for many turkey hunting situations. When you hunt in open country, a decoy or two can help pull gobblers across long, open areas and get them in position for a shot.

Hevi-Shot entered the turkey hunting market in 2002. Despite its irregularities in shot size and other imperfections (note the two pellets in the front with tiny pellets attached), this heavier-than-lead tungsten alloy delivers devastating downrange punch. The author predicts Hevi-Shot or an equivalent load will own the market in 10 years.

These turkey eggs were broken by a crow.

Combining a turkey hunt with a fishing trip is a good idea, provided you can tear yourself away from turkey hunting long enough to go fishing. Killing a turkey helps, particularly when you're hunting in a state with a one-bird-a-day rule, or when you're hunting in a morning-only state.

The Ouachita National Forest of Arkansas and Oklahoma was one of the first large public hunting areas in the country to have good turkey numbers in the late 1960s and early 1970s. Now, many other national forests and wildlife management areas throughout the country provide good turkey hunting.

A fall turkey hunt can often be combined with a deer hunt, especially when using archery gear.

Jakes often run in gangs. Although they're often whipped into submission and kept from the breeding activities by dominant gobblers, they still have all the urges.

Radio-telemetry studies have unwrapped much of the mystery of turkey management that plagued early wildlife biologists.

The fastest-growing segment of the hunting population is women, and they're proving they have what it takes to be turkey hunters.

Although turkeys can usually get enough water from their foods, in hot or dry weather they need permanent water sources. Ponds can fill this need, and give you a place to fish as well.

Trap-and-transplant efforts by state and federal agencies have restored turkeys to almost all their former range, and to lots of places where the birds never existed before.

Gobblers get the mating urge earlier than hens.

Topo maps are an invaluable aid for the turkey hunter, no matter where he's hunting and no matter how well he thinks he knows the territory.

Removing the sinew from the adductor muscles of a turkey's breast (the long, small muscle that lies against the keel) makes the already-tender meat even more so. It's easy to do with a small, sharp knife – don't cut, just use the edge of the blade to scrape the meat away from the sinew.

Face paint, while messy and a lot of bother, isn't a bad idea, especially if you're in a camp for a few days and don't have to be seen in public.

If there's a creek or other potential obstacle between you and a gobbling turkey, the best move is to get across it if there's any way possible.

Outdoor writer Monte Burch shows off the white tail and rump of a fine Merriam's gobbler.

The remote bottomlands along the lower Mississippi River were one of the last strongholds of the Eastern wild turkey during the gloomy days of the 1930s and 1940s. This gobbler lived in the Mississippi River bottoms not far below the mouth of the Arkansas River and was a direct descendant of one of those remnant flocks that hung on there.

New York outdoor writer Glenn Sapir with an Osceola gobbler, the first leg of a Grand Slam.

A successful early-morning hunt in the lower Mississippi River bottoms.

Marty Eye knows what he's doing when it comes to turkey hunting. After the author blew one chance at a gobbler by sneezing at an inopportune moment, Eye found another one.

Keep a journal of your turkey hunting experiences. It's not only a source of enjoyable reading during those long months between springs; it will also help you learn more about turkey hunting.

If a hunter had one of each brand and style of diaphragm caller on the market, he'd have to build a spare room to store them in.

Orange hats and/or vests may make you feel foolish in the turkey woods, but when you're moving from place to place and not working a turkey, it's not a bad idea to wear one or the other.

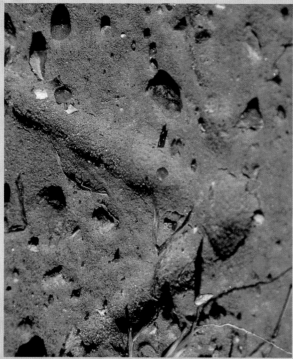

This track is smoking fresh. This fact can be determined because the damp soil retains the pattern of tiny ridges and creases on the turkey's toes. Evaporation and subsequent crumbling of the track's lining usually eliminates these details from a turkey track within an hour or two.

Spurs come in all shapes and sizes, even on old, dominant birds.

Chapter 24

Bad-Weather Turkeys

When it's raining, or when vegetation is still wet following a rain, turkeys avoid heavy cover and gravitate toward short-grass openings.

The spring turkey season was 4 days old, and there hadn't been a dry day yet. It may be true that April showers bring May flowers, but they don't do much to help turkey hunting. I was getting pretty disgusted with this whole string of lousy weather. I'm sure I wasn't alone.

Apparently the turkeys were tired of it, too, because when I went out on the fifth morning, anticipating more silent turkeys and yet another soaking from the threatening clouds that blotted out the stars, I ran into one of the gobblingest turkeys I've ever heard.

He was already gobbling when I got out of the truck at first light on that gray morning, but the wind was blowing so hard I could barely hear him. If he hadn't been upwind, I'd never have known he was there. I was running a little late that morning because of my discouraged state of mind, and he was on the ground before I could get to him. But it didn't make any difference in the rate or intensity of his gobbling. He was really hammering, sounding off every few seconds. He gobbled at wind gusts, woodpeckers, cardinals, owls, everything. If I'd blown a police whistle or shouted the Pledge of Allegiance, I believe he'd have gobbled at that, too.

I got in as tight on him as I could in the open woods, about 150 yards. When I started calling, he gobbled at every peep I made. He quickly closed

Turkeys will often gobble ferociously at thunder, but that doesn't mean they'll come to your calling.

One of the prime times to be on the hunt is when the sun pops out right after a heavy rain.

the gap to that familiar, maddening 60 yards or so, and I saw him once or twice as he came. But then he hung up just out of sight and just out of range, in a little bottom fringed with a screen of low-hanging stuff. I think I might have been able to see him if the light had been better, but it was pretty dim at ground level and I just wasn't able to make him out.

I never had any doubt as to exactly where he was, though, because he ripped off gobble after gobble. At one point, I clocked him at 17 gobbles in 60 seconds. He sounded as exasperated at the weather as I was, and he seemed determined to scare the clouds away.

If that was his plan, he failed at it. He moved back and forth in a 50-foot pattern in that little bottom while the dark-blue line of a serious thunderstorm advanced on us, flashing lightning and belching out thunderclaps one after the other. Each time the thunder would roll, the turkey would gobble six or seven times as fast as he could pull his head back. He gobbled until he literally ran out of air, and the last gobble in each series came out as a strangled little warble. But as soon as he could suck in another lungful of air, he'd start it all again.

And then the blue cloud line was on top of us, and the bottom fell out. When it did, that turkey shut up as quickly and as completely as if one of those lightning bolts had struck him dead.

Up until then, that hunt was an almost identical replay of a hunt I'd made three or four years earlier in that same general area. In that first hunt, though, when the rain started and the gobbler shut up, I gave up in disgust and went back to camp, wet as a carp and mad as a trapped bobcat. But over the intervening years I'd thought a lot about that hunt, and I'd made a contingency plan if such a situation ever arose again. So, this time, I didn't go straight back to camp.

This time, I gave the gobbler a few minutes to get good and wet, and also to make sure he wasn't going to gobble again. When he didn't, I got up and eased straight toward where I'd heard him last, carrying my shotgun at port arms and squinting through the curtain of rain that coursed off the bill of my cap.

He was humped up like a wormy coon hound when I first saw him, squatting under an ironwood bush and looking as miserable as you'd ever expect a turkey to look. He was so caught up in

Nasty weather doesn't put a stop to turkey activities. Unlike turkey hunters, turkeys don't have the option of going inside to wait it out. Savvy turkey hunters don't do that, either.

his own misery, he didn't even see me coming. I closed the gap to 25 yards, stopped, got the gun on him and yelled "Hey, turkey!" When his head snapped upright, I squeezed the trigger, and subsequently I carried back to camp the wettest gobbler I've ever seen this side of the scalding tub.

Call that a dirty trick if you want to. You won't be the first. I call it "assessing a bad situation and making it work" making lemonade, if you will. You bet, I'd much rather have called that gobbler all the way to the gun and taken him that way, but the weather precluded it and it just wasn't going to happen. By *carpe*-ing that wet *diem*, though, I turned it into a memorable and successful hunt. It's an example of the unorthodox tactics that can work for you when the weather is less than ideal – and incidentally, that same tactic has worked for me on two more occasions since.

The sad fact is, most of us don't have enough free days available during the all-too-brief spring season that we can afford to bypass any of them

because of some trifling, piddling, unimportant factor like lousy weather. If you work five days a week and can only hunt on weekends, and it's raining on Saturday … well, what are you gonna do? If you're as addicted to this sport as I am, it's a no-brainer: You're going to go hunting. It won't be as enjoyable as a bluebird day, and your odds may not be as good, but they're a lot better than if you don't go at all.

Your rainy-day odds really aren't all that much worse than normal, though. It's true that if it's raining at daybreak, there's a good chance the turkeys are going to stay in the trees later than normal. The harder the rain, the more likely they are to stay on the roost. However, if it's not raining at daylight, in most cases the turkeys will fly down even if it's cloudy and threatening rain. And even if it is raining, unless it's the sort of stuff that made Noah build his boat, they're eventually going to hit the ground and go about their business. It's the only way they have of making a living.

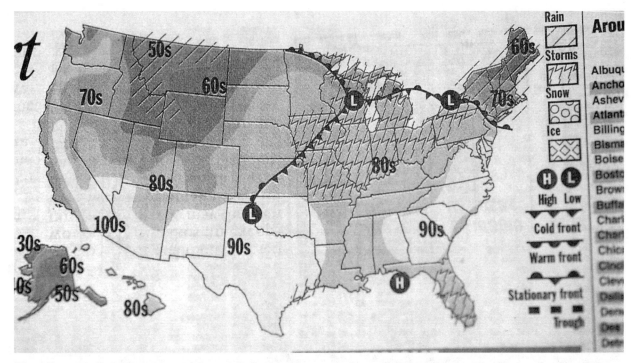

Frontal activity bringing rainy, cooler or windy weather – sometimes all three – is a standard part of turkey seasons throughout the country. Learn to deal with these weather shifts and you'll tag more turkeys.

But they often conduct that business differently in bad weather, and that's where many hunters miss the – no pun intended – boat. In most cases when vegetation is wet, turkeys gravitate toward short-grass pastures, plowed fields or other areas where they can move around without brushing against wet bushes and grass. A turkey is pretty much waterproof until he brushes against something, at which point moisture can break through the bird's feathers the same way it breaks through a canvas tent when you brush against it. So the savvy wet-weather hunter will concentrate his hunting efforts near these open places, to give turkeys their most comfortable and least traumatic approach options, and because it's where they're going to be in the first place.

Where fields and pastures are scarce or absent, turkeys tend to use roads and open ridgelines more heavily in wet weather. If you set up on a rainy-day gobbler in heavy woods, your odds of calling that bird in will vastly improve if there's an open, brush-free travel lane between you and the turkey. Calling him through wet brush is theoretically possible, but attempting it is a very good way to save your tag for another rainy day.

Another quirk of wet-weather turkeys – the hunt at the beginning of this article aside – is they don't usually gobble as much as nice-weather birds. The exception is when there's thunder. Even when they do gobble on these days, it's harder for you to hear them. And, of course, it's almost impossible to hear a turkey approaching your position through wet leaves if he's not gobbling. You won't hear him walking, that's for sure, and I've found out the hard way that the sound of dripping water masks the sound of drumming almost perfectly.

Naturally, this puts a pretty big crimp in your game, since hearing is so much a part of turkey hunting. Which, of course, is another reason hunting near open areas is a good idea. You'd be surprised how many turkeys you can locate by easing slowly and quietly along the edges of fields and roads, using binoculars to scan the territory as far ahead as you can see. Once you've spotted a gobbler, you can then use whatever cover is available to get into the best possible position before trying to call the bird.

Bad weather doesn't have to be wet. Windy conditions are chronic during the spring turkey season in many parts of the country, whether it's raining or not. In the East, extremely windy days often shut down both turkeys and turkey hunters, but in, say, South Dakota, turkeys would go extinct if they didn't court and breed in the wind. It blows there almost all the time or so it seems.

I've hunted in Kansas, South Dakota, Colorado, New Mexico, Oklahoma and Texas on days when it was hard to stand upright in unprotected areas. I've also called in and killed gobblers in those states in wind so strong I considered leading the stationary bird as if it were a flying duck, so the wind wouldn't blow my shot string off course.

Hunting in the wind is another case where visual contact with turkeys becomes important. On many occasions on windy days, I've called to turkeys I could see, and it was obvious that the birds never heard me. On other occasions, it's been obvious that they did hear me, because they perked up and gobbled back at my call, and although I could see the gobble, I couldn't hear it. This happened once in New Mexico at a range of less than 75 yards.

Wind like that puts you at even more serious a disadvantage than rain, in my opinion. The best way to deal with wind, first of all, is to concentrate your hunting in sheltered areas such as valley bottoms or creek beds. Try to locate a gobbler visually at a distance, and then try to get as close as possible, preferably upwind or at least crosswind of the bird, before calling. If you have no choice except to call upwind to a gobbler in high wind, get absolutely as close as possible, then use a box or tube call so you can get maximum volume. Call hard and long, and maybe a few notes will leak through a momentary quirk or lull in the wind and reach the bird. Leave the soft stuff for other hunts; it's impossible to overcall to a gobbler if the bird can't hear you.

Many turkey hunters carry some sort of rain gear. I used to be one of them, but gave it up as a bad effort. I've tried everything from $3 Army surplus ponchos to $200 breathable rain suits, and nothing works. If the material is made so the rain can't get in, then the sweat can't get out, no matter what the manufacturer says. So with rain suits or without them, you're wet. I just dress normally, make the best of it and try to find shelter if it rains too hard. On many occasions, I've waited out a sudden shower holed up in a roofed deer stand, like a possum in a hollow tree.

Regardless of your particular method of dealing with bad weather, the most important thing is that you do indeed deal with it. Turkey season is short and each day is precious. Just cowboy up and get out there. That's the best strategy of all.

Hunting in the wind is tough. Your calls don't carry as far, so it's wise to use loud, high-pitched calls to cut through the wind. Often, you won't hear a gobbler unless he's right on top of you.

Rainsuits seem to be some sort of expensive, elaborate joke, like neoprene waders. Both leave you just about as wet as if you'd not worn them at all.

Chapter 25

Living on Turkey Time

On those days when turkeys aren't gobbling, it's a good idea to set up in an open area where you can see them coming even if they're quiet.

For once, a silent gobbler showed up where I predicted he'd be. It doesn't happen often. This particular gobbler ghosted onto the ridgetop at 7:50 a.m., barely 50 yards from where I'd been sitting since flydown time.

Even though I was expecting him, his arrival nonetheless startled me. Therefore, I did what I often do when I'm startled while turkey hunting: I promptly forgot everything I ever knew about killing turkeys.

While I watched, with my skull full of mush churning ineffectually in an effort to come up with some sort of plan, the bird slowly closed the distance. As he moved regally toward me along the narrow, level ridgetop, I took the opportunity to make my first mistake. All I had to do was remain motionless for a few more seconds and he would have walked behind a big oak tree, giving me plenty of time to raise my gun. But instead, I started easing my gun up while he was still in the open, and of course he picked me out.

That's when I made the second mistake. The gobbler stopped abruptly and ran his head up in that all-too-familiar I'm-about-to-vacate-these-premises pose. And rather than making a slow, smooth, non-threatening movement that just might have worked, I tried to quick-draw him, jerking the gun the rest of the way to my shoulder in an awkward, panicky maneuver reminiscent of a rabbit hunter stumbling into an unexpected covey of quail.

Here's a rule of thumb for your future turkey hunting reference: Don't do that.

You get three strikes in baseball, but one strike is usually the limit when a gobbler is in sight. I had just taken two wild swings in as many seconds, and the result was inevitable.

Back in camp, I took what comfort I could from the fact that, in one sense, I had already beaten the gobbler before I gave him the chance to beat me. I had followed his movements for two mornings, listening to him from across the valley as he climbed the ridge. I had a pretty good notion he'd show up on that same ridge again the next day, and I figured he'd get there sometime in the midmorning. Sure enough, he did.

I had set foot in that part of the world for the first time only three days before. I'd located the gobbler on his roost at first light two mornings before the season opened. By studying a set of topographical maps for several nights in my living room two states away, and by doing some on-the-ground reconnaissance the day I got there, I'd located several likely roosting areas. This bird had been sleeping in one of them, and I'd kept up with his movements by the sound of his gobbling until he wound up on the ridgetop at midmorning both days. Both days, he was back at the same roost at sundown.

This was a patternable turkey, and poring over my maps by the campfire the night before opening day, I had decided on the most logical travel route between the bird's roosting area and his daytime strutting area. At first light on the big day, I was positioned in what I thought was a good spot along that route.

It was a good spot, but he ignored my calls and got by me anyway. I let him go and took rounders on him, hustled to the ridgetop and set up again to await his majesty's arrival. I guessed right, had him in my lap and then let him beat me. Or, rather, I beat myself. There's a difference between losing the game and throwing it away.

Two days later, I got a second chance at that same gobbler. This time he again ignored me when he flew down, and again I retreated and set up as close as I could to the area he'd been using for a strut zone. This time, I didn't try to quick-draw him when he showed up. Drop by my office some time and I'll show you his spurs.

There are many important aspects of successful turkey hunting, and good calling certainly ranks high on the list. That's why five chapters of this book are devoted to the subject. Possessing the

Jill Easton with a silent gobbler she took by setting up in a known strutting area – in this case, an old log yard used in a recent logging operation.

183

ability to sit absolutely still is another important thing. But if you want my take on the subject – and I guess you do, since you're reading this book – the most important factor in targeting and harvesting a particular gobbler is patterning the bird's movements and behavior, and then plotting your hunting strategy accordingly.

Patterning a gobbler isn't all that hard, but it is time-consuming. And that's why not many hunters do it; they're either unable or unwilling to invest the time. It's understandable; most turkey hunters have limited vacation and off time, and they'd rather save it for the actual hunt instead of spending part of several mornings following one or more gobblers around as they go about their business.

However, if you want to be the most deadly turkey hunter you can be, you'll pattern turkeys before you hunt them, whenever possible. Patterning is often the only real chance you'll have at tagging many of those old, sharp-spurred patriarchs that have survived on their wits through four or five hunting seasons.

Patterning a turkey is an advanced form of scouting. And like other scouting, it requires topographical maps for maximum effectiveness. Once you have the maps of your hunting area in hand and have located several potential roost sites, it's time to get started. Plain old listening comprises the first step of patterning a gobbler, but there's a lot more to it than just finding the roosting places of a few birds. It's keeping track of what they do after they fly down that's the most important part of patterning.

Once you've located a strong-gobbling turkey, try to move in fairly close to him, but don't push the envelope the way you would if you were hunting him. You don't want to bump him; that would destroy your plan. Get within 200 yards or so, depending on the terrain, and wait for him to fly down. Your objective is to be close enough so you can determine the gobbler's direction after he hits the ground.

This part should go without saying, but I'll say it anyway: Do not, under any circumstances, call to the gobbler, not even with owl calls or other locators. You've already got him located; don't screw it up. You don't want to influence his behavior in any way. You just want to figure out how he likes to spend his day.

Take note of the time he leaves the roost (relative to sunrise, not the clock). If you can, trail along behind him or on a parallel course, maintaining your distance from the turkey and attempting to pinpoint his location on your topo map as he travels. Mark each location on the map and note the time he was there.

Often, as we all know, a gobbler will shut up not long after leaving the roost. If and when this happens, maintain your position and just listen. Sometimes I'll bring along a book to read for just this eventuality. You no longer know where your gobbler is, so any attempt on your part to find him might spook him instead. Sometimes a gobbler that goes silent right off the roost will crank up again an hour or three later. When he does this, he'll usually be on or near one of his favored strutting areas (most dominant gobblers have several). This is what you were sitting around and waiting for, alternately napping and reading the latest Tom Kelly book. Mark the gobbler's location on your map, note the time and get out of there as quietly as possible.

On your next patterning trip, again try to locate your gobbler on the roost. If you hear him in the same general area, forget about him for a while and go try to find another bird or two. Then, along toward the time when turkey No. 1 started gobbling from his strutting area, go to a good listening spot and see if he's there again. Use a crow or owl call if necessary, but only sparingly, and if you hear him gobble even once, don't call at him again. If he's close to the same area the second time you find him, you're in business.

A dominant gobbler, as mentioned, will usually have two, three or even more favorite strutting areas, and he'll rotate from one to another on a schedule that may be regular as clockwork or completely erratic. If your scouting time permits, you may be able to nail down more than one of these favored areas, but since you can only hunt one of them at a time, anyway, there's really not much point in it.

Except for one thing: Locating these favored strutting areas will help you in future years. Radio-telemetry studies in Arkansas, Florida and elsewhere have revealed that a gobbler returns to the same strutting areas each spring until he's either deposed or killed. Even after one gobbler is dead and gone, whatever it was about the site that made it attractive to him will also make it attractive to other gobblers, and another bird will almost certainly take over the spot.

On a patterning trip long ago, I followed a talkative gobbler over a long route through the Ouachita Mountains of western Arkansas. He gobbled enough for me to keep track of him from first light until after 6:30 that evening, and during the course of the day he visited four widely spaced strutting areas. He stayed at each one for periods of time ranging from 35 minutes to more than two hours.

Not only did I kill that gobbler that spring on the first of those strutting areas he showed me, but in the years since, I've taken almost a dozen other gobblers from those four places that gabby, traveling tom stopped that day. They were natural showoff places for him, and they're still natural showoff places for his great-great-great-grandchildren.

Patterning a gobbler is valuable for right-off-the roost, early-morning hunts, but where it really shines is during midday. When they first hit the ground, gobblers are often unpredictable and are liable to strike off in practically any direction, whether there's a hen calling to them or not. But after morning's bloom is history, they often settle down and are much more likely to follow a pre-established route – or, at least, show up in a pre-established favorite place.

Patterning is also valuable for late-season hunting, after many of the gobblers have already been harvested and the wise ones left are even wiser. An old gobbler will generally continue to follow the schedule you discovered through pre-season patterning, making his rounds just as he did before the season started. But he may do so silently or nearly so, especially in heavily hunted areas. If you don't have anything going, setting up near one of these favored strutting areas and doing some soft, contented calling will give you a pretty good chance to fill a tag.

In fact, any day the turkeys aren't gobbling is an excellent day to play the pattern game. The turkeys are still out there, you know, even when they won't even give you a courtesy gobble. Blundering around looking for one of them is usually fruitless, unless you consider it fruitful to bump a bunch of turkeys.

If you know where they like to strut, you might just arrange for one of them to bump into you instead of the other way around.

There's not much sense in blundering around through the woods when turkeys are in a quiet mood. You'll spook birds, but you won't get many of them to answer you. Instead, get a good book, blind up in an area you know turkeys are using, and wait them out.

185

Chapter 26

When He's in Sight

Sometimes when you're going to a distant gobbler, you'll find yourself out of hearing at times during your approach, and this can happen in flat country as well as in the hills. Always take a compass bearing on a gobbler before beginning your approach, and come at him at a slight angle rather than going directly toward the bird.

I was hunting a remote walk-in area on a slow, uneventful spring morning, and I'd been covering a lot of ground and prospecting for more than two hours without hearing a gobble. When I finally heard this turkey, though, he seemed like a good candidate. I wish I could tell you I raised him by my expert calling ability, but that's not how it happened. He was gobbling on his own and more or less raised himself, climbing into range of my hearing by coming up the opposite side of a long ridge that lay across the valley.

The first two or three gobbles were faint and muffled, but as he gained altitude and crested the ridge, the sound grew clearer and louder. Once he reached the top, I could hear him plainly, since there was nothing but air between us. He started gobbling frequently then, and after a while it seemed he was happy to stay more or less in the same place.

He wasn't far away, but I can't fly. The only way I could get to him was by crossing a deep, steep valley, and I knew it was going to be rough going. But he was gobbling, you know?

When I dropped into the valley on the compass bearing I'd shot, it wasn't long before I couldn't hear him any more. I stuck to my course, stumbling over logs and rocks, pushing hard to get there as quickly as possible. When I was two-thirds of the way up the opposite slope, I began to hear him again, still gobbling from the same spot.

Altering my course so as not to come up right in his face, I reached the spine of the ridge about 75 yards west of him. I was able to get that close thanks to a jumble of rocks that hid my movements as I crept onto the flat and carefully made my set. He double-gobbled at the first soft run of yelps, and I heard him drumming just before I saw him come around the rockpile, strutting and moving steadily toward me at a range of 50 yards.

This is perfect, I remember thinking. My gun was on him, and I watched as he closed the gap. Forty-five yards, then 40, then 30. I could have dropped him, but it had taken me so much time and energy to get to him, I didn't want to end it that quickly. At 25 yards he walked behind a cedar blowdown and stopped. I was looking down the barrel at his big white head through a softball-sized hole in the blowdown, and he was staring suspiciously at me through the same hole. I could have shot him then, too, but I decided to hold off until he cleared the brushpile so I could watch him go down. As confident as a hawk pinning a field mouse, I waited calmly for him to move.

That's when I blinked.

The next thing I knew, the turkey was rocketing off the side of the mountain. No putts, no warning, just an explosion of violent motion and flying leaves, and he was gone. I struggled to my feet in time to watch him set his wings and sail across the deep valley to the ridge where I'd been standing when I first heard him.

That was many springs ago, and I've replayed it in my mind a thousand times. I still have a hard time believing it happened. I'm certain I made absolutely no body movement, and he couldn't have seen it anyway because I was hidden by brush. All I could see of that gobbler was his technicolor head, and all he could see of me was my face, hand and gun barrel. And he got away because I blinked my eyes.

Turkey hunters all over the country have similar tales regarding the uncanny eyesight and unforgiving paranoia of these great birds. I've heard hundreds of them, and you have, too. If you'll listen to most of these tales about the ones that got away, it doesn't take long to figure out that most of them involve a gobbler that was already in sight of the hunter when it spooked. Getting a gobbler to answer the call is relatively easy, but calling him those final few yards into sure shotgun range is a lot tougher.

A big part of the reason many hunters have trouble with that second half of the job is they don't think far enough ahead when they set up on a gobbler. The tendency of most hunters, inexperienced

When he's close, don't even blink.

By setting up so that an approaching gobbler is already in gun range when he comes into view, you can neutralize his amazingly acute eyesight and tilt the odds a little more in your favor.

If you think a seat cushion is a luxury item on a turkey hunt, think again. It can help you sit still during those long, agonizing minutes when he's in sight but still not killable.

Sit in the shade, wear good camo and choose a setup that gives you a wide backrest so you won't be silhouetted.

and veterans alike, is to choose a calling position that affords a good view. After a quarter-century of chasing gobblers, I still have to fight that tendency in my own hunting. Other experienced hunters have told me they do, too.

It's an understandable urge. We want to be able to see a long way, and we want to watch our quarry come in. That may be the appropriate strategy for deer hunting, but a turkey isn't a deer. If you can see him, he can see you. Twitch a muscle – or blink an eye – and it's over.

The best setup on a turkey, most of the time, is where you can't see the approaching bird until he's in shotgun range. Setting up just below the crest of a ridge, for example, is a good technique for a gobbler that's on top or is coming up the other side. Using a rockpile, log, treetop or other obstacle also works at times, as it did for me that long-ago morning. I beat that turkey, and I'd have killed him if I'd taken the shot at the first opportunity – or even the second.

By using this strategy, you neutralize the gobbler's amazingly acute eyesight, and you rob him of the opportunity to use a long, slow, cautious approach to scrutinize every leaf, twig and bump as he comes in. This is a good thing, because one of those bumps is going to be you.

Which is not to say he's going to gallop toward you because you're out of sight. Using the terrain this way may keep a gobbler from spotting you at long range, and it'll sometimes keep him from hanging out there at 80 to 100 yards, but it probably won't do much to speed up his approach. That's why it's very important to make yourself as comfortable as possible when you set up. You're liable to be there a long time. Even when a gobbler is in range, he's often not killable. You may have to wait for what seems like forever for him to move into the open or go behind a tree so you can swing your gun barrel.

Part of getting comfortable is selecting the right place to sit. Soft pine needles or peaty soil are best, but often a turkey hunter doesn't have the luxury of sitting where he wants to. Instead, he must sit where he has to. At the very least, if you have time, scoop out a slight depression for your butt and clear it of any rocks.

If you think a seat cushion is a luxury item on a turkey hunt, think again. It's a necessity. And a turkey vest with a back cushion also comes in handy on long setups, because the bark of an oak tree can get pretty rough when all that separates it from the skin of your back is the thickness of your shirt.

Check the ground out a foot or two from your butt, as well. At some point, you're going to need to raise your knees so you can rest the shotgun on them. Loose rocks, sticks or other uneven footing out there where your feet are going to be have been the salvation of more than one in-sight-but-not-in-range gobbler.

So much for creature comforts. What else can you do beforehand to reduce the chances of spooking a gobbler when he's in sight?

You can stick a few limbs in the ground and make a rudimentary blind, for one thing. Sometimes you can find a natural hide, but if not, it doesn't take much time or effort to cut a few leafy branches and stick them up in front of you.

These two photos, taken at different times of day at the same tree, illustrate the difference between sitting in the sun and sitting in the shade. Which do you think hides you better?

This can help immensely to break your outline and reduce your conspicuousness when a gobbler is staring a hole through you at 45 yards. Don't overdo it, because too much vegetation doesn't look natural in most turkey woods, and you don't want it to interfere with your vision. A little goes a long way.

If possible, set up between the turkey and the sun. This puts the glare at your back and in his eyes – the best of all possible worlds. Setting up with the sun off one shoulder is also acceptable, but the gobbler has a lot more chance of spotting you this way. If you have no choice except to set up facing the sun, try to pick a spot where there's enough vegetation or tree trunks to allow you to sit in the shade. You still won't be able to see as well as you need to, but sometimes it'll be the best you can do.

Sitting in the shade is important, no matter which direction the sun is. A turkey hunter is conspicuous as a bullfrog on a card table when he's in the sun, and every tiny body movement is spotlighted. I've killed some turkeys while sitting in bright sun and expect to kill some more before I'm through, but I never set up that way unless I have absolutely no choice.

When he's in sight, don't wiggle. You should have already had your gun on your knee and pointing in his general direction well before he got there; if you didn't, shame on you. If you have to move your gun barrel to get on him, wait until his head goes behind a tree before making your move, and then do it smoothly and quietly. And be cautious here. On quite a few occasions, I've had gobblers start to go behind a tree, then suddenly stop and crane their neck and head backwards to look around the trunk one last time before committing. Several of them burned me that way, but now I know better and I wait that extra half-second to make sure.

Calling is tricky when he's in sight. You've already gathered from reading the preceding portion of this book that I use a box or slate for most of my turkey calling, but not for close work in most cases. I keep a diaphragm call stuck in my cheek at all times, and I switch to it for close-range stuff, or to a pump-action yelper, which is easy to operate one-handed. Sometimes it's possi-ble to use a friction call when a gobbler is visible by laying the call on the ground and working it one-handed as well, but in my case, this has a tendency to produce inferior sounds.

Call sparingly, if at all, if you can see the gobbler – and never call when he's standing still and looking in your direction. Turkeys have an uncanny ability to pinpoint the source of a sound, and if he hears you call and is looking at the spot where it came from and doesn't see a hen, he's going to get suspicious.

It's probably not necessary to call at all when he's in sight. If you pulled him that far, he'll eventually come the rest of the way. However, if he doesn't, and you feel you absolutely have to call or bust, do so only when the turkey is moving or gobbling. He can't pinpoint the sound as well that way.

Never try to quick-draw on a turkey. The best that'll happen is you'll be shooting at a rapidly departing bird. If he handcuffs you and won't hide his head so you can get the gun on him, wait until he's in the open and then *smoothly and gradually* swing the gun into position. This is a last-ditch technique and one you should never try unless you have reason to believe the gobbler is about to leave, but it will sometimes work. The gobbler will almost always see the movement, but because it's gradual instead of jerky and violent, he'll probably run his head up and stare at you for a second or two before starting to leave. You should have time to get off a shot at an erect, fairly motionless target. But don't dawdle; once you decide to make that move, things are going to start happening pretty quick.

Patience and forethought are the two keys to closing the deal on a gobbler when he's in sight. Think ahead and take care of as many variables as you can beforehand, and after he shows up, bide your time and don't do anything stupid. Keep as still as the tree you're leaning against, be extremely judicious with your calling, and wait for the right moment to make your move.

Oh, and one last thing: Don't blink.

While it's possible to successfully work a friction call by laying it on the ground and working it one-handed, a better option when a gobbler is close is to switch to a diaphragm call.

Chapter 27

Boating to Your Gobbler

When you're hunting near a large body of water, simple acoustics dictate that most of the turkeys you hear will be on the other side. By using a boat, you can cover both sides of the waterway and eliminate that particular problem. Of course, you still have to outsmart the turkey, but at least you'll be in a position to do it.

This gobbler created some minor problems by roosting near a lake where the bank sloped so gradually, it was impossible to get the boat all the way to dry land. Simple solution: Take off your boots.

It was a gobbling session as aggressive as any I've heard. The three turkeys cranked up in full darkness, almost half an hour before the first blush of light in the east. Well before normal gobbling time arrived, each of them had already gobbled at least a hundred times.

The birds were roosted together in a ridgetop stand of big pines only 250 yards away, close enough for me to have been set up on them in an ideal calling position in a matter of two or three minutes. I only had one small problem: 200 of the 250 yards between us consisted of cold, deep water. I was hunting near the shore of a large hill-country reservoir in western Kentucky, and one of the lake's many narrow arms snaked up the valley that separated me from the gobblers. I could have fired my gun and rained shot down on their heads from where I stood, but the creek arm extended more than 5 miles up the valley. It would have taken me at least three hours to get around there on foot. Those turkeys were as safe from me as if they'd roosted in Pennsylvania.

There was always the remote possibility of calling one of them across the water, of course. There were no other gobblers sounding off within hearing distance, and anyway, I was sucked into the vortex of their ferocious gobbling. I sat down and gave it a try.

You'll get a gobbler to cross a wide expanse of water like that every so often, but you'll win a long-shot trifecta every so often, too. It happens, and it may be worth a try if you're already at the track, but don't bet the mortgage on it. The turkeys cluster-gobbled at every call I made, and when it was light enough they left the roost and came down toward the edge of the lake. Twice I even saw one of them as he strutted in a little open spot in the trees across the bay. I can see the moon, too, but I can't shoot it with my 12 gauge, and my only profit that morning was practice in my ability to endure frustration.

I've had similar experiences on many other turkey hunts in probably seven or eight states. I expect you've had them as well. It seems every time I get within a quarter-mile of a hard-to-cross body of water, almost every turkey I hear will be on the other side of it. (See Chapter 29 for more on this.)

There's at least a partial explanation. Every experienced hunter knows it's much easier to hear the turkeys on the next ridge than those sharing the ridge with you. You don't have any tree trunks or wrinkles in the ground getting in the way of the

Small mountain streams often wind through prime turkey country. A canoe is just the ticket for this type of hunting.

sound waves, and the audio just works out better. This is especially true when the next ridge lies across a lake or river, because sound carries better over water. Habitat and turkey numbers being equal on both sides of the water, over the long haul you'll hear more unreachable gobblers than reachable ones.

This is a decided disadvantage for the land-bound hunter, but there's a good way to combat it: Start those close-to-water hunts from a boat. By adding a boat to the picture, you transform the water from a barrier into an approach route, and you also gain the advantage of being able to hear turkeys equally well on both sides of the waterway.

The conventional wisdom of modern-day turkey hunting is to find a high listening point that overlooks one or more potential roosting areas. Obviously, that's impossible when you use a boat, because all the turkey roosts in the area are going to necessarily be higher than your position at water level. But that disadvantage is outweighed by the two advantages mentioned above, plus one more: In a boat on open water, you're not closely surrounded by the profusion of lush spring growth that is so effective at dampening sound. I've heard turkeys gobbling at a measured 2 miles across open water on a calm morning, and that's much farther than you can hear a turkey from the best ridgetop listening post in the world.

What type of boat? That depends on the situation. When hunting around big reservoirs like Lake Ouachita in Arkansas, Truman Lake in Missouri or Lake Barkley in Kentucky and Tennessee, a bass boat is probably the best craft because of its speed and seaworthiness. A faster boat will let you cover more water and therefore more good listening areas during gobbling time, and big lakes can get pretty rough if it's windy.

On the other hand, a bass boat is sadly out of place on a small mountain stream, and these small headwater creeks are sometimes ideal for water-based hunts. Here, the canoe or johnboat is king. By launching at one access point and taking out at another farther downstream, the turkey hunter can borrow a page from the float-tripper's book and penetrate areas an on-foot hunter would be hard-pressed to reach.

Overnight floats, as well as hunts lasting several days, are also possible with the aid of a canoe or johnboat. Many float streams flow through national forests or other public lands with good turkey populations, and by simply floating along with the current, it's possible to cover a good bit of territory in a short time. Naturally, this increases your chances of locating a gobbling turkey, and it can also put you in contact with turkeys that are less educated than their easier-to-reach cousins.

One of the most enjoyable turkey hunts I've ever made was a solitary three-day float through a wilderness area, on an Ozark stream I'm not going to name. The float distance was 22 miles, and it took me through some of the most beauti-

It's easy to hear turkeys from a canoe on a mountain stream, but climbing up to where they are can be a problem.

ful country I've ever seen, country made even more beautiful by the fact that during the whole three days, I saw only one other hunter. He was standing on a rock promontory overlooking a sweeping bend in the stream, listening for a gobbler and taking in the view.

He was just a little vertical, greenish-brownish line on the highest part of the rock, 600 or 700 yards away. He could have passed for a lightning-shattered snag if he hadn't raised an arm in response to my experimental wave from far below.

In my gravel-bar camp that night, I consulted my topo map and learned that the shortest route to that particular rock outcropping involved a hike of more than 4 miles from the wilderness boundary, through some of the roughest country between the Mississippi River and the Rockies. No wonder I only saw one other hunter in three days.

I didn't kill a turkey on that float trip, by the way. But I worked four gobblers and heard more than 20 others, and as far as I could tell I had every one of them all to myself. My two overnight gravel bar camps were perfect, and I had fresh-caught rock bass for supper both nights. Both mornings, I heard my first gobbler of the day while I was still puttering around camp, and both times, the birds were on the opposite side of the river. No problem, though, for a hunter with a canoe.

A hunt like that would be impossible on foot. The both-sides-of-the-stream factor is one thing,

of course, but equally important is the fact that I covered four or five times as much territory during prime gobbling time as I could have covered on foot. Using a boat geometrically increases your range.

Boats are also handy on larger streams. I've hunted by boat on the Arkansas, White, Osage, Tennessee, Missouri, Yazoo, Ouachita and Mississippi rivers, and there are some situations on these and other rivers when you either use a boat or you just don't hunt. Spring flooding can render all other forms of transportation less than useless, unless you happen to be a fish.

But it's during these very periods of flooding that you can often hunt river-bottom turkeys without competition from other hunters. Turkeys congregate on ridges and high spots that remain above the floodwaters, and the hunter with the right equipment to reach them can often find quality hunting.

The right equipment, in this instance, is usually a flat-bottomed aluminum johnboat 14 to 16 feet long and with a beam of 40 to 48 inches. These boats ride high on plane and have a shallow draft. With a trolling motor or with the outboard trimmed for shallow running, they can operate in less than a foot of water, and they can be just the ticket for weaving back through the flooded bottomland jungles to reach that hump of ground the gobblers are on. Carrying a small wooden or fiberglass "sneak-boat" (a modified Cajun

195

An overnight float trip through big country can get you to places few other turkey hunters are willing to go.

pirogue with a flat bottom) in the larger boat can also allow a hunter access to high ground that's unreachable with the johnboat. But if you do this, it's important to make sure you can find your way back to your bigger boat when the hunt is over.

Even at normal water levels, using a boat is often the best way to hunt these big-river systems. Bottomland habitat is often chock full of turkeys, but it's flat as a one-egg cake. That's a disadvantage for the turkey hunter because you can't hear a gobbler as far across flat, heavily forested land as you can when you have some elevation on him. This difficulty becomes even more pronounced as the season advances and the spring greenery gets thicker. Sometimes it's hard to hear an on-the-ground river-bottom gobbler for more than a couple hundred yards.

Just like on the big lakes, hunting from a boat is an advantage here because you can hear a bird farther in this flat country when he's still in the tree,

and you can cover a lot more territory by boat than by foot. And if you think that leafy, sound-absorbing spring growth is lush in the mountains, you ought to see it in the bottoms. Getting out on the water helps hugely in such places.

This was brought home to me one morning long ago. I was hunting from a boat on the lower White River in southeast Arkansas, floating through a long, straight reach at first light, when I heard a gobbler on the west bank. He was a considerable distance from the river, but because of the stillness of the morning, the open-water acoustics and all that, I could hear him and course him easily.

I got to the bank and started through the woods toward the bird without taking time to see if I could hear him from land. He was gobbling quite a bit, and I figured I'd pick him up somewhere along the way as I moved toward him.

Wrong. I plowed along through the greenery, stopping every 75 yards or so to listen and hoot, but the only things I heard were woodpeckers and blue jays. After 30 minutes, I returned to the river, figuring the gobbler had dummied up.

Wrong again. When I got back out into the middle of the river, I could clearly hear him again. He was still in his tree, gobbling lustily.

This time, I did it the way I should have in the first place: I took a compass bearing on the sound of his gobbling, went back to the bank and followed my compass bearing into the bottoms. I'd about decided he had shut up again when I heard him out there on the ragged edge of imagination, right along my compass line.

He weighed 21 pounds, pretty big for a river-bottom bird, and once I finally managed to find him, he proved to be one of those anxious, come-a-running birds that give you inflated ideas about your abilities as a turkey hunter.

As it turned out, he was roosted more than 700 yards from the river. I'd been within 150 yards of him when I gave up and went back to the boat the first time. I hadn't been able to hear him at that relatively short distance, even with him still in the tree, yet I could hear him plainly from nearly a half-mile away from the middle of the river.

On a few occasions, I've used float tubes to cross water to get to my turkey hunting spot. Usually, though, this has been only when I needed to cross a fairly narrow stream that was either too swift or too deep to wade. I tried a 3-mile turkey hunting tube float on a stream one time, and if I ever try it again, you can book me a one-way ride on the loony wagon. Float tubes, as it turns out, are much better suited to bream fishing and duck hunting than turkey floating. It was tough enough just keeping my gun, hunting vest and boots dry during the float (I was wearing waders in the tube), but then I heard a turkey on a ridgeline, went to him and, as bad luck would have it, killed the bird. And that's when the juggling act began.

He was a big, heavy gobbler, and I broke a wing when I shot him, so he was even more unwieldy than usual. By the time I floated down to my take-out point, the turkey was wet, I was wet, and the inner tube had sprung a leak and was about to sink with all hands on board. Try a float tube if you want to, but consider yourself warned.

Regardless of the situation in which you use a watercraft, you have options that aren't available to the landlubber. For one, it's much easier to change your angle of approach to a gobbler when

The big bottomland areas along large rivers such as the Mississippi and Mobile have excellent turkey populations, but hunting these birds can be difficult because of the abundance of sloughs and backwaters often found here.

Woods roads through the dense ground vegetation found in many river bottom areas are good turkey travelways.

197

you're on the water, and any hunter who's had to climb or descend a cliff or steep ridge to get to a bird will have no trouble appreciating the magnitude of this advantage. If you're floating along and you hear a gobbler atop a bluff, it's often possible to go one way or the other and climb to the bird along a much gentler slope. Avoiding other obstacles such as clear-cuts, rockslides, canebrakes or briar thickets is much easier as well.

Also, you often don't have as far to go to get to a gobbler when you hear him from a boat. You can usually cover part of the distance with the boat, and turkeys frequently roost near the water, anyway. This factor makes boat hunting easier for youngsters and injured or disabled hunters, all of whom usually have more trouble navigating rough terrain. Not all of the turkeys you hear from a boat will be easy to reach, but a good proportion of them will be.

Hunting from a boat, in many cases, also provides the opportunity for combination trips. My three-day wilderness float-hunt is a prime example; I caught dozens of smallmouths and several hundred panfish of five or six species during my trip, even though I did almost no fishing during the mornings. Carrying a trotline or two and running them at night and just before first light is another way to make an enjoyable turkey/fishing combo trip.

Of course, a boat isn't going to make you a better turkey hunter in and of itself. A turkey along a lake or river is still a turkey, and just because you can get to him doesn't mean you're going to tag him. But with a boat, you can reach pockets of less-pressured turkeys, and that always helps. Even where you're hunting harder-pressured gobblers, the simple fact that you're targeting a bird from the water side means you're more than likely coming at him from a direction he hasn't been approached before. That's not going to hurt your chances much, either.

All in all, boating to a gobbler is an effective hunting technique. No turkey hunter's equipment inventory is quite complete unless there's a boat in it.

Hunting from a boat provides the opportunity for combination hunting/fishing trips. In the boat with this hunter, in addition to turkey gear, are two rods and reels and a tackle box. Guess what she's going to do if the birds aren't gobbling?

A boat can be one of the most valuable pieces of a turkey hunter's equipment.

Chapter 28

Open-Land Gobblers

When you've done most of your turkey hunting in the heavily forested Eastern states, a trip to the Black Hills can be a confusing experience.

There wasn't so much as a blade of grass between the big Merriam's gobbler and us as he strutted 250 yards away. We'd heard this particular bird while he was still on the roost, but it hadn't done us much good. At the time, we were at the bottom of a ridge and the gobbler was on top. He was already on the ground with his hens, strutting in an overgrazed pasture that occupied the top of the ridge, before we could climb up there with him.

The sun wasn't even up yet, and already we were working under a heavy handicap. Back home, where I'd done most of my turkey hunting up to that time, I'd learned it was usually fairly easy to get to a gobbling turkey before he flew down. Here, in the much more open country of the Black Hills, things were somewhat different.

The gobbler was strutting with his hens at the edge of a steep drop-off bordering the far edge of the flat, bald ridgetop, and approaching him from the steep side was out of the question. We're talking *seriously* steep here. The best we could do was belly-crawl to the last scrubby ponderosas on our side of the open pasture, set up and hope for the best. The two trees we had our backs against were no bigger than goal posts at a high school football field. Our job was to call that gobbler to our ridiculously inadequate hide across 2 1/2 football fields worth of winter-grazed shortgrass prairie.

We managed it, but it took a while. My hunting partner was doing most of the calling that morning – and a good thing, too. I don't think I could have made enough sustained racket by myself to bring the gobbler across the pasture to the gun.

The buddy system can be especially effective in open country. Two sets of eyes are better than one when it comes to spotting distant gobblers.

Matter of fact, I don't think I'd have ever thought to attempt such constant calling.

My partner went through most of his inventory of turkey calls before hitting the right combination. Following the playbook, he started with soft yelps and purrs, and I chimed in with a few gentle, contented clucks now and then. We switched back and forth from one diaphragm to another. The turkey turned toward us and displayed, and even gobbled once or twice in our direction, but it was pretty clear he wasn't very interested.

Then we switched to friction calls and ran through three or four of them apiece, my buddy playing lead and me backing him up. We gradually increased the tempo as we progressed through the calls and, after almost an hour of nearly non-stop calling, we hit the gobbler's hot button. We were playing dueling box calls at the time, and when my buddy walked on my box call notes with a loud, raspy series of cutts and yelps, the gobbler finally broke out of his hang-up. Here he came, strutting slowly across the open ground, and 30 minutes after he took his first step in our direc-

tion, I pulled the trigger. He never broke out of strut all the way across the ridgetop, and he didn't gobble a single time after he started his move.

That successful South Dakota hunt illustrates two of the many differences between open-land turkey hunting and the big-woods version of the sport most of us know best in the East and South. On the minus side, in open country, it's often impossible to get as close to a gobbler as you'd like. The plus side is you can locate these open-land birds easier than woodland birds when they're not gobbling, and you often get to watch the bird respond – or not respond – to your calls. This gives you clues as to how to call and allows you to change calling strategies in an attempt to find something that will work.

Everybody has an opinion, and here's mine: The advantage provided by being able to see a gobbler's reaction to your calling far outweighs the disadvantage of having to set up farther from your bird. I offer that opinion based on the strength of having hunted open-land turkeys of all four United States subspecies: Merriam's in South Dakota, New

Mexico and Colorado; Rio Grandes in Texas, Oklahoma and western Kansas; Easterns in Mississippi, Missouri, Arkansas, Kentucky, Georgia, New York and eastern Kansas; and Osceolas in south Florida. I've been beaten far too often by these open-land birds to have any illusions about my level of skill at hunting them, but at least I consider myself a veteran open-land hunter.

When I started turkey hunting in the late 1970s, few hunters could make that claim. Open-land gobblers are a relatively recent phenomenon over much of the modern-day turkey range. As late as the 1950s, nobody thought turkeys would be able to thrive in open areas – not even Rios, Merriam's and Osceolas, all of which are more adapted to open spaces than Easterns. This belief is understandable; by the 1950s, turkeys had in large part ceased to survive in open places.

The biological crash that occurred during the first half of the 20th century left wild turkeys teetering on the brink of extinction. This is covered in a more detail in Chapter 2, but here's a thumbnail history in case you skipped it: Originally we had a lot of 'em; then we almost wiped 'em out; now we have a pretty good slug of 'em again.

By sometime in the 1930s, wild turkey populations were teetering on the ragged edge of extinction. By 1940, only Arkansas, Mississippi and Alabama had spring hunting seasons, and in retrospect, those states probably shouldn't have. By the time turkey populations finally bottomed out – probably in the late 1930s or early 1940s – the only places wild turkeys existed were on a few strictly protected large, private holdings and in the most-remote, hard-to-reach backwoods mountain valleys and river swamps. Leading up to this dismal time, turkeys had been exterminated from the vast majority of their range, and even in this remote backcountry, most of the easy ones got themselves killed.

More than anything else, it was this accelerated process of survival of the fittest that shaped the American wild turkey into the paranoid ghost he is today – but that's another story. What this process also did was plant a faulty idea in the heads of pioneer wildlife managers. Because the only places turkeys hung on were in large, unbroken tracts of near-virgin hardwood forest, biologists understandably developed the notion that turkeys required vast, continuous hardwood forests for survival. True, the birds survived, but for reasons that dif-

Binoculars are valuable in almost any type of turkey hunting, but they're almost a must in open country. Buy the best you can afford; good optics don't come cheap.

fered from the biologists' perception. The turkeys were there not so much because the forest was, but because the people weren't.

We know now these early biologists were wrong. It's a good thing, too, because if turkeys actually did require large expanses of unbroken forest for survival, there'd be few birds for us to hunt today. I wouldn't have bothered to write this book, and if I had, you wouldn't have bothered to read it, for the same reason you'll never read a book on how to hunt passenger pigeons.

Today there are healthy, vigorous turkey populations throughout the West, and also in areas of the East, with as much as 80 percent open land in Alabama, Missouri, Iowa, Kansas, New York and other non-Western states.

We've been mostly talking about Eastern wild turkeys in these last few paragraphs, of course. Easterns are the most woodland-oriented of the four United States subspecies, and they still do occur in substantial numbers in national forests, state wildlife management areas, corporate tim-

201

When you see turkeys, freeze, because they may not have seen you yet. The author spotted this Rio Grande gobbler strutting on a power line at less than 100 yards, waited until the bird turned its back, laid flat on the ground, and then called the gobbler in and shot him at less than 25 yards.

berlands and other large expanses of forest habitat. But even where the trees start to play out and give way to pastures and prairies, those same forest-loving Easterns are taking to the open places like they've been waiting for the chance. And perhaps they have.

Easterns do require a bit more forest cover than Rio Grandes, Merriam's or even Osceolas, but it's surprising how little actual forest a flock of Easterns needs to survive and thrive. As it turns out, Eastern turkeys actually prefer woods interspersed with open areas – a notion whose sponsor would have been hooted out of the tavern 60 years ago. Nowadays, though, it's evident that turkeys do better when they have some open ground, and

we now know the truth: Those scattered flocks of turkeys that hung on in the remote backwoods of the 1930s were there not because they preferred to live in the big woods, but because they were adaptable enough to survive there.

The ability of turkeys, even Easterns, to thrive in open areas has geometrically increased our turkey hunting opportunities today. That's unquestionable. But hunting these prairie and pasture birds is a different ball game from hunting them in the big woods.

Probably the most common mistake made by first-time open-land hunters is moving too fast and too incautiously. They bump turkeys they didn't even know were there, and sometimes they do this at very long distances. Often they bump birds without ever seeing or hearing them, and never know it happened.

The solution to this problem is to move as slowly and carefully as a rat in a room full of sleeping cats, paying attention to the terrain as it unfolds in front of you so you can take maximum advantage of brushpiles, weed patches, scrolls and strands of timber and the roll of the land itself to hide your movements. Never just barge over a ridgeline or around the end of a strand of brush or trees. Instead, snail your way over or past these things one step at a time, cresting those ridges as slowly as the sunrise while using whatever cover is handy to break your silhouette, carefully scanning the landscape as it comes into view.

A good pair of lightweight binoculars are valuable for any type of turkey hunting, but in open areas, they're indispensable. If I had to give up one or the other, I'd sooner hunt open-land gobblers without camo than without a good set of glasses. Mine are a little bulkier and heavier than I wish they were, but because they're so much better than any of the shirt-pocket versions I've tried, I've decided to put up with the extra bulk and weight. With good glasses and a lot of patience and care, it's usually possible to spot distant turkeys before they spot you. Sometimes you get lucky with close birds, too; more than once, I've detected open-land turkeys within 40 yards without being seen.

Regardless of the range, once you've found a turkey or turkeys without being detected yourself, you're a step ahead of the game. Don't blow it at this point. When you first see turkeys, freeze. Stay that way until you can assess the situation and you can be absolutely sure you're not being scrutinized, either by the bird or birds you've seen or by other nearby turkeys you haven't made out yet.

Even if a gobbler sees you at long range, you can sometimes fool him into thinking he hasn't. It might take a long time, but you can do it if you can stand still long enough. Two examples prove the point:

I was hunting at Bent Creek Lodge in western Alabama in early April, and Bill Martin and I were trying to get something going one afternoon after a disappointing morning. We were walking down a railroad track to reach a creek bottom, when I spied a gobbler crossing the tracks a quarter-mile ahead.

Open-land turkeys key on terrain features like fence-lines, roads and gullies. Setting up near these travel-ways with a decoy can produce big results.

203

Bill saw the bird at the same time I did, and the bird spotted us at the same time we saw him. All three of us abruptly stopped between the rails. Bill and I looked wistfully at the gobbler. He stared suspiciously back at us.

Having no brilliant plan at the ready, and not knowing what else to do, we did nothing. It was a warm afternoon, and mirage waves shimmered in the air over the shiny rails and creosote crossties. We all three did some more staring. Nobody moved, not muscle nor feather. Finally, after what seemed like an hour but truly must have been 10 minutes (which is a lot longer than it sounds like when you're standing absolutely still in the hot sunshine), the gobbler broke his petrification, shook himself unconcernedly and wandered off the tracks toward the right-of-way border and the cool shade of the creek bottom. But half-in, half-out of the brush, he stopped abruptly and eased his head and neck backwards, the way turkeys sometimes do when they're just about to go behind a tree. Just checking one more time, you know.

But we didn't fall for it, and he was satisfied and disappeared for real. After giving him about two more minutes to get well into the timber, we ducked into the woods and headed in his direction. Not quite 30 minutes later, I pulled the trigger on him as he came in a half-strut to the call.

Another day in Oklahoma, I was walking a paper-company gravel road in the Kiamichi Mountains north of Antlers. I'd been working a gobbler and had lost the battle with him, but all the while I'd been hearing a second gobbler hammering pretty good a long way west, in some big pine timber off the edge of the paper-company road. I was hot-footing it westward on the road toward the now-silent gobbler, when I saw him break out of the pines into the road a scant 300 feet ahead. He was broadside and in full strut when I first saw him, taking those little short patty-cake steps gobblers take at such times. I guess he was so mesmerized with his own grandeur, he didn't have enough brain cells left to notice me, and as soon as I saw him I stopped walking and dropped to my knees in the middle of the road.

He strutted onto the middle of the road, too, turned toward me … and popped out of his strut like somebody had shot him with a bean flip. He went from round fuzzball to periscope-up in a split second, and after taking two or three nervous sidesteps, he got still. I stayed that way. Five minutes later he fluffed a little and shrank down a few inches, and two minutes after that he was in strut again. He tootled around in the road for 10 more minutes while I sat there in plain sight. Then strutted back into the pines. I gave him a few more minutes, and without rising from the ground I scooted into the woods and cut the distance by 35 yards. When I called, he cut me off with a double-gobble. I had him over my shoulder 15 minutes later.

It doesn't always happen that way. Most of the time the party's over if the turkeys see you, but not always, as those two incidents prove. Therefore, the first thing to do when you spy turkeys, whether they've seen you or not, is freeze. I've gotten away with it a lot more than just those two times.

It's always better, of course, if the birds don't see you. When that's the case, do everything you can to keep it that way. Just stand still and watch for a while, if possible. Are the turkeys moving or holding? If they're moving, in which direction? How fast? Is there a way for you to use the terrain to either get closer or at least get ahead of them? Are there any obstacles between you and the gobbler that might cause him to hang up? Does he have an easy, convenient travelway to come to you, or is there a better spot you can move to without being seen? Is he alone? With other longbeards? With jakes? With hens?

In short, is there anything you can do, while you still have the advantage and the gobbler doesn't yet know you're in the world, to improve your odds? If so, now's the time to do it. Once you make that first call, you're going to get his attention. He may not come, but he'll know you're there, and the element of surprise is gone. Never, never, make that first call to a gobbler you've spotted until you think you're in the best position you can achieve, relative to the turkey and the terrain.

Traveling turkeys in any habitat are hard to deal with (see Chapter 20 for more on this), but in open country they're really a challenge. Not only do you have to figure out where he's going and how long it's going to take him to get there, but you also have to be able to flank him, get ahead of him or just simply keep up with him without letting him see you. It can be more like antelope hunting than turkey hunting.

It's almost impossible to know for sure a turkey's final destination, but luckily, that's not necessary most of the time. Open-land gobblers seldom have a "final destination" the way big-woods birds usually do; their usual pattern is to just sort of mosey around all day, moving in a more or less circular (or at least out-and-back) route that brings them back to their roost at night. Sometimes they'll hole up in a shady spot in the heat of the day, but mostly they just mosey. So if you can manage to stay with a gobbler in open country long enough, you can usually figure out a place to get that will put you in his path. The trick is being able to get there undetected.

Open-land turkeys tend to avoid high grass and areas of thick brush if they have a choice, just like their cousins in big timber. You can use these features to help predict the route of a traveling gobbler. If there's a thicket or patch of weeds in a turkey's line of travel, it's a safe bet he'll skirt one side of it or the other; making a setup at the edge of this thick stuff can be a good strategy.

But which side? Other terrain features may give you a hint. Open-land turkeys, like their big-woods cousins, like to walk along two-track roads, cattle trails and other types of paths, even if the going is just as easy off the trail. If a field road, cattle track or sendero passes by one side of the thicket, that's your best bet.

Open-land turkeys also tend to walk fencelines, gullies and ridgelines if these features are running in their desired travel direction. The thin strip of weeds and brush along a barbed-wire fence can provide you with a good setup spot in otherwise coverless territory, and it's also a likely travelway for the turkeys.

Assuming you can figure out the turkey's travel route and arrive at the predetermined rendezvous point ahead of the bird, you still have to get him into shotgun range. On the plus side is the fact that it's easier to call a turkey to where he plans to go anyway, but on the minus side is the whole topic of this chapter in the first place: The terrain is wide open. A gobbler may refuse to come to your calling or he may pick you out as he approaches.

If you've plotted the turkey's course accurately enough, you may not need to call to him at all – or at least, only enough to satisfy your conscience and allow you to tell your buddies back at camp you called the bird in. The thing to avoid in this

Loud, penetrating calling is important for locating turkeys in open country.

situation is the tendency to call too much or too aggressively, thereby hanging the turkey up or moving him in another direction. Remember, you're already pretty much where the turkey wants to be. Don't blow the deal by getting too pushy.

Using a decoy or two can be another big aid in getting a traveling gobbler within that magic 40-yard circle, but I confess I rarely use them. (See Chapter 37.) I travel light in open country, because I figure I'm going to make a lot of footprints between sunrise and sunset. Since I've had decoys hang my bird up or run him away in some cases, I usually just opt out. However, decoys can be extremely effective in open country, particularly when you're blind-calling and attempting to attract a gobbler.

As we've said more than once in this chapter, being able to see a long way can be a definite advantage when you're working a gobbler, because you can see how he's reacting regardless of whether he's gobbling or not. The flip side is, the gobbler can see a long way, too. This means good camouflage, effective setups and absolute motionlessness become even more important than normal. Use whatever cover is available when setting up on an open-land turkey. In the woods, you have heavy shadows and big objects to work with, but you have little of that stuff in many open-country situations, and you need to make maximum use of whatever you find. I usually don't bother with it in woodland hunting, but in open land, if I have time, I almost always try to fashion some sort of rudimentary blind. Just a few broken branches stuck in front, or a dead limb or two piled close by, can make the difference between turkey meat and turkey tracks.

Setting up along those likely travel lanes mentioned earlier – two-track roads, fencerows, dry stream courses, pond dams and the like – can also improve your odds in open country, whether you're hearing and seeing birds or not. Blind-calling in these areas can be especially productive for afternoon hunts. Many open-land gobblers travel several miles from their roosts during the day and tend to use easy travel routes so they can cover ground fast as they head home in late afternoon.

Use loud calls when prospecting in open land. Those big-sky areas swallow up a lot of sound, and the wind that's often present doesn't help, either. Play the wind when you can, using it to carry your calls into likely turkey-holding areas.

Above all, be patient. If you have several days to hunt an area, don't try to make tracks on every square foot of it the first morning. Ease around quietly, try to figure out what's happening and work your way into the natural pattern. If you see a gobbler in a particular place at a certain time of day, odds are excellent he'll be there the next day, too – unless you disturb his routine.

A Kansas buddy and I located such a predictable open-land gobbler on public land in southeast Kansas several springs ago. Our first contact was a late-morning encounter that had him within 50 yards before we ran into interference from real hens.

We were back on him at daylight the next morning, setting up at the spot where he'd hung up the day before – in a sparse stand of cottonwoods at the edge of a large, open area. This time he came a little closer, but he had three jakes with him. He let them do the looking while he hung up just beyond sure killing range. Alan and I had our pockets full of tags, and we could have taken the jakes, but we held off. Eventually, everybody walked away unharmed and still unspooked.

The third morning found us back within yards of where the gobbler had stopped the day before. We listened to him gobble on the roost and kept our calls in our pockets until he was down. Then we hit him with hard yelps and cutts until we got him to gobble back several times. We then shut up and got ready.

He was there in three minutes, but again he hung up just out of range, in good sight through the skimpy cottonwood saplings, but as safe as if he'd been on the moon. I held the bead on his apple-red wattles and watched him spit and drum, silently daring him to come just 5 yards closer. After a one-hour stand-off, that's what he did.

He was only a 2-year-old with blunt, short spurs, but he'll always be one of my most satisfying trophies. Alan and I had two magnificent opportunities to screw that gobbler up (three, if you count that hour-long wait on the third morning), but we held off each time and never spooked him, and eventually we found ourselves in a sure-kill situation. We kept ourselves from disturbing his routine, and it finally paid off.

Hunting open-land gobblers gives you a wider window of opportunity to make things like that happen, provided you have the patience and discipline to hunt carefully. The opportunities are there, but you shouldn't force things.

Chapter 29

River-Bottom Turkeys

River-bottom turkeys are even more water-oriented than mountain birds. In bottomland situations, turkeys almost always roost over water.

The gobble came so quickly after our loud calling — and from such an extreme distance — I thought maybe I might have almost felt like I could have heard it. That's probably the clumsiest sentence I've ever written, full of weasel words, but it's accurate and appropriate in this context. If you're a turkey hunter, you know exactly what I mean.

We were deep in the Mississippi River bottoms of southeast Arkansas, my Kansas buddy J.R. and I, hunting turkeys on a 19,000-acre lease. It was straight-up 1 o'clock, and we'd hunted hard all

The Round Pond gobbler takes a ride.

morning without any action. When we'd gone back to camp two hours earlier, Sid Riley drew us a map in the dirt of the front yard and sent us out again after we wolfed down one of his patented BELTs (bacon, egg, lettuce and tomato sandwiches.). "There's been a bird gobbling back toward Round Pond," Sid said. "He hasn't been doing anything early, but you might be able to get him going in the middle of the day."

Sid has been hunting those bottoms for more than 50 years, and his dirt map was accurate. We found Round Pond and fresh gobbler tracks in the mud of the road, but after an hour of fruitless moving and calling, we lost our enthusiasm for the hunt. We stayed out there, sure, but we'd already mentally given up. I can't speak for J.R., but my thoughts had turned toward another BELT, a beverage and a nap.

On our way out, we stopped for one last effort at the junction of two logging trails. I pulled out my battered old Lohman box and ran off a loud series of cuts and clucks, trying to elicit a shock gobble from the silent woods. No dice.

"How do you do that cutting stuff, anyway?" J.R. asked, pulling his own box call out of his vest. "Show me what you're doing."

So the turkey hunt ended and the calling seminar began. I showed J.R. the same basics of cutting on a box call I'd learned from Brad Harris, then listened and watched as J.R. tried it. Then I did it again, and so did he, and so on, until we were both cutting and putting and clucking nonstop, in a long frenzy of turkey racket that must have sounded like date night at the turkey loony bin. Finally we stopped, and that's when I sort of thought maybe I might have almost heard something, right as our racket died out, off to the northwest at the limit of hearing.

Understandably enough, J.R. didn't believe me. He and I have a long history of playing pranks on each other, and while my hearing is nothing to brag about, his is even worse. But he went along with the joke, and soon we were seated at the base of a huge pecan tree, looking out on what seemed like 80 acres of flat, open woods.

The bird gobbled three more times in the next 45 minutes, and J.R. finally heard him the last time he gobbled. Each time he was closer. How he got past us in those open woods I still don't know, but 20 minutes after his last gobble out front, I

A favored roosting place in bottomland areas is a cypress/tupelo swamp.

heard him drumming and walking in the leaves behind.

When these damaged old eardrums of mine can hear a turkey drumming, the turkey is already kill-able. But he was – naturally – behind the only rise of ground in the neighborhood, and that's where he decided to stay. I tried some soft, seductive stuff and coaxed another two or three gobbles out of him, but 30 minutes after I first heard him drum, he was still in the same spot. So I shut up calling and switched over to rustling the leaves with my hand.

It took another half-hour, but the new tactic finally did the trick. I heard him break from his spot and start walking purposefully to the left, angling toward us and getting closer. When his warty old head finally popped into view, he was only 15 yards off the gun barrel. He was a heavy 2-year-old, J.R.'s first river-bottom gobbler.

Bottomland turkeys are nobody's pushovers. You'll find the occasional easy bird that comes a-running, the same way you'll find eager, coopera-tive birds in hill or farm country. But it seems, from my experience and the experience of other hunters I've talked to, these kamikaze gobblers are less common in the bottoms.

One reason for this (if indeed it's true and not just a faulty impression on my part), is the terrain. Not only is the typical overflow bottomland as flat as a tabletop, it's also mostly barren of ground-line vegetation – in the spring of the year, anyway. This makes for a wide-open, park-like setting, one in which an approaching turkey has a field of view that sometimes extends 300 to 400 yards through the woods. You can find open settings like that in the mountains, too, but you can usually avoid these wide-open setups when you're dealing with a turkey.

You can't avoid them in the bottoms, though, because usually that's all you have to work with. As a further problem, these seemingly flat woods aren't completely flat. They often have small dips and drains too shallow to hide a hunter from an approaching turkey, but plenty deep to hide an approaching turkey from a hunter. And if there's such a drain present, be assured the turkey will use it. I'm pretty sure that's how J.R.'s gobbler got around us that day.

It's not that bottomland turkeys are smarter or more wary. Put the same gobbler in a mountain situation or a flatland situation, and he'd be more

difficult to hunt in the flatlands. That's because the terrain gives a hunter fewer options. Bottomland turkeys live in places that make it harder for the hunter to get in good position, and every experi-enced turkey hunter knows good position is the key to killing turkeys.

Hunting Eastern gobblers in river-bottom situa-tions is similar in many ways to hunting the Western subspecies in more open terrain. Open-land gobblers, like Rio Grandes in central Kansas, or Merriam's in the South Dakota prairies, will often fly down right out in the middle of a square-mile pasture, because it's safer out there where they can see well. It makes things tough for the hunter, but there are several ways to cope. Getting in posi-tion early, using the cover of darkness, is one way. Being patient, slowing down your hunt, is another way. And, sometimes, being very aggressive with your calling is another way. All those approaches will also work with bottomland gobblers.

Getting in position earlier than normal is the most common tactic used by veteran bottomland hunters. Bottomland gobblers are more pre-dictable in choosing their roosting sites than mountain birds. They tend to roost over water when possible, and in the typical overflow area, roosting over water is almost always possible. Therefore, it's not a bad strategy to set up in a likely fly-down area near a watery roost site well before first light, using the cover of darkness to get close to where you suspect a gobbler is sleep-ing. This is a good idea even if you don't have a gobbler roosted; you have to start the morning somewhere, and it might as well be in a good fly-down spot near a potential roost.

Which brings us to another point: Bottomland gobblers, for some reason, tend to start gobbling earlier than mountain birds. They may not start gobbling on their own, but they're generally more susceptible to shock-gobble tactics. It's often pos-sible to knock a gobble out of a bottomland bird a full hour or more before first light, and this gives you ample time to move in close.

Normally, it's not a good idea to call much to a gobbler before he comes to the ground, because he might hang up in his tree and wait for hens to walk under him. Hens aren't going to walk under a turkey roosted over a cypress brake, though, so you can call more aggressively. In fact, I've dis-covered through trial-and-error in this situation that aggressive calling is the right choice most of

When you locate a gobbler across a slough or lake in bottomland country, do whatever it takes to get on the turkey's side of the water.

the time. Don't forget, there's an opposite side to that water the gobbler is roosted over. He could very well fly out that way if you don't give him a reason to come toward you.

Which, in turn, opens still another subject. Bottomland gobblers have an aggravating habit of being on the opposite side of a body of water from wherever you happen to be. Sometimes this water body is substantial – a river, for example, or an arm of a lake. Or it may be ridiculously small and insignificant, such as a thin ribbon of advancing or receding backwater no more than a few inches deep. Usually it's something in between.

Regardless of how much or how little water is between you and the turkey, though, it's a problem. Both bottomland and mountain turkeys routinely cross water in the course of their daily business, and three times I've seen them flying across the Mississippi River itself. But when you're trying to call in a gobbler, it seems like water will hang him up every time. When I locate a bird on the other side of a slough, lake or other water body, I make every effort to get on the same side as the turkey before attempting to call to him. Even if you have to give up a lot of distance on the bird and set up farther away, you're better off.

If moving to the turkey's side of the water isn't an option, another tactic is setting up as close as possible to the water's edge and shooting across the water to kill the gobbler. Of course, the waterway must be fairly narrow for this to work. If you do succeed, you're then faced with the problem of having to retrieve your bird on the other side of that water. However, on the three occasions I've successfully done this, I didn't really mind getting wet.

If the water is too big to get around and too wide to shoot across, your only other option is to try to call the turkey across it. This can work, but that's like saying buying a lottery ticket can work. (See Chapter 27.) It's possible, but it's nothing to bet the mortgage on. I've hunted bottomland gobblers for 21 seasons, and I've called birds across water only two times. I tagged one of them, and for all I know, the other one is still out there.

In both cases, I relied on complete silence to finally pull the hot bird across the water.

The first time, the silence was because I gave up and left. I had worked on this loudmouth gobbler for more than two hours. He was across a deep but narrow slough, and although I could catch a glimpse of him every so often, he wouldn't come close enough to the edge for me to be able to close the deal. I tried moving away from the water a time or two, calling as I went, but he wasn't having any of it. At 11 a.m., when he went out of sight yet again, I slipped out of the area and went back to camp. I came back at 2:30 and was easing toward the edge of the slough when the turkey gobbled at the sound of my footsteps in the leaves, no more than 25 yards away and out of sight behind the edge of a thick stand of switch-cane – on my side of the slough this time. He'd evidently gotten antsy when I shut up calling and left, and flew across to look for the AWOL hen.

But getting the bird on my side of the slough didn't help that time. He caught me by surprise, and that was all the advantage he needed. While I was doing a one-man Keystone Cops routine, trying to decide where to sit, the gobbler walked around the cane, spotted me and flew back across the slough where he'd been all morning. He didn't look much bigger than an emu.

Three springs later, I remembered that disaster when I found myself in a similar situation. After playing yoo-hoo with the gobbler until we were both tired of it, I quit calling, got comfortable and deliberately took a nap. Two hours later, a loud gobble woke me up. The turkey was on my side of the slough, less than 80 yards away, walking briskly straight at me and looking for the hen he thought he'd lost. All I had to do was wait until he closed the gap and walked behind a tree. He weighed 24 pounds, which in terms of Mississippi River bottom turkeys, made him a monster.

If you had to put it in a nutshell, I guess that verb I used in the last paragraph just about sums up the key to successful bottomland turkey hunting: *wait*. Take your time. Take a nap. Go early. Stay late. Move cautiously in between.

Wait. Good things come to those who do.

Chapter 30

Mountain Turkeys

"Get high to listen" is good advice.

The gobble came from … where? It was clear but distant, and when we heard it, Bill and I pointed in directions 180 degrees apart. It was the only bird we'd heard all morning, and it was well past desperation time. Legal hunting ends at 1 p.m. in Missouri, and it was after 11 when we heard him.

We tried a hawk call, a crow call and two or three cackles and cuts on a loud, raspy box, but the turkey stubbornly refused to gobble again. This never is a good thing, but it was particularly undesirable in this case. We needed to be sure we'd coursed the bird correctly before we committed to him, because we were standing on a steep, narrow backbone of high ground with a deep valley on each side. We knew the ridge would prevent us from hearing him again if we guessed wrong and dropped off the opposite side from the turkey.

Finally, Bill outargued me, and we went in the direction he'd pointed. Maybe he was right, too, but you couldn't prove it by me. The end of shooting hours came and went, and we never heard another peep from that bird or from any other.

We were pulling the long, steep slope back to the high ground we'd left two hours earlier, trying to reach the top without going completely rubber-legged. We were hot, thirsty and waterless, and we still had a 2-mile hike back to camp even after we made the ridgeline. Halfway up, Bill plunked down on a limestone outcropping to catch his breath. He dragged a shirtsleeve across his dripping brow, leaving a glaring splotch of pink skin where he rubbed off a few square inches of face paint.

"You wanna know something?" he asked, trying to work up enough saliva to spit. "Mountain turkeys are tough."

In the mountains, look for places that catch the early light. These places attract early-morning gobblers and hens.

My hunting buddy was right. Mountain turkeys are tough, and in more ways than one. Turkeys, as we all know, are characteristically wary and paranoid no matter where you find them. If you're lucky, you'll run across one of those five-minute kamikaze gobblers once every season or so. They're the ones that carry us through lean times and make us feel like turkey hunters. They're rare, though, because they usually don't live long. By and large, we have to work for our turkeys. And when you compound the normal, everyday paranoia of your average gobbler with the up-and-down topography of the Ozarks, Smokies, Adirondacks, Catskills, Ouachitas, Black Hills or even the Rockies, what you come up with is a really tough situation.

In many cases, though, it's unavoidable. Many of us have to do at least part of our turkey hunting on public land. And most public-land turkeys are in mountainous (or at least very hilly) terrain, because that's where most of the national forests are. There are exceptions to this rule, of course, and some of them are sizable. One example is Delta National Forest in western Mississippi, where the highest land features are road berms. But mostly, if you're going to hunt public-land turkeys, you'd better be prepared to climb.

This, by the way, is not entirely bad. Back in the 1970s when I got interested in turkey hunting, I went to a turkey seminar at a sports show. By modern standards, it was a primitive and rudimentary affair – no slides, visual aids, famous names or designer camo. The speaker, a man named Bob, simply stood in front of the sizable crowd, wearing street clothes, and told us pretty much everything he knew about turkey hunting. It took maybe 20 minutes. The only specific piece of advice I remember from that night was when Bob told us how to locate a gobbler.

"Get high to listen," he said.

Sitting down front were two good ol' boys with long hair, scraggly beards, wild-looking eyes and tie-dyed shirts. "Shoot," one of them said loudly, elbowing his buddy in the ribs, "I've been doing that for years."

It brought the house down, but Bob didn't mean it the way the space cadet took it. The advice was sound. Hunting turkeys in the mountains lets you locate gobbling turkeys over a much wider area than is possible in flatland hunting, because the acoustics are better. But only if you "get high."

In steep country, it's sometimes possible to get ahead of a traveling gobbler and bushwhack him, if you're in good enough shape to do it.

However, that's only part of the strategy. There are relatively few prime listening spots in a given stretch of rough country. You need to be high, but you also have to be where you can hear one or (preferably) several potential roosting areas. Further, you have to be able to get to them in reasonable time and with reasonable effort. Listening for gobblers from the lip of a 500-foot cliff may let you hear a lot of turkeys, but hearing them from there won't do you much good unless there's a parachute in your vest.

A short finger ridge coming east off a main ridge is often a good bet, especially if there are good roost trees in the hollows on either side of the ridge. East-facing ridges catch the early sunlight and provide well-lit stages for early-morning strutting activity.

A high place that looks west across a valley to the east slope of a mountain is another good bet, since you'll be able to hear a large expanse of country that's going to catch the early light, says Marty Eye, an accomplished mountain gobbler chaser who lives in Missouri. "The problem, of course, is that anything you hear will probably be across the valley from you, and you'll have to cross it to get to them. In gentle country, this may not be much of a problem. In some of the mountains I hunt, it's a big one."

In heavily hunted areas, sometimes the "get high" strategy doesn't work very well. Turkeys in these places – the survivors, anyway – soon learn

that locator calls and hen calls coming from above are often associated with danger. If you run into this problem, forget the high-ground strategy and try starting your hunts on the valley floor rather than on the ridgetops. You can't hear as far, obviously, and you'll probably have to climb to any turkey you hear. But when you find one, you'll stand a better chance of doing something with him because your calls will be coming from the opposite direction of the hunters who've worked him before.

Those east-facing exposures are important areas throughout the day, not just at first light. Not only do they catch the early sun and provide a spotlit stage for a gobbler, they also provide afternoon shade. Also, there's usually better mast on the east slopes because of the more moderate summer temperatures there. Gobblers don't spend much time eating during the spring, but hens do, and where there are hens, there will be gobblers.

Everybody who's hunted turkeys for long has made contact with a few of those aggravating gobblers that sound eager but are constantly on the move. These birds often gobble at everything you throw at them, but the problem is, they're gobbling over their shoulders as they move steadily away. These birds are tough to handle in any terrain, but at least when you're hunting in the mountains, the land tends to funnel turkey movements. This is important. Often, the only way to kill one of these gobblers is to get ahead of him and a) call him in; or b) bushwhack him. (See Chapter 20 for more on this subject.)

Footwear is also important for hunting in mountains. Forget about the lug-soled, low-topped, lightweight, fabric-and-suede, fashionable, silly things advertised as hiking shoes or boots. Hikers are creatures of the trails, where the going may sometimes be steep but usually is relatively easy. Turkey hunters need shallow-textured soles that provide traction without making them stumble, good ankle support and heavy leather. A 10-inch boot is about right for most situations.

Carrying a pair of clean socks and a little cornstarch, foot powder or baby powder in a film canister or pill bottle can be a foot-saver on rough-country hunts. Midway through the morning, I like to find a creek, wash my feet and let them air-dry, then powder them and put on the clean socks. It's amazing how much this simple ritual refreshes.

To put together some of the things we've just talked about, let's examine a hunt I had a few springs ago. Scene: the Ozark Mountains of Franklin County, Ark. – a steep, fertile region awash with hardwood timber and wild turkeys. Jill Easton and I were hunting together, and we'd double-teamed an Ozark gobbler the previous morning.

Sturdy footwear with shallow-textured soles and good ankle support are best for mountain hunting.

We were leaving for a Kansas hunt at noon, and it had been an uneventful morning. It was almost time for us to depart, and we were easing along an old logging road that traversed a narrow bench on a steep, north-facing slope. It was a good prospecting area. We could hear a lot of country, and all of it was reachable if we were willing to sweat a little. At 10 a.m., far across the valley, we heard a faint gobble.

The bird answered my crow, then my box, and after a while he decided he liked gobbling and wanted to do a bunch of it. We stood on the road and listened, and in 10 minutes he gobbled 25 times.

"Well," Jill said, "he's a long way. But he's a turkey."

My philosophy exactly. We consulted a wrinkled topo map and determined the gobbler was probably on an east-facing spur ridge extending into the valley from the base of the next mountain. There was a road on top of the mountain, but the turkey was far below it. By crossing the wide, deep valley to reach him, we'd be coming in on the side from which he probably hadn't been hunted.

Jill was right. The bird was a long way. But he was eager, and we were, too. We bailed off the road and descended four or five benches to the

In mountainous country, these traveling salesmen almost always stick to the same level. This means on a ridgetop, in a valley or along a bench partway down the side of a mountain. Knowing this, you can look at your map, then exploit the terrain to take rounders on a moving gobbler, get ahead of him and set up along his projected route.

Notice I mentioned maps. If you're hunting in mountains without a topo map, you're handicapping yourself. No matter how well you think you know a particular mountain or group of mountains, you don't know the country as well as the topo map does. A standard 7 1/2-minute topo map reveals saddles, flats, hollows, trails, springs, drainages and dozens of other terrain features you're not even aware of.

Washing your feet, letting them air-dry, then applying talcum powder and putting on a fresh pair of socks is a refreshing midmorning ritual.

bottom, then started seriously cutting the distance across the jumbled valley floor.

When we came to a mostly dry creek bed, we found the spur ridge rising on the other side. Sure enough, the gobbler was on it. It wasn't high, maybe 50 feet above the valley, but its sides were a steep, jumbled fortress of truck-sized rocks and 20-foot drops. We set up on the flat valley floor below the spur and tried to pull the bird down to us.

He'd been steadily gobbling as we advanced on him, and he went crazy at my first series of sharp cuts and yelps. Jill chimed in with her box call, and he got crazier yet.

Back and forth along the edge of the spur ridge he marched, gobbling insanely all the while. He was close enough to kill several times and, judging from the sound of his gobbling, he was com-

ing to the edge of the ridge and gobbling straight down at us. But green-up was well advanced, and we were looking up through the crowns of the trees that grew at the base of the slope. It was the only time I've ever tried to look up through trees to see a turkey that wasn't perched in one, and I can testify it's no easier than seeing a bird through heavy ground cover.

We never caught so much as a glimpse of him. After 30 frustrating minutes, we were ready to try something else. Figuring if we couldn't see the turkey, he couldn't see us either, I eased to Jill's side and we held a battlefield conference.

"I think we need to get up there with him," I said.

Jill looked at the sheer side of the ridge. "How?" she whispered. "Fly?"

I bullied her into making the move, though. We

Hunting in the mountains is rough duty.

Mountain turkey hunting is rewarding, but don't make the mistake of going there if you're badly out of shape. An exercise regimen of walking and jogging is a good idea beforehand.

waited without calling, and the gobbler slowly decompressed and his gobbling rate diminished. When he moved far enough back from the lip, we crossed the creek and inspected the formidable bluff. We found a seam leading steeply upward between boulders, and soon we were creeping up to the edge of the flat.

I was leading, trying to get us onto the flat ground on top, but to cover the last 5 yards, we had to wade through some dry, wind-piled leaves. With the first crunch, the turkey gobbled explosively, so close I could hear the rattle at the tail end of it. I ducked, motioned for Jill, and we traded places on the narrow trail. With only her head and shoulders above the bluff, she had to stand to the turkey rather than sit to him, and the only thing available for a rest was an 8-inch blackjack oak growing just below the lip. She leaned against it and shouldered her Beretta.

An almost inaudible cluck on my diaphragm was all it took. The turkey gobbled again, and we could hear him drumming. Jill shifted her barrel slightly left an instant before I saw the gobbler. Head up, half-strutting, he looked suspiciously in our direction, but the camo and the blackjack oak did their work. Behind a tree he went, and Jill completed her move. Seconds later, it was over.

Struggling back up the steep slope to the logging road with a heavier load than we'd been carrying when we left it two hours earlier, Jill stopped and looked back across the valley toward the now-invisible spur ridge. Then she looked at her watch.

"We're going to be late getting to Kansas," she said. "Know what, though? I don't mind a bit."

218

Chapter 31

Public-Land Turkeys

Not all good listening spots are spots from which you really want to hear a turkey.

It's one of those ideal listening places from which you hope you won't hear a turkey.

You know the kind of place I'm talking about. First off, it's naturally camouflaged by a slight rise that hides it from the smooth gravel Forest Service road that runs only 200 yards to the north. On top of that, the timber on both sides of the road has been heavily cut. The landscape between the road and the listening spot looks like the downrange section of a heavy artillery firing range. It's not a very likely looking place to stop and listen for gobbling.

But when you walk through the nasty cutover and top the 50-foot rise, you find yourself on the brink of a rocky outcropping that overlooks a wide, forested valley. From the outcropping, you can see forever and hear a gobbler half that far – and therein lies the problem. Any turkey you hear from that spot is going to be downhill, unless the turkey happens to be flying overhead at the time or sitting in the gnarly 20-foot blackjack oak that somehow clings to life in the middle of the rockpile.

Since both those possibilities are extremely remote, you know any turkeys you hear from the outcropping are going to be downhill – steeply downhill – and through stuff an aging, out-of-shape turkey hunter like me has no business going through. Getting from that listening spot to a gobbling bird entails scrabbling down through a 100-yard boulder field, then crossing a deep valley filled with scrubby, clothes-grabbing brush before reaching the more open timber on the other ridge, where the turkeys always seem to roost.

But you can hear about two square miles of good turkey country from that knob, so that's where I went that opening morning. Sure enough,

Use a compass or GPS in mountain country; it can save you a lot of misery.

I heard one. Sure enough, he was away off on the backside of yonder, on the ridge beyond the boulder field and the brushy valley. I shook my head, took a compass bearing on the sound and headed turkey-ward.

Nearly an hour later, sweaty and scratched, I eased into the area where I'd figured the bird to be. An exploratory run of yelps from my box call yielded nothing, so I moved toward the top of the ridge. Stopping just below the crest, I yelped again. The gobbler answered from so close by, I wondered as I scrambled to sit down how I'd kept from bumping him. I barely had time to get my face mask in place and raise the gun when he came strutting over the ridge, his backlit tail fan glowing like a Halloween pumpkin in the golden morning light.

He was already in easy killing range when I first saw him, but I wasn't ready to end the show just yet. He evidently liked that little patch of sunlight, because that's where he stayed for the next five minutes, spinning and drumming and gobbling about twice a minute. I watched him over the gun barrel, savoring the moment. But then a hen started yelping farther down the ridge, and when the gobbler started easing that way, I clucked sharply with a diaphragm call. When he raised his warty old head to look for me, I removed his genes from the pool.

Two sweaty hours later, I climbed back out onto that perfect listening spot and stumbled the last 200 easy yards to the truck, swearing to myself with every step I'd never again stop and listen for turkeys at that particular spot.

But, of course, I have. And will again.

Since the vast majority of public turkey hunting land in the United States is on national forests, for simplicity's sake, "national forests" is the term we're going to use in this chapter. Keep in mind, though, these remarks also apply to public turkey hunting on state-owned wildlife management areas, Corps of Engineers property, national wildlife refuges, national grasslands, U.S. Army posts and other types of public land open to turkey hunting.

Nine states – Connecticut, Rhode Island, Massachusetts, New Jersey, Maryland, Delaware, Iowa, Kansas and North Dakota – have no national forest land, but the rest do. That's fortunate for the nation's turkey hunters. National forests were the first large public areas to have huntable turkey populations during the early years of the Great Turkey

Military installations across the country offer good turkey hunting opportunities, but in the wake of Sept. 11, gaining access has become more of an obstacle.

Comeback in the 1960s and 1970s, and on most of them, turkey populations are still good. Better than ever, in fact. I killed my first turkey in 1981 in the Ouachita National Forest in western Arkansas, and my turkey logbook reveals that nearly half of the 80-odd gobblers I've taken since have been from a dozen national forests in 10 states.

I'm not the only hardcore hunter who takes advantage of public land. Brad Harris has access to more private land than a dozen average hunters put together, well-managed property where hunting pressure is minimal and turkeys are more plentiful and less wary than public-land birds. Even so, he spends a portion of each spring chasing gobblers on Forest Service, Corps of Engineers and state-owned lands in Arkansas, Missouri, South Dakota, Oklahoma and other states. He does this for several reasons, but the biggest one is simple: Our

nation's public forests and turkeys go together like prime rib and horseradish.

"It's true that hunting pressure can be pretty bad on some national forests, especially early in the season and on the first weekend," Harris says. "But if you'll go back to those same places after the first few days of the season, and after the first weekend, you'd be surprised at how uncrowded most national forest lands are."

Of course, some of the available gobblers will also be gone after those first few days, hauled out of the woods over the shoulders of lucky or skillful hunters. And it's likely that most of those hot-to-trot 2-year-old birds that make us feel like real turkey hunters will have either been killed or given a crash course in paranoia.

One alternative to Harris's wait-a-few-days approach to public-land hunting is to simply out-

221

Fort Bragg, N.C., and a good military gobbler.

last the competition each day. Hundreds of magazine articles, videos and book chapters (including one in this book) have been devoted to the subject of late-morning or midday turkey hunting, but even so, the vast majority of hunters are out of the woods by 9 a.m. Some of those hunters must leave the woods early to go to work, but many others who could stay out there longer simply don't. They get bored, discouraged, or both, when the early-morning gobbling frenzy fades into silence. Then they head for town to grab a late breakfast and commiserate with their buddies about the sorry state of that morning's hunt.

But while these early quitters are swapping lies and tales of woe in the coffee shop, the savvy hunter will still be in the woods. Granted, it's not as easy to find a gobbling turkey after 9 a.m., but when you do locate one, you can very often do something with him.

Harris also likes national forest hunting because of its expanded scope. He's a roamer, and he needs room for it. "When you're hunting a lease or a piece of private property, your options are limited by the boundaries of the property," he explains. "When you're hunting national forest lands, you have a lot more flexibility. There's so much acreage available, you can often find an unpressured area even during the high-use times

of the early season. Even when you can't find an unpressured area for early-morning hunting, you have more room to wander and look for a cooperative late-morning turkey."

On those mornings when nothing much is happening, Harris likes to cover a lot of ground in search of a workable turkey – or at least a gobbling one.

"It's hard for me to find a chunk of private property big enough to hold me on those slow days," he says. "Many turkey hunters look down their noses at public-land hunting, and that's fine with me. Let them go elsewhere and pay big money for the privilege of hunting on a tract of leased ground or on a relative's or friend's farm. While they're bumping up against the neighbor's lease and listening to turkeys gobbling across the fence, I'll be hunting without fear of hitting a property line I can't cross." Harris hunts private land, too, as mentioned, but says when he feels the need to stretch his legs, he heads for a national forest.

There are 155 separate national forests in the 48 contiguous states, with more than 187 million total acres. Not all that acreage has turkeys, but most of it does. Finding those birds, however, can be a daunting proposition – especially for the first-timer who doesn't quite know how to go about it.

Maps are the keys that open this vast public hunting ground to the likes of you and me. The U.S. Forest Service publishes maps of all its national forests, and they're available at nominal cost from each national forest headquarters office. Studying a map of your chosen forest is an excellent way to find likely looking hunting grounds.

Once you've narrowed your search to three or four likely spots, it's a wise move to buy topographical maps of those particular areas. Topo maps are much larger-scale than Forest Service maps, and they have the added advantage of showing elevation contours, and other details that aren't shown on national forest maps. Using maps is covered in greater detail in Chapter 13.

When I'm doing my broad-based search for hunting areas with the national forest maps, I like to look for larger expanses of roadless, or at least road-poor, country. Those are the areas least likely to be heavily hunted, and on public land, that's always an important consideration.

Another often-overlooked opportunity for hunting unpressured birds can be found by searching out the smaller outholdings of national forest land surrounded by private stuff. Most national forests have scattered 80s and quarter-sections of public land that are isolated from the main Forest Service property, and these get overlooked by most hunters. They get hunted, sure, but not usually as much as bigger sections of land. I've taken several turkeys off these small outlying parcels, and have rarely encountered other hunters.

Wilderness areas and designated walk-in hunting areas are also good places to look for unpressured turkeys. Not all national forests have designated wilderness areas, but many do. Most of the larger wildernesses are in the Western states, naturally, but there are wildernesses in the East, too. My home state of Arkansas, for example, has 10 wilderness areas on national forest land and three more on National Park Service land, totaling more than 113,000 acres. Although the largest of the 13 is only 22,500 acres – a tiny scrap of real estate compared to many Western wildernesses – that's still a big place to make a turkey hunt. See Chapter 32 for more on this topic.

The run-and-gun approach to national forest turkey hunting is widely practiced by many hunters, and it's one of the reasons public-land turkeys are so spooky after the first few days of the season. This method of hunting can be done on foot, but most often it involves driving the

On public land, maps are a real help because of the large expanses available for hunting.

Many states provide walk-in hunting areas on public land, to give hunters willing to walk the extra mile a place to find less crowded hunting conditions.

When "driving and hooting" to locate turkeys on public land, the hunters should stand a considerable distance apart. The hunter who's not calling has a better chance of hearing an answering gobble that way.

roads and stopping every half-mile or so to hoot, caw, call and otherwise try to get a turkey to gobble. Then the hunter goes to the bird and attempts to make a hunt.

Despite the number of people who do it, this can still be an effective way to locate a gobbler on public land. You can cover a lot of ground in a short while, and it's a good strategy when you arrive in a new area blind, without any knowledge of terrain or turkey distribution. I also sometimes resort to it during the mid-day hours, on those days when I'm unable to get anything going early, simply because I can cover more ground this way and increase my chances of striking a gobbler.

The key to successful drive-and-hoot, drive-and-caw, drive-and-call hunting is this: Once you've located a bird, tone down your calling and play coy and hard to get. Most run-and-gunners can't – or at least don't – do that. They stop on the side of the road, get out, and hoot or cutt or whatever, and when a bird fires back they charge turkey-ward like their hair was on fire and start calling like the most sex-crazed hen in the woods.

After a couple days of this, the turkeys get wise to it. They'll still shock-gobble at your locator calls, maybe, but they're onto that other stuff. The best approach, once you've located a bird from the road, is to try to circle (or at least flank) the gobbler so you can call to him from some direction other than toward the road. Keep your calling low-key, too, because most of the other hunters, their fires stoked by too many hot-action turkey videos, will have already hammered at the bird with loud, aggressive calling.

Clucks and purrs and a few soft yelps are the best-percentage play in this situation. Don't get in a hurry. No matter what you think about it, a turkey doesn't really have to do anything. He can come to your calls or not, and if he does, he'll do it in his own good time. Patience and finesse are the tricks that work most often on road-located gobblers.

Going the extra mile is important for national forest turkeys, whether that means searching out roadless areas, hiking far into a wilderness area before daylight, or being willing to outlast the other hunters and stay out there all day.

However, spouting statistics and how-to-do-it advice is one thing; putting together a successful hunt is another. Let me wrap this up with an example of how it can work:

In a recent spring, a friend and I hunted southwest Mississippi's Homochitto National Forest. Two weeks of heavy pressure, lousy weather and several recent poor hatches in the area combined to make our first four days a frustrating string of zeros. On the final morning we decided to try something different and started prospecting on the smaller portions of Forest Service land hemmed in by private holdings.

At the third stop, we hit paydirt. The turkey was gobbling on his own when we got out of the truck, and the fact he was a long way from the road was an advantage in this case. A long, narrow strip of national forest property bordered the road, and it was only a quarter-mile wide for a half-mile east before broadening into a half-section of national forest surrounded by private land.

National Forests usually have small outlying parcels that are surrounded by private land and disconnected from the main holdings. These small blocks are ignored by most hunters and can be surprisingly good.

The bird pulled us the half-mile through the narrow strip and midway through the half-section before we were able to set up on him. It was rough going all the way, through cutovers and up and down the steep folds of the Tunica Hills.

When we finally got to him, he came in on a string, acting like an opening-day bird rather than a three-weeks-into-the-season one. He strutted and drummed and gobbled his head off, and he made it to the 25-yard marker before my buddy stopped him. An hour later and 250 yards farther along the ridge, I called in a second longbeard.

"We're coming back to this spot," my partner informed me as we made our way back to the truck.

And we will. Right after I go back to my perfect, horrible listening spot in Arkansas.

Top Public Lands

Singling out the best national forests for turkey hunting is a matter of personal preference and experience. A Pennsylvania hunter's choices might be vastly different from those of a Georgia hunter. However, here are a few candidates for anybody's top-10 list:

Missouri: Mark Twain National Forest, 401 Fairgrounds Rd., Rolla, MO 65401, (573) 364-4621.

South Dakota/Wyoming: Black Hills National Forest, RR 2, Box 200, Custer, SD 57730, (605) 673-4954.

Georgia: Chattahoochie National Forest, 1755 Cleveland Hwy., Gainesville, GA 30501, (770) 297-3000.

Kentucky: Daniel Boone National Forest, 1700 Bypass Rd., Winchester, KY 40391, (606) 745-3100.

Vermont: Green Mountain National Forest, 231 N. Main St., Rutland, VT 05701, (802) 747-6766.

Pennsylvania: Allegheny National Forest, P.O. Box 847, Warren, PA 16365, (814) 723-5150.

Chapter 32

Wilderness-Area Gobblers

Wilderness areas are not for the short-of-wind or faint-of-spirit, but they're there for those who can hack it.

It was getting on up in the morning, and I was walking a narrow, green valley between steep-sided ridges. I was already losing concentration and enthusiasm for the hunt and beginning to think about the 3-mile hike and the three steep ridges that lay between my weary feet and my truck.

All that negativism vanished, however, when I came past the toe of one of the ridges and yelped into the mouth of a side hollow that wound back to the north. A gobbler answered me at the limit of hearing up the valley, and I took off after him. Never mind that he was another 800 yards farther from the truck. He was a turkey, and that was all that mattered.

Although most Eastern wildernesses are much smaller than their Western counterparts, the word "small" shouldn't be used to describe a 10,000- to 20,000-acre chunk of roadless land.

It was 10:30 when I first heard him, 11:00 when I first saw him, and 12:30 when he finally gave up and came marching in, chasing his two jake acolytes out of the way as he strutted to the call. I didn't mind a bit that I had to haul him nearly 4 miles through rough country. I hadn't heard or seen another hunter all morning, and while that may be a rarity in most public-land turkey hunting, it happens more often than not when you're hunting in a wilderness area.

The controversy over the wilderness area system in our national forests and national parks has been going on for a long time, and there's no relief in sight. On the one side are developers, timber interests and county and state governments who want zero acres of wilderness because tax and payroll revenues will be higher if the land is available for timber production and regularly scheduled logging. Facing them across the divide are the preservationists who want huge and many wilder-

ness areas because they think man is an abomination on the landscape and we ought to turn as much of the world as possible into a hands-off Eden, where man can visit but not meddle.

In between are the large majority who either don't care one way or the other, and then there are the rest of us, we right-minded ones, who think that a) we ought to have a reasonable amount of wilderness acreage; and b) everybody ought to shut up and live with it.

Without exception, the turkey hunters of my acquaintance fall into that latter group. We most definitely are in favor of having wilderness areas, but we don't want all of them to be so large that the interiors are inaccessible, and we don't want too many of them. We feel this way for some very specific reasons.

Wilderness areas give a hunter the opportunity to find uncrowded conditions and relatively unpressured turkeys, provided he is willing and

Carry snacks and water. This hunting is different from a jaunt into the back 40.

able to go the extra mile or three. That's a big plus for hunters who have the time, the drive and the physical ability to access these areas on foot.

But that last requirement is the very reason most of us don't want wilderness areas to be too big or too numerous. I'm like many of you in that I'm getting longer in the tooth and am starting to notice it. While I can still reach down inside myself and find what it takes to bushwhack my way 4 or 5 miles into a wilderness area to make a hunt, I've noticed in the past few years it's getting harder to pull together enough want-to to get the job done. I can see the day coming when I won't be able to gather up enough gumption to pull those hard miles in and out … and it's because I'm selfish and because I can see that day coming that I don't want wilderness areas to be too large or too numerous. Many of my fellow hunters have already reached that point, due to age or handicap. They don't begrudge more physically able hunters their wilderness areas, but they also don't want these areas to slurp up too much of the land they're able to hunt.

There's one more reason many of us don't want to see the wilderness area system take in an excessive amount of acreage, and it's an important one: Wilderness land, over time, becomes pretty sorry wildlife habitat in general. The wilderness area concept does away with all manipulation by man, and regardless of what the Sierra Club types believe, over the long haul a hands-off forest management approach doesn't bode well for wildlife in an Eastern hardwood forest.

But right now, in terms of tree life and the vigor of the forest, most of the wilderness areas in the Eastern national forests are relatively young. Therefore, most of them still have productive forests and still harbor good turkey populations. That won't be the case 100 years from now, but none of us hunting today will be around to bemoan that fact. For now, the wilderness areas of the Eastern national forests are good prospects for turkey hunting – assuming you have the time, desire and physical stamina to handle it.

The wilderness areas in the states east of the Great Plains are for the most part much smaller than the mega-wildernesses of the Rocky Mountains. That's a good thing from the aspect of turkey hunting, because in huge wildernesses that cover several hundred thousand acres, most of the

Many wildernesses have honor-system check-in points where visitors log in and out. If the area you're entering doesn't, leaving a note at your vehicle saying where you're going and when you'll be coming out is a good idea. A broken ankle 5 miles deep in rough country isn't a good thing.

interior is effectively sealed off from hunting because of the time and difficulty required to reach it. Moreover, many states have laws on the books (unconstitutional laws, but laws nonetheless) requiring that hunters in wilderness areas hire the services of a professional outfitter, and this raises an economic barrier as effective as a 10-foot electric fence for many of us.

No such regulations exist on Eastern wilderness areas, though, and their smaller size makes them accessible for most hunters willing to get there. Hiking 3 miles may not take you to the middle of one of these places, but it'll get you well into the interior of most of them, since they're more likely to cover 20,000 acres than 200,000. Hike 3 miles into the million-acre Bob Marshall Wilderness in Montana, and you haven't even scratched the surface.

Most of the larger Eastern states have designated wilderness areas within their national forests. Most states have walk-in turkey hunting areas as well. We can include these walk-in areas in the rest of this discussion, since vehicular traffic is prohibited and these areas are frequently larger

than the wilderness areas they often abut.

As already mentioned, these no-vehicle areas offer top-quality turkey hunting, because the turkeys that live in them don't get bothered nearly as much as their cousins on the surrounding lands. However, making a hunt into one of these places usually requires a little more preparation and forethought.

A map and a compass (and a GPS) are more than handy for any turkey hunting situation; they're downright essential when you're planning to park your truck in the predawn darkness and bail off into a wilderness area. Remember, you're not going to have many man-made landmarks such as roads, rights-of-way, cutting-unit boundaries or flagged survey lines to help you get your bearings. Most wilderness areas – at least, most of the ones I've hunted – have self-serve stations set up at the major entrance points and trailheads. These stations usually have cheaply printed black-and-white maps of the area, depicting trails and major terrain features. These maps are OK for hikers who plan to stay on the ridges and major trails, but they're not good enough for turkey hunting. Instead of relying on these dinky maps, I always photocopy the part of a topo map that depicts the wilderness area – or, at least, the part of it I'll be hunting. I used to have to sometimes photocopy parts of two maps and tape them together, but with the advent of CD-ROM-based electronic map programs like those from DeLorme and All Topo Maps, I can usually print out a single map that covers my potential hunting area. If you have to cut and paste maps to cover your territory, though, do it. I've been lost in several wilderness areas before, and even in our relatively small Eastern wildernesses, it's not much fun.

Carrying food, water and a few lightweight emergency supplies is also a good idea for a wilderness area hunt. Don't overdo it, but remember you're likely to hike 10 miles or more during your hunt. Unless you're in training for the next reality TV series, you're going to need refreshments. I usually carry a few granola bars and candy bars, maybe a small orange or two, some jerky and a 1-liter pop bottle filled with water, plus a few water purification tablets for an emergency. They make the water taste terrible, but it's better than getting giardia, or worse, from drinking contaminated water. These days, you can't count on finding pure water even in the middle of a wilderness area.

Speaking of emergencies, let someone know where you're going and approximately when you think you'll be back. Some of the self-serve entrance stations have sign-in logbooks, and if there's one where you go in, by all means sign it. The nature of turkey hunting being what it is, it's impossible to know for sure which direction the morning's hunt is going to take you, but be as specific as you can when you tell somebody your plans.

Backpacking and making an overnight camping trip is a great way to take advantage of the interior solitude of a wilderness area. However, some states require hunters to check their harvested birds within a designated time frame, and this effectively limits the extent to which you can put this plan to work. If circumstances allow, though, putting a backpacker's tent and a few minimalist supplies in a pack frame, and spending a night or two "way back in there with 'em" is a good way to fully live the wilderness hunting experience. There are few things more thrilling than to hear the first gobble of the morning while you're still in camp drinking the last sip of coffee … and knowing you're the only hunter within 2 miles of that bird.

"Hunting through" is another way to effectively hunt a wilderness area. This strategy requires two hunters who are both experienced enough with GPS or map and compass that they can negotiate rough, unfamiliar terrain and come out at a predetermined spot, but it's a great way to get the most out of your hunting time.

First, pick a portion of a wilderness or walk-in area that has two entrance points 5 to 10 miles apart. The actual distance isn't important, but remember you both will have to cover all of it in a day's hunt. Then, one hunter drops his partner off at one of the entrance points, drives to the other area, and parks. (Alternatively, each hunter can drive his own vehicle.) The hunters then hunt their way through the wilderness, each of them working toward the opposite entrance point. If they're using a single vehicle, the hunter who arrives at the truck picks up his partner at the opposite entrance point. If they're using two vehicles, each hunter drives his partner's vehicle home or to a pre-arranged meeting place.

Obviously, this type of hunt plan involves close coordination, mutual trust and a system for either hiding car keys or making sure both hunters have keys to the vehicle(s). On the plus side, though, it offers an opportunity for some very efficient backcountry hunting.

Wilderness area turkey hunting isn't for everybody, nor is it the type of thing you want to tackle every day of the season. But if you've been looking for a way to avoid some of the hunting pressure, you might try a wilderness or walk-in area. You may very well run into another hunter back in there somewhere, but if you do, you can bank on one thing for sure: You'll be looking at a serious turkey hunter, not some fair-weather, opening-weekend type.

One good way to hunt a wilderness is to use the buddy system. Drop your partner off, then drive to a pre-arranged spot and leave the vehicle to begin your hunt. Your partner then hunts his way to the vehicle and picks you up at another pre-arranged spot.

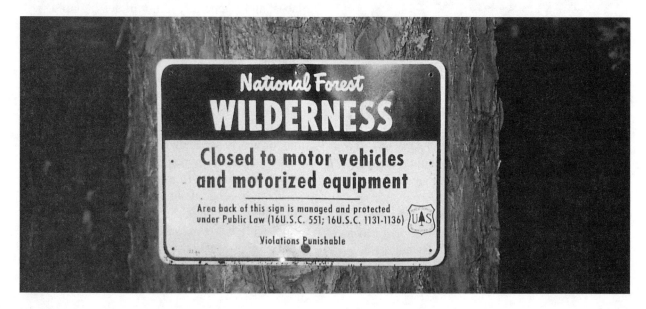

Chapter 33

Suburban Turkeys

You don't have to have big country to have turkeys. Many of them live within walking distance of suburbia, even inside the city limits of cities like St. Louis, Orlando, Memphis and Kansas City.

It was the first-ever turkey hunt on this particular wildlife management area, and since the word hadn't gotten out very well, I was lucky enough to draw a permit. The area was a 25,000-acre military reservation, and I lived north of it and worked south of it. By adding a few miles to my commute, I could drive through the area every morning on my way to work.

And on almost every workday that March, that's just what I did, stopping along the way and listening for turkeys. You won't believe this, but it's the truth: By the time the three-day permit hunt rolled around in April, I had more than 40 gobblers located and a dozen of them patterned. I had little trouble filling my tag.

That was an ideal situation, and most of the time something like that just can't be laid out. Because of the drive time involved, most of us who work for a living are largely limited to hunting on weekends or using vacation days.

It doesn't take a time-management specialist to figure out that the more driving time you can eliminate from a hunting trip, the more minutes you can spend actually hunting. Still, a good percentage of the turkey hunters I know rarely hunt within 50 miles of their homes.

By now, you've no doubt figured out that I do a lot of that, too. I love traveling to hunt new places, and I generally hunt turkeys in half a dozen states each spring, but I can't do it every day of the season. Like I said, most of us have to work for a living.

That's where suburban turkeys come in. I have permission to hunt on nearly a dozen private properties within 25 miles of my house, where I can get in a 90-minute hunt and still get to work on time, or nearly so. They're much smaller than the 25,000-acre military reservation, but they all have turkeys, and they're fine for a short hunt.

This tight-schedule hunting doesn't allow time for dealing with those difficult gobblers we all like to fool with, but over the course of an average season it gives me an extra 16 to 20 hours of time in the turkey woods. I usually take a bird or two during those bonus hours, too. But even when I don't,

Here's a sneaky but effective trick for gaining permission to hunt on private land: Take a female hunting partner with you when you ask.

they're still a bonus. A sunrise watched from a listening spot in the spring woods beats a sunrise watched from almost anywhere else I can think of.

Time was, most turkey biologists and turkey hunters believed the only place wild turkeys could survive was in the remote backcountry, that ragged, unkempt, uninhabited landscape out back of beyond. But as turkey trapping and turkey management techniques developed, as biologists learned more about what turkeys need to survive, we all began to realize these birds are more adaptable and tolerant of humans than formerly believed.

Given protection from overhunting and excessive disturbance by humans and dogs, turkeys can, and do, live in surprisingly tame places. Today, there are thriving turkey populations in small chunks of suitable habitat in many major metropolitan areas, including, to my personal knowledge: Jackson, Miss.; Kansas City and St. Louis, Mo.; Little Rock, Ark.; Rapid City, S.D.; Orlando, Fla.; and Memphis, Nashville, Knoxville and Chattanooga, Tenn. From conversations with

turkey hunting friends around the country, I know big cities with turkeys are far from rare. The same holds true, of course, for smaller cities.

This relatively recent rapid expansion of turkeys into suburbia has created many new hunting opportunities. And because this expansion has been so recent, hunters haven't caught on to it in many cases. Turkey hunters are accustomed to going that extra mile to the Big Woods, and old habits are hard to break. These suburban birds, although they're literally next-door neighbors with large numbers of humans, are often subjected to far less hunting pressure than their wild cousins in remote, uninhabited forests.

Another reason for this relatively light hunting pressure is difficulty of access. In some instances, the birds are actually within the city limits or on otherwise inaccessible territory. For example, there's a fine flock of Osceola turkeys behind chain-link fences on the property of Orlando International Airport, and a dense population of Easterns live on President's Island, a major indus-

233

Scouting is easier when you're hunting suburban turkeys, because sign is more concentrated and you don't have as big an area to search. Either they're there or they aren't, and you can find out in a hurry.

trial area on the south city limits of Memphis. Both of these areas, though non-residential, are off limits to hunters.

Other suburban turkey populations are found in blocks of habitat completely surrounded by residential areas, and there's no way to reach them without parking on a neighborhood street and walking though somebody's back yard. This stymies many would-be hunters, but it can be a simply solved problem in many cases. Sometimes one or more streets will dead-end against the edge of the property, in which case you can park at the end of the street. Another possibility is to walk across an empty lot or the lot of a vacant house to gain access. A third way is to ask for access permission across the lot of an occupied house.

If you must resort to that last one, try to find a house with a boat, ATV or other evidence of outdoor interest. You're likely to find a friendlier reception. Another hint: Don't knock on the door while wearing camouflage, and most assuredly not with your shotgun slung over your shoulder. You'll look less threatening in street clothes.

Sometimes the land isn't posted and no permission is required. Speculators and investors who are

biding their time, waiting for land prices to increase before developing the property or selling it, own much of the suburban turkey habitat. Usually they don't care what happens on the property as long as it isn't abused or vandalized. However, some states have closed-door laws that make all private land posted, whether signs are present or not. And sometimes suburban turkey habitat consists of an old family holding that's slowly been engulfed by creeping suburbia, in which case getting permission to hunt may be tough. Still, it doesn't hurt to ask.

Getting permission to hunt in a suburban woodlot is no different than getting permission to hunt anywhere else. Try to catch the landowner when he or she isn't busy. Dress neatly and conservatively and ask permission in person rather than over the phone. Make yourself as non-threatening and unobnoxious as you can.

Finally, promise to treat the land with respect. Then, if permission is granted, live up to your promise. Send a thank-you note or small present afterwards.

Hunting techniques for neighborhood gobblers differ little from those you're accustomed to using

Suburban turkeys are much more likely to roost in the same spot night after night, simply because travel is restricted and therefore suitable roosts are, too. When you find such a roost, the evidence is obvious.

in the big woods, except that the block of country you have to hunt is usually smaller. This dictates a slower, more thorough and methodical approach – no running-and-gunning here, if you want to be successful. If you storm through a 200-acre wood-lot cutting and cackling, trying to fire up a gobbler, chances are you'll bust through more turkeys than you fire up. It's entirely possible to spook every single turkey on a small hunting property in a single morning.

Because they have limited living space, you already pretty much know before you leave the house where the turkeys are. Your job is therefore both simplified and made more complicated. The good news is you don't have to find them; the bad news is, you still have to figure out how to get them to come in.

That's why pre-hunt scouting is so important for suburban turkeys. It doesn't seem like it would be, since your entire hunting area may be no bigger than a dozen city blocks. Knowing the lay of the land is even more important for these neighborhood hunts than for deep wilderness ones. The reason is simple: In the big woods, you usually have enough room to back out and look for anoth-

er setup if what you're trying on a particular gobbler isn't working. Or, you can go look for a different gobbler. But in a woodlot measuring a quarter-mile by a half, you're pretty much going to play the hand you're dealt. You may be forced to stick with a single setup the entire hunt. If this is the case, that setup had better be a good one.

Fortunately, it's easier to effectively scout suburban turkeys. Obviously, you don't have as much territory to cover, which makes it easier to figure out the birds' movements and habits within the smaller habitat. Also, since you don't have to drive or walk as far, you can scout with less invested time.

Locating suburban gobblers during the pre-season can be pretty easy. Two of the several wood-lots I hunt are completely surrounded by roads, and in each place it's possible to hear the same gobbling turkey from at least two sides, sometimes three or four. By using topographical maps and a compass, I can listen to the same turkey from two or more points, use the compass to determine a direction from each, and by triangulation pinpoint the roost location of that turkey within a few yards, without ever leaving the roads. This has obvious advantages, among them

Hunting close-in turkeys lets you spend a lot more of the average turkey season in the woods, because there's not as much travel involved.

speed, accuracy and reducing the possibility of getting too close and spooking the bird.

Roosting a bird the evening before your hunt can be much more valuable in hunting suburban turkeys than in hunting their big-woods cousins. As they say, roosted ain't roasted, but knowing where that gobbler is sleeping will help you avoid bumping him off the roost when you enter the hunting area at first light. Spooking a roosted bird is a much greater possibility in a 200-acre patch than a 10,000-acre one. Further, when you've spooked a bird in one of these small patches, you've probably ruined your chances that day. You can't go somewhere else and hunt up another bird the way you can in big woods.

"Conservative" is the key word in hunting suburban turkeys. Move slowly, call softly. Cover ground as if it were full of booby traps. Your hearing will often be diminished in suburban settings because of traffic, dogs and other sounds of civilization, so you'll need to proceed more cautiously than when hunting the big woods. And, after fly-down, these suburban turkeys are usually less vocal, possibly due to harassment by dogs. Remember, the gobbler you're hunting in a 200-acre woodlot is almost certainly able to hear your calling, regardless of your respective locations

within that block. More often than not, hunting these places becomes a waiting game.

You'll also encounter aggravations in suburban woodlots that you rarely have to face in the big woods. More than once, I've had kids and adults scare turkeys off me by running or riding bikes through my hunting area, and, as mentioned, neighborhood dogs are often a problem. I once had a suburban gobbler spooked off of me by the roar from a hot air balloon giving free rides at an automobile dealership next to the patch I was hunting.

In addition to the aggravation factor, of course, are matters of safety and legality. If non-hunters or people's pets are likely to be in the woods with you, it behooves you to take extra precautions in identifying your target and what's beyond it. This is a must for turkey hunters anyway, but it's especially important in suburban situations.

Many suburban areas have ordinances governing the discharge of firearms. Some prohibit it altogether; others have limitations on how far you must be from a dwelling before shooting a firearm. In some cases, archery or crossbow hunting may be legal in these places even though gun hunting is not. Be sure to check local ordinances and wildlife regulations before making a hunt in these areas.

Because of all these extra worries, suburban turkey hunting is not my favorite thing. I'd much rather put on my hiking boots in some wilderness camp, start walking a full hour before daylight, and listen for the morning's first gobble from a high ridge on the back side of nowhere.

But spring turkey season is brief, and I have to work through a depressingly large portion of it. By utilizing the opportunities presented by suburban turkeys in close-in woodlots, I can get in a lot more woods time during the season. That's not a bad thing.

Incidentally, last spring, after 10 years of unsuccessful applications, I once again drew a permit to hunt that 25,000-acre military reservation near my home. Once again, I had a good number of gobblers located (though not 40, admittedly) before the season. Once again, I easily filled my tag.

That wasn't a bad thing, either.

Chapter 34

The Tough Ones

Some spurs from a few of the tough ones.

Some turkeys are easy. They're our occasional reward for putting in the long hours and hard work in the turkey woods. They come along just often enough to keep most of us from giving up in disgust.

When one of these birds drops into our lives like manna from Heaven, we start to feel like turkey hunters again. After most of a season's worth of getting whipped by gobbler after gobbler, having one of these eager fellows come galloping to the call is a welcome change. Never mind that most of these easy birds are lovesick 2-year-olds with pencil beards and spurs like Hershey's Kisses. Never mind that they'd probably have come running to any vaguely turkeylike sound we made. Never mind it was being in the right place – not skill – that killed the turkey. The easy birds give us confidence and they give us hope, and that's what counts.

What makes these birds so memorable is that they are so rare. Most turkeys are what insurance agents and automobile dealers call "a hard sell." They may be interested in the product, but they're resistant to the sales pitch. They make us work for them.

Tough gobblers, in short, are the majority, and they come in many types. Here are 10 categories of tough gobblers and brief suggestions for how to deal with them. Some of these types are covered in greater detail in other chapters, and others appear only here. These methods won't work all the time, of course, but maybe they'll give you a starting place.

The Hung-Up Gobbler: This type of problem gobbler is so common as to almost be a cliché. The truth of the matter is, though, most of the rea-

Get as close to a gobbling turkey as you can before trying to call him in. Sometimes this means crawling to set up a decoy, or crawling to your setup tree. The shorter the distance you have to bring a bird, the better your chances of tagging him.

sons a gobbler hangs up are hunter-caused, and most of them are avoidable.

First, learn as much as you can about the area you're hunting. On familiar ground, try to learn every little wrinkle and rock in the landscape. In new territory, study and carry maps, talk to other people more familiar with the place than you are, pay attention to your surroundings and do everything within your power to familiarize yourself with the hunting area. Second, get as close as possible to a gobbling turkey before you start trying to call him in. Doing these two things alone will reduce your hung-up turkeys considerably, because it minimizes the chance you'll set up with a serious obstacle between you and the bird you're trying to work.

Don't set up where it's too thick. A gobbler doesn't like to get into thick stuff when he can avoid it. But also don't set up where it's too open, or the approaching bird will be able to see too far and might either hang up or pick you out. One of the best setups, if you can manage it, is just over the crest of a ridge or other rise that hides you from the approaching gobbler and puts him in killing range when he first comes into view.

Don't overcall to an approaching bird, and especially don't overcall to one that's still on the limb. Having a gobbler come to the call and gobbling every step is exciting, but if he's not in the mood to get this way (which is usually), calling too much can hang him up. Don't be so timid that your gobbler loses interest and leaves, but don't call more than necessary, either. Take your cue from the turkey. If he's closing the distance in response to your moderate calling, don't get anxious. If he starts to leave, pick up the intensity.

If he hangs up despite all this, first try to change calling locations if you can do so without getting burned. If calling from several different setups doesn't work, try ceasing to call altogether. This can break a reluctant tom loose if you can convince him his sweetie is about to leave. Only after changing setups and giving a bird the silent treatment should you try to overpower a hung-up bird with hard, aggressive calling. This is a desperation tactic that should only be tried when you have nothing else to lose.

The Fickle Gobbler: Aggressive calling isn't always a no-no; it's just not the best thing to try on a turkey that's hung up. If you're competing with a

The fall-back technique for dealing with a reluctant gobbler is easier when you're hunting with a partner. The hard part is deciding who falls back and who stays put to shoot the bird.

real hen or two that are also calling to the gobbler from other locations, you're probably going to have to lean into your calling or lose the gobbler to the feathered competition.

First, though, try to determine if your competition is a real hen or another turkey hunter. If it's another hunter, the safest option is to back off and go looking for a different gobbler. No turkey is worth the risk of getting shot, and this situation is responsible for a high percentage of turkey hunting's accidental shootings.

If you're sure you're dealing with another hen, one way to get rid of the competition is to simply *get rid of the competition.* On more than one occasion I've walked over and chased away the competing hen, then called in the gobbler from the new location. Obviously, this only works when the gobbler is out of sight and you can get away with moving, but when conditions are right, it can be a very effective tactic.

If you can't manage it, though, you can still outcall the hen. The best way to do this, I've found, is not so much with volume as with quantity. Use a diaphragm and run a box or slate call

simultaneously, or use a couple of push-button calls to stage a turkey fight. Or, alternatively, call to the hen rather than the gobbler, mimicking her every sound and trying to pull her in. If you can do that, the gobbler will likely come as well.

The Henny Gobbler: This is possibly the toughest of all birds, because he has no incentive to come to your calling. In fact, he has a definite disincentive. If he does respond to your calling, some other gobbler is likely to slip in and steal his girlfriends.

However, there are ways to fool these toms. One effective but unorthodox technique involves separating a gobbler from his hens. The easiest time to do this is very early in the morning, when the birds are still on the roost, or right after fly-up in the evening. Since a gobbler seldom roosts in the same tree with his harem, it's sometimes possible to get between them and scare them in different directions. Then you can set up on the gobbler and attempt to call him back.

An evening scatter, as opposed to a morning scatter, usually results in a calmer, less-spooky gobbler for the next morning's hunt. However, an evening scatter means the hens will be calmer,

Hay bales can sometimes be used as makeshift setup spots in open-land hunting.

too, and will make a fast beeline for the gobbler when daylight comes. It's also sometimes possible to scatter a gobbler and his harem by keeping track of them as they move along, then rushing the flock and scattering them the way that's so effective for fall turkeys. Again, this results in a badly spooked gobbler, which means the hunter will usually have to wait several hours before the gobbler will become callable again.

Another way to deal with a henny gobbler is to simply wait the hens out. In the early part of the mating season, the hens will stay with a gobbler all day, but as mating gives way to nesting, a gobbler's hens will start to desert him by midday. If you can just maintain contact, or merely hang around in a gobbler's primary use area until the midday hours, it's often possible to find that gobbler when he's bereft of female companionship and more susceptible to your calling.

The Back-and-Forth Gobbler: This gobbler is a variation of the hung-up gobbler. He doesn't stay in one place, but he won't come in, either. Usually the reason is the same: The hunter is calling too much, or there's an obstacle between him and the bird.

The most obvious way to cope with this situation is to change calling locations. Don't give up after just one move, however. You may have to look hard for a place the gobbler will come to. It's not unusual to have to move a half-dozen or more times before finding a spot the gobbler will approach.

The silent treatment occasionally works with back-and-forth gobblers, but I rarely try it anymore. What usually happens when you quit calling is the gobbler just keeps on going when he gets to the end of his track.

Another way to deal with a gobbler like this is to wait until the bird is at one end or the other of the back-and-forth route he's established, then hotfoot it to the opposite end and wait him out. This is most easily accomplished when you're hunting with a partner, because one of you can stay put and continue to call to the gobbler while the other makes the move. It's a risky tactic, though. In most cases the track that one of these back-and-forth gobblers establishes isn't all that long, and there's a good chance the bird will spot you when you make your move.

The Open-Land Gobbler: Sometimes a gobbler in the open can be a pushover, but often he'll waste half your day and then go on his way. It's hard to leave a gobbler when you can see him.

Using a decoy or two is one of the best ways to deal with these wide-open gobblers, but the obvious problem here is getting the decoys out while the turkey is in sight. However, open-land birds are often pretty predictable about being in a certain field or pasture at a certain time, so it's often possible to anticipate, get in position and set up before the bird shows.

On occasion, it's possible to get right out there in the open with the bird and call him in. Last spring, I took a gobbler in a pasture while sitting at the base of a scrawny persimmon that was the only tree within 100 yards. I also once put myself in killing position on an open-land gobbler by carrying a square hay bale into the field and putting it near his usual midmorning strutting ground. I'd been lying on my belly beside that bale for an hour when the gobbler showed up at the edge of the field. After suspiciously eyeing the new addition to his strutting ground, he marched right on in. The fact that I missed him at 25 yards is beside the point.

Watching a gobbler enter and/or leave an open area is another way to get the drop on him, but it often requires several days of hunting the same bird. In most cases, he'll enter or leave the field by fairly predictable routes, and you can be there waiting at the appropriate time.

The Retreating Gobbler: One of the most difficult birds to conquer is the one that enthusiastically answers all or most of your calling, but moves steadily away from you, forcing you to follow and set up on him again and again. One way to cope is to just bide your time with a bird like this, trying to maintain contact until he get to where he's headed. In most cases, he does have a destination in mind – a favored strutting area, usually.

If you can just stay with him until he gets there, it's sometimes possible to ease as close as possible and then go to work with aggressive calling, to try to break him from that spot and bring him to the gun.

However, often you can't stay with a gobbler like this until he reaches his destination. He'll quit gobbling, move onto land you don't have permission to hunt, or simply outdistance you, and you'll lose contact. One tactic that sometimes pays off is

Keeping up with a traveling gobbler until he reaches his destination is tough. However, if you can pinpoint one or two of his favored strutting areas, this particular type of tough bird can be relatively easy – sometimes.

Subdominant gobblers often form gangs and roam the country, looking for action but reluctant to come in. If you encounter such a group, tone down your calling and use the subtle approach.

Never make a call until you've already set up. It takes a minute or so longer, but if you make a habit of doing this, you won't get blind-sided by those eager birds that come galloping in.

to return to the area the next day and set up somewhere along the bird's previous travel route – preferably at a pinch point such as a saddle, logging road or field edge. When he comes through this time, you may be in position to do something about it.

The Silent Gobbler: If turkeys didn't gobble, hunting them wouldn't be as much fun. But on some mornings, the woods are as silent as a Tuesday morning choir box. On these mornings, go to places with good visibility where you've seen gobblers or gobbler sign, make yourself comfortable, maybe put out a decoy or two, and settle in for a long day. Call softly and regularly (but not too often), and keep your eyes skinned.

Listen hard, too. Just because they're not gobbling doesn't mean they're not making noise. Many times you'll be alerted to the presence of a gobbler by the sound of drumming, or by footsteps in the leaves.

If a gobbler that's been answering your calls suddenly goes silent, don't think he's left. Instead, get ready. There's a good chance he's sneaking in for a look-see.

The Across-the-Water Gobbler: If the turkey you're working is on the other side of a creek, pond, lake or other water body, don't despair.

First, make every effort to cross over and get on the same side of the water with the gobbler. If you can't do that and the waterway is narrow enough to shoot across, crowd the shoreline and try to work the bird down to the water's edge and shoot him across the water.

If the water is not crossable and too wide to shoot across, back up 50 to 60 yards from the edge and pour on the calling. Try to "fire the gobbler up" and get him excited. Occasionally you can get a gobbler to fly across the water to your side.

If that doesn't work, try the silent treatment. Give it a good hour before giving up, or else simply leave the area and return in a couple of hours, ease within calling distance of where you were when you stopped calling, and give it another try. Sometimes a gobbler will get curious enough to cross the water after all the calling ceases, and when you hit him again after a couple hours of quiet, he may well be on your side of the water and ready to play.

The Bachelor Party: In some cases, subdominant gobblers will form bachelor groups and roam the countryside during the mating season. They'll

This hunter has thought ahead before making a call. If a nearby gobbler answers, he can be in a good setup and ready to shoot in two seconds flat.

cluster-gobble at almost anything, but are hesitant to come in.

If you think you're dealing with a group of bachelors, tone down your calling to a few clucks and purrs and scratch occasionally in the leaves with your hand. Don't try to overpower them, because the reason they're in a bachelor group in the first place is because they're afraid to challenge the boss for his hens. But they may well come sneaking in to check out what sounds like a lone hen.

The Come-too-Fast Gobbler. Again, this turkey is difficult only because of hunter error. He shows up before you're ready, catches you off guard and makes his escape before you can get the gun on him.

To avoid this problem, think ahead. Never make a call until you've already picked out a good setup tree. Better yet, never make a call until you've already set up. It takes a minute or so longer, but

if you make a habit of doing this, you won't get blind-sided by those eager birds that come galloping in while your first string of yelps is still echoing from the trees.

*   *   *

There are plenty of other tough turkeys, of course, and this discussion only scratches the surface. However, if you'll think each situation through, make adjustments and allowances as necessary to shift the odds more in your favor, you'll begin to improve your score on the tough guys.

Chapter 35

The Confidence Factor

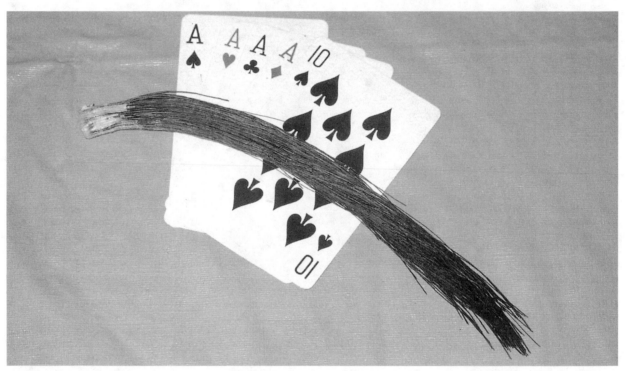

The beard from the author's first turkey, called to the gun by another hunter who had little actual skill but a whole lot of confidence.

After the gobbler came off the roost going downhill and away from us, I wouldn't have bet a nickel against a dollar he'd come our way. We were above him, on a flat, narrow ridge at the head of the little hardwood cove where he'd spent the night. After quite a bit of on-the-limb gobbling, the longbeard pitched down the slope, out of the cove and all the way to the floor of the valley, where he started gobbling in earnest as he drifted slowly away.

I was a rookie at the time and had yet to kill a gobbler. Robert, my hunting buddy and guide, had shot 15 or so – enough to be cocky and confident, but not enough to have learned he really didn't know all that much about turkey hunting. Because he was in that know-it-all, in-between stage, he had what Mark Twain once called "the calm confidence of a Christian holding four aces." He just knew he could turn that bird around and bring him back up that mountain.

And sure enough, he did. We repositioned 100 yards closer to the gobbler but still well up on the slope from him. Robert went to work with a diaphragm call and got into a spirited conversation with the turkey. After almost an hour of it, it

If you feed enough quarters into the slot machine, some money is going to fall into the tray. However, thinking each situation through and doing your best to improve your odds will serve you better.

became apparent the gobbler was slowly closing the gap. He shut up 100 yards out, still out of sight under the break of the hill.

This happened a long time ago, and my hearing was still fairly good. By the time the longbeard quit gobbling, I could already hear him drumming.

My inexperience almost cost me that tom, just as it had cost me a dozen or so others over the past five seasons of bumbling around in the woods. First, even though I heard him moving to the left as he drummed and crunched in the leaves, I let him come into sight 45 degrees left of my gun barrel. That's especially bad because I shoot left-hand-ed, and it's as awkward for me to swing left while sitting as it is for most hunters to swing right.

Second, I got excited and swung on him when he was in the open, and the result was predictable. The gobbler reversed direction, started alarm-putting and headed back downhill the way he came, walking rapidly but erratically in that jerky-necked, spastic, high-stepping fashion that tells you they're not thoroughly panicked but are leaving anyway. But luck smiled on me, and somehow I centered the pattern on that jinking, juking white head just before it disappeared over the break of the hill.

Mark Drury and Tad Brown (with turkey) are both supremely confident hunters, but they know when to raise the bet and when to fold the hand.

He wasn't much of a gobbler by trophy standards, but he was my first one, and I'll never forget anything about that hunt – not the golden light slipping in under the new, green leaves, nor the sheen of his breast feathers as he came up the slope, nor the truck-in-the-distance sound of his drumming as he slowly closed the gap. Another thing I'll not forget is that Robert's confidence in his ability to call that bird to the gun was what closed the deal that morning.

Never mind that my mentor's confidence was largely misplaced. We were behind a traveling turkey, first off, and that's almost never a good place to be. We were far up a steep slope from him, too, and while that's better than being far downslope from one, it's still not a very high-percentage calling position. We could have gotten closer to the gobbler before setting up, could have even gotten in front of him with only a little more trouble, but Robert wasn't having any of it.

Without question, Robert was a far better and more experienced turkey hunter than I was, but the fact remained that he still didn't know very much about the sport. He used one call and one call only – a double-reed diaphragm, announcing to everyone who would stand still for it that a diaphragm was all the turkey call anybody needed to carry. I thought his calling sounded like the angels singing, especially with that dead turkey at my feet, but I've since come to know better. His yelp was OK, but his cackle sounded less like a turkey and more like a guinea hen caught in a fence. And he used that cackle almost exclusively, yelping only occasionally to relieve the monotony. Cluck? Robert? Never heard of it.

All those things point to Robert's inexperience as a turkey hunter, but you have to keep coming back to one central, indisputable fact: The pencil-shaped, 8-inch beard of that 2-year-old gobbler hangs today on my office wall, and the reason it hangs there is because my long-ago turkey hunting mentor had confidence in his ability to call the bird in. He didn't say "Oh, well" and go look for another gobbler when that one flew off our mountain; instead, he moved to a slightly better position and went to work. A Christian with four aces.

It's that sort of confidence that turns rookie turkey hunters like I was into 15-gobbler know-it-alls like Robert was – and it's that sort of continuing confidence that enables those 15-bird hotshots to finally develop into truly good turkey hunters. It's not something that happens overnight, and for some turkey hunters (perhaps most) it never happens.

"Confidence may just be the most important tool in a turkey hunter's arsenal," an accomplished turkey hunter told me one morning a long time ago. Over the years since, I've come to agree with him wholeheartedly.

Nobody is unbeatable when it comes to turkeys. Difficult birds leave expert turkey hunters just as frustrated and bewildered as they do you and me. But where the experts differ from most turkey hunters is that they don't let it get them down when they get beat by a turkey.

I followed an expert hunter one morning while we made half a dozen setups on a talkative but uncooperative gobbler, and each time the expert tried both conservative and aggressive calling with a number of instruments – diaphragms, box calls, slates. I'd have given up on that turkey, but the expert didn't. I killed the bird at 25 yards, more than three hours after we started fooling with him. The episode gave me more confidence in my own chances of killing difficult turkeys, and that increased confidence has helped me on many hunts since then.

My buddy's type of confidence differs from the kind my other buddy, Robert, displayed on that long-ago hunt. Robert was convinced he could make that gobbler change his mind and come back up the hill to a place he'd already vacated, but if he'd really been an expert, he'd have known better than try it. He'd have done what Robert and I should have done but didn't – improved his position on the turkey before calling to him. Robert's confidence was the type of mentality that causes some people to keep feeding quarters into a slot machine: Do it long enough, and something will eventually fall into the tray.

Likewise, if you sit on enough mountains and call down to turkeys that have already left your calling position, one will eventually retrace his steps, climb the slope and commit suicide. That's what my first gobbler did; we just hit the jackpot with the first quarter, that's all. In the same situation, a good turkey hunter would have moved fast along the ridge until he got well ahead of the bird, dropped into the valley and gotten into position along his expected line of travel, then tried to call him in the direction he was already wanting to go.

One of the biggest differences between the rookie hunter and the veteran is that the rookie is scared he's going to make mistakes, while the veteran knows he's going to.

It won't work every time, but that's the way to scotch your bet.

On another spring hunt, I tagged along with Mark Drury and Tad Brown, the twin driving forces behind the success of M.A.D. Calls. Hunting on extensive but widely scattered private properties in central Missouri, we started the morning by running into another hunter almost underneath a gobbler Tad had roosted the previous evening. No big deal; it happens. But it caused us to waste the prime time of the early morning, and by the time we found action on another property, all the gobblers were on the ground and henny. We spent an hour or so in a long-distance shouting match with six or seven gobblers, but they wouldn't come, and there was no way we could approach and make a decent setup. So we went elsewhere. About 10 a.m. we struck a gobbler on a third property, went to him and got wooled around pretty well for another hour and a bit. I won't go into the details, but it was frustrating.

Running short of time, we were moving slowly through a pasture when Mark spied two long-beards feeding in the woods 150 yards away, across a little valley, and we somehow managed to drop to the ground before they spotted us. The orchard grass pasture had been close-cropped by winter-grazing cattle, and there wasn't any more cover than you'll find on a well-tended golf green. So Mark and I belly-crawled across 50 yards of open ground to the edge of the woods, where I took up a standing position behind an oak as big around as a restaurant table. Peeking around the edge of the tree, I watched as the two gobblers slowly closed the gap in response to Mark's soft calling. The one I killed weighed 25 pounds.

That bird, too, died as a result of confidence. At 12:30 p.m. when we spied those gobblers, Mark and Tad were still hunting as hard and with as much intensity as they'd been when we met that other hunter underneath the first gobbler at first light. Even though I knew better than to do it, I'd already given up and was thinking about how good a ham sandwich would taste. My guard was down, and even if I'd still been in the woods that morning if I'd been hunting alone (which I doubt), I'd never have seen those two gobblers before spooking them.

Mark and Tad, though, are confident hunters. They'd already been beaten by circumstances and bad luck on three separate turkey encounters that morning, but they both kept their confidence level high, and it paid off.

"Confidence" may not be exactly the right word to use here, but I'm stumped for a better one. I'd give the nod to "optimism," except that optimism without experience is the stuff of long shots – like when Robert called that gobbler back up the mountain. When Tad Brown or Mark Drury – or for that matter, any of the other excellent turkey hunters I've been privileged to share the woods with – makes contact with a gobbler, the first thing they do is assess the situation. If there's a way these hunters can improve the odds, by mov-

ing, climbing, descending, getting out of a thicket, crossing a fence, creek or whatever, they do it immediately and cautiously, but at the same time with confidence. If it doesn't work out, they shake it off and get ready for the next opportunity.

It boils down to a matter of attitude. With the number of books, videos, seminars and magazines devoted to turkey hunting these days, inexperienced and beginning hunters have little problem gaining the technical knowledge required to start participating in the sport. But knowledge is only as good as a hunter's ability to put it to use on the playing field, and that's where the experienced hunter has the edge on the two-days-a-season guy or gal.

Experience, measured in the number of hours logged in the woods, translates quickly into cockiness as a neophyte hunter tags a few birds. But by the time 15 birds have become 50, in most cases that cockiness has matured into genuine confidence, and the result is a pretty good turkey hunter. Here's the basic difference between a rookie and one of these veterans: The rookie is afraid he's going to make mistakes and lose a good number of the turkeys he encounters, and the veteran knows for certain he's going to.

Like I said: attitude. The veteran hunter realizes he must make a multitude of small and large decisions on every turkey he sits down to, and the odds are excellent some of those decisions will be wrong. But he doesn't worry about it, because he knows he can often make another decision on the same turkey that will erase the effects of his mistake.

Attitude. Call it confidence, optimism or something else. But whatever you call it, you can't be a good turkey hunter until you have it, and you can't have it until you earn it. And you can't earn it without getting in there and swinging the bat, as often and as diligently as possible. You'll strike out and you'll hit foul balls and little dribblers back to the pitcher, but you'll also hit some home runs.

Make your decisions and learn to live with your mistakes. But as you live with them, also learn from them. It's the way we learned to walk when we were babies, and it's the only way to achieve excellence in turkey hunting.

I like to think I'm about halfway there.

Chapter 36

Primitive Weapons

Muzzle-loading shotguns, especially modern ones with choke tubes and special loads, are effective gobbler-getters. Still, the author doesn't think most turkey hunters have the temperament or discipline to pass up risky shots, and therefore considers the muzzle-loader a choice for the experts.

There are those who hunt turkeys with muzzle-loading shotguns and bow and arrow. I am not among them.

I realize I'm walking the thin edge of anthropomorphism and maudlinism here, but here's my personal opinion: The American wild turkey is the most valuable, most worthy game animal in the United States – maybe in the whole world. As such, he is too valuable to be trifled with by hunting him with weapons that are not as deadly as human engineering can make them. Muzzle-loading shotguns

and archery equipment simply don't stack up to modern guns. Sure, I'm aware that with extended screw-in choke tubes and tweaked loads, some front-stuffers are capable of delivering patterns as dense and deadly as conventional shotguns, but if that's the case, what's the point of using a muzzle-loader? Am I missing something here?

OK, now that I've not only flung down the gauntlet in front of all you primitive-weapons fans, but also slapped you in the face with it, let me lay out my case:

Turkeys can't trample you or eat your arm off. The only way one can draw blood is with his spurs.

There are animals more elusive and harder to find than wild turkeys, if that's what trips your trigger. Africa's bongo and bushbuck come immediately to mind, and if you don't use bait or dogs, our good old American black bear fits that category as well.

Certainly much larger game animals are available, too. The adults of even the smallest whitetail race, the Key deer, weigh approximately three times as much as an adult turkey, and if you want to talk moose and elk, there's not even a remote comparison.

As far as danger to the hunter goes, the wild turkey can't even play. Oh, these big birds no doubt cause heart attacks each year when out-of-shape hunters have coronaries negotiating rough turkey country and when excitable hunters pop blood vessels as vocal turkeys approach. However, no wounded turkey gobbler ever bit off a hunter's arm the way a grizzly bear can, or trampled a hunter into the topsoil the way a Cape buffalo can. If you want to hunt game animals that can hurt you back, go to Africa or Alaska. The only time a turkey gobbler has ever drawn any of my blood

was when I got careless subduing a flopping bird and one of his spurs gouged a hole in the heel of my left hand. I show people the scar all the time, but they never react like I imagine they would if I were showing them claw marks left by a wounded leopard.

The American wild turkey is a phoenix risen from his own ashes. We're not going to repeat the story here, but if ever there was a game bird that missed a good chance at extinction, the wild turkey is it. So that's one reason he's special: because we almost didn't have him around to hunt.

The wild turkey is cautious to the point of paranoia, which makes him hard to dupe except under specialized circumstances, and that's another reason he's a worthy adversary. This paranoia is directly related to the fact that we almost exterminated turkeys; only the most secretive and survival-oriented birds survived the holocaust, and those few ultra-spooky survivors provided the seed for this new turkey population of the 21st century. Each spring and fall over the past five or six decades, we've further refined that spooky nature by systematically removing the less wary birds from the gene pool.

The thing that puts the above paragraph in the plus column is that the wild turkey gobbler, in the spring of the year, becomes susceptible to calling. This chink in his armor leads to some very exciting, highly uncertain contests in the woods, as the gobbler's lust and wariness struggle for dominance. Wariness often wins, of course, and other times the hunter does something (or fails to do something) that gives the decision to the bird, but it almost always makes for an entertaining morning. And the soft underbelly created by the gobbler's urge to breed lets us win just often enough to let us maintain our attitude of hope and positive thinking – most of the time, anyway.

The wild turkey is fairly accessible to most hunters and is becoming more so with each passing year. This makes him an extremely important game animal, putting him head and shoulders above moose, elk, geese, ducks and almost every other animal except maybe white-tailed deer.

A turkey is a big bird, but not so large we can't carry him out of the woods over our shoulders after we shoot him, and this – in my mind, at least – gives him another decided edge over elk, moose and even deer. I've passed up more than one deer because of the degree of difficulty that would have been involved in getting the animal out of where I was hunting, but I've never had to make that decision with a turkey. If you can get out of there yourself, you can walk out with your gobbler.

The wild turkey is also delicious, but not so tasty that we feel reluctant to share his flesh with family and friends. Thus, he is the centerpiece of many happy extended-family meals, and while he is big enough to feed a dozen or more hungry people, he's not so big you get sick of eating him before he's all used up.

A mature gobbler is also beautiful in his own way, with his iridescent feathers and patriotic head and all, but at the same time his breeding antics and his general behavior both in and out of the breeding season are goofy enough that most of us are saved from deifying him too much. He is, after all, a bird.

But what a bird! And for all those above reasons, and a lot more besides, I think it is irresponsible for most hunters to go after turkeys with primitive weapons. It's not the shooting of a

If you can consistently put an arrow into a target the size of a coffee cup at 20 yards, you're accurate enough to hunt turkeys with a bow. But do you have the discipline for it?

turkey that's the challenge; it's getting him into the proper position and location to be shot. Turkeys require a considerable amount of killing, and call me cynical, but judging from what I've seen over the past quarter-century, the average turkey hunter lacks the patience, ability and restraint to get turkeys into effective primitive-weapons range.

You have only one shot with either a muzzle-loader or a bow. In addition, the effective range with a bow is no more than 20 to 25 yards (and that's for an expert archer), and no more than 30 yards for the average muzzle-loader. And, like I said, there's no backup shot in case something goes wrong. It's hard enough for a hunter to pass up a 45-yard shot with a tightly choked modern shotgun delivering a 2-ounce payload. Do you have any idea how much harder it is to pass up a 35-yard shot when you're toting a smokepole?

Well, I do. Not long ago, I went on a several-day turkey hunt and let my host talk me into carrying a black-powder shotgun.

"Oh, this thing shoots tight," he said. "It's deadly out to 30 yards. I killed a bird with it just yesterday."

Against my better judgment, I left my dependable old Mossberg in my room and walked out of the lodge carrying the front-stuffer. It was a pretty thing, all right, and it was lighter and easier to carry than my heavy pump gun, and everything went swimmingly for two days. That is, until we called in those four longbeards that stopped like they'd hit a hog-wire fence, exactly 35 yards away. For more than 20 minutes I looked down the barrel of that light, pretty, inadequate gun at first one and then another of those four birds as they strutted, gobbled and suspiciously craned their necks, looking for the hen they'd heard but couldn't see. Then they faded back and disappeared from sight.

The next morning, we got right back on those four birds, and this time they topped a small rise on a little woods road, stopped again and stood there looking our way. The range – I'm sure you've guessed already – was 35 yards. Again I watched them strut and gobble off the end of my bead, and for another 20 minutes none of the four turkeys moved a single inch closer. When they left that time, I was very proud of myself for not throwing that gun into the nearby Mississippi River, but I wasn't polite enough to keep on hunting with it. I made my host take me

– right then – back to the lodge, and for the rest of that hunt I danced with the one who brung me – my old Mossberg. But, of course, we never saw another gobbler.

In the hands of the experienced hunter willing to practice (with a bow) or pattern and experiment (with a muzzle-loader), I'm well aware that using a primitive weapon to bag a gobbler can add an extra feeling of accomplishment for the hunter who can get the job done. And I'm perfectly willing to take my hat off and stand aside while you walk by if you are one of those people, because you are a better person than me.

But if you use primitive weapons and leave crippled turkeys in your wake, then you need to rethink your approach to this whole business. Your priorities are out of whack.

If you elect to use primitive weapons, go back and read the previous two paragraphs again. Bows and muzzle-loaders are deadly when used correctly and with the proper restraint, and they add an extra degree of difficulty to an already difficult enterprise. But they're not for the inexperienced hunter.

If you can't call turkeys in close, if you can't make yourself wait for the proper shot and pass up risky ones, if you can't accurately judge distances out to 25 yards to the nearest yard or two, if you can't consistently put your arrow in a target the size of a coffee cup at 20 yards, you're not good enough to hunt turkeys with a bow. Practice, practice and then practice some more. And when you practice, do it from a sitting or kneeling position, because that's the position you're going to be in when you shoot at a turkey. If you use a muzzle-loading shotgun, pattern it relentlessly until you know which load patterns best, and at what range it ceases to be effective.

With either muzzle-loader or bow, develop the discipline to pass up shots that are beyond the effective range for your choice of armament. If you don't think you can do all these things, don't use primitive weapons.

Chapter 37

Decoys

Decoys can completely fool a gobbler, but sometimes they'll send them running the other direction. You just never know.

It was as early as I've ever seen a gobbler hit the ground. The eastern horizon was awash with the pink glow of dawn, but the sky in the west hadn't yet gotten the news. Back toward Wichita, it was still night. We were walking across a wide Kansas pasture, heading toward the north edge of the field where we planned to set up. As we walked, we listened to the first sleepy gobbles of the turkeys we'd roosted the evening before. Mike glanced east, toward the glow of the coming day, and froze in his tracks like a deer in the headlights.

"Dang it!" he whispered. "That turkey just flew down!"

I looked that way in time to see the gobbler silhouetted against the light as he flared out, landed in the middle of the shortgrass pasture, and disap-

peared in the poor light. Just as he vanished, another large shape glided in behind him.

"Stand still a minute," I whispered, bending over at the waist, walking slowly toward Mike and grabbing him by the belt loops. "OK. Walk straight to the treeline. Don't get in a hurry, but don't stop either."

We got away with it. I don't know whether our makeshift deer/cow/whatever fooled the birds, or whether it was simply still so dark they couldn't see us at all. Whatever, it worked, and we were soon snugged into the edge of the treeline and listening to the two still-invisible gobblers sound off from the middle of the pasture.

Using the cover of the lingering darkness, I duck-walked back out into the pasture and stuck

Many hunters swear by decoys. Others swear at them.

two decoys, jake and hen, at a range of about 30 yards, thus making two mistakes at once.

The light slowly gained strength, and we began to be able to see the gobblers in the pasture. At first, all we could see was the white of their warty old heads as they strutted and gobbled. Then we could make out the dim blobs of their bodies, and a few minutes later the blobs morphed into turkeys, and the day was upon us.

We thought the turkeys might spot the decoys on their own, but after 10 minutes, that didn't appear to be happening. Mike looked at me, I looked at him, and after shrugging our shoulders at each other, we went to our box calls. A couple of yelp runs later, the two gobblers slicked down, craned their necks at our motionless decoys, held what appeared to be a two-turkey huddle, then calmly marched the other way, down the length of the field and out of sight over a rise at the far end. It was as definitive a display of utter rejection as

I've ever seen, and it left Mike and me sitting there shaking our heads, wondering what in the world we'd said.

But not for long. Less than two minutes after the first two gobblers strolled out of our lives in one direction, another longbeard entered the pasture from another. Mike saw him first. I followed his line of sight and picked the bird out myself, already puffed up and homed in on the decoys at a range of 200 yards. He advanced quietly and slowly but steadily, closing the distance at a rate of about a foot a second.

That is, he closed the distance at that rate until he was 30 yards on the other side of the decoys, which put him 60 yards off our gun barrels. And that's where he hung, as firmly as if he'd stuck his foot in a steel trap. We looked at that gobbler down our gun barrels for more than an hour as he strutted and drummed and gobbled back and forth along an invisible line that kept him at 60 yards,

While a single hen decoy is often effective and is probably the most common setup, using a jake-and-hen combination appeals to both of a gobbler's spring instincts – mating and dominance.

and then he lost interest and went back the way he'd come.

Like I said, two mistakes at once. The first was putting the decoys out at all for the first two birds we encountered that morning, and the second mistake was putting them too far from our position for the next bird that showed up.

That's not the way decoys are supposed to work, of course. They're supposed to bring the gobblers in and give them something on which to focus their attention while you bring your gun up and shoot them in the head. And sometimes it works exactly like that.

Trouble is, decoys don't always work that way. Sometimes they run off the very bird or birds you're trying to shoot. That's why, frankly, I'm not much of a fan of using turkey decoys in most situations. I don't share the opinion of the state of Alabama, the only state that bans their use; I don't

think decoys are unethical, unfair or anything like that. I just don't think they work well enough to be worth the bother, that's all.

There are other reasons I don't like decoys much. For one, a decoy (or two or three) is just one more thing to keep up with and lug around. For another, I'm a firm believer in being rapidly mobile on a turkey hunt. I believe one of the most important aspects of being an effective turkey hunter is being able to shift positions and set up again at the drop of a hat, and if you've got to pull up and reset your decoy or decoys each time you move, it detracts from that quick-draw, quick-change ability.

OK, having said all that, there are times and places where decoys can definitely help. If your hunting territory has a lot of open country, decoys can help pull turkeys across long, open areas and get them in position for a shot. Or, if you don't have a very big area to hunt and are limited to staying in one spot or in a relatively small territory for long periods, decoys can help because you don't have to move them often. If you're trying to get video footage or still shots of a hunt, decoys can be valuable because they focus a close-in gobbler's attention and allow you to do your thing with the camera with a lesser chance of getting busted. Ditto if you're trying to kill a gobbler with a bow – but you can read the previous chapter and find out what I think about that, too.

Last spring, since I spent so much time hunting open country and trying to kill birds on video, I used decoys much more often than is normal for me. Most times, it was a jake-hen combination. And I have to admit, I had considerable success with them; of the seven birds I took last season, decoys figured in four, and I watched two other birds die in front of decoys as well.

Expert hunter Brad Harris is a firm believer in decoys:

"I like to use more than one decoy," Harris says. "But 'more' doesn't mean a whole flock. It usually means two, one jake and one hen. Lately we've been having good success with a hen and two jakes – a standing, submissive decoy and a strutting, dominant jake."

Harris says the hen-jake combo works on both of a gobbler's spring mandates – breeding and dominance. The strutting jake adds another level of dominance challenge, and sometimes brings the boss gobbler at a run to thrash the interloper.

"You can even use the jake to position a gobbler for the best shot, because the gobbler will almost invariably address the jake decoy head-on or at least quartering from the front," Harris says. "By setting your jake decoy or decoys in a certain position, you can almost draw an 'X' on the ground where you want the gobbler to stop."

Harris is also a fan of the "breeding position" decoy setups, with a jake positioned over a squatting hen in the mating position. He says this also often stirs the fighting blood in a dominant gobbler and can goad him into doing something unwise.

Harris agrees that decoys focus an approaching bird's attention and helps the hunter remain undetected. He says this is especially important when you're dealing with a gobbler and his harem, because there are so many more eyes available to spot you.

As far as decoy placement goes, Harris has some definite ideas there, too. He prefers to position his decoys fairly close to his setup location, to avoid the kind of thing Mike and I experienced that Kansas morning when the longbeard hung up 20 yards outside gun range. Whether he's using a standard, strutting or breeding jake, he wants it facing more or less toward his setup position. "When a gobbler comes to a jake decoy, it's usually to display his dominance," he explains. "In order to do that, the longbeard will face the jake down, and when he does, I want him facing away from me so I can complete my move with less chance of being detected."

Harris says that while a single jake decoy is often effective, multiple jakes may scare off even a dominant gobbler. If you've ever seen a flock of jakes gang up on a longbeard and send him packing, as I have on several occasions, you understand the logic of this reasoning, and you understand why Harris often uses a single jake.

Because turkey hunters are gadget-oriented, and because all of us are continually looking for new tricks or trinkets to help us be more successful with gobblers, there will continue to be more and more innovations regarding turkey decoys and other tools of the trade. Witness the moving decoys that operate by means of a hunter pulling on a string, or the suspension rigs that allow decoys to swing freely in the breeze, or the stake-mounted push-pull yelpers that let you make turkey sounds from the precise location of your decoy by pulling on another string.

But keep in mind that decoys also sometimes scare turkeys, they definitely slow you down, and they're one more thing to carry. Whether to use them or not is a personal decision.

Despite my considerable success with decoys last spring, I expect my personal decision, most often, will continue to be "not."

Chapter 38

State-Hopping for Turkeys

Traveling to hunt not only gives you the opportunity to stretch your season, but you also get to see new places.

March 26: The turkey started gobbling before daylight, but he was unreachable over the swampy water of a cypress brake. One thing led to another, though, and he eventually flew out to dry land. Before the morning was over, I outmaneuvered him and wore him down, and he made a fatal mistake.

April 15: The bird gobbled hard at the loud cutting on the box call, but he was on the other side of a small river. Alan and I had permission to hunt the other side, though, and we were over

Make a list and check it twice. It was good advice for Santa, and it's good advice for the traveling hunter as well.

there in no time. It wasn't long before he came strutting in with one of his buddies. We got 'em both. Alan's was a lot bigger.

April 19: Easing through scattered mesquite, I raised a cluster-gobble from a group of four long-beards. They were on me almost before I could get ready. All of them were good birds, and once they were under the gun I relaxed and watched as they strutted, gobbled and sparred with one another in a small clearing 30 yards off the barrel. Finally, I ended the performance with a load of 5s. The one that stayed behind had 1 1/2-inch spurs.

April 24: He was one of those aggravating birds that gobble at you while walking away. After following for a while, I circled and gained ground. I was still behind the gobbler, but close enough to turn him and get him headed the right direction. He came walking through the dew-wet grass of a little creek-bottom pasture, looking for the hen that had chased him down. He never knew what hit him.

Each of those hunts in one of my recent seasons was successful, but each differs from the others in one important respect – each took place in a different state. The first was in Mississippi, the second was in Kansas, the third was in south Texas, and the fourth was in Missouri. When it comes to turkey hunting, I'm like the gobbler described in the April 24 hunt – I'm a traveling man.

So are many other turkey hunters. Turkeys are legal game in every state except Alaska, not to mention southern Canada and northern Mexico, and many hunters are taking advantage of the expanded turkey hunting opportunities outside their home ranges. They're discovering the only thing more satisfying than getting out there on opening day is getting out there on two opening days. Or three. Or four.

Given the growing popularity of state-hopping for turkeys, you'd think folks would be getting pretty good at it. But according to my own observations and the stories I've heard from other hunters, that's not necessarily so. Hard-luck stories of botched out-of-state trips are as common as diaphragm calls at an NWTF convention. Tell a bunch of turkey hunters how your early-season Alabama hunt got spoiled by an influx of other

Breasting your gobbler reduces the bulk of the bird considerably and makes it easier to transport. Take the legs, too; if you separate the thighs and drumsticks, you can pack a 20-pound gobbler's breast and legs in a gallon freezer bag. That's hard to believe, but it's true.

hunters, and you'll get trumped by someone whose Black Hills trip was ruined by an outfitter who didn't know his butt from his binoculars.

In order to make the most of these away-from-home hunts, you have to plan ahead. Many hunters, myself included, have learned the hard way that a successful out-of-state turkey hunt involves more than just throwing the camo in a duffel bag and hitting the road. Here are a few tips that can get you off on the right foot:

Start your fact-gathering and planning well in advance. The military doesn't call this process "intelligence" for nothing.

"One of the best ways to avoid problems on a trip is to not get in a big hurry to do it," says Harold McAlpine, an old friend and boondocking buddy of mine who's about as experienced and capable a trip planner and trip maker as anyone I know. I've shared trips with him to Wyoming, Missouri, South Dakota, Oklahoma, Arkansas and elsewhere after turkeys, mule deer and antelope, and this I know from experience: When you travel with Harold, you're going to be fine. Everything's been thought out, and there are few possible contin-

gencies or mishaps that haven't been provided for.

"Think well ahead," McAlpine advises. "If you're planning an April turkey hunt, September isn't a bit too early to start making plans and getting ready. Many states have advance permit application periods and drawings, and it's important to start planning early to get in on them."

Know where you're going before you start. That sounds like the worst sort of condescending, unnecessary advice, but you'd be surprised how many hunters head out for a new state with little more advance planning than looking at a road map to find the shortest way to the state line. I'm not real big on making predictions, but here comes one: If you have to stop when you get to your chosen state and ask directions to the nearest national forest or wildlife management area, you're probably not going to shoot a turkey. Or see one, for that matter.

Unless you're luckier than a six-footed rabbit, it will take more planning than that to have a successful hunt. Outdoor magazines such as *Turkey & Turkey Hunting* often run where-to-go articles, and these can be excellent sources of information.

When you begin your state-hopping career, the natural tendency is to go to as many different places as possible. There's nothing wrong with adding new places, but don't abandon all the old ones, either. The better you learn a piece of out-of-state territory, the more successful you'll be there.

The problem with going to a place that's recently been profiled in a national magazine is pretty obvious. If you read about it, other hunters did, too, and unless it's a big area, you're likely to find yourself in a crowd.

A better way to gather intelligence is to first decide on a state for your turkey hunt, then narrow it down to a specific hunting area by using other sources. There's an in-depth discussion of this process in Chapter 13.

Make a list and check it twice. Keep it on file for future reference as well, amending and updating it as you discover new things you need to take – or, almost as important, things you can leave behind next time.

"After you've made a trip or two, your packing will get a lot simpler and more efficient," says McAlpine. "You learn what you need to take and what's excess baggage. This is much more important when you're flying to a destination than when you're driving and have more room for luggage, but there's no sense in taking stuff you know you're not going to need, no matter how much room you have. If you keep a running list of necessary equipment, and add or subtract things you learn you need or don't need, after a while you can pull out your equipment list and put your gear together pretty easily."

Don't neglect to make provisions for taking care of the meat. A turkey isn't an elk, but he's still a fair-sized critter. If you're driving and camping, the ice chests you'll use in camp will serve. But on a plane, a big ice chest can be a hassle. I usually try to freeze the bird, if possible, wrap it well in newspaper, and then carry it on board in a soft collapsible cooler I carry empty in my luggage on the way out. Or you can buy a medium or small cooler before returning, and check it as baggage on the return trip.

Guides and outfitters can either be a godsend or a disaster. If you find a good one, it makes the trip a lot easier and more worry-free. Also, good outfitters usually have access to private land where the hunting is better – or they are more familiar with the public hunting territory – and can usually put you on birds. The downside, of course, is that using a guide/outfitter is considerably more expensive than doing it on your own.

Another downside to using an outfitter is you might get a bad one, but there are ways to mini-

There's traveling, and there's traveling in style.

mize that possibility. First, ask around in the state you're researching. When you talk to biologists and other turkey hunters, ask them to recommend a few reputable people in the industry. Then call those people and discuss the possibility of booking a hunt, being specific about what you're looking for (i.e., remote hunting far away from the nearest roadhead, or an area that's within easy driving distance of the airport you'll be flying into, or whatever other stipulations you wish to make). If they tell you they can meet your needs,

ask for a list of references. If they don't want to or can't furnish references, don't book a hunt with that outfitter. Trust me, you don't want him.

Once you get the list of references, call several of them and ask questions. Were these former clients satisfied? How was the hunting? Any problems or heartburn? If you get satisfactory answers from three or so former clients, it's probably safe to send a deposit.

The only other thing to really worry about when booking a hunt is the possibility of clashing personalities. People are different. Some of us simply don't like others of us, and there's not much anyone can do about it. However, it's usually possible to get a pretty good read on a guide or outfitter during your telephone conversation, and anyway, most people in this business are there for two reasons: They like hunting, and they like people. They're sure not in it because they think they'll get rich.

Pick an area and stay with it from year to year. Hunting out of state is like hunting close to home, in one major respect: The better you learn the territory, the more effectively you can hunt it. Returning to an area in future years is a good way to improve the productivity of these long-range trips.

Carried to its extreme, though, this strategy defeats one of the most attractive features of state-hopping – to see new places and have new experiences. There's a lot to be said for becoming intimately familiar with your hunting area, but it's also nice to make footprints where you've never made them before. Strike a happy balance to achieve both goals.

Most state-hopping turkey hunters concentrate their efforts on public land. This is logical, because when you go to a new area, you don't know the landowners, and it's difficult to gain permission to hunt.

Or is it? I've been hunting more and more private out-of-state land over the past years, simply through the process of screwing up my courage, knocking on doors and asking. Often I get turned down, but sometimes I don't, and it's opened up a lot of land to me that isn't as heavily hunted as the nearby public areas.

Some property owners allow hunters on their land for a daily trespass fee, but I've never hunted under those arrangements. What I do, though, is offer the landowner the dressed turkey I've taken from his property, if my hunt is successful. Whether they accept or decline the bird, the gesture makes a favorable impression, and it nearly guarantees my welcome on that property in future years. Landowners talk among themselves, too, and it's also gained me access to nearby properties.

This next is just common sense, but it's worth a mention here: If you gain admittance to private land, don't abuse the privilege. Don't show up with a crowd of buddies, don't rut up the roads, don't litter, don't leave open gates closed or closed ones open. In short, don't make a nuisance of yourself.

Consider the possibility of a late-season hunt. In early-opening states like Alabama and Mississippi, this can make a big difference in the amount of crowding on public land. Granted, there will be fewer turkeys to hunt, and the survivors will be smarter, but I'd rather hunt one savvy old gobbler that's been fooled with and have him to myself than hunt a lot of birds with six other hunters sharing my patch of woods. Also, in Northern turkey states like Montana and South Dakota, late-season hunts are much more likely to provide you with decent weather. It's no fun to sit in your motel room while a blizzard dumps 13 inches of snow outside on the first day of your hunt. Trust me on this, too.

You can easily find out if waiting until later in the season is a good option for the state you're planning to hunt. Just ask the biologists and other hunters when you call them in the intelligence-gathering stage.

Consider making a multi-state jaunt to increase your hunting opportunities and cut down on travel time. There are many places where this is possible – for example, the Black Hills and its surrounding prairie country. It's entirely feasible to hunt Wyoming, Montana, South Dakota and Nebraska on the same trip, given enough time. By making a multi-state hunt, you can stretch travel dollars farther and increase your chances of finding an out-of-state hot spot.

In the end, don't let the logistics of planning a state-hopping trip or two scare you away. It requires attention to detail, but it's not brain surgery. The bother of planning an out-of-state hunt is a small price to pay for the experience of seeing new country and hunting turkeys in new places.

Just remember the advice of my buddy Harold McAlpine: "The more you plan, the better your trip will probably be."

Chapter 39

Fall Turkeys — A Different Species?

Fall hunting is a different ball game, and fall gobblers can be especially tough.

Fall hunting is fun. It is as gay and bright and frothy as light summer literature. It smells good and it looks good and it feels good, but like making love to chorus girls, there ain't no depth to it."

That's Tom Kelly, who wrote the foreword to this book, in his landmark turkey book *Tenth Legion*.

It's not a bad description, except for that last part. As a long-time advocate and ardent practitioner of fall turkey hunting, I summon up all the gumption I have and beg to differ with the man who's widely recognized as the poet laureate of turkey hunting: There is, too, some depth to it.

Admittedly, hunting fall turkeys rarely results in that spine-tingling, palm-sweating, jitters-begetting excitement often produced by a spring hunt, because in fall it's rare for turkeys to gobble much. It happens sometimes, but you can't count on it.

Aside from the lack of gobbling, there are other important differences. In spring hunting, we use the mating urge of a turkey gobbler as the basis for most hunting tactics. In fall, that urge is even more absent than gobbling. This makes mature gobblers even more difficult to hunt than they are in spring. Not only are they mostly silent; they usually aren't very interested in your calling.

Luckily, fall turkey hunters aren't restricted to gobblers in most states. There are three reasons for this: 1) Turkey populations are highest in autumn; 2) Hunting pressure is lower than in spring; and 3) A significant natural mortality in

In spring, you stand about as much chance to locate turkeys by sound as by sight. However, because gobbling is much less prevalent in fall, most of the turkey sounds you stand to hear are subtle – soft yelps, clucks and purrs, and the sound of turkeys walking or scratching in dry leaves. Many hunters, especially older hunters with ears deadened by years of shooting with inadequate hearing protection, need help hearing these subtle sounds. Products like these, manufactured by Walker's Game Ear, Inc., can be a big help.

the juvenile turkey population between fall and spring means carefully regulated fall seasons cause no detectable reduction in spring turkey numbers. Because hunting pressure is so low over-all, any turkey, regardless of age or sex, is legal in most states during fall seasons. This levels the playing field a bit, and as we've already mentioned, hurts the population not a whit.

The initial step to successfully hunting fall turkeys is finding the birds. The Catch-22 is that although this task sounds simple, it's often quite challenging.

It's challenging for several reasons. Turkeys, as any hunter knows, are shy, retiring birds, as allergic to human contact as the wildest buck in the woods. That's one thing. Another is the lack-of-gobbling factor we've already mentioned. Turkeys yelp and cluck in the fall, but a yelp or cluck doesn't carry as far as a gobble, so locating turkeys by ear becomes more difficult. Third, turkeys tend to form large flocks in fall, with hens and poults gathering together and old gobblers doing likewise. As the poults mature, young-of-the-year gobblers break away from the hens and

form flocks of their own, but in October, most of the young gobblers are still with the hens.

In areas with good turkey populations, hen-and-poult flocks often number from 25 to 40 or more. Rio Grande and Merriam's birds in the open country of the Western states sometimes come together in huge flocks numbering 200 or more. Mature gobbler flocks are usually much smaller, from 20 or more birds in the West to eight to 10 birds in the East. Both West and East, you'll sometimes spot old gobblers running in pairs or even going it solo. Later in the fall or early winter, as mentioned, the jakes break off from the hens and form their own groups, clustering together in gangs of five to 20 or more.

These numbers vary from year to year, of course, depending on factors like food availability, but in general, hen flocks are the largest, jake flocks are second and mature gobbler flocks are the smallest.

All of this flocking means most of the landscape is devoid of turkeys, because they're all bunched up in a few places. The job of the fall hunter, then, is combing through a big chunk of

Finding fresh sign in the fall, like this dusting bed, is a good first step to finding turkeys. They form large flocks in fall and winter, and much of the spring turkey range is devoid of birds.

territory looking for those concentrations of birds. This is usually easy in the more open country of the West, because a flock of 40 or more birds the size of turkeys have a hard time hiding. In the heavily forested country of the East, however, locating birds can be a real challenge.

Most experienced fall hunters, just as they do in spring, try to spend as much time in the woods as possible before the season opens, covering as much territory as they can and looking for sign – scratchings, feathers, tracks, dusting areas, droppings. Likely places to find it are along waterways or ponds, along old logging roads or the soft shoulders of main and secondary gravel roads, and in open woods with a good complement of oaks, pecans, dogwoods and other hard-mast trees. Ridges, saddles, valley bottoms, firebreaks, hiking trails and other natural and manmade travelways are also likely places to find sign.

Once you locate a concentration of turkey sign or the birds themselves, at least part of the battle is won. A fall turkey flock may have a large home range, but it's a safe bet they'll be back on a regular basis through the area where you found the sign. A hunter who's located abundant turkey sign in several spots a mile or so apart can often piece together a logical set of travel routes (usually the

path of least resistance) connecting these places. By simply walking this projected route, it's often possible to find turkeys.

Don't just blunder through the woods, though. If you do, most of the turkeys you encounter will see or hear you first. Instead, ease quietly along, following trails or roads when possible to minimize noise. Stay below the crest of a ridge when you're walking along it, but close enough to the top so you can listen for the soft, contented clucks and purrs and scratchings of a flock of feeding turkeys. Despite the fact that fall birds are quieter, hearing them is still the best way to locate them.

When you find birds, of course, you have to do something about it. It's the old dog-catches-the-car dilemma: *Omigosh! What now?*

Here's the wise, imprecise, wishy-washy answer from this corner: It depends.

Well, it does. Are the turkeys aware of your presence? If they are, you've got only one play: run at the birds as if they'd stolen your wallet, yelling and making as much racket as possible. You want to panic the birds and make them flush wildly in separate directions, like a covey of quail. More about this later.

265

After scattering a flock, move 100 yards or so in the direction most of the birds went, find a good open place as if you were setting up on a spring hunt, and wait.

Detecting the turkeys before they detect you is the most desirable scenario. It gives you many more options, as well as time to think about which ones to put into play.

Some hunters try to get in front of the birds and let them feed their way past (maybe prompted a little by soft yelping, purring, clucking and kee-keeing). Others try to call the birds in without attempting to get in front. Both options are pretty boring, frankly, and they're low-percentage tactics anyway, especially when you're dealing with mature gobblers. Hens and poults can sometimes be called into range this way, but if you're dealing with longbeards, you've got your work cut out for you.

Personally, I prefer the rush-and-scatter method. The objective isn't to run within gun range and shoot a bird (although this can sometimes be done), but to split the flock up so you can call them back together. Get as close to the flock as possible, then follow the instructions given three paragraphs ago: Try to scare their feathers off.

As a safety precaution, it's probably best to lay your shotgun down where you're sure you can find it, and then rush the flock empty-handed. However, I can't look you in the eye and tell you I follow that advice. I used to do it that way, but after I lost my camo shotgun in the leaves and spent an hour kicking around for it while my nicely scattered flock got back together 200 yards away, I gave it up as a bad idea.

If the birds all fly or run off in one direction, forget it. Go find another mob of turkeys, because all you've done is inconvenience the one you just ran at. But if the birds fan out when they leave, you're in business. Move 100 yards or so in the direction most of the birds went, find a good open place as if you were setting up on a spring hunt, and wait.

If you're dealing with a flock of longbeards, your wait is going to be a long one. In fact, if you scatter a flock of mature gobblers later than about 2 o'clock, chances are they won't try to get back together until the next day. (This is not necessarily bad; come back and hunt them the next morning, as discussed later in this chapter.)

But if you're dealing with hens and/or young birds, you'll usually hear them start calling to one

266

another within an hour or less as they start trying to get back together. Sometimes it only takes a few minutes for them to start calling.

However long it takes, mimic the sounds you hear. Yelp back at yelps, and kee-kee when you hear kee-kees. In a short time, you're probably going to be looking at turkeys – unless, like I said, it's longbeards. They'll take their own sweet time.

Make no mistake: Hunting adult gobblers in the fall is a challenging business. Gobblers aren't interested in sex this time of year, and the birds are warier.

Still, there are ways to specifically seek out, hunt and kill gobblers in the fall. It just takes more work than it does in the spring. Basically, there are two fall hunting philosophies: Hunt conservatively, or pull out all the stops.

The Conservative Approach
"Hunting fall gobblers successfully is 99 percent scouting," says John Vaca, a veteran fall gobbler chaser from northwest Missouri. In the fall, says Vaca, turkeys are concerned with three things: feeding, flocking and survival. The breeding instinct lies dormant, not to awaken until the growing day length of spring triggers the annual mating ritual.

Vaca says he likes to scout two to three weeks prior to the fall season, to pattern turkey movements in the area he intends to hunt. He tries to actually see the birds, but tries not to spook them in the process. Toward this end, he does a lot of sitting, watching and listening.

"They're usually not as vocal in the fall, but they're still there," he says. "By knowing their habits, you can set up an ambush between Point A and Point B. Hunt all day in the fall. You might make contact with turkeys at any time. Since fall gobblers usually roost in the same area night after night, if you don't do any good during the day, you can set up near the roost and hunt them as they come back in the afternoon."

Vaca says breaking up the flock and calling them back in is also another good way to hunt fall gobblers – although he agrees it requires more patience than scattering a flock of young turkeys and doing the same thing.

"When you break up a flock of adult gobblers, watch closely as they disperse," he advises. "If you see a good gobbler fly or run in a particular direction, go that way yourself. If you set up in the

Breaking up a flock of fall longbeards and then calling them back together is the traditional way to hunt them, but when you break them up, you're going to be in for a long wait.

direction you see a particular gobbler run or fly away, you'll have a better chance at that bird."

Knowing the lay of the land is also extremely helpful when targeting fall toms. "Turkeys are like people in that they take the easy route when they're not being pressured," he says. "Use natural bottlenecks and funnels such as saddles, forest roads and such to your advantage.

"Nothing is 100 percent effective, spring or fall," Vaca says. "But the more you know about the habits of the turkeys you're hunting in the fall, the better off you'll be."

Aggressive Tactics for Fall Toms
Brad Harris agrees with Vaca's philosophy for hunting fall gobblers – but only up to a point.

"There are two ways to hunt fall gobblers – conservatively or aggressively," Harris says. "The conservative approach is effective, and for a long time I believed that was the only good way to hunt them. Bushwhacking, stalking, calling softly and sparingly – all those things are part of the conservative style of hunting. But over the years, I've begun to notice a change in the behavior of fall

Spending a lot of time in the woods is the best way to increase your odds of being successful with fall turkeys, and a good way to do that is camp out and hunt all day long.

turkeys, and I've modified my fall hunting techniques to take advantage of it."

Harris says when he was a youngster hunting deer or other game in the hills and hollows of the eastern Ozarks, it was rare to hear a turkey gobble in the fall. Nowadays, he says he hears them all the time, and often they gobble as aggressively as if it were spring. He says other hunters are telling him the same thing, and I've noticed it myself.

"I don't know the reason, but I suspect it's partly due to the fact that we have higher turkey densities in many areas than we've ever had before," Harris says. "Fall turkeys aren't very vocal on bad-weather days, but when the weather is mild, they can really crank up."

Harris says he lets the weather dictate his hunting tactics. On cloudy, windy, cold days, he relies on the traditional, conservative tactics described by John Vaca, doing a lot of slipping along and looking for turkeys, calling softly, being patient and stealthy. But when the day is nice, he gets unconventional. And it works.

"In bluebird weather, I've found it's very productive to get aggressive with fall gobblers," Harris says. "I call to 'em just like it was spring, with locator calls, loud, fast hen yelps, cutts, gobbles, fighting calls, gobbler yelps, you name it. I try to cover as much ground as possible, just like I do in the spring, looking for a gobbler or group of gobblers that wants to play."

However, "play" is probably an inaccurate word to use in this context. Harris believes that, to a certain extent, turkeys are susceptible to the same social pressures humans are. In higher population densities, turkeys, like humans, become more irritable. Too many individuals crammed into too little available space inevitably causes friction, and this leads to open conflict. It's why you read about road rage on the LA freeway system, but rarely hear of any overt driver aggression in Tiptonville, Tennessee, or Spotted Horse, Wyoming.

It's Harris' contention the increasing density of turkey populations in many areas of the country – his home state of Missouri, for example, and in neighboring eastern Kansas – is causing gobblers to be more aggressive toward one other. Turkeys aren't exactly territorial, but Harris believes they get grumpier as their populations increase.

"In the past two or three years, I've learned that this loud, aggressive stuff is working," he says. "We're making longbeards come in gobbling and strutting, just like they do in the spring. Surely it's not a breeding impulse that's causing them to do this – it's bound to be tied to dominance – but whatever it is, it's happening more and more."

Harris has long been on record as believing the dominance factor is more important than the breeding instinct in influencing turkey behavior. "The turkey breeding season lasts only a few weeks," he says, "but the struggle for dominance goes on all year long. It never stops, and it's present in all segments of the turkey population. Adult gobblers in a given area have a pecking order, and so do immature gobblers. Hens do, too. And all these pecking orders are constantly changing."

Harris says that even in spring, when turkeys are all in a fizz over the mating season, the dominance factor overrides the breeding instinct.

"That's why a big gobbler will go to face off a jake decoy rather than going directly to a hen decoy when you have a mixed decoy spread," he says. "For the moment, at least, the big gobbler is more interested in establishing his dominance over the jake than he is in servicing the hen."

Harris says that although he hasn't been doing it long enough to be absolutely sure of what's happening, he believes it's easier to fire a turkey up in the fall where turkey densities are highest.

"The gobblers are all bunched up this time of year, but there are getting to be more and more bunches of them. That not only makes them easier to find, but also easier to fool into thinking their dominance is being challenged. It's a lot easier to set 'em off."

Harris says he hasn't abandoned the tactic of breaking up a flock of gobblers and calling them back together, but he has some pretty specific ideas about the timing of this enterprise.

"If you're going to bust up a bunch of gobblers, do it late in the afternoon or even after they've flown up," he advises. "It's much harder to get a wide dispersal when you're breaking up a gobbler flock during the day, and it takes a lot longer for a bunch of old birds to get back together in full daylight. But when you break them up late in the day,

In cold weather, conservative tactics usually work best for fall gobblers.

The best time to break up a flock of gobblers is late in the afternoon. It takes gobblers longer to settle down than hens and young birds after they're scattered, and when a fall longbeard spends the night alone, he's much more susceptible to calling the next morning.

they won't be able to find each other before dark, and each of them will have to spend the night alone. The next morning, if you get out there among the scattered gobblers, you can call them back much easier." Harris says he uses a lot of coarse gobbler clucks for this, but he's also had success by staging a gobbler fight.

"We're in the heyday of turkey hunting," Harris says. "Nationwide, it's never been better. You probably need a pretty good turkey population to make these aggressive tactics work, but so far I've seen them work in Texas, Missouri and Kansas, and they will work in other states, too."

So if you've been lukewarm about hunting fall turkeys because young birds aren't really your thing and fall gobblers are too tough, maybe you ought to give Harris' aggressive tactics a try on your hunting grounds. If you feel silly out there cutting and cackling when the trees are losing their leaves instead of growing them, so what? Who's gonna see you?

I can testify his aggressive tactics work for fall gobblers in Arkansas, too – or at least, they did once, and I doubt it was an accident. I called in a mature gobbler last October using the aggressive approach.

If the aggressive longbeard tactics don't work for you, you can always take a page out of the traditional playbook and hunt fall longbeards a la John Vaca. Or forget about targeting gobblers and try to break up a flock of young birds, which are both easier to find and to call back together.

But when they're coming in, whether they're 9-pound jennys or 22-pound longbeards, I promise you this: Your level of tension and excitement is going to rise. You'll sit there looking down your gun barrel, your eyes darting frantically from spot to spot as you search for that warty, wrinkled head you just know is going to appear any second.

And somewhere during those moments, I'm betting this fleeting thought will cross your mind: *I'm glad I didn't have to wait until April to do this again.*

Section 5

Putting Something Back

Chapter 40

Private Lands Turkey Management

Turkey numbers are on the rise, but so are the numbers of turkey hunters.

If you want to grow tomatoes in your back yard, the procedure is simple and straightforward: Dig up a patch of soil, maybe fertilize it a little and plant tomato seeds or set out small tomato plants. Then you weed and water the growing plants, dust them with insecticide if needed, and finally you harvest your crop.

If you want to grow turkeys on your back 40, the general procedure is much the same, though the specifics are different. You must prepare a favorable environment, do what you can to nurture the growing crop, reduce competition, if possible,

and harvest the surplus at some future time. It's as simple – and as complicated – as that.

Most of us understand the basic principles of wildlife conservation, although we don't always follow them. We haven't always known these principles, however, and we almost lost our native wild turkeys because of our ignorance and thoughtlessness.

The history of this big-game bird is a story of riches to rags and back to riches again. From a population low of approximately 30,000 birds nationwide during the 1930s and early 1940s,

Many hunters limit their hunting to private land, but not all of us have access to property that contains a huntable turkey flock.

today's total wild turkey population is over 5.6 million and still climbing.

With this surge in turkey numbers has come a corresponding surge in the number of turkey hunters. Our nation's public lands, while they still provide a lot of high-quality turkey hunting, are becoming more and more crowded as the population of turkey hunters continues to increase. Accidents, though statistically rare, are far too common, and confrontations between hunters – most of them friendly but some of them, well, confrontational – grow more numerous with each passing year. Even when it's unintentional, two people working the same gobbler degrades the hunting experience. Worse still, nobody kills the bird in most of these situations, and the gobbler receives an education and becomes much harder to hunt.

That's why more and more hunters are searching out privately owned property for their turkey hunting. Usually the acreage you have to hunt is smaller, but at least you can eliminate a lot of the competition.

There's a catch, of course. If you're hunting private property, there has to be a gobbler on the land before you can engage him. Going back to the tomato-patch analogy for a second, you can't pick tomatoes unless there are tomato plants in the garden. Just as obviously, you can't shoot a turkey if there aren't any on the property. So how do you make sure turkeys will be there? By giving them what they need to survive and prosper, that's how.

Turkeys need as cornerstones for survival the same things you and I require: food, water, shelter, space and protection. This ought to be a no-brainer, but you'd be surprised at how much private land would be great turkey habitat, except for one little fact: Turkeys would starve to death on it. Many landowners don't think about the fact that turkeys need a dependable food source 365 days a year. If at any time during the year there's an absence of food on the land, turkeys will be absent as well. Generally they'll be absent for the whole year, too, not just when food is scarce. The same holds true for the other four basic requirements. These things must be present not only around the clock, but also around the calendar, because turkeys are resident wildlife and don't migrate.

According to Mike Widner, former turkey project leader for the Arkansas Game & Fish Commission and a long-time member of the NWTF's Technical Committee, a good turkey

273

Good turkey habitat has woods, openings, crops, brushy areas and water.

property comprises several thousand acres. Ideally it consists of 30 to 60 percent mature hardwood forest, 10 to 30 percent scattered pasture or other grassy openings, 10 to 20 percent old fields or other brushy habitat, and 10 to 30 percent small grain crops such as soybeans, corn or wheat. While we usually can't control the size of the property – and most of us have to settle for considerably less than the several-thousand-acre ideal – we often have a lot more control over those other requirements.

In most places, the ratio of forest to open areas is the most significant thing out of kilter. Good turkey habitat has both openings and mature forest. Let either component get too scarce and your turkey flock will suffer.

In spring, turkeys feed heavily on greenery – clover, alfalfa, winter wheat and grasses. If your property doesn't have food plots, cover strips, field borders or woods edges that provide the open areas where these grasses, legumes and forbs grow, you won't have as many turkeys on your land as you could have.

The size and distribution of these open, grassy areas have a lot to do with how valuable they are to your home turkey flock. If you have 20 percent grassy openings in a 1,000-acre turkey management area, it's a lot more desirable to have ten 20-acre grassy openings scattered throughout your

thousand acres than to have one 200-acre field smack in the middle of it. Even better, probably, would be to have twenty 10-acre openings, or forty 5-acre ones.

The shape of these openings is important, too, especially the larger ones. Irregularly shaped or long, narrow openings are much better than perfectly square or round ones. The critical factor here is "edge" – the border between field and forest that provides food, escape cover and security for turkeys and other wildlife.

Pastures or fields containing alfalfa or clover, perhaps in combination with orchard grass, ryegrass, winter wheat or bahia, are more valuable to turkeys than pastures dominated by fescue or bermuda. Unfortunately, fescue looks so green and healthy during the winter months, it's been a pasture grass of choice for many years throughout much of the country. If you have fescue in your grassy areas and want to make them more attractive to turkeys, there's only one suitable course of action: *Get rid of the stuff.*

Open areas are important to turkeys year-round, but they're especially vital in late winter, when mast crops have largely been depleted. This is the time of year when food is most scarce. The green vegetation planted in pastures and small fields provides a high-protein food source also rich in Vitamin A. Both of these nutrients are needed by hens to produce good egg clutches. Later in the spring and early summer, the openings provide hens with a good place to bring their broods to catch insects, which the chicks and poults need for early and middle development. Ripening seed heads also supply high-quality food for turkeys of all ages during summer and fall, before the hard mast crop ripens in the woods.

Not all of the forest openings in our theoretical 1,000-acre turkey management area should be grassy fields, though. Turkeys also need some old-field-type cover where brush is beginning to invade and overtake the grassy stuff. This is good escape cover, but its primary value for turkeys is to provide good nesting areas.

Since the advent of modern agriculture, old-field habitat has become a scarce commodity in many areas. However, on a well-managed property, it's possible to plan a forest harvest rotation and use small clear-cuts in place of old-field sites.

The ideal percentage of old-field habitat quoted above – 10 to 20 percent – is probably a little on the high side, since brushy areas provide little food and turkeys don't use them as much as they use open fields. If the brushy areas are too small, however, it becomes much easier for predators to find and destroy turkey nests. For this reason, it's not a good idea to get much below the 10 percent figure for brushy areas, despite the fact that they provide less turkey food than other types of habitat.

The distribution of these old fields or brushy clear-cuts is important, too. Sticking with our 1,000-acre model, you should have at least five old-field sites scattered around the property. Ten would be better, but we must keep the realities of timber economics in mind here, and 20 acres is about the minimum-size clear-cut that's economically feasible under most conditions. Again, irregular-sized openings are preferred. It's important, though, to keep from making the clear-cuts too long and narrow, thereby making things easier for nest predators. Long and narrow is OK if you're talking about a food plot; it's the kiss of death if it's nesting cover.

As these old fields or clear-cuts grow up and revert to young timber stands, you can bring other new areas into the old-field status with other timber harvests.

*   *   *

The shape of food plots and openings in the forest is important. Irregularly shaped plots provide more "edge" and are therefore more valuable than square plots.

Clover is a good choice for food-plot plantings, since it provides good early-season and summer greenery.

Old-field sites are extremely important for nesting success.

The turkeys were smack in the middle of the north Arkansas pasture, and they weren't showing any inclination to leave it. Five strutters competed for the attention of a dozen hens, and although they'd gobble and turn toward us in full display every time we called, they were doing it from a distance of 250 yards. For all the good they were doing us, they might as well have been in Cleveland.

The stand-off continued for two hours, but then we noticed there were only 10 hens left. A half-hour later, there were eight.

"Things are looking up," my hunting partner said. "I'm gonna try something. Wait right here." Larry rolled carefully around his side of the big bur oak we were using and slipped back into the woods. I could hear his footsteps recede, then move to the left. Soon he was back in my peripheral view, low-crawling toward the edge of the field with a hen decoy in his hand. Using for concealment the winter-ragged fringe of milo that ringed the edge of the field, he wiggled forward 6 inches at a time until he was fully exposed but flat on the ground in the new 6-inch-high ryegrass. Fifteen feet out into the field, Larry stopped where the shade ran out, eased the decoy into an upright position and firmly pushed the stake into the ground. Then he wiggled slowly backwards, retracing his path through the short grass, and soon I heard him crunching in the leaves behind me. He rolled back around the tree, reclaimed his spot against the trunk and said, "Now we wait."

The eight hens had dwindled to five. This time when we called, one of the strutting gobblers broke away from the cluster of birds and moved 50 yards in our direction. During the next 30 minutes, he closed the gap to 75 yards, and another of the longbeards joined him. Four hours and a few minutes after we first found the flock of turkeys in the field, the two gobblers finally drifted into range and we took them with a quick one-two.

That's one way to use a cover/food strip at the edge between pasture and woods, but, of course, it's not the reason you ought to plant one. Supplemental feeding of turkeys by planting such seed-bearing crops as milo (grain sorghum), corn, browntop millet, cowpeas, soybeans or sunflowers is an important factor in properly managing your land for wild turkeys. These crops may be used sparingly, or maybe not at all, in an area with

Using fields and food plots for hunting over decoys is effective, but it helps to get there before the turkeys do, so you don't have to crawl to set out your decoys.

abundant mast-bearing trees when there's a good acorn crop. In the spring, however, when it's time to plant these supplemental foods, you don't have any way of knowing whether you've got a good mast crop coming or not. If you want to be one of those land managers who consistently carries turkeys on his property, you should plant some of these crops every year, especially if your land runs heavily to pine.

There's no need to overdo it, however. Studies in Minnesota have shown that a wild turkey needs the energy equivalent of about 2 bushels of corn to make it through an average winter. It doesn't take a math wizard to figure out that even if coons, deer, squirrels and other wildlife are also present, you don't have to convert your property to a big row-crop farm to provide enough supplemental grain to get your turkeys through until spring. In general, more than 10 acres of standing grain within the home range of a flock of turkeys is overkill. Three or four 2- to 5-acre foot plots per square mile, when combined with the grassy openings we discussed above, are plenty. If you're combining a farming operation with managing

turkeys, you can provide the desirable volume of standing grains with a minimum of trouble: Simply leave two or three rows of your crop standing along woods edges.

If fences are necessary between woodlands and pastures or food plots, avoid woven wire or hog wire. Turkeys are ground-dwelling birds, and they evolved before fences existed and are therefore poorly equipped to deal with them. If you've ever tried to call a gobbler that was on the other side of a fence, you know what I'm talking about here. Fences create a barrier to turkey travel, if not physically then at least psychologically, especially for young turkeys. In some cases, fences can help predators catch birds.

Artificially feeding turkeys by scattering corn or other grains in woods or fields isn't a good idea, for several reasons. First, it concentrates them and makes them more vulnerable to both poaching and predation. Also, feeding birds this way sets the stage for disease, since it greatly increases contact between turkeys. Finally, aflatoxins produced by a fungus that grows on wet grain can kill or weaken turkeys and other wildlife. On

If it's necessary to fence, use barbed wire instead of woven wire or hog wire so turkeys will have no trouble getting through. Not only do fences hinder the hunt, they can also act as a trap and allow predators to catch turkeys more easily.

top of all those reasons, it's expensive. Better to spend the money planting food plots or improving habitat in other ways.

One of those ways is by managing the forested areas on your property. Done correctly, this provides food for turkeys for the life of the forest. Contrast this with the short-term benefits of food plots, which usually only provide food for turkeys for a single year. In addition, manipulating a forest is the one aspect of turkey habitat management that has income potential.

It's also, however, a trickier proposition, and you have to live with the consequences of your decisions for a long time. Goof up planting a food plot, and you can correct it next year. Goof up cutting an 80-acre block of forest, and your grandkids will still be cussing you 30 years after you're dead.

This chapter doesn't offer nearly enough space to get into even a superficial discussion of how to properly manage a forest for turkeys. But the techniques are different from managing a forest strictly for timber and pulp production, because often the most valuable trees for forest products

are also the most valuable for wildlife. This creates a conflict between dollar signs and turkey tracks, and the landowner has to decide which is more valuable.

Take cherrybark oak, for example. Whether you leave a vigorous 18-inch-diameter cherrybark or cut it depends on whether you're managing for maximum timber production or maximum turkey production. It's valuable in both equations, but you have to cut it to realize its value in the former and leave it standing to realize its value in the latter.

Most state wildlife agencies have private-lands biologists who will help landowners and land managers draw up a timber management plan. The biologist looks at your whole habitat situation rather than just at your woods, because these other habitat components will heavily influence his recommendations for timber management.

If the wildlife agency in your state doesn't have any private-lands folks, your state Cooperative Extension Service can usually provide some help. Or, you can hire a consultant forester to help you draw up a timber management plan. In the latter case, though, make sure your consultant has a

Decisions can be confusing when it comes to managing land for turkeys. Most states have biologists who will come to your land and make suggestions for improving it.

strong wildlife background, and be careful to explain that you want to manage the land for turkeys, not timber. These private foresters are accustomed to maximizing the dollar yield of their recommended forest treatments, and this may or may not be what's best for the turkey flock on your land. It's usually not, as a matter of fact.

If your forest is predominantly of the oak-hickory type, you're in luck. This forest type can be beneficial to turkeys with less hands-on management than other forest types. If you have a lot of pine stands, you'll probably want to begin to convert at least some of it to hardwoods through selective cutting. On the other hand, if all you have is oak-hickory, it might be best to convert a small portion of it to pine. Remember, diversity is the key to having top-notch turkey habitat. Pine seeds, small as they are, can get a turkey flock through the winter when the acorn crop fails.

Water is also a key. The water source must be dependable and must be there the whole year through, without any interruption. Ask a biologist about how many watering places you'll need in a given chunk of turkey range, though, and you'll

probably get an imprecise response. "Well-watered land" or "land with sufficient watering places" are the kinds of answers you'll hear.

The fact is, no one really knows. Turkeys in good habitat have smaller home ranges, usually, and turkeys in poorer habitat have larger ones. Paradoxically, therefore, turkeys in poorer habitat can probably get along with fewer water sources than their richer cousins, because they have to cover more ground to make a living. Broadly speaking, though (and this is the best consensus I've been able to come up with among the many turkey biologists I've talked to), a permanent spring, pond or flowing creek on every 160 acres – four water sources per square mile, in other words – should be sufficient. More would probably be better, but they're not really necessary.

Protection from harassment (not just from poaching) is another critical component of good turkey management. Give your turkeys the best habitat conditions possible, but subject them to undue bother by man, livestock or free-ranging dogs at the same time, and you might as well bulldoze the whole property flat and sell it to

279

No one really knows just how many dependable watering sites turkeys need on a per-acre basis, but everyone agrees permanent water sources are crucial for good turkey habitat. One dependable source per 160 acres is probably a safe figure, but more would no doubt be safer.

Wal-Mart for all the turkeys you're going to have on the place.

This doesn't mean you have to tiptoe around on your property like a thief in the night. It just means you ought to consider the timing of certain management practices to cause minimum problems for your resident birds. For example, haying is an acceptable practice on the openings in your turkey property, but don't cut too early. Delaying the first cut until after the turkey eggs have hatched will save the lives of many of the current year's crop of poults – to say nothing of the hens themselves, which often sit on the nest until the mower runs over them.

Keep dogs out of the woods at all costs, year-round if possible but certainly from early March through the end of summer. Mature turkeys can usually escape dogs, but poults often can't. Even when a flock of young birds all manage to escape, they're usually split up and the hen has to assemble them again. They're exceptionally vulnerable to other predators at this time, and the hen doesn't always manage to reassemble her entire brood.

Livestock and turkeys, while they do sometimes coexist on a piece or property, are not a good mix. The turkeys don't have much impact on the cows, but the reverse sure isn't true. Livestock compete directly with turkeys for available food, destroy nesting habitat, and even break up nests with their clumsy hooves. Make up your mind whether you want livestock or turkeys, and act accordingly. At the very least, fence livestock away from wooded areas and food plots.

*　　　*　　　*

"I'd like to give you permission to hunt my property this spring," said the unfamiliar voice on the telephone. "It's loaded with turkeys."

That sort of thing doesn't happen often, and I sat straighter in my chair. The man said he was an absentee landowner and was looking for somebody to keep an eye on his place. I'd been recommended by a mutual friend. Since I lived less than an hour from the property and at least a hundred miles closer to it than the owner did, he offered me a key to the gate and the run of the place, if I'd just keep an eye skinned and question anybody I saw on the place to see if they had any business being there.

I jumped at the chance, of course. Sure enough, it was a honey of a hunting spot. A bit over 1,100 acres, it butted up against a sizable tract of timber company land that was excellent turkey habitat. The property had two ponds, several creeks and spring seeps, a pretty network of mountaintop pastures interspersed with groves of trees, hills and hollows cloaked in pretty hardwoods, several dense pine stands and good protection from unauthorized entry. Watchful neighbors lived on each side, the front was bounded by a paved county road and a steep ridge, and the back butted up against the big timber-company tract. And the owner was right, as I found out during a pre-season scouting trip – the place was loaded with turkeys.

It was as promising a turkey hunting property as I've ever seen. The only thing missing, I learned when the season opened, was enough land to accommodate all the hunters the landowner had given permission to hunt there. Evidently the guy really wanted somebody to keep an eye on his property, because I ran into hunters everywhere I turned on that property that year. I talked with everyone I saw, as the landowner had asked me to do, and without exception, they'd been given permission to hunt from the same guy who'd given it to me and had the paperwork to prove it. I hunted the property four times, got messed up by other hunters every time, and finally gave it up.

I've tried that property once or twice a season every year since, and have found other hunters on the property every time. Nowadays, there aren't very many turkeys to be found there. On a property that ought to yield six to 10 gobblers a year, the mob of hunters who run all over the place take maybe two or three birds each spring.

That's a prime example of how you can do everything possible to make your property attractive to turkeys, and then destroy your advantage by allowing too much human activity. If my landowner friend would cut the hunting pressure in half, the turkey harvest on that property would more than double.

But I don't expect him to do that, because he's basically a nice guy and likes to let people hunt on his property. So, for the foreseeable future, I have

Delaying the first haying until mid-June, after most of the hens have brought off their young, is a good management practice.

Finding turkey sign and seeing turkeys on your land in spring is desirable, but if you don't provide for their needs when times are tough in late winter, you might just be out of luck come gobbling time.

281

When a landowner gives you permission to hunt, he's granting you a precious gift. Don't abuse the privilege.

permission to hunt on 1,100 acres of good-looking property in prime turkey country, and it's within reasonable distance of my driveway … and it's not worth my time to hunt it.

If you manage your land according to the guidelines presented earlier in this chapter, your property is going to be attractive to turkeys. If you don't want to waste a good part of the money and hard work you invested in attracting those birds, pay attention to that little story. Give the turkeys some breathing room and protection from human disturbance during turkey season as well as at other times of year, and you'll have more birds on your land and better hunting for them.

Limiting the access of other people to your land becomes more and more important as the size of the property decreases. If your property is 2,000 acres, the turkeys on it will put up with a lot more human aggravation than if you've only got a quarter section. But not even on the largest property will turkeys put up with relentless, day-after-day disturbance, whether it's in the form of hunting, farming, horseback riding, dirt biking or whatever.

I have a friend in Missouri who owns a 1,000-acre tract of mixed pines, hardwoods and pasture that abuts a 15,000-acre chunk of national forest land. He manages his land for turkeys to the extent he can, while still conducting his dairy cattle operation, and he has turkeys all year.

"But man, you ought to see how the population of birds on my place jumps after about the first five or six days of spring turkey season," he told me. "I go from hearing four or five gobblers on my place to hearing a dozen or more, and where there were one or two birds strutting in a pasture, suddenly there are five or six."

That's not coincidence. My friend hunts his land, but no one else does – not legally, anyway. Meanwhile, right across the fence on the public land, the pressure is high. And it doesn't take the gobblers long to figure out where the living is less hazardous. Shortly after the close of turkey season each spring, the excess gobblers disappear from the farm. But my friend knows they'll be back again next spring.

If your land lays so that you can split it up into two or more hunting units, alternate your hunting efforts around the farm according to a planned rotation. You can vary from the schedule if there's a particularly aggravating or tantalizing bird you're after, of course – after all, it is your land. But don't

Some private property gets hunted even harder than public land.

concentrate too much of your effort on one segment of the property or you'll damage it, hunting-wise.

If the property is too small to break up into hunting units, you'll need to exercise a little restraint if you want to maintain quality hunting for turkeys that aren't a) ultra-spooky; or b) living on your neighbor's property until hunting season is over. As we all know, it's hard enough to do anything with birds that haven't been excessively fooled with. Dealing with educated, heavily pressured gobblers can be … well, you know how it can be.

Unfortunately, there's no hard-and-fast rule that can tell you how much hunting pressure turkeys on a small property will tolerate. A good turkey hunter can get away with far more hunting than a poor one, though, because the good hunter won't "booger" as many birds as the poor one will. Still, a small property needs to be rested regularly, no matter how skillful and cautious the hunter or hunters. On a tract of land less than a square mile, four days of hunting a week is probably about as much pressure as you ought to exert. If the property is less than 300 acres, two days a week is safer.

There's been considerable disagreement for at least the past 25 years on whether or not shooting juvenile gobblers hurts the adult gobbler population. As of the copyright date of this book, Mississippi has had a no-jakes rule statewide for spring turkey hunting for four or five years, and Arkansas has had a one-jake-per-season rule for three springs along with its two-gobbler season limit. Other states are considering similar moves. The jury is still out on whether this helps much in the quest to put more gobbling 2-year-olds in the woods each spring. On its face, the theory seems sound, but on the other hand, turkeys – especially young ones – have a high annual mortality rate, and there's no assurance the jake you pass up this April is still going to be in the population next spring.

So should you shoot jakes on your property, or shouldn't you? The answer to this question lies strictly with the landowner, unless state regulations settle the question for you. If you want to shoot a jake or two every spring, it's probably not going to make any noticeable difference in the number of 2-year-olds you have next spring. However, there's a certain amount of moderation in order here. Just as you don't want to shoot all your longbeards, neither do you want to shoot all your jakes. One legal gobbler for every 100 acres of forested habitat is a good harvest figure to try for, regardless of beard length. In years of high gobbler populations in good turkey range, you can probably double that figure. In lean years, you might be wise to cut back a little.

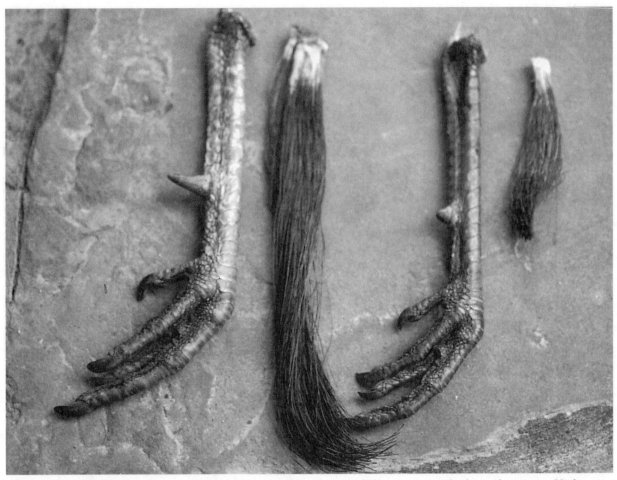

The question of whether to shoot jakes or let them walk is a personal decision, not a biological concern. Under normal conditions, removing jakes from the population has no discernible effect on the number of 2-year-olds the next spring.

Some restraint is in order, regardless of the age of the gobbler. Just as you don't want to shoot too many of your jakes, neither do you want to shoot too many of your longbeards. One legal gobbler per 100 acres of forested habitat is a generally safe harvest rate, regardless of the age of the birds harvested.

Some private-land hunters build elaborate blinds in areas frequented by turkeys, and hunt them like most of us hunt deer – by hiding in the blind and waiting them out. While this is unquestionably an effective method for harvesting a bird or two, it robs you of the ultimate challenge of turkey hunting – playing chess with a gobbling bird on the turkey's game board, trying to maneuver into a position the bird will approach. Another downside of hunting from permanent blinds is that eventually, if you do it enough, the birds will begin to avoid them. If the blinds are in food plots or other valuable habitat components, as they usually are, you're not only killing turkeys, but also the goose that laid the golden eggs.

Don't get me wrong; I've killed a few turkeys from the comfort of a permanent ground blind. No doubt I'll kill a few more the same way. But I'd rather hunt one the old-fashioned way and not kill him than sit in a blind and shoot the biggest leaf-raker in the county.

Turkey management is as much a seat-of-the-pants operation as is turkey hunting. Some things, like weather and predation of nests by skunks, coons, foxes and crows, are largely beyond your control.

To each his own. There's nothing wrong with hunting out of a blind. Just be careful you don't overdo it and cause the birds to shy away from your hunting spot and their feeding spot.

No doubt you've noticed a lot of weasel words as you've read this chapter. There's a simple explanation: Turkey management is as much a seat-of-the-pants operation as is turkey hunting. Like every turkey hunt, every parcel of land is different, and requires slightly different management techniques and strategies to become the best it can be for the resident turkey flock. It's only by thinking things through first, applying common sense and basic wildlife management principles, then jumping in there and trying various things, that the landowner will be able to figure out what works best in his particular situation.

Just like turkey hunting.

Chapter 41

Passing It On

Despite the huge volume of learning materials available today, a neophyte turkey hunter can still benefit from a little coaching by a more experienced hunter. This fellow is a daunting adversary for the beginner.

You don't have to be an expert to help a less experienced hunter get off on the right foot.

Hi. You don't know me, but I've read a lot of your turkey hunting stuff, and I want to ask you a big favor."

The words came through the receiver in a nervous rush, as if the caller was afraid I'd hang up before he finished saying his piece.

"I want to go turkey hunting with you," the caller continued, and the further he got into his spiel, the faster his words came out. "I won't take a gun or anything; I just want to tag along on a hunt with you so I can learn a few things from an expert. I'm really interested in turkey hunting, but I've been chasing them for three years now and I haven't had any luck at all and I can't figure out what all I'm doing wrong. I'm a safe hunter and I don't drink when I'm hunting and I really want to learn at least a little bit turkey hunting and please-wouldyouletmegowithyousometime?"

I had mixed emotions about the request. I was flattered that someone would think enough of my meager abilities as a turkey hunter to want to go hunting to learn from me, but I've had plenty of personal experiences in the turkey woods that leave me no room for any delusions of grandeur where my abilities as a turkey hunter are concerned. Anyway, I'm pretty persnickety about choosing my hunting partners, especially turkey hunting partners.

Part of my feeling in this regard is based on … well, I suppose you could call it snobbery if you wanted to. That's not entirely accurate, but it's close. In case you haven't figured it out from reading this far in this book, I have a love, respect and abiding regard for this big bird and the ceremony of hunting him that borders on the religious, and I have scant truck with those who don't share my feelings. I've met enough turkey hunters over the years to fill a college football stadium, but the ones who had what I feel is the proper attitude toward turkey hunting would fit inside the visitor's locker room, with room left over for the cheerleaders.

There's also the not inconsiderable matter of safety. My father, one of the most safety-minded hunters you'd ever want to meet, shot another hunter one time when he was squirrel hunting. The guy was trespassing and wasn't supposed to be there, and the late-afternoon sun was in Dad's eyes, and there were several other mitigating factors we won't go into here, but it happened. And be assured here, my Dad was as old-maidy with a firearm as the most paranoid hunter education instructor you ever saw. He took away my first gun, a single-shot .410, less than a month after he gave it to me because I'd set it in the closet without breaking it open to make sure it wasn't loaded. (It wasn't, but I lost the gun for a month, anyway.) And yet, safety-conscious as he was, Dad shot another hunter thinking he was shooting at a squirrel. The other guy wasn't injured badly, but that's beside the point.

While squirrels are squirrels and turkeys turkeys, that incident convinced me long ago that none of us who hunt are safe from the possibility of either shooting another hunter or being shot ourselves. No matter how many precautions we take, there's always the risk of either. While we can't eliminate the risk, we can minimize it, and one of the ways we can minimize it is by being careful about who we take to the woods with us to share the experience.

I didn't know this faceless (still nameless, for that matter) caller from Adam's off ox. So, all things considered, my first impulse was to give him a polite but firm brush-off.

"Well, I really don't know all that much about turkey hunting myself," I began when he paused for breath, trying to be as nice as I could while I worked up to telling him no. I was telling the truth. Just that morning I'd been whipped by not one but three separate longbeards, and I was perched on a pretty low limb.

"Maybe not," the caller replied, "but you know a lot more about it than I do."

Instant flashback. I remembered a time, years ago, when I was an unsuccessful and frustrated beginner and a more experienced turkey hunter took me under his wing and called in my first bird for me. The story of that first-bird hunt is covered in Chapter 35, but what I didn't tell you in that chapter was how it came to be that Robert and I were hunting together that day:

After several frustrating springs of chasing gobblers around and committing all manner of grievous and stupid blunders, I gave up turkey hunting in disgust. I was writing a weekly outdoor column for my hometown newspaper at the time, and I devoted one whole column to my decision to quit, saying something to the effect that turkeys were unkillable in the first place and turkey hunting was screwing up my spring fishing in the second place.

Robert, the guy who called up my first gobbler, read that column and called me. He was going to take me on as a project, he said. He was going to show me it could be done. He talked me into going hunting with him, and though it took two Saturdays, he got the monkey off my back. (Or lashed it securely in place there, depending on how you want to look at it.)

Whichever, the real thing of value I got out of those two days in the woods with Robert was just watching the things he did and asking him why he did them. Despite the fact that Robert was one of those 20-turkey experts with more confidence than his skill level warranted, I learned more through those two days in the woods with him than I'd picked up in the four or five years I'd tried to kill a turkey on my own. The very next spring, using in large part the tricks and techniques Robert showed me, I called in and killed my first solo gobbler.

I was daydreaming with the receiver at my ear, thinking how there had been plenty of highs and lows since, but remembering too that it was Robert's willingness to take a rookie in tow that had given me the opportunity to experience those highs and lows, when the guy on the phone brought me back to the present.

"Hello? Are you still there?"

Instead of politely explaining why I wasn't going to agree to take him turkey hunting, I found myself telling this faceless voice, this unknown quantity, how to get to the spot where we'd meet the next morning.

"Be there at 4:30, and if you're late I'll leave without you," I warned gruffly, in a final, futile attempt to salvage something out of the conversation.

The smile came through the phone as plain as if we were face to face. "Don't you worry about that. Me being late ain't gonna happen."

It didn't, either. As far as I could tell, my rookie guest – his name was Robert, too, and I thought that somehow appropriate – spent the night in the parking lot of that little country store. The hood of his truck was cold as an iceberg when I got there at the designated time.

It was a lousy morning for a turkey hunt: cloudy, windy, with one rainstorm just past and another

An expert hunter might kill more turkeys than a rookie, but the remaining turkeys will be less bothered when he leaves.

threatening. The air temperature was better suited to hunting mallards than turkeys. That's why, when we heard the gobbler sound off on the next ridge at first light, I had a hard time masking my surprise.

It was a long, difficult hike to get to him, but that matters little when you're young and there's a bird hammering over there. We descended through a thick cutover, crossed an icy, knee-deep creek and climbed a steep, boulder-strewn slope, not quite at a run but as close to one as we could manage. Still, we got there too late. By the

time we reached the top, two other hunters had converged on his roost tree and were already at work, calling too much and calling too loud, trying to pull him in opposite directions.

Lesson One, therefore, turned out to be not about turkey hunting strategy but about turkey hunting protocol. Trying to keep the disappointment and discouragement out of my voice, I explained that the other hunters had beaten us to the bird, and while we could set up on the bird as well, it wasn't the right thing to do.

"Well, then, let's give this bird to those guys and go find another one," Robert said with an optimistic grin, and that's when I began to think maybe this guy had the right stuff.

Later that morning, with the wind still gusting, we located another turkey. When we made our set and I started calling, it was only a few minutes until not one but two gobblers showed up, and Robert bestowed upon one of them the honor of becoming his first turkey. That the bird was a jake did not then nor does it now detract from either the importance or the memorable nature of that moment. As we stood over the bird, grinning and shaking hands and both of us trying to talk at once, I knew my decision to help Robert get started turkey hunting was the right thing to do. He did have the right stuff. He still does.

Admittedly, there was some luck involved all around. Before Robert's phone call that day, I'd never heard of him, and it was only because somebody did for me what he was asking me to do for him that I agreed to it in the first place. He turned out to be a winner, but he could just as easily have been a jerk, and I'm not advocating for a minute that other hunters do what I did – which, in effect, was to go on a blind date.

But I do think it's a fine idea for those of us with a little experience to help initiate other beginning turkey hunters into this grand spring sport. We ought to be helping people get off on the right foot, and not just because we're all such wonderful people, either. We're not all so wonderful, in case you hadn't noticed. I am, of course, and you probably are, too, but somebody's turning loose a whole lot of folks out there who ought to be kept in the yard. They bump our turkeys, they crowd into our space. They do all sorts of things they shouldn't be doing to make the hunt harder and less enjoyable for those of us who try to do right. As if it weren't hard enough already.

Some of those folks are just, well, jerks, and there's nothing to be done about it. But many of them are nice folks like you and me, and the only reason they're making pests of themselves is because they're new to the game and nobody's taken the time and trouble to show them the ropes. It would help upgrade both the quality and the safety of turkey hunting in general if we could get these rookies educated and up to speed as quickly as possible. If you've had any amount of experience in the turkey woods at all, I'm sure you share my preference for sharing a given stretch of woods with an expert hunter instead of a rookie. The expert may kill a turkey where the rookie won't, but he also will leave the woods relatively undisturbed and will practice the proper turkey hunting etiquette.

I'm not suggesting that we should all make an effort to bring new hunters into the fold. If your next-door neighbor is a golfer or gardener, by all means leave him to play with his clubs or his tiller on April weekends. Those hobbies will keep him out of the turkey woods, and if you ask me, there are enough of us out there already. The numbers are going to continue to grow without us dragging any reluctant neophytes into the woods. But all of us know hunters who want to or have already started turkey hunting but don't have a clue how to go about it. These hunters are out there floundering around and making the same mistakes you and I made, rediscovering the potholes and traps we fell into. If they're going to be out there anyway, they might as well be going about it properly; it makes things better for everybody.

It's easy to look down on these folks and feel superior. What's not so easy, but is much more rewarding, is to take one of these beginners hunting once or twice and show them a few of the ropes. Videos, seminars and books are fine, and by using them today's beginner can start his or her career a lot farther up the learning curve than those of us who started before this plethora of information was available. Even so, there's nothing like being out there with a more experienced hunter.

Keep in mind that your name doesn't have to be a household word in turkey hunting circles for you to be able to make a valuable contribution to the education of a beginning turkey hunter. At the time I helped Robert kill his first gobbler, I was one of those 20-bird experts myself. But my 20 were 20 more than he'd taken, and as he told me on the phone that day, I still knew a lot more about it than he did. When you know nothing at all, even mediocre help can be invaluable.

I still enjoy hunting turkeys all by myself, going one-on-one with a longbeard in the classic style. Therefore, I don't let myself get too carried away with this Good Samaritan schtick. Still, I try to take one rookie each year, if I can find one I think has the right stuff, just to get him or her started right. Sometimes, we kill a bird; more

The classic turkey hunt is still a one-on-one encounter, but it's a good investment in the future of the sport to help a rookie get started.

often, we don't. Both outcomes are OK, because learning humility is also an important part of becoming a right-minded turkey hunter.

There's a lot to be said for helping a newcomer take his or her first turkey. I've been fortunate enough to have been there looking on more than a half-dozen times so far, and those kills stand out in my mind even more vividly than many of my own.

If you don't believe me, take a rookie next spring and see for yourself. Not only will you be helping a fellow turkey hunter, but you'll also be helping improve the sport.

291

Section 6

Laginappe

Chapter 42

Defensive Turkey Hunting

Turkey hunting is an exciting sport. While this is a desirable thing, that very excitement sets the stage for "hunter-mistaken-for-game" accidents. That's why it's important to hunt defensively.

W hen Ron arrived at the emergency room, they took one look at his ruined eye and taped two metal guards over it and his good one as well, to minimize eye movement until the doctor could take a closer look. The eyeguards had holes in them, like kitchen utensils designed for scooping French fries out of hot grease, and they made him look bizarre, like an extra in a low-budget horror flick. The effect would have been almost comical – except for the blood.

It was everywhere. It's always surprising how much blood the human body actually holds, and how much of it a body can give up and still operate. Ron looked like he'd given up about as much of it as he needed to for the moment. It had run out of the holes in his arms, chest, neck and head, caked in his hair, painted about two-thirds of the surface area of his upper body, and dried there. Part of it had also run on down and soaked into the upper part of his camo pants, turning them a strange, camouflage-patterned maroon color.

Ron was the victim of a turkey hunting accident, shot by another hunter. He'd been hunting with two friends in a remote area, and they were walking through open woods when it happened. Single file, they topped a ridge, with the sun at their backs. The next thing Ron knew, he was lying on his back, hurting, dazed and unable to see very well.

Another hunter had shot him, at fairly close range, with a load of 3-inch No. 2s. Ron's two companions were untouched, but Ron himself took a heavy dose. It might well have killed a lesser man, but Ron was – still is – an iron-pumper, and his massive upper torso muscles absorbed the shot and kept them from getting into his body cavity. Even so, his eyes were no tougher than yours or mine, and one of the pellets ruined one of his corneas. After a transplant, he regained some of the sight in that eye, but he still doesn't have full vision in it. He never will.

The other hunter, who helped Ron's buddies get him out of the woods and to the hospital that morning, said he had heard a gobbler and was set up on the bird when, looking into the bright, rising sun, he saw three shapes come over the ridge. To the excited hunter, the shapes took the form of three strutting gobblers, and he shot the one in front. It was a bad mistake, and it serves as a stark example of what can happen when turkey hunters get excited.

It's not as though you're going on a suicide mission every time you put on your camo and step into the turkey woods. In 1989, the year Ron absorbed the load of 2s, an estimated 30,000 people hunted spring gobblers in my home state of Arkansas. Five others besides Ron were shot, and one of them died. If you expand that ratio, it works out to about 20 accidents and three fatalities per 100,000 hunters.

That's way too many, but consider: 27,041 of every 100,000 young athletes who play high school football this year will be injured on the field. Basketball, thought of as a no-contact sport, results in injuries to 1,810 of every 100,000 participants each year. Even tennis players are 5 1/2 times more likely to be injured than turkey hunters.

But consider also: There's an undeniable differential in seriousness between turning an ankle on the tennis court and taking a load of 2s in the face. The relatively low probability of getting shot while turkey hunting is of little comfort to those dozen or so per 100,000 on the receiving end of the shot swarm. That's why we owe it to our fellow hunters to be careful, and why we owe it to ourselves to hunt defensively.

Most turkey hunting accidents fall into two categories: self-inflicted, and hunter-mistaken-for-game. Most of the self-inflicted accidents result from carelessness and/or stupidity – a hunter rests his gun barrel on his boot and blows away part of his foot; another pulls a loaded gun barrel-first across the seat of his truck and shoots himself in the stomach; a third crosses a fence with a loaded

An approaching longbeard, setting the woods athunder with the sound of his gobbling, doesn't bring on a mood of calm and peace.

295

gun, gets a foot tangled in the wire and blows his own head off.

There's not a lot to be gained here by a discussion of how to avoid these kinds of turkey hunting accidents. We all know better than to do those things, and those who continue to do them anyway stand a good chance of demonstrating Darwin's "survival of the fittest" principle by suddenly and unexpectedly removing themselves from the gene pool.

But hunter-mistaken-for-game accidents are almost always preventable. Not only can we do things to avoid shooting another hunter, we can also do things that will help us avoid getting shot.

The one basic rule of safe turkey hunting is simple in the extreme: Positively identify your target and what's beyond it before you pull the trigger. If all turkey hunters would do this one small thing, there'd be no need for any of the defensive turkey hunting measures we're going to talk about a little later in this chapter.

In the spring of the year, only gobblers are legal game. This automatically invalidates one of the most common excuses heard when one hunter shoots another: "I thought he was a turkey." If a hunter doesn't even take the time to make a proper determination between man and bird, it makes you wonder just how many hen turkeys such a hunter has kicked under logs over the course of his hunting career.

Still, such mistakes are understandable, if not exactly forgivable. You've been there, just like I have. An approaching longbeard, setting the woods athunder with the sound of his gobbling, doesn't bring on a mood of calm and peace. Your pulse is racing, your mouth is dry, your hands are sweaty, and your blood pressure, if you knew what it was right then, would scare you to death. It's not the frame of mind that lends itself to reflective, rational thinking.

Therefore, to make sure you never find yourself in the position of having to explain how it came to be that you shot a fellow hunter, it's important to develop safeguards. A sort of shooting ritual, if you want to think of it that way.

For example, I have one friend who says he never shoots a turkey until he's not only seen the bird's beard, but mentally measured it as well.

"It's not that I have a minimum beard length in mind," he says. "I don't mind shooting a jake once in a while if it's been a slow season. But making

an estimate of the length of a turkey's beard forces me to concentrate on the bird and helps me stay just a little bit calmer, too. Those two things give me a good chance to make absolutely sure I'm looking at a turkey and not another hunter."

It's good advice. Waiting through those last agonizing minutes with your gun to your shoulder for a vocal gobbler to step into the open gets the old adrenaline pumping pretty good. Anything that can inject a little calmness and rational thinking into the situation is not a bad thing. Caught up in the heat of the moment, it's not too hard to convince yourself you're seeing a gobbler when you're really not.

That's experience talking there, in case you were wondering. A friend and I put a big Missouri gobbler to bed one afternoon, and morning found us sitting 60 yards apart on the bench above him, waiting for him to fly down. I could see Bill's tree, but there was some brush in the way and I couldn't see Bill. Just after daylight, when the bird should have been gobbling but wasn't, I glanced over my right shoulder and saw the bird already on the ground, silent but in full strut beside a big oak about 30 yards behind Bill and 45 yards from me. When the bird strutted behind the oak, I shifted my body a little to the right so I could bring the gun to bear. I was convinced I was looking at a gobbler, but for some reason I didn't raise my gun just yet.

The gobbler strutted back into view, black as a bowling ball in the half-light of early morning. He was a little farther away than I like to shoot a turkey, but I had a choke/load combination I had confidence in to 45 yards. This turkey was at the edge of that range, but killable.

Still I held off, though. I didn't know whether Bill had seen the bird or not, and if he had, he was much closer.

You've guessed the rest of it by now. The turkey I was looking at turned out to be my hunting partner, bent over and scraping the leaves back from the base of the oak so he could sit down. When he stood up straight and I figured out what was what, it left me in a cold sweat.

Bill had moved from his planned setup because he couldn't see well enough from there, but in the pre-dawn gloom, I hadn't seen him do it. When I looked around and saw his rear sticking out from behind the other tree, my eyes convinced my brain (or maybe it was the other way around) I was looking at a strutting gobbler. And I wasn't even particularly pumped up at the time.

Since that long-ago morning, I've developed a variation of the same trick my beard-estimating friend uses. But instead of mentally measuring the beard and thus taking my concentration away from the desired target area (the turkey's head and upper neck), I concentrate instead on that head. If the light is good enough and the bird close enough, I try to focus on the turkey's eye. If his head is in shadow, I try to focus on some other feature – the beak, the wattle, the snood. Like estimating the length of the beard, this is simply a brief exercise in discipline, a little pre-shot ritual that forces me to concentrate closely enough on my target to see a specific part of it – and to make doubly and triply sure what I'm about to shoot is really a turkey gobbler.

On the other side of the coin is defensive turkey hunting, which for our purposes here can be defined as the subtle art of making sure other hunters know you're not a gobbler.

A good many hunters get shot while they're simply walking through the woods, the way my buddy Ron did. The use of hunter orange would eliminate many of these cases of mistaken identity, and at least one state requires turkey hunters to wear an orange hat when moving in game cover.

I carry an orange hat in my turkey vest, and while I confess I don't always wear it when I'm moving, I do when I'm in heavily hunted territory. It's easy enough to take it off and either sit on it or stuff it back in my vest when I sit down to a bird.

I don't really like wearing orange in the turkey woods, though; for me, it detracts from the overall quality of the experience, and I feel more like a deer hunter than a turkey hunter when I wear the stuff. That I feel safer, though, is undeniable, and I don't think the orange is a disadvantage to my hunting success. If you don't let the gobbler see you, you can trick yourself out in blinking lights, like Robert Redford in *Electric Cowboy*, and it won't matter. There's almost always plenty of time to take your orange off and hide it before you start to call.

This book talks a lot about hunting on public land, and for good reason: There's lots of public land available to hunters across the country, and much of it has excellent turkey populations. The problem is, hunting on public land often leads to

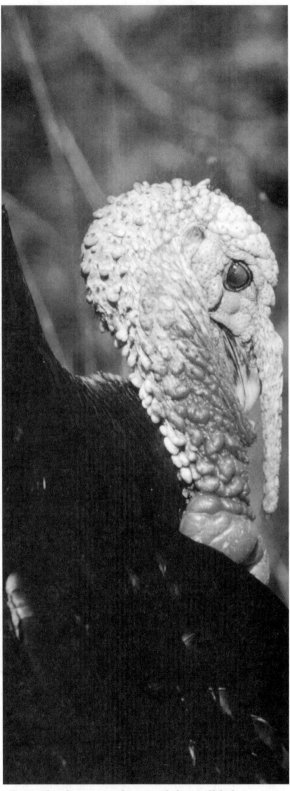

Try to develop a pre-shot ritual that will help you positively identify your target as a gobbler and ensure that the bird is in range. Don't just look at the whole turkey; instead, concentrate on some specific part of that bird – the beard, eye, beak, snood, whatever. It will calm you down and help you not only to identify your target, but also to make a better shot.

Visibility is poorest in early morning, when light is poor and the sun's angle is low. Most hunter-mistaken-for-game shooting accidents occur at this time.

situations where more than one hunter is working the same gobbler. (See Chapter 43.)

Sometimes this is unavoidable, when two hunters set up on opposite sides of the bird a considerable distance from each other. Neither may know the other is in the picture. If you do become aware of another hunter on a bird you're working, the safest thing to do is abandon that bird and go look for another one.

Of course, a little common sense is called for here. If you're working a gobbler from a decent setup and you hear another hunter calling to your gobbler from the next ridge over, the other guy is probably not a serious contender and has no ethical claim to the bird, anyway. In such a situation, there's no foul involved in getting in the best possible position and keeping right on with your hunt. But a hunter who's achieved a good calling

Wear orange when moving through the woods, especially if you're carrying a gobbler.

position on a gobbler you're approaching deserves the courtesy (and you both deserve the safety) of being left to work that gobbler in peace … and that's exactly what an ethical and safety-conscious hunter will do. Every time, no question.

True hunting accident: A man and his 10-year-old son were sitting against a tree, working a gobbler. The man had just made a call and gotten a response from the bird, and he was in the process of laying his slate call on the ground when another hunter walked up, saw the hand movement, thought it was the gobbler, and fired from a range of 25 yards.

The kid wasn't hurt, but the man nearly died from his wounds. He didn't do one thing wrong, but he got shot anyway. He was sitting down. He was working the gobbler, which was responding to his calls. He had heard no other calling, and to the

299

A blue-and-red decoy head sticking out of your vest isn't really a good idea.

best of his knowledge there were no other hunters in that stretch of woods. He never knew the other hunter was there until after he'd been shot.

If you're in a good calling position and you get moved in on by another hunter, you can assume one of two things: Either the encroaching hunter doesn't know you're there, or he doesn't care about ethics and safety. Neither of those possibilities is desirable.

I usually make a loud call or two to make sure the other hunter knows I'm already on the bird, but if he doesn't back off, I pick up my stuff and get out of there. My chances of killing the bird just went in the toilet, anyway, and remember, you don't have to do anything wrong to get shot.

If you see another hunter approaching, speak to him in a normal voice to get his attention. Under no circumstances should you make a turkey call or move your hand or arm to get the other hunter's attention. Those are dandy ways to get shot.

Another true hunting accident: A hunter was sitting in a dry creek bed (why, I don't know) when he saw a turkey hunter coming down the hill. When he raised a hand and waved, the other hunter mistook the seated man's hand and arm for the head and neck of a gobbler. The victim caught most of a load of copper-plated 4s in the neck, face, chest and arm.

And still another one: A father and his son were hunting turkeys, and they split up and went their separate ways. Later in the morning, the son eased into position and sat down less than 50 yards behind his father and, to pull a joke, made a few yelps. The joke backfired. Dad turned and fired at the sound, putting 22 pellets in his son's chest, arms and neck.

To repeat: speak. Don't wave. Don't call. *Speak.*

Furthermore, do it while the approaching hunter is still out of shotgun range, or nearly so. Don't wait until he's right on top of you.

I made that particular mistake less than a week after I stood beside my blood-streaked buddy Ron in the emergency room, when a hunter approached me through wide-open woods. I was sitting in the deep shade of the only cedar tree on that hillside, and I was as well hidden as if I'd been underground. I watched that guy coming for 150 yards or more, and he was 15 yards from me when I said "Good morning."

This guy reacted like a Vietnam vet hearing a bus backfire. He was carrying his gun over his shoulder, and he brought it into play as fast as Clint Eastwood ever did in a spaghetti Western. I saw what was happening and started yelling "NONONO!" at the top of my lungs, and the man got himself under control just before he would have had me covered.

I apologized and he did, too, and we chatted for a few minutes while we both calmed down. Before we went our separate ways, though, I had to ask the question or bust wide open from wanting to: "Do turkeys normally say 'good morning' to you?"

He didn't have an answer.

Don't gobble on public land, even if you think there aren't any other hunters within hearing. Gobbling has limited usefulness as a turkey call, anyway, in my humble opinion (mostly because so pitifully few hunters can realistically reproduce this weird sound). It won't fool many turkeys, but for some reason it often fools turkey hunters.

Don't wear solid-black clothing, or anything that contains even a little bit of red, white or blue. These are all turkey gobbler colors, and they can all get you shot.

Be careful when you're using decoys, too. Chapter 37 covers this subject in more detail, but here are the basics: Make sure the heads of your collapsible decoys aren't sticking out of your vest when you're carrying them around. When you set them out, make sure you have a large opening out front so you can see any approaching hunter, or make sure there's a large tree directly beyond your decoy(s) so it will block a hunter's shot from coming toward you.

Don't let your guard down after you've killed a gobbler. More than one hunter has been shot while carrying a bird out of the woods. It's not a bad idea to put on that orange hat when you're walking through the woods with a gobbler over your shoulder, and to wrap the bird in an orange vest or carry bag as well. Several companies make tote bags for just this purpose.

These basic principles of safe hunting sound very simple, and they are. But every year, a small but disturbing percentage of hunters continue to ignore them. If you're among the majority who try to hunt safely, thank you. If you're in the unsafe minority, shape up. A little self-discipline and common sense might save your life.

Better yet, it might save mine.

Several companies make turkey tote bags of hunter orange material. Making use of one when you're carrying a gobbler out of the woods isn't a bad idea, particularly on public land.

Chapter 43

Ethics in the Greening Woods

If there's already a vehicle parked at your planned hunting spot, go somewhere else.

It's first light, that magical time between the owl and the cardinal. You're standing on a high ridgeline on heavily hunted public land, straining the muscles in your ears and hoping you'll hear a turkey gobble. You hear one, all right, but he's on a distant ridge when he cranks up – too far away and too hard to reach to be very tempting if another bird gobbles closer. Unfortunately, that fails to happen. Five minutes later, you've listened to the distant bird gobble a dozen times, and it's becoming obvious what you're going to have to do. Swearing softly under your breath – the habit of being quiet in the turkey woods is too deeply ingrained for you to cuss out loud – you take a compass reading on the sound of his gobbling and fall off the ridge into the first valley.

You're moving fast to make up for the time wasted standing around listening to him gobble, and when you top the first ridge, you're sweating like an August cow pony. But the turkey is still on his limb and still gobbling hard, one more hole and one more ridge away. You huff and blow for a minute or two, then recheck your compass bearing to the bird, swear softly once more, and drop into the next valley.

Near the top of the second ridge, you stop to listen and let spirit catch up to body. The bird will almost certainly be on the ground by now, and you don't want to pop up in his face and bump him. It's important right now to locate him, preferably by just standing here and letting him gobble on his own.

Five minutes pass, disguised as hours, and the turkey never utters a sound. All sorts of unhappy possibilities come to mind: *Did he fly down into the middle of a bunch of hens and shut up? Did he glide down into the valley on the other side of the ridge? Did a coyote try to get him and make him quit gobbling? Did he …*

… and then he gobbles, hard and insistently, not 200 yards along the ridge and barely uphill. You're within working distance of him where you stand, but there's enough curve to the slope that you can safely cut the distance by at least another 50 yards. Since closer is better in everything but hand grenades, you do it. You've already picked out a tree and plopped down against it, and you're pulling on your head net when another hunter calls to the bird from a position 100 yards to your right and slightly uphill.

OK, that's where you are. Whose bird is it?

Well, first of all, you're on public land. Technically speaking, the bird doesn't belong to anybody until a tag goes around its leg. But ethically, it's not a tough call. My philosophy in such a situation is to let the other hunter have the bird and go try to find another one. It's a hard pill to swallow, but it's best from the standpoint of both safety and sportsmanship. Not that I'm overly fond of being a Good Samaritan, but it usually works out best.

Two hunters working the same gobbler usually results in a hung-up bird anyway, and the frustration index of the average turkey hunt is high enough already without setting yourself up for even more. There's also safety to consider. Safety and ethics often go hand in hand in the turkey woods, and the above situation is a prime example.

If it bothers you to see things like this in the woods, don't be guilty of such behavior yourself, even on a smaller scale.

Just because a hunting method is legal doesn't mean it's ethical. A wild turkey is too valuable a bird to take except under fair-chase conditions.

But what if the shoe is on the other foot? What if you're already set up on the bird and calling to him when the other hunter shows up?

First of all, don't get in a hurry to do anything. Call or hoot loudly to let the other hunter know you're there, then sit tight for a while without calling and see what happens. If you're lucky, the other hunter will back off. Good Samaritanism and good sportsmanship work both ways, and that's what I hope for whenever this happens to me. But, of course, it doesn't always play out that way. The other hunter may not be able to hear my calling, or he may think I'm a turkey instead of a fellow hunter. (Yes, I'm good enough for that to be a possibility.) Or, maybe, the other hunter just doesn't care. For whatever reasons, sometimes the competing hunter stays and goes to work on "your" gobbler from a different direction.

In that case I always, *always*, give up the bird, even though I feel I have the better claim. I didn't do this when I was younger, but I do it now. It's maddening to walk away from a hot gobbler, but safety is the prime consideration here. The biggest gobbler in the woods isn't worth running the risk of getting shot. What's right and what's fair have little to do with it.

Ethical considerations are an important part of any hunting effort these days, and these considerations get more important each spring as more and more people take up turkey hunting across the country. But what are good ethics, anyway? It's a cloudy issue. Like one's morals, one's ethics are largely self-defined.

Most of you who are reading these words probably consider yourselves to be ethical hunters. I know I do.

But are we? Consider:

• Have you ever found yourself competing with another hunter for the same bird, as in the scenario that began this chapter, and instead of backing off, hung right in there and tried to call the turkey away from the other guy? Me, too.

• Have you ever shot at a gobbler you felt was a few yards out of sure killing range, hoping you might get lucky? Me, too.

• Have you ever known a friend to violate a "minor" game law – take more than the legal limit of gobblers in a season, say, or fail to check a bird so he could keep on hunting – and kept your mouth shut about it because it's not nice to snitch on a buddy? Me, too.

• Have you ever left litter in the woods, even something so small and insignificant as a candy wrapper or cigarette butt? Have you ever stretched a hunt a few minutes past legal closing time because of a hot-gobbling bird that wasn't quite killable when time ran out? Have you ever followed a gobbler onto land you didn't have permission to hunt? Have you ever used someone else's tag on a gobbler? Have you ever let another hunter use one of yours? Have you ever shot a turkey on the roost? Hunted over bait? Breasted out a gobbler and thrown the legs away? Taken more than the legal limit of gobblers in a day or in a season? Failed to tag or check a turkey, or looked the other way when one of your buddies did?

Maybe we're not so ethical after all.

Ethics. Sportsmanship. We hear these terms all the time, and we roll them glibly off our tongues at NWTF chapter banquets, turkey-calling contests and campfires.

But what are those things, anyway? And, just as important, how are we supposed to apply them to this sport we love so much?

If you're looking for firm answers, suitable for carving in stone, look somewhere else. You won't find them here. Many writers better than me have tried for years to get a handle on this slippery subject, and they've all failed. If they couldn't lay it out in black and white, I'm certainly not conceited enough to think I can do it. But here are some of the thoughts I have on the subject:

Most folks are intellectually lazy, and they don't want to go to the bother of actually thinking things through for themselves. So they comfort themselves with the notion that the state regulations dealing with turkey hunting are acceptable guidelines for what's ethical and what's not. After all, that's the job of state and federal wildlife managers, to tell us what we can and cannot do when we're hunting or fishing. So they doubtless have a firm grasp of ethics, the same way they do with wildlife biology. Right?

Hardly.

Unless I missed something while researching this chapter, it's perfectly legal in every state to move in on another hunter who's already set up on a turkey and start working the bird yourself in an attempt to call him away from the other guy. Legal, maybe, but don't waste your breath trying to convince me it's acceptable.

Is it ethical to hunt over bait? Is a food plot considered "bait"? Hmmmm.

In every state except Alabama, decoys are legal. Are they ethical, though? It's an individual decision.

Wildlife officers have a firm grasp on what's legal. But regarding the question of what's ethical, they're just as confused as the rest of us.

In some states, it's legal to put out bait for turkeys in the form of corn or other grain. In other states, it's not. But everywhere it's legal to sit over a pre-prepared bait site, although in most circles they're known as "food plots" – or, if you prefer the techno-speak of professional wildlife biologists, "wildlife openings."

These two things stand in sharp contrast in the minds of most hunters. There are corn-pilers among the ranks of turkey hunters, sure, and I'm certain some of them are reading these words now, but most of us would no more hunt over a baited site than we'd try to catch a gobbler by the foot in a steel trap. But then again, we think nothing of sitting around on a slow day beside a food plot and bushwhacking a turkey when he comes in to eat a few leaves of clover.

What's the difference, aside from the fact that one is illegal and the other is not? It's an interesting question, especially when you consider that, as Tom Kelly says so concisely in *Tenth Legion,* planting a food plot is simply baiting six months before the fact.

See? This ethics thing is slippery.

Not always, though. In some states, it's illegal to shoot a gobbler out of a tree. This is a case of ethics lining up with legality. But in other states, my home state of Arkansas included, you can shoot your annual limit of gobblers out of trees, take out ads in the local newspaper to brag about it, complete with pictures, and never get in a smidgen of trouble with the warden. It's one more case of a thing being legal but unethical.

Let me, though, throw another scenario into the mix:

You're hunting in the lowlands of the Deep South, and you locate a gobbler roosted far out over the backwater. The bird eagerly answers your calling, but you can't make him come to dry land. At 8 a.m. he's still gobbling back at you, but he's still out over the water.

There are no other turkeys gobbling within hearing, so you do what any red-blooded turkey hunter would do: You throw logic to the winds and plunge into the blackwater swamp. Leaning against a tree like a duck hunter, thigh-deep in the tannin-stained water, you call again to the bird. The change in calling positions does the trick, and the gobbler flies toward you through the tupelos and cypresses. But, as mentioned, you're in 2 feet of water, and this is a turkey gobbler and not a drake wood duck. He lands on a waist-thick limb 30 yards away and immediately puffs into a strutting position.

What do you do?

Well, I'll tell you what I did, when this very thing happened to me in Mississippi near the beginning of my turkey hunting career: I rolled the bird off his limb with a load of 5s and subsequently picked up a soggy, unphotogenic but otherwise magnificent 20-pound gobbler.

After all these years, I still worry about my decision that morning. I gave the bird ample time, more than 2 1/2 hours, to come out of the swamp and play the game on dry land. When I went in after him, I called him in fair and square. The tree I shot him out of wasn't his roost tree, and he'd have been on the ground if there had been any ground for him to be on. He was in good killing range, and he died immediately and cleanly without ever knowing I was in the world.

But it troubles me still. I killed the gobbler legally, but did I kill him ethically? Yes, I think … but I'm not completely sure. I guess I never will be.

See?

Decoys are yet another area of controversy in this business of turkey hunting ethics. Is the use of decoys ethical, or are decoys just a form of visual baiting, as detestable to the right-minded turkey hunter as a fresh pile of corn in a logging road? Alabama thinks they're unethical, and decoys are illegal there. In every other state, they're legal.

Where do you stand on the issue? Why do you feel the way you do? Are decoys OK? Are they an unfair advantage? It's enough to make your head hurt.

Regardless of state-to-state differences in such turkey hunting controversies as baiting, tree-shooting and decoys, the result of any successful turkey hunt brought to its intended culmination is a dead turkey. This is true whether he's "Arkansaw-ed" off the limb he slept on in Georgia or called to the gun at 10 minutes before quitting time in Missouri (where, incidentally, they apparently think it's unethical to hunt in the afternoons, so they make it illegal to do so). In both dead-turkey instances, the kills would be legal. But if you want my take

on it, the Missouri bird was killed ethically, but the Georgia bird was not.

In the event the Missouri hunter called in and killed the bird 10 minutes past closing time instead of 10 minutes before, the act would be illegal, but still not unethical – except, of course, in the sense that it's automatically unethical to break game laws.

But – and here comes another wrinkle to think about – is it always unethical to break game laws? If you answer the question quickly and without thinking, your answer would almost certainly be yes. But just as some things are legal though unethical, the reverse is also sometimes true. Here's a true story:

A friend and I were hunting near Abilene, in the hill country of Texas, on a ranch that belonged to my friend's uncle. We separated to hunt different areas, and about 7 a.m. I heard a volley of gunfire from a portion of the ranch that wasn't supposed to have anybody hunting on it. My buddy heard it, too, and we met in the mesquite a half-hour later as we converged on the area to check things out.

We spied a truck parked along a road bordering the property, but when we were still several hundred yards from it, a camo-clad hunter walked out of the brush carrying a shotgun and some unidentifiable burden. He saw us and dropped whatever it was, jumped in the truck and sped away before we could get close enough to read the license plate. When we reached the site, we found what the trespasser had dropped – two hen turkeys.

My friend wasn't on good terms with the local wildlife officer. They'd gone to the same high school and had been enemies for years. If we called the officer, he said, we'd be accused of killing the birds and there'd be a big hassle. So we threw the carcasses into the bushes and went away, and neither of us ever mentioned it to anybody. We've both fretted about our decision ever since. We still talk about it every time we get together, and we're no closer to making up our minds about it now than when it happened many years ago.

Ethics, when you wade through all the flowery rhetoric, is what you do when no one is looking. And there's the trouble in a nutshell: Almost everything a turkey hunter does, he does when no one is looking. We have plenty of opportunity to do things wrong or to do wrong things.

Ethics are important in turkey hunting because there are usually no referees standing around watching the game. It's an honor system, and many of us often fail.

Like baseball, turkey hunting has rules that are based at least in part on ethics and sportsmanship. But unlike baseball, there's usually no umpire standing around in the turkey woods to enforce the rules, and statistically speaking, there's very little chance of getting caught if you break them.

That's why ethics are so important for the turkey hunter. There's no one standing around in a white shirt to make us play by the rules. Miss the ball three times in a baseball game, and the ump will make you go sit down, whether you want to or not. Set up on a gobbler another hunter is already working, and there's no penalty even if someone does see you, because this is one of those examples of an unethical act that's not illegal.

Ethics are an expression of personal values, of personal morality. And since one's values and morals are one's own, neither can be effectively legislated.

Most state wildlife agencies and conservation organizations give ethics a lot of lip service in hunter education classes, how-to seminars and press releases, but it's my opinion this is largely a waste of time and effort. By the time kids appear in a hunter-ed class at age 11, 12 or 13, their mindset is already established. Either they're already on their way to becoming ethical hunters, in which case you're preaching to the choir, or they're headed the other way, in which case you're preaching to the deaf.

But still we have to wrestle with it. Turkey hunting, by its solitary nature, is particularly vulnerable to violations of ethics. And as the sport continues to gain popularity and the woods become crowded with more and more hunters, it's inevitable that conflicts among those hunters will increase. How we handle those conflicts will bear heavily not only on our enjoyment of turkey hunting, but also on our right to continue doing it.

The basic issue with which we must individually tussle isn't just "Is it legal?" but also "Is it right?" The first question is easy.

It's the second one that's hard.

Chapter 44

Field Care and Cooking

Field-dressing a turkey can be a good idea or a bad one, depending on how fast you're going to be able to get the bird home or to camp so you can care for it properly. Insects are also a factor; opening the body cavity increases the bird's exposure to flies and other undesirables.

Isaac Walton, the great pioneer of fishing literature, once wrote: "Treat him as though you loved him, that he may live the longer." I'm probably misquoting by a word or two there, but I'm too lazy to look it up, and that's the gist of it, anyway. Walton, of course, was talking about fish, specifically trout, and about how you should always treat a fish properly regardless whether you were going to kill it for the table or release it. Your taste buds depend on that proper care in the former case, while the fish's very life depends on it in the latter.

Walton lived in England, and since no wild turkeys ever lived there, he couldn't possibly have been a turkey hunter. But if he had been, his advice for getting the best flavor out of a wild turkey would no doubt have been similar: Treat him as though you loved him, so that he may taste the better.

We can't practice catch-and-release turkey hunting, of course, although often that's more or less how turkey hunts work out. Still, sometimes we do manage through some combination of luck and skill to actually kill a gobbler. And it's what happens in the hours following the harvest that ultimately determines how that bird is going to taste. That, of course, and how you choose to cook him.

I can tell you some real horror stories about the improper handling of wild turkeys, but you may have eaten recently, and I don't want to cause a revolt in your digestive system. Suffice it to say that judging from what I've seen, there are a heck of a lot of hunters out there who don't have the foggiest idea what to do with a gobbler after it quits flopping.

Actually, the proper handling of a turkey in the field begins before you shoot it, not after. In many cases, turkey hunters aren't operating out of their house, but rather from a tent camp with no electricity or running water, sometimes many hundreds of miles from home. Even when you are hunting close to home, "close" is a relative term. It may be several hours to half a day before you can get the bird to a place where you can process it. Since one of the major differences between spring turkey hunting and most other types of hunting is that it's much warmer during the turkey season, proper care of the bird during those first couple of hours after you've killed it is critical.

What you do (or don't do) in that first two or three hours can make you or break you when that bird shows up on the Thanksgiving table. Likewise, having the right items on hand can also save the day or ruin it.

Following the Shot

Getting a gobbler cooled down is a lot more important than most hunters realize. It's also not quite as simple as you'd think. A turkey's body temperature is about 106 degrees in the first place, so you're already in the hole before you start. When you've got a 20-pound bird covered with a thick layer of insulating feathers and the air temperature is in the 80s, getting him cool can be a real challenge.

All of us are duty-bound to do a little admiring and picture-taking with a freshly slain turkey, but don't let this process drag out until you ruin the flavor of your bird. If possible, get the turkey out of direct sunlight immediately and keep him in the shade while you do your glad-handing and take your photos.

Hanging a gobbler by one foot (not both) in a shady, well-ventilated place is the best way to get the body heat out of him. Hanging him by one foot allows his free leg to fall away from the body, and the head-down position causes his feathers to fall away from the carcass and expose the bird's skin to the breeze. Despite what you see on turkey videos, it's highly advisable to hang a gobbler this way for a little while before you stuff him in your vest or into a hunter-orange tote sack and haul him out of the woods. Fifteen to 20 minutes of hanging upside down in the shade will cool a gobbler considerably, even when it's hot. Conversely, packing a gobbler into a vest or bag right after

Taking time for the obligatory photo shoot is fine after shooting a gobbler, but don't let the process drag on so long you ruin the bird.

311

Hanging a bird by one foot in a shady spot allows for rapid cooling, except in hot weather. A breeze helps, of course.

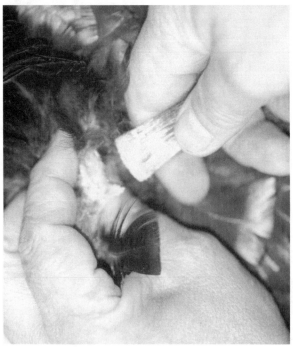

Don't cut the beard off; just grasp it and pull firmly, and it'll pop right out. The author has beards done this way that are more than 20 years old, and they're holding up fine.

shooting him pins his feathers and wings against his body and traps all that body heat in – not to mention adding the heat from your back as you struggle across the rough country between you and your truck.

If you're more than an hour away from a place where you can dress the bird, field-dressing him at the site of the kill is a good idea, in which case you can eliminate the hanging-him-up routine. However, when you open a turkey's body cavity, you also open up the possibility for flies and other insects to invade it, so you need to be mindful of this.

To field dress a gobbler, pluck away a few feathers around the vent so you can see what you're doing. Next, cut a slit through the skin into the body cavity in the soft spot right below the point of the bird's keelbone, and extend the slit down to just above the anal opening. Cut a circle through the skin all the way around the opening, being careful not to nick the gut in the process. Then grasp and pinch off the intestine with your hand, and haul the intestines free of the body. Reach into the body cavity (roll your shirt sleeve up or remove your shirt first; this is a bloody operation) and remove all the innards up to the neck. Be careful not to nick, cut or break the intestines or stomach, to prevent contaminating the body cavity with bacteria-loaded fecal matter.

If you want to save the giblets (highly recommended, if you're going to roast your gobbler), separate the heart, gizzard and liver from the rest of the guts and store them in a resealable plastic bag. Wipe the excess blood out of the body cavity with a *clean* absorbent rag like an old T-shirt, but *do not* wash the body cavity out with water until you get the turkey to a place where you can complete the preparation process. The film of blood left inside the body cavity will help seal it and retain moisture, and washing the body cavity can introduce other undesirable organisms or spread fecal matter or other contamination throughout the bird's interior, if any such material is present.

The next step is to waste no time getting the bird back home or to camp. Then, postpone the congratulatory toddy and the mandatory telling and retelling of the story until you've finished taking care of this bird you're so proud of.

The Second Phase – Care in Camp

If you're planning to roast or deep-fry the turkey, it should be plucked, not skinned. And the

If you have multiple gobblers to clean, getting an assembly line going is a good way to get the job done. Assign somebody to picking, somebody else to gutting, and somebody else to another chore.

longer you wait, the harder the chore is going to be. Some folks recommend scalding the bird with hot, soapy water to loosen the feathers, and while this definitely makes the picking chore easier, it's not really a good idea – especially that part about the soap. If you want a turkey that tastes like a bar of Irish Spring, go right ahead.

Scalding a bird with clean hot water is acceptable, if you're careful not to overdo it and parboil the skin, but this parboiling is a real risk and will adversely affect the taste of your bird. The best way, truly, is the old-fashioned, a-few-feathers-at-a-time way, starting and finishing with a dry turkey.

Don't get in a big hurry. If you try to take off too many feathers at once, you'll rip the skin. Grasp a few feathers firmly in one hand, use the other hand to hold down the skin near the roots of the feathers, and snatch them out "with the grain," that is, in the direction the feathers are growing. Pick the wings out to the first joint, and then cut them off at that joint.

Once the turkey is picked, it's important to singe off the remaining bits of down and hairlike feather filaments. The best method, by far, is to run portable propane torch quickly over the bird's skin. If you don't have one handy, you can use

any ready flame source. One good alternative is a rolled-up piece of cardboard. Rolled-up paper will also work, but it tends to get ashes on the turkey, and these should be quickly hosed off.

Washing the turkey thoroughly is the next step after singeing, anyway. I like to do this in the bathtub or in a washtub outside, since a big wild turkey gobbler is a little too much for the average kitchen sink. Wash the body cavity thoroughly, scrubbing it with a vegetable brush to loosen the dried blood and unwanted tissue. Pay particular attention to removing the spongy lung tissue from between the ribs on each side of the backbone. You'll probably have to dig most of this stuff out with your fingers.

If you're in a primitive camp, of course, you probably won't have a bathtub or washtub at your disposal. In this case, do the best you can with a 5-gallon bucket or other large container. Rinse the bird thoroughly inside and out with clean water once you're through scrubbing it, and then prop it in an upright position and let the body cavity drain for a few minutes. Then, put the bird in at least two, preferably three, large plastic bags, tying each bag separately, and get it on ice or into the freezer. Always use unscented bags, to avoid possible taste contamination. Don't put any ice in

Pouring near-boiling water over a turkey loosens the feathers and makes picking a breeze. Use a container to catch the hot water, and you can pour it over the bird a second time. It doesn't take much; a 3-quart saucepan will hold enough hot water to scald a turkey, provided you recycle the water once.

If you dry-pick a bird, either do it while he's still warm or do it a few feathers at a time, to keep from ripping the skin.

the body cavity, but do keep the bird well-iced until you can freeze it, and keep the melted water drained off.

If you're going to pan-fry the turkey instead of plucking it, you can simply fillet the breasts and cut off the legs. Wash and drain these parts the same as you would a whole turkey, and get them on ice as soon as possible. By separating the drumsticks from the thighs, you can fit both breasts and both legs of a 20-pound gobbler into a gallon freezer bag and still get it zipped. When you get home, freeze each breast in a separate bag, and freeze one thigh and one drumstick in separate packages for making soup or stew.

Turkey hunters are itchy-footed types, and many of us fly to various destinations to hunt gobblers far from home. To bring home a bird on the plane, treat it in either of the ways described previously, then wrap it one final time in newspaper and in one more fresh, dry plastic bag. Stuff the bird into the middle of your suitcase or duffel bag and surround it with your hunting clothes for extra insulation. Check the bag rather than carrying it on, so it will be stored in the baggage compartment of the plane, which is much cooler than the cabin. A turkey packed in this manner will be good for 24 hours or more without damage, provided you handled it properly before you packed it in your luggage.

Cooking the Bird

There are as many turkey recipes as there are turkey hunters, I guess, and there's not nearly enough room in this chapter to do justice to the topic. However, here are several ways I've made very tasty meals out of spring gobblers:

Roasting: This is the classic way of preparing a turkey, but there are some considerable differences between your wild gobbler and a Buttterball from Piggly Wiggly. The wild bird is leaner, and if you're not careful you'll dry him out in the cooking. While turkey jerky is tasty in its own right, you don't want your Thanksgiving main course to turn out that way. Weigh the bird, season him inside and out, stuff him with dressing or (better) quartered raw apples, onions, celery and mushrooms, drape several strips of bacon over the breast and cook 15 minutes per pound at 325 degrees. If you want to be scientific, the bird should be perfectly done when the temperature in the middle of the thickest part of the thigh reaches

185 degrees. If the turkey isn't brown enough to suit you when the time is up, remove it from the oven, turn it to broil and let it reach maximum heat, then put the turkey back in and watch it carefully until it's the proper shade of brown.

Deep Frying: If you're set up for it, with a large enough pot and an outdoor fish cooker, you can fry a turkey whole. First, put the turkey in the pot and add enough water to barely, but completely, cover the bird. The pot should be big enough so that the water level is still 5 to 6 inches below the rim, to allow for the bubble-up factor when you add the moist turkey to the hot grease. Now remove the turkey from the pot and allow it to drain. Mark the level of the water in the pot after you remove the bird, then get rid of the water, and dry the pot. Now add oil (peanut oil is best) up to your mark and heat it to 350 degrees. While the oil is heating, season the bird heavily inside and out, and bind the drumsticks tightly together with sturdy wire, wrapping each drumstick with several tight wraps so the wire won't slip off the end of the leg. When the oil reaches the desired temperature, slowly lower the turkey into the pot, using a long-handled hook to hold the bird by the wire. You may have to raise it out of the hot oil a time or two until the excess water boils off. Cook for 3 minutes per pound, plus 5 minutes. (For a 10-pound bird, for example, the cooking time would be 10 X 3 + 5, or 35 minutes.) Then use the hook to lift the bird out, letting it drain over the pot, and then place it on a tray with several layers of paper towels to catch the excess oil.

Pan-Fried Turkey Breast: Cut the breast in strips about the size of your index finger. Season and flour, and cook quickly in hot oil until golden brown. "Quickly" is the key word here.

Grilled Turkey Breast: This is my favorite cooking method. Butterfly the turkey breast to reduce its thickness, then marinate in Italian dressing for 3 to 4 hours. Then pin several strips of bacon to each side of the butterflied breast with toothpicks and cook over coals or propane. Stay with it, or the grease from the bacon will catch fire and give you a charcoal slab instead of the delicious meal you're looking for.

That should get you started toward some delicious eating. Remember: Treat him as though you loved him. Your taste buds – not to mention the turkey – deserve it.

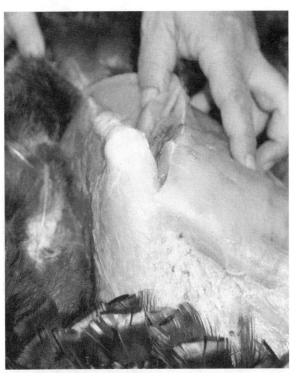

Filleting the breast of a gobbler and taking the legs for soups and stews gets more than 90 percent of the available meat off the bird.

Even though wild turkey is much better-tasting than domestic turkey, it's still turkey. For those who like more flavor in their meat, making turkey jerky is a good option. Slice it thin, use your favorite marinade or a conglomeration of kitchen spices, and dry the meat for 16 to 20 hours in a low-heat oven or dehydrator.

Words of Wisdom
on a Grand
Spring Sport

Turkey hunting usually isn't a fatal disease, but it is seasonally debilitating. And the season, of course, is spring.

It was during the spring of 1978 that the turkey virus first entered my blood. I haven't been the same since.

Because you've made it this far through this rambling, often contradictory book, it's a pretty safe bet you're similarly afflicted. Therefore, you have some idea of what I'm talking about here. "This thing of ours" isn't a fatal disease, but for many of us, it's seasonably debilitating. And the season, of course, is spring.

The only cure for it is dressing in what my youngest daughter calls a "tree suit" and prowling the mountains, swamps and piney woods on as many spring mornings as we can manage, our eyes red and stinging from lack of sleep, searching for a bird whose call sounds like a cross between a mugging and a train wreck. If we do find him, it's even money we won't quite know how to deal with him.

I'm now well into my second quarter-century as a turkey hunter. When that thought crosses my mind – and it often does – my only major regret is that I waited until I was past 30 to take it up. I wasted a good 15 springs of my youth and young adulthood on silly, pointless pursuits like bass, bream and crappie fishing, and I'll never forgive myself for it.

Even as late as I got started, though, I've now been at it long enough to have survived hundreds of encounters with turkeys in – at last count – 17 states. Most of the turkeys survived those encounters as well, but that's fodder for another chapter. Another book, actually.

Still, some of those birds honored me by coming home slung over my shoulder. If I continue to hunt with my normal intensity (my basic game plan, if you haven't figured it out by now, is to move slow, keep my head in the game, try to keep from making stupid mistakes, avoid carelessness, and mostly just stay out there until something *happens*), I expect I'll kill a few more.

Because I get out there as often as I can, and because I stay out there as long as I can, I've begun to learn a few things the hard way. It would have been difficult not to have picked up a thing or two, actually, when you've hunted turkeys as much and as vigorously as I have.

Some of the things I've learned are valuable and useful, and some aren't. It can be hard to tell which is which. Many of these lessons are covered in more depth in other chapters of this book.

Getting your ears even a foot or two higher can mean the difference between hearing a distant gobbler or not. If there's a rock or stump handy to your listening spot, get on top of it.

While elaborate blinds are usually too much trouble, selecting a well-concealed setup spot is an advantage.

A few of the tidbits that follow are tongue-in-cheek. Some of them are dead serious; others aren't. A few of them may be both. At any rate, here they are, in no particular order:

• If you "roost" a turkey late in the afternoon on the day before you're planning to hunt, the bird will either change locations, develop lockjaw or get himself eaten by a bobcat before daylight the next morning.

• Always go to high places to listen for turkeys. Climb to the top of a ridge rather than listening from the valley floor, because you can hear much more country from up there. Never mind that the turkey you hear gobbling will be back down in the bottom of the valley you just climbed out of. Get on up to the top, anyway.

• Never hunt within hearing distance of a stream you're not willing to wade or swim, unless you're heavily into beating yourself over the head with stout limbs or other forms of masochism.

When you hunt close to one of these unwadable streams, every gobbler you hear will be on the other side, and there won't be a boat within 5 miles.

• A corollary to the above item says that on smaller, deeper, colder streams, there will usually be a crossing log that looks like it just might bear your weight. But it won't.

• Elaborate blinds are generally not worth the trouble for hunting turkeys. A gobbler can see into one of these much better than a turkey hunter can see out. Also, blinds slow you down on those all-too-frequent occasions when you need to pick up stakes and change locations in a hurry. Just sit still. You can do it.

• The frequency of a turkey's gobbling is directly proportional to the number of competing hunters within range of his voice. Stated another way, if you are the only hunter within 5 miles of a turkey, he'll gobble once just to let you know he's there and then shut up for the rest of the day.

Turkeys are allergic to shiny objects – like faces and hands.

If there are six other eager hunters on the same mountain with you and the bird, he'll gobble with every breath.

• A turkey possesses the ability to see up, down and behind itself, all at the same time. It is a fallacy, however, that turkeys can see through rocks. Only Superman can do that. Instead, turkeys see around them.

• Turkeys cannot hear your heart beating at 40 yards, as some hunters believe. That's ridiculous; no bird can hear that well. Instead, they feel the pressure waves your pulse sends through the air.

• Turkeys are allergic to many things, the most noticeable of which are: movement; the sound of twigs breaking underfoot; shiny objects such as glasses, oily noses and uncamouflaged gun barrels; and any object in their home range that has not been in the same spot for at least three years.

If there are three possible directions from which a turkey can approach your calling, and two of them afford good visibility, the bird will always come in via the third route. That is, if he comes in at all, which is highly unlikely in the first place.

• Turkeys have the ability to become invisible at will. I think they do this with mirrors.

• Calling turkeys is very simple. Anybody can do it. Making a turkey come to your calling is what's hard.

• There are five basic calls from which to choose – yelp, cluck, purr, cutt and cackle. All are equally effective at making turkeys ignore you or go the other way.

• When you do succeed in calling a gobbler within shotgun range, most of the time he will a) come up directly behind you and gobble in your ear; b) come into view while your shotgun is still in your lap or lying on the ground; c) let you get your gun lined up on the spot where he last gobbled and then come into view a full 90 degrees away from where your gun is pointing; or d) stay just out of sight under the crest of a hill and gobble and drum until some other hunter comes along and scares him away or kills him.

• If you stop to answer a call of nature when you are turkey hunting, a gobbler will pick that moment to walk up and catch you, literally, with your pants down. Turkeys have a perverse sense of timing on this.

• Contrary to what other hunters will tell you, a gobbler is very predictable in his habits. For example, it is possible to accurately predict the exact tree a gobbler will roost in for the six nights just before the season opens, and then it is possible to predict that the night before opening day, he will move to an undetermined location at least a mile away.

• In any given hunting situation, you'll only get one shot at a stationary turkey. Make the shot count.

• A double corollary to the above rule states: a) a running or flying turkey is nearly impossible to hit; and b) any turkey that has been shot at and missed is awash with so much adrenaline, he's practically bulletproof.

*   *   *

We could go on and on with this; my wisdom in this particular aspect of turkey hunting is boundless. But my editors gave me a maximum word count for this book, and we have to spread it around among more chapters than just this one. Anyway, this is a good place as any to stop. It would be a shame if I told you everything I know and thereby robbed you of the true joy of turkey hunting.

A hunter needs to learn some of this stuff on his own.

Many things can go wrong when a gobbler approaches, and more often than not, one of them will. But sometimes we win, and it keeps us going back.

Chapter 46

The Story of a Turkey Hunter

The turkey played his part flawlessly in The Great Turkey Caper.

Call him Bill. It wasn't his name, but it'll do. He died in 1991, when his 70-year-old heart got tired and quit. He was a friend of mine, and this is his story:

Born to a poor rural family during the Roaring Twenties, Bill fell victim to a raging, dangerously high fever. Medical care was distant, expensive and rudimentary, so his parents did what all poor rural folks did in those days in similar situations: tried to keep liquids in their sick baby, did everything they could think of to fight the fever, and prayed. Bill survived the ordeal, but the fever left him … well, not quite right.

In some ways, Bill had the intellectual powers of a Harvard graduate. He never forgot a name or a face or a detail of any long-ago conversation, and you sure didn't want to play dominoes against him. But in other ways, he remained childlike and innocent.

A country boy, Bill grew up in a hunting-oriented family in the Arkansas Ozarks. Although his limited physical coordination kept him from becoming a proficient wingshot, he nevertheless got pretty good at hitting squirrels. Over the years, he tagged a buck or two as well.

Inevitably, as turkeys were reintroduced to his home area and the flocks took hold and began to grow, Bill got interested in turkey hunting. "Interested," though, is too mild a word. "Obsessed" is closer. Bill joined the National Wild

Turkey Federation, and he read each issue of *Turkey Call* from cover to cover. He attended local calling contests and hunting seminars. He talked turkey, to the point of exhaustion, with anybody who would listen or who couldn't figure out a way to escape.

This next thing is difficult to explain without sounding snotty and superior, but I don't mean it that way at all. Please don't read it wrong. But … turkey hunting is a game of strategy and finesse, and with Bill's arrested mental development and lack of sophistication, he just wasn't up to the task. In the matter of hunting these grand birds, my old friend was in over his head.

And so, after watching Bill become more and more frustrated at his inability to call in and kill a gobbler, a mutual friend decided to help a little. Call him Tom.

Tom tried to do it the straightforward, honest way at first. He solicited the help of another mutual friend, a famous turkey hunter whose name you'd recognize if I mentioned it.

The Famous Turkey Hunter accepted the challenge, and he tried hard to get Bill in front of a turkey, or vice versa. But Bill had other health problems, too, and he wasn't able to walk very far or very fast. That greatly increased the degree of difficulty in an already difficult undertaking, and the FTH wasn't quite able to pull it off.

After several unsuccessful tries, they managed to locate a hot bird one morning that was close to a road on gentle terrain, and it looked like Bill was going to kill his first gobbler at long last. But the turkey was gobbling with every step as he approached, and the closer he got, the more Bill trembled and shook. Finally, just as the bird was about to show itself, Bill got so rattled he dropped his shotgun on the rocks at his feet. End of gobbling. End of turkey hunt.

End of Bill, too, nearly. "I thought he was going to die on me right there," the FTH told me later. "He was trembling and breathing hard and grabbing his chest. I asked him, 'Bill, are you OK?' and he said yes, he thought so, but he felt the same way the time he had a heart attack."

Back in camp, the FTH told Tom he didn't think the legitimate approach was going to work, and they might kill Bill if they kept trying. So they drafted two more friends – call them Dick and Harry – and the Great Turkey Caper was born.

Early the next spring, the Famous Turkey Hunter went to a nearby farm and bought a good-looking bronze domestic gobbler with a thick, bushy beard. A week before the opening of the turkey season, he cooped the bird in a ramshackle shed on a hunting property he had under lease, leaving the turkey with plenty of water but no feed.

On the first morning of turkey season, Tom brought Bill to the lease before daylight and comfortably installed him in a roomy, portable, roof-and-wall archery blind the FTH had set up at the edge of a green patch, just a couple hundred yards from the shed housing the domestic gobbler. Tom put a decoy in front of the blind and closed all the openings except the one overlooking the decoy. Then he got in the blind with Bill.

When all was ready, Tom gave a loud series of yelps. Dick, standing by at the shed, heard the pre-arranged signal and went into action. He entered the shed, caught the gobbler and headed for the blind, bird riding calm and peaceful under his arm. The turkey had been getting this same ride every day for a week, getting his daily ration of feed and unknowingly training for his part in the pageant. Once Dick was in position, slightly behind and a few yards to the right of the blind, he yelped softly back at Tom.

Meanwhile, Harry was setting up a video camera just to the left of the blind. When he was ready, he yelped, too.

Inside the stuffy blind, Bill and Tom peered out the front window at the decoy. "Tom, I think I hear one!" Bill whispered excitedly.

"Me, too," Tom said. "Maybe we better call a little." And so he did, thus giving Dick the signal to release the gobbler.

They had rehearsed this part with the gobbler, using a small pile of corn at the decoy to train him to walk to the proper place and stop. The corn was missing this morning, it being turkey season and baiting now illegal. Still, the gobbler played his part perfectly, as befitted the star of the show. He walked along the edge of the woods, toward the decoy, and stopped precisely where the corn was supposed to be – at point-blank range, squarely in front of the blind.

The gobbler didn't have much time to puzzle over the absence of his little corn pile. Eight yards away, the muzzle of Bill's old double-barrel poked out of the shooting port of the blind, wavered, then steadied. Kaboom!

On the video, you can see the bird flinch as the tennis ball-sized swarm of 6s goes whizzing by his head. He takes a few nervous steps away from the noise. Kaboom! again. A flaw in the plan was becoming obvious: The Great Turkey Caper team hadn't allowed for enough range to ensure adequate pattern development, and Bill's nervousness and hoochie-koochie gun barrel weren't getting the job done with the bird so close.

On the audio, you can hear muffled curses and clanks as Tom and Bill struggle to reload the shotgun in the close quarters of the blind. The blind sways and trembles as they jostle back and forth. By the time they succeed in reloading the gun, the gobbler is 25 yards away, showing signs of rethinking his part in the whole affair. But he is finally far enough out for Bill's pattern to develop. Three's the charm, and this time the bird goes down. Despite an attack of uncontrollable giggling, Harry managed to capture the entire event on film. I have a copy of that video, and I promise you don't have enough money to buy it.

It's a wonderful piece of footage, especially the post-hunt recap. That part features a grinning, still-shaking Bill, who, despite his own excitement, still has the courtliness and generosity to offer the use of his lucky blind to Harry for the next day's hunt.

Some will say it was a dirty, dishonest trick. Others will fault the fact that an unsuspecting barnyard gobbler was summarily executed. Some will say it was probably illegal. I've been told all those things by some of the people I've told the story to. And all those things may be true, but before you pitch your tent in any of those camps, consider this: Until the day Bill died (which wasn't many springs later), the spurs, beard and fan of his first and only gobbler hung in a place of honor in his simple little house. If you asked – or even if you didn't – Bill was always happy to tell you the long, involved story of how he dueled for hours with this magnificent bird before skillfully and single-handedly bringing him to the gun. Bill's innocent, childlike mind, you see, had taken the event far beyond its facts, and the old man sincerely believed he had called that gobbler in all by himself, overcoming immense difficulties all along the way.

As you sat and listened to Bill's story, as I did many times, you were invariably struck by the awe and reverence in the eyes and voice of this generous, good-hearted man-child. His chest swelled

The feeling that bonds all turkey hunters together is real but intangible: impossible to explain to an outsider; unnecessary to explain to each other.

with pride and excitement, and his face alternated with that curious mixture of happiness and regret a turkey hunter feels when recalling a job well done, a kill well made, a bird fairly taken.

That feeling is what bonds turkey hunters one to another. It's a thing we all share, if we're worthy of being called turkey hunters. It's impossible to explain it to an outsider; it's unnecessary to explain it to each other.

It's a feeling that came to Bill only once in his lifetime. But, as you nodded your head and exclaimed at the appropriate places during his story, as you watched his faded old eyes flash, as you saw the smile play around the corners of his mouth, you realized once was going to be enough. Bill had the feeling captured. It was never going to escape.

Yep, the critics are right. The Great Turkey Caper was dishonest. It was an execution, not a hunt. And it may well have been technically illegal. Any way you look at it, the whole elaborate scheme was a complicated, premeditated, unmitigated lie, and lying is a sin.

Still, I suspect there are some sins a person will go to Heaven for.

Chapter 47

Climbing the Learning Curve

A hunt that ends with no turkey isn't a failure. That's what non-turkey hunters so often fail to understand.

At first light on the first day I ever went turkey hunting, a day before which I had never heard the gobble of a wild turkey, I heard seven Mississippi gobblers sound off, row-row-row-your-boat style, in response to the hoot of a considerate barred owl. I became an instant turkey hunting junkie.

But not a good one, you understand. Not even a mediocre one. The guy who took me that first morning of my turkey hunting career didn't know much more about it than I did, and so we failed to kill a bird that day. Looking back on it from the accumulated experience of a quarter-century of chasing turkeys, it's easy to pick out several occasions on that turkey-rich hunt when we should have tagged gobblers. But we didn't capitalize on any of those opportunities because we were too far down the learning curve.

Following the tradition established on that inaugural hunt, I spent the next four Aprils chasing gobblers without killing any of them, either. I blundered and bumbled and botched chance after chance. I made mistakes I didn't even know were mistakes. I did every stupid thing you could think of doing in the turkey woods, and then for good measure I went back and did them all again.

After four springs of it, I got fed up. I tried one last time, got ring-around-the-rosied by two gobblers on the same morning, and swore off turkey hunting for good. Spring mornings were too good for bass fishing to waste any more of them on hunting oversized birds that wouldn't cooperate, I explained to everyone who would listen.

If you have read the rest of this book, you know what happened next: A friend heard about it, called me, bullied me into trying again and subsequently called in my first gobbler.

Sometimes, in an April when things are going badly, I still wonder whether that was a good thing or a bad thing. He wasn't much, that first gobbler of mine – 18 pounds, an 8-inch beard not much thicker than a milkshake straw, spurs that looked like miniature Hershey's Kisses – your typical late-hatched 2-year-old after a poor mast crop and a tough winter. But there he lay, all right, shot in the head, and that counted for a lot. As we stood on opposite sides of that gobbler, shaking hands across his still-quivering body, Robert spoke two sentences I remember as clearly as I remember everything else about that fine spring morning.

"OK," he said, "the ice is broken. Now you're on your own."

When you knock all the feathers off it, that's what turkey hunting is all about – being on your own. Sure, it's nice to go hunting with someone who knows a lot more about the sport than you do, because it gives you a fast track on picking up some good stuff about turkey hunting. Other chapters of this book deal heavily with this aspect of the sport; it's an important part of the overall picture, and it's no doubt the best way to get started in this frustrating sport. But your goal as a turkey hunter should be to get past the point of needing this in-the-woods mentoring.

I've been lucky in my turkey hunting career. As a guy who writes magazine articles (and now books) about this sport, I've had the opportunity to hunt with some of the best in the business – people named Salter, Harris, Walker, Brown, Drury, Norton, Haas, Strickland, Pittman, Jordan, Waddell, Eye, Kelly. Those guys. And I've learned a lot from every one of them.

However, these famous names aren't the only top-shelf turkey hunters out there. There are hundreds, maybe thousands of turkey hunters every bit as good as these well-known hunters, but who haven't been in a position to get the publicity required to make them famous outside their local area. They're just regular men and women, local hunters who have achieved expert status. Chances are, you know a few of these people. If you want to get a crash course in turkey hunting, somehow wrangle a hunting invitation with one of them.

The only trouble with that plan is, these experts are often older hunters, people who learned to hunt gobblers in those dim, bleak days of the 1940s, 1950s and 1960s, when turkey populations had quit falling but still hadn't started showing

"OK, the ice is broken. Now you're on your own."

much in the way of recovery. There weren't many turkeys then, and even fewer turkey hunters, and reliable information on the sport was practically non-existent. These guys learned about hunting turkeys in the school of hard knocks, and they learned to guard their intelligence with the care of wartime generals. Most of these old-guard hunters can't seem to break that habit. Many of them are loners, and some are downright unfriendly. Their attitude seems to be, "Hey, I learned this stuff on my own. I'm not going to show any of it to you."

Fortunately, the brightest bulb on the tree isn't the only one that sheds light. There are plenty of lesser luminaries who are still pretty good turkey hunters, and while this group also has its share of loners and information misers, there are also a lot of folks who'll take the time to help you get off on the right foot. You might not have much luck in getting invitations to go turkey hunting from them, but it's not that hard to find somebody who'll let you pick his or her brain. The only thing a dedicated turkey hunter likes more than talking about hunting turkeys is actually hunting turkeys. Take

The only thing a dedicated turkey hunter likes more than talking about hunting turkeys is actually hunting turkeys.

advantage of this at seminars, calling contests, sport shows and NWTF banquets.

Speaking of which, involvement in a state or local National Wild Turkey Federation chapter is one of the best ways for a neophyte hunter to upgrade his or her skill level. As a former 5-year banquet committee co-chairman and former board member of the NWTF's Arkansas State Chapter, I know first-hand how much knowledge and know-how just sort of rubs off on you when you spend time working on projects with other turkey hunters.

It also helps to hunt with a partner when you're trying to climb the learning curve. Bill White and I formed a loose partnership when we were still pretty far down the curve, and we hunted together more often than not for about 10 learning-intensive years. When we were trying to double-team a bird, we held whispered conversations to discuss almost every move of every hunt, thinking things through before we did them. Some of our conversations got pretty heated, and I'm sure some of them went on so long, the gobblers we were trying to dupe got bored and went somewhere else. But we taught each other a lot in the process, too, and we killed our share of turkeys.

When we didn't hunt together during those years, we'd meet afterwards and share our experiences through lengthy conversations and explana-

tions that sometimes lasted longer than the hunts themselves. We dissected each hunt, discussing the pros and cons of this strategy or that, and what we could have done differently to make things turn out better. When one of us got lucky and killed a gobbler, we dissected those hunts even more meticulously, striving to understand what we did (or didn't do) to kill the gobbler and why it worked. This, too, made us better hunters.

There's a wealth of second-hand information out there today that wasn't available even as recently as the early 1980s, and this accumulated knowledge can also help you climb the learning curve. There are turkey hunting seminars at almost every sporting convention and sport show in the country, and these interactive seminars feature some of the best, most articulate hunters in the business today. An hour spent at one of these seminars is worth a whole spring's worth of "uh-oh, wish I hadn't done that" lessons in the woods.

And don't even get me started on books and videos. My personal turkey hunting library contains more than 80 videos and 50 books, and I buy every new one I hear about. (I have three new books on order as I write these words.) And if I've ever thrown away an outdoor magazine that had a turkey article in it, it was by accident.

However, reading about turkey hunting and watching seminars and videos about turkey hunting, will only take you so far up the curve. These educational opportunities are extremely valuable, sure, but there's no way they can take the place of OJT. You simply gotta get out there and take your lumps while trying to put all that book knowledge into practice. That's the only way it will actually sink in.

Pay attention to what's happening when you're in the woods. That sounds like the worst sort of useless advice, I know, but I've watched beginner after beginner go through a turkey hunt like a steelie ball in a pachinko machine, bouncing from bumper to bumper and not learning a blessed thing in the process. Every action – or non-action – has its consequences in the turkey woods, and the hunter who takes note of these cause-and-effect relationships and thinks about how to deal with them in the future is the hunter who'll get farther up the learning curve, and get there faster as well.

Take your time when you're hunting. One of the biggest mistakes turkey hunters of all levels of experience make is to get in too big a hurry. Remember: A turkey isn't on a timetable. He has all day to do whatever it is he's going to do – and if he doesn't get around to it today, there's always tomorrow. Some turkey hunting situations require quick decisions and fast action, but most of the time speed is not only unnecessary, but also detrimental to your success. Be deliberate. Think things through.

One way to help yourself in this learning-curve business is by keeping a hunt log. When you spook a turkey or screw up a hunt in one of the myriad ways possible to screw it up, record it – honestly – in your log. Also write down why you think your mistake was a mistake, and speculate on paper about what you could have done differently.

This process will make you think. What's more important, it will create a permanent record of your experiences as a turkey hunter. I re-read my turkey log every year during the off-season. Not only does it help me get through the awful heebie-jeebies that come over me on long February evenings, it reminds me of the things I've learned through my own lengthy enrollment in the school of hard knocks. It helped me immensely in writing this book.

And don't forget, as you begin to accumulate the knowledge that helps you climb the curve, that

Keeping a hunting log is a way to help yourself up the learning curve.

you don't have to be a terribly good turkey hunter to be of invaluable assistance to another hunter who's farther down the curve than you are. I've called in several first birds for beginning and/or struggling hunters, and if I can do it, it can't be all that hard to do.

And every time, when the new hunter and I are standing on opposite sides of the freshly fallen gobbler, I've spoken the two sentences I heard from my own mentor all these years ago: "OK, the ice is broken. Now you're on your own."

It felt good saying it. It feels even better today when I think about the fact that several of the hunters I helped get over the hump have gone on to become pretty fair turkey hunters in their own right. Some of them have even done their own share of mentoring other beginners, and it feels good to think about that, too.

I think it's fair to say I'm a better turkey hunter than I was 15 years ago, when I first called in a

Bill White with one of his trackers.

gobbler for a beginning hunter. Certainly I'm a better one than I was when my own mentor, Robert, called my first one in for me in 1981. I've still got a long way to go, but I've hunted these magnificent birds long enough to have learned the two most important things I will ever learn about turkey hunting:

First, you can never take anything for granted, because there will never be any two turkey hunts that play out the same.

Second, there is no end to the learning curve, because becoming a good turkey hunter isn't a destination.

It's a direction.

Directory

Camouflage

Mossy Oak Camouflage
Haas Outdoors Inc.
P.O. Box 757
West Point, MS 39773
(662) 494-8859
www.mossyoak.com

Realtree Camouflage
P.O. Box 9638
Columbus, GA 31908
(1-800) 992-9968
www.realtree.com

Trebark Camouflage
3434 Buck Mountain Road
Roanoke, VA 24014
(540) 772-2790
www.trebark.com

Decoys

Buckwing Products Inc.
2650 Lehight St.
Whitehall, PA 18052
(1-800) 555-9908
www.buckwing.com

Carry-Lite Decoys
3601 Jenny Lind Rd
Fort Smith, AR 72901
Phone (479)782-8971
www.carrylitedecoys.com

Feather Flex Decoys
4500 Doniphan Dr.
Neosho, MO 64850
(417) 451-4438
www.outland-sports.com

Flambeau Products Corp.
P.O. Box 97
Middlefield, OH 44062
(1-800) 232-3474
www.flamprod.com

Higdon Decoys
Number 7 Universal Way
Metropolis, IL 62960
(618) 524-3385
www.higdondecoys.com

Outlaw Decoys
624 N. Fancher Rd.
Spokane, WA 99212
(1-800) OUTLAWS
www.outlaw.com

Sceery Game Calls
P.O. Box 6520
Santa Fe, NM 67502
(1-800) 327-4322

Game Calls

B & R Game Calls/Deer Hollow Ranch
Barney LaRue
P. O. Box 104
4315 Kenner Chapel Road
Rudy, AR 72952
(1-800) 833-5351

Haydel's Game Calls
5018 Hazel Jones Road
Bossier City, LA 71111
(1-800) HAYDELS
www.haydels.com

Hunter's Specialties
6000 Huntington Ct. NE
Cedar Rapids, IA 52402
(319) 395-0321
www.hunterspec.com

Knight & Hale Game Calls
PRADCO Outdoor Brands
3601 Jenny Lind Road
Fort Smith, AR 72901
(501) 782-8971
www.knight-hale.com

Lohman Game Calls
4500 Doniphan Dr.
Neosho, MO 64850
(417) 451-4438
www.outland-sports.com

Lynch Worldwide, L.L.C.
500 West Jefferson St.
Thomasville, GA 31792
(229) 226-5019
www.lynchworldwide.com

MAD Calls
4500 Doniphan Dr.
Neosho, MO 64850
(417) 451-4438
www.outland-sports.com

Penns Woods Game Calls
P.O. Box 306
Delmont, PA 15626
(724) 468-8311
www.pennswoods.com

Primos Hunting Calls
604 First Street
Flora, MS 39071
(1-800) 523-2395
www.primos.com

Quaker Boy Game Calls
5455 Webster Road
Orchard Park, NY 14127
www.quakerboygamecalls.com

Southern Game Calls
545 Oakhurst Ave.
Clarksdale, MS 38614
(1-800) 881-1964
www.southerngamecalls.com

Woods Wise
P.O. Box 681552
Franklin, TN 37068
(1-800) 735-8182
www.woodswise.com

Footwear

Browning
One Browning Place
Morgan, UT 84050
(801) 876-2711
www.browning.com

Danner
18550 NE Riverside Pkwy.
Portland, OR 97230
(1-800) 345-0430
www.danner.com

Georgia Boot Co.
1810 Columbia Ave.
Franklin, TN 37064
(1-800) 790-4229
www.georgiaboot.com

LaCrosse Footwear, Inc.
18550 NE Riverside Pkwy.
Portland, OR 97230
(800)-345-0430
(503) 766-1010
www.lacrosse-outdoors.com

Rocky Shoes and Boots
39 Canal St.
Nelsonville, OH 45764
(740) 753-1951
www.rockyboots.com

Outdoor Suppliers

Bass Pro Shops
2500 E. Kearney
Springfield, MO 65898
(1-800) BASS-PRO
www.basspro.com

Cabela's
One Cabela Dr.
Sidney, NE 69160
(1-800) 237-4444
www.cabelas.com

Shotguns

Beretta USA
17601 Beretta Dr.
Accokeek, MD 20607
www.berettausa.com

Browning
One Browning Place
Morgan, UT 84050
(801) 876-2711
www.browning.com

Ithaca Gun Co.
901 Rt. 34B
King Ferry, NY 13081
(315) 364-7171
www.ithacagun.com

Remington Arms Co.
870 Remington Dr.
Madison, NC 27025
(1-800) 243-9700
www.remington.com

O.F. Mossberg & Sons
7 Grasso Ave.
North Haven, CT 06473
(1-800) 989-GUNS
www.mossberg.com

Winchester Firearms
U.S. Repeating Arms Co., Inc.
275 Winchester Ave.
Morgan, UT 84050
(801) 876-3440
www.winchester-guns.com

Shotshells

Hevi-Shot
P.O. Box 834
1307 Clark Milll Road
Sweet Home, OR 97386
(541) 367-3522 (phone)
www.hevishot.com

Federal Cartridge Co.
900 Ehlen Dr.
Anoka, MN 55303
(763) 323-2300
www.federalcartridge.com

Remington Arms Co.
870 Remington Dr.
Madison, NC 27025
(1-800) 243-9700
www.remington.com

Winchester
427 N. Shamrock St.
East Alton, IL 62024
(618) 258-3568
www.winchester.com

Maps

DeLorme Mapping Co.
Two DeLorme Dr.
Yarmouth, ME 04096
(1-800) 452-5931
www.delorme.com

Optics

Burris Co, Inc.
331 E. 8th St.
Greeley, CO 80631
(970) 356-1670

Bushnell Sports Optics
9200 Cody
Overland Park, KS 66214
(1-800) 423-3537
www.bushnell.com

BSA Optics Inc.
3911 Southwest 47th Ave.
Suite 914
Ft. Lauderdale, FL 33314
(954) 581-2144
www.bsaoptics.com

Leica
156 Ludlow Ave.
Northvale, N.J. 07647
(1-800) 222-0118
www.leica-camera.com/usa

Minolta Corp.
101 Williams Dr.
Ramsey, N.J. 07446
(201) 825-4000
www.minolta.com

Nikon, Inc.
1300 Walt Whitman Road
Melville, N.Y. 11747
(631) 547-4200
www.nikonusa.com

Pentax Corp.
35 Inverness Dr. E.
Englewood, CO 80112
(1-800) 877-0155
www.pentaxlightseeker.com

Redfield
P.O. Box 38
Onalaska, WI 54650
(608) 781-5800
www.redfieldoptics.com

Steiner Binoculars
97 Foster Road
Suite 5
Moorestown, N.J. 08057
(1-800) 257-7742
www.steiner-binoculars.com

Simmons
201 Plantation Oak Dr.
Thomasville, GA 31792
(912) 227-9053
www.simmonsoptics.com

Swarovski Optik North America Ltd.
2 Slater Road
Cranston, RI 02920
(1-800) 426-3089
www.swarovskioptik.com

Tasco Worldwide, Inc.
2889 Commerce Pkwy.
Miramar, FL 33025
(1-800) 368-2726
www.tascosales.com

Carl Zeiss, Inc.
13005 North Kingston Ave.
Chester, VA 23836
(1-800) 441-3005
www.zeiss.com

Turkey Conservation

National Wild Turkey Federation
770 Augusta Road
Edgefield, SC 29824
(1-800) THE-NWTF
www.nwtf.org

INDEX